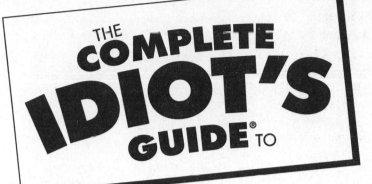

THE
COMPLETE IDIOT'S GUIDE® TO

The Music Business

by Michael Miller

ALPHA

A member of Penguin Group (USA) Inc.

To Sherry: It's nice to have someone to share the music with.

ALPHA BOOKS

Published by the Penguin Group

Penguin Group (USA) Inc., 375 Hudson Street, New York, New York 10014, USA

Penguin Group (Canada), 90 Eglinton Avenue East, Suite 700, Toronto, Ontario M4P 2Y3, Canada (a division of Pearson Penguin Canada Inc.)

Penguin Books Ltd., 80 Strand, London WC2R 0RL, England

Penguin Ireland, 25 St. Stephen's Green, Dublin 2, Ireland (a division of Penguin Books Ltd.)

Penguin Group (Australia), 250 Camberwell Road, Camberwell, Victoria 3124, Australia (a division of Pearson Australia Group Pty. Ltd.)

Penguin Books India Pvt. Ltd., 11 Community Centre, Panchsheel Park, New Delhi—110 017, India

Penguin Group (NZ), 67 Apollo Drive, Rosedale, North Shore, Auckland 1311, New Zealand (a division of Pearson New Zealand Ltd.)

Penguin Books (South Africa) (Pty.) Ltd., 24 Sturdee Avenue, Rosebank, Johannesburg 2196, South Africa

Penguin Books Ltd., Registered Offices: 80 Strand, London WC2R 0RL, England

International Standard Book Number: 978-1-61564-013-3
Library of Congress Catalog Card Number: 2009910485

12 11 10   8 7 6 5 4 3 2 1

Interpretation of the printing code: The rightmost number of the first series of numbers is the year of the book's printing; the rightmost number of the second series of numbers is the number of the book's printing. For example, a printing code of 10-1 shows that the first printing occurred in 2010.

Printed in the United States of America

Note: This publication contains the opinions and ideas of its author. It is intended to provide helpful and informative material on the subject matter covered. It is sold with the understanding that the author and publisher are not engaged in rendering professional services in the book. If the reader requires personal assistance or advice, a competent professional should be consulted.

The author and publisher specifically disclaim any responsibility for any liability, loss, or risk, personal or otherwise, which is incurred as a consequence, directly or indirectly, of the use and application of any of the contents of this book.

Most Alpha books are available at special quantity discounts for bulk purchases for sales promotions, premiums, fund-raising, or educational use. Special books, or book excerpts, can also be created to fit specific needs.

For details, write: Special Markets, Alpha Books, 375 Hudson Street, New York, NY 10014.

Publisher: *Marie Butler-Knight*
Associate Publisher: *Mike Sanders*
Senior Managing Editor: *Billy Fields*
Acquisitions Editor: *Karyn Gerhard*
Senior Development Editor: *Phil Kitchel*
Senior Production Editor: *Janette Lynn*

Cover Designer: *Kurt Owens*
Book Designer: *Trina Wurst*
Indexer: *Celia McCoy*
Layout: *Brian Massey*
Proofreader: *Laura Caddell*

Contents at a Glance

Contents

Introduction

It's tough trying to make a buck in the music business. Heck, it's tough trying to make a buck in *any* business, but the music business is particularly challenging. That's at least partially because most musicians would rather be playing than doing business stuff.

Hey, I know how it is. You see a contract or hear somebody talking about points and percentages and you start fantasizing about playing your next big gig. But if you snooze, you lose—and in our business, that could mean giving up some big bucks. So it pays to pay attention, and to run your music like a real business.

Now not every musician needs to have Donald Trump–like business skills. If all you do is play an occasional weekend gig for grins and beer money, that's cool. But when you start making real money—and relying on that money to help pay the rent—then you need to start taking your music seriously. At that point it's not a hobby anymore, it's a profession—and you should treat it as such.

In the old days (say, sometime before yesterday afternoon), the music business was dominated by big record labels and driven by radio play. That's not the case anymore, and that's a good thing. A hard-working musician today can do just about everything the record labels used to—record, distribute, and promote your own music, from the comfort of your own home. Digital technology makes it relatively easy to cut your own tracks, while the Internet lets you sell your tracks as digital downloads. Just as important, the Internet lets you create your own web page and connect directly with your fans. It's a much different world than it used to be.

The challenge is, how do you take advantage of today's technology and social networking to jumpstart your music career? Do you still need to hire a manager and agent, and sign with a big record label—or can you do some or all of these things yourself?

The Complete Idiot's Guide to the Music Business answers these questions—and more. Whether you're playing local lounges or touring big concert halls, whether you're recording your first CD or negotiating a new record deal, whether you're a burgeoning songwriter or in a popular cover band, this book helps you plan your music career and shows you how to do what you need to do to be successful. It doesn't matter whether you play rock, country, jazz, or hip hop, I'll show you how to assemble your team, negotiate better deals, put together an online presence, and make more money from the music you create—as well as protect yourself against the scam artists who are only out to get your money.

Who This Book Is For

The Complete Idiot's Guide to the Music Business is written for musicians of all types and at all levels. If you're just starting out, you'll learn how to create a roadmap to success and assemble the team to take you there. If you're a more experienced musician you'll learn new ways to promote your business and get a bigger cut of the profits. And all musicians will benefit from the expert advice for taking advantage of new technologies and opportunities.

By the way, I don't assume that you have a lot of business experience. Just the opposite; I figure you spend more time practicing your instrument than you do balancing your checkbook. Even though there's a lot of business stuff in this book, I try to explain things in terms that even a drummer can understand. (I can say that; I'm a drummer, in addition to being a writer.)

There's even information in this book for nonmusicians—specifically, for music lovers who want to be part of the music business. So if you're an aspiring manager or agent or A&R person, there's something here for you, too.

One thing, though. For reasons that will become apparent, this book is very U.S.-centric. While music is global, business practices are quite local, and I can't present every legal nuance for every country on this big blue ball of ours. So I cover U.S. contract and copyright law, and focus on American companies and organizations. The basic principles apply in other countries, of course, but the legal and corporate details will differ. If you're reading this in another country, sorry about that.

What You'll Find in This Book

The Complete Idiot's Guide to the Music Business is your step-by-step guide to making your way in today's music business—turning your music into a paying profession. While it doesn't have to be read from front to back, it helps if you pick up the initial concepts first before you proceed to the more advanced stuff.

To that end, I've organized the book into five major parts.

Part 1, "Welcome to the Music Business," is a gentle introduction to how the music business works. You'll learn why you need to treat your music like a business, what business skills you need, and where exactly the business might be headed in the future.

Part 2, "Becoming a Business-Oriented Musician," covers a lot of the big-picture stuff you need to know. You'll learn how to put together a business plan for your music, what kind of business team you need to assemble, how to work with a personal manager, and why you need a business manager to handle your financial affairs.

Part 3, "The Music Business for Musicians," is the nuts-and-bolts part of the book, aimed squarely at today's professional musicians. You'll learn all about recording your music, dealing with major record labels, distributing your own music, promoting your music, making money from performing and touring, selling all sorts of merchandise, songwriting and publishing, and licensing your songs for movies, TV shows, and other media. In addition, you'll learn all about distributing and promoting your music online—from creating your own website to having iTunes offer your songs for download.

Part 4, "The Music Business for Nonmusicians," explores all sorts of jobs in the music business for people who don't play or sing. Music lovers will find advice on careers in artist management, booking, recording and production, and music publishing—as well as all the various jobs found at major record labels.

Part 5, "The Legal Side of the Music Business," is all about contracts and copyrights. You'll learn how contracts work and how to put together and negotiate your own contracts. You'll also learn about the various types of copyrights, licenses, and royalties—including mechanical, synch, and performance royalties.

The Complete Idiot's Guide to the Music Business concludes with a glossary of relevant music and business terms. This is a great place to look up those words and phrases that you've heard but were never sure what they meant.

How to Get the Most Out of This Book

To get the most out of this book, you should know how it is designed. I've tried to put things together in a way that makes learning about the music business both fun and easy.

I end each chapter with a section covering the big picture—some of the most important issues in the music business today. These sections contain a fair amount of opinion, so take them as such.

In addition to the main text, you'll find a number of little text boxes (what we in publishing call *margin notes*) that present additional advice and information. These elements enhance your knowledge or point out important pitfalls to avoid, and they look like this:

Behind the Music
These boxes contain additional information about the topic at hand.

 Smart Business

These boxes provide additional tips and advice beyond what's present in the main text.

Scam Alert

These boxes contain important warnings about people and practices to avoid when working in the real world.

def•i•ni•tion

These provide quick and simple definitions of industry lingo and jargon so you can keep up in any professional conversation.

Let Me Know What You Think

I always love to hear from my readers. Feel free to e-mail me at musicbusiness@ molehillgroup.com. I can't promise that I'll answer every e-mail, but I will promise that I'll read each one!

And just in case a few mistakes happen to creep into the printed book, you can find a list of any corrections or clarifications on my website (www.molehillgroup.com). That's also where you can find a list of my other books, so feel free to look around— and maybe do a little online shopping!

Acknowledgments

Thanks to the usual suspects at Alpha, including Karyn Gerhard, Phil Kitchel, Janette Lynn, and Marie Butler-Knight, for helping to turn my manuscript into a printed book. Thanks also to David Olson of the McNally Smith College of Music, who offered much-needed initial input and guidance for the book—and is just a fun guy to swap stories with.

Trademarks

All terms mentioned in this book that are known to be or are suspected of being trademarks or service marks have been appropriately capitalized. Alpha Books and Penguin Group (USA) Inc. cannot attest to the accuracy of this information. Use of a term in this book should not be regarded as affecting the validity of any trademark or service mark.

Part

Welcome to the Music Business

Just when does your music become a business? And how does this so-called music business work, anyway? Read these chapters to learn the history and the future of the music business—as well as all the essential business skills every musician needs to know.

Minding Your Business: Why You Need Business Skills

In This Chapter

- ◆ What business skills does a gigging musician need?
- ◆ What business skills does a recording musician need?
- ◆ What business skills does a songwriter need?
- ◆ Learning how to protect yourself from unscrupulous characters
- ◆ Discovering how the changing business requires even more business skills

You're a working musician, just trying to make a buck. Or maybe you're in a successful band, thinking of recording some tracks or perhaps signing a contract with a label. Or maybe you're a music student, hoping someday to make some sort of a career in music.

Whatever you're doing in the music world, you need to know a little bit about the music *business*. Yes, you're a musician first and foremost; and, yes, the whole business thing stinks of crass commerciality; and, no, you wouldn't know a mechanical royalty from the British royalty—but that's all beside the point. If you want to make any money with your music and not be ripped off, you have to learn yourself some business skills. It's as important as learning your scales.

Welcome to the Business World

That's right, being a professional musician is more than just playing the right notes; it's about managing your career so that you can make a little money doing what you love. And that means learning some essential business skills that you can apply whether you're booking a gig, recording your music, selling your songs, or promoting yourself and your music.

What kinds of business skills are we talking about? Fortunately, you don't need an accounting degree; the skills you need are a mix of common sense and industry-specific practices. Things like learning how to read a contract, knowing what's the standard practice and what isn't, and understanding how various types of copyrights and royalties work. It's a matter of getting the most from your music—and not getting ripped off by those unscrupulous types who unfortunately tend to hang out around musicians.

You might think that, in your little part of the music world, business skills aren't that important. Maybe you're just playing an occasional local gig or selling a few digital downloads from your own website. Maybe you have no dream or intention of signing with a major recording label. Almost every musician, however, deals with issues that require some degree of business savvy: you're working with contracts (or should be), dealing directly with experienced businesspeople, and promoting yourself, your band, or your music. When it's your money and your reputation on the line, you need to make sure you're playing on an even playing field—which you do by bringing your best business game.

Business Skills for the Gigging Musician

Let's start with probably the most common type of musician today—the local gigging musician. You're in a band, or maybe you play solo; you play cover music or some original tunes; you play rock, country, blues, jazz, whatever. Maybe you're playing small clubs or lounges, maybe you're playing wedding receptions or the local VFW hall, or maybe you're on the road, playing the regional circuit. What's common is that you're *playing*, week in and week out.

When you're playing, you have to deal with everything that goes with the gig—starting with the booking, going through the set up and tear down, and ending with getting paid. It also means dealing with club owners and promoters and the like—the guys on the other side of the table.

So what business skills does the gigging musician need—and why? Let's take a look—starting at the very top.

Marketing Skills

Before you can get a gig, you need to know what gigs are available, and then sell yourself or your band to the club owner or promoter. In other words, you have to market yourself—which requires, you guessed it, *marketing* skills.

Now any marketing major at the local business school will know how to do this naturally, but the average working musician probably has zero marketing experience—and might have zero marketing savvy. In essence, it revolves around telling others about how great you are, so that they'll either sign you for a gig or come and hear

def·i·ni·tion

Marketing is the act of presenting products or services—or, in this instance, you and your music—in such a way as to make them desirable.

you play. If you don't market yourself, club owners or booking agents won't know about you. And if they don't know about you, they won't sign you—and you won't get a single gig.

On the other hand, if you market yourself well, club owners and booking agents will have heard about you long before you place your first phone call. In fact, they may even call *you*, if you've done a good job establishing your reputation. If you do your job right, you may even be able to negotiate a better deal; after all, an in-demand artist is worth more than an unknown one.

Beyond that, you need to market yourself to your current and potential fan base. Good marketing establishes a strong relationship between you and your fans—it makes them feel as if they're close to you and invested in your success. Good marketing also creates new fans, by drawing audiences to your shows and your recordings. It's all about getting the word out—and getting the crowds in the clubs.

Marketing is actually a combination of several related skills, including promotion, advertising, and public relations. Marketing activities include everything from writing press releases to handing out flyers to creating print advertisements. It's all in service of making potential fans aware of you and your music; effective marketing can sell both tickets and recordings.

Bottom line, you need marketing skills in order to promote yourself or your band—both to club owners and booking agents and to your fans and the general public. Market yourself well, and you'll get more and better-attended gigs; market yourself poorly, and you'll be sitting home on Friday night playing *Guitar Hero* by yourself. (Learn more about marketing skills in Chapter 12.)

Contract and Negotiating Skills

So you do the marketing thing and find a club owner who wants to sign you for an upcoming gig. What comes next?

Well, what comes next is that you have to negotiate with the club owner. You have to agree on a price (you want to make more money; he wants to pay you less), the hours you'll play (you want a half hour break between sets; he wants 10 minutes), and other details (you want a big dressing room, snacks and sandwiches laid out, and a free tab at the bar; the club owner wants you to arrive fully dressed and charge you for everything you eat or drink). Somewhere between what you want and the club owner wants is what you'll probably get, but the better you are at negotiating, the more you can work it out in your favor.

def•i•ni•tion

A **contract** is a formal record of the terms negotiated between two parties.

After you've agreed on all the details, big and small, you have to put it all in writing. The *contract* formally lays out what you're obligated to do (show up at such and such a time and play for this many hours) and what the club owner is obligated to do (pay you this amount and provide these amenities).

But here's where it gets tricky. Assuming that you're not a lawyer and haven't gone to law school, it's very, very easy for a wily club owner to throw a spanner in the works somewhere in the fine print. Yes, the club owner is obligated to pay you X amount (it's right there in paragraph 23, sub-paragraph 4, clause C, point B-1), but first he can subtract the cost of cleaning the dressing room, dressing the stage, renting an extra cymbal for the drum kit, and providing toilet paper and napkins for the band's use. Don't laugh; this sort of thing happens all the time. These hidden details eat away at the money you thought you were going to make, which is why you need to know what to look for when you read the contract.

So you need to know how to negotiate and read a contract to keep unscrupulous club owners and promoters from taking advantage of you. You need to know what's standard business procedure and what's not. You need to know that what you negotiated is there in the final contract, and not undercut by unwanted *holdbacks*. And you need to know what to do if the club owner doesn't hold up his end of the bargain—that is, what steps you can take if you don't get paid what you thought you were owed.

def•i•ni•tion

A **holdback** is part of a promised payment that is withheld by the paying party until a specified contingency has been met by the payee.

It's the same thing, by the way, whether you're playing a small club, a large concert hall, or an intimate wedding reception. You need to negotiate terms (including, but not limited to, how much you'll be paid) and then set those terms in writing. This is an important skill for any musician, no matter what size or type of gig you're playing. It's how you protect yourself. (Learn more about negotiating and writing contracts in Chapter 23.)

Merchandising Skills

Playing a gig these days isn't just about playing the gig. For many musicians, a gig is also a forum for selling merchandise—CDs, T-shirts, pictures, you name it. That's right, you can make money not just from your music, but also from selling sounds and images of yourself. It's called *merchandising*, and it's an important revenue stream for all types of musicians. Bruce Springsteen does it, as does the saxophonist at your jazz club; it's a big deal.

def•i•ni•tion

Merchandising is the exchange of goods for an agreed-upon sum of money; in the music business, the sale of items somehow related to the musician to his or her fan base.

Now in order to merchandise yourself, you need to have something to sell. CDs are a logical choice, but anything souvenir-like will do. And that means getting into the manufacturing thing; if you're selling T-shirts, after all, somebody has to make the darn things. So you need to arrange manufacturing, which will require some money upfront, and then pay someone to sit at a table at the gig and sell the stuff. A savvy artist can make as much or more selling merchandise as they do from the gig itself; it does, however, require some skill in picking the sorts of things that your particular fans want to buy. (Learn more about selling your stuff in Chapter 14.)

Online Skills

I almost hate to mention this as a separate thing, since the Internet is so integrated into everything a musician does today, but obtaining online skills is essential for the gigging musician. You can use the web to reach out to your fan base and to promote yourself to potential employers. That means creating and managing a website, creating and managing MySpace and Facebook pages, running an e-mail mailing list, managing fan message boards, and more.

Do you have to be an Internet wizard to be a successful musician today? Well, it helps to be Internet savvy, but if HTML coding is beyond your skill set, you can hire out just about everything Internet-related. That might mean hiring your tech-savvy cousin to be your webmaster, or signing with a professional firm that specializes in online artist management. So don't worry if you don't know a mouse-click from a click-track; you need an online presence, but you don't have to do it all yourself. (Learn more about online marketing and distribution in Chapter 17.)

Business Skills for the Recording Musician

Recording your music is important for almost every musician. Not only does it provide a historical archive of your music, a recording can also generate income and help promote you and your music.

To that end, you need to know how to create a good-sounding recording. Do you need to go into a professional recording studio and spend big bucks on a big production? Or can you do it on the cheap, using computer-based recording software to make a recording with your own PC in your own home? And however you proceed, how big of a budget do you need? Find out the answers to these questions—and more—in Chapter 9.

def•i•ni•tion

Royalties are payments made to the holder of a patent or copyright—such as the copyright held by the writer of a song—for the use of that patent or copyright.

Then there's the music you record. If you record your own songs, that's one thing, but if you record someone else's songs, you have to deal with *royalties*—paying the songwriters for the songs they wrote. It gets even more complicated if you're lucky enough to get your music placed in a television show, movie, or commercial. Now we're talking about synchronization royalties, in addition to mechanical royalties. And if you don't have any idea what synchronization or mechanical royalties are, you're not alone; you should, however, think about adding a lawyer to your team to deal with issues like these.

As you can see, recording is a big subject, and only gets bigger when you consider all the things you can do with the recordings you make. If you want to sell your music, do you just produce a few CDs to sell at your gigs, or do you look for a record label to do the distribution for you? And what about downloading your music—do you make your music downloadable for free from your website, or do you look for a digital distribution partner? Information about the whole self-distribution issue can be found in Chapter 11.

And that's not all. If you go the label route, should you sign with a big company or an indie label? And what kind of label deal is a good one? How much of an advance should you receive—and how likely is it that you'll ever earn it out? And what does "earn it out" mean?

As you can see, once you get into the recording thing, the distribution thing follows, and that leads quickly to the independent versus major label discussion. I'll be honest with you: an artist today has few reasons to consider a traditional major label contract; you can do just about everything you need to do yourself, and take home a larger percentage of the proceeds. Major labels are good at promoting major acts, but take a very large cut in return; most artists never earn out the advance they get from signing. Learn more about choosing a record label in Chapter 9.

That said, there's a time and a place for everything, including major labels. Let's face it; you may be the greatest guitarist around, but not know a lick about record distribution. You may need to pay somebody who knows how to get your record played, whether it's a major label or an independent promoter.

In any case, you *will* be dealing with contracts and negotiations, so those business skills come into play once again. If you choose to record in a pro studio, you'll need to negotiate studio rates and services, and find a way to pay for it all. If you decide to produce and sell your own CDs, you have to deal with manufacturing, distribution, and merchandising issues. And if and when you sign with a record label, there are lots and lots of contractual issues to deal with.

And here's the thing. At every stage in the game, someone will be lurking in the shadows, just waiting to take a bigger cut than they're entitled to. It's the way of the world, especially the business world; sharks exist, and they like to eat little fishies just like you. We've all heard tales of big-name artists who sell a million CDs but go bankrupt. There's a reason for that, and it all revolves around business skills—or the lack of them.

Business Skills for the Songwriting Musician

Things get even more complicated when you write your own music. Not only do you have to deal with placing your songs with other artists (in addition to recording them yourself, of course), but legal issues suddenly take precedence. That's because to make money from your songs, you have to deal with all manner of copyrights and royalties. (Learn more about publishing your music in Chapter 15.)

That's right, the songwriting business is part of the music publishing business, which is a big part of the music law business. When a song you write gets recorded, you're owed one type of royalty (mechanical); when a song of yours gets performed live, you're owed another type of royalty (performance); and when a song of yours is licensed for use in a TV show, movie, commercial, or other media, you're owed yet another type of royalty (synchronization).

You're owed these royalties, that is, unless you've sold or given away all or part of your copyright, in which case you may not be owed anything—which isn't a good thing, especially if your song becomes a hit or gets placed in a major motion picture or TV show. You'd want to get paid for that, right?

These rights are typically managed by a music publishing house, and through one of the three major music rights organizations (ASCAP, BMI, and SESAC). You sign a contract with a music publisher, and (for a cut of the royalties) they manage your music placements. Or maybe you're in desperate straits and sell the rights to your song for a flat fee; while it might be nice to get a big payment today, you forfeit the rights to any royalties in the future, which could grow over time. The whole royalty thing can get quite complicated; learn more in Chapter 24.

So what we have here is a need for contract and negotiating skills, again, but also for specific legal skills. Now I'm not recommending that all potential songwriters go to law school, but it is a good idea to have a reliable music lawyer as part of your team. Again, you need to know what standard practices are, but you also need to know how to make informed business decisions—and look out for those sharks in the chain.

Vultures, Vultures Everywhere!

You need business skills to make the most out of what you do, but you also need them to protect yourself. As the line goes from the movie *Casablanca*, "This place is full of vultures, vultures everywhere, everywhere."

It's true, you know: vultures *do* exist in the music business. Not to be an alarmist, but a lot of people are willing to take advantage of your talent for their benefit, and others are eager to rob you of every thin dime you might otherwise earn. There are so-called "agents" who take their cut off the top even if there's nothing left for you afterwards. There are club owners who always seem to end up short on cash when it comes time to pay the band. There are record labels who charge back the band more for expenses than they earn on record sales. There are music publishers who will buy your music for a song and then retain all future royalty streams. Vultures, vultures everywhere!

And it isn't just the obvious vultures who'll do you in. I've heard several stories of musicians who agreed to play a gig or record a song for some local organization, only to find out afterward that their contribution was indeed expected to be a *contribution*, with no payment forthcoming. These folks put in a lot of effort preparing for the gig or recording, and end up with nothing to show for their time. Intended charity is fine, but if you expect to get paid and then don't, then charity becomes a crime. A little business savvy upfront and things would have worked out better—for the musicians, at least.

Of course, new technologies lead to new ways to fleece the unsuspecting musician. Many musicians whine about all the money they're losing from free or illegal downloads, but it's more likely that you're not getting your fair share of legal downloads from legitimate music download services. That's especially true if you're signed to a major label; you get to share your online sales not only with the download service but also with the label, which probably won't leave much for you.

The major label issue, of course, extends well beyond the digital domain. Labels are in it to make money for themselves; advancing your career, if it happens at all, is a secondary part of the process. The way major-label contracts work, most artists get an upfront advance, but then get charged back for every single expense the label can think of, from renting studio space to shooting promotional videos to paying the lawyers who negotiate against you. In most cases, the expenses end up exceeding the advances, so that you never see a penny of royalties from music sales.

Then there is the issue of *consolidators*—operators who package together different services, but in so doing end up controlling more of your business than they should. For example, beware the big-name singer who wants her name added to the songs you write. That way she gets not just performance royalties but also songwriting/publishing royalties, essentially double-dipping in your pool.

Even worse are producers who demand publishing rights. I've heard cases where a producer works a deal where he gets to use the songs he publishes as he sees fits. That might, for example, end up with another act recorded by this producer using your song for free, just because your producer is also your music publisher. It's a conflict of interest that works against you.

The same thing happens today with record labels. In the old days, labels didn't want to have anything to do with artist tours, which were seen as money-losing propositions. But now that most artists make more money touring than they do from record sales, the labels want to manage your tours and merchandising, too—which, of course, they can cross-collateralize against your recording and marketing expenses. They get their cut, and you end up with less—or nothing.

> **Smart Business**
>
> Musicians today have options that didn't exist in the past. For example, you don't have to sign with a major label; you can sign with an independent label that won't take as big a chunk of your earnings, or you can use the Internet and other tools to distribute your music yourself—and keep *all* the money you earn.

Knowing all of these potential pitfalls, if you opt to stay ignorant of business details, someone sharper than you will be more than happy to con you out of what's rightfully yours. This is why too many musicians are poor or have day jobs; they give away their money needlessly.

Business Skills in a Changing Business

Taking everything we've discussed into account, a successful musician today also needs to be a marketing genius, a flesh-pounding PR maven, an in-your-face salesperson, a tech-savvy online wizard, a hard-nosed negotiator, a numbers-oriented accountant, and an experienced attorney. Oh, and you need to know how to play your instrument and make interesting music; we can't forget that.

Moving full-bore into the twenty-first century, there is every indication that business skills will become more and more important to the working musician. Not only can't you rely on major labels, producers, or even managers to act in your best interests, you may not even be dealing with these entities.

For better or worse, technological and cultural changes have put more of the music business in the hands of musicians, not the big companies. Thanks to personal computers, the Internet, and social networking, you can do more and more things yourself; you can record yourself at home, sell your music online, and connect with your fans via Facebook and MySpace. Yes, you'll still play live at clubs and concert halls, but now you can book yourself and manage all your own tour arrangements. You can even arrange the manufacture of merchandise to sell at your gigs, and keep all the profits for yourself.

To do all this, however, you have to know every aspect of the music business. You have to know marketing and promotion, you have to develop online savvy, you have to learn recording skills, you have to develop your own means of distribution, and you must—you *must*—become a savvy negotiator and stickler for contractual details.

Your success depends on developing these business skills—and neglecting them can result in failure. Let's face it, it's no secret that the average musician is not naturally business savvy; in fact, some musicians I know are especially business ignorant. This ignorance, whether naturally earned or willful, will cost you.

For all these reasons, building the appropriate business skills is a necessary evil for even the most humble musician. You don't want to be taken advantage of, and you do want to maximize the potential of your music. You need business skills to build your own personal music business—and to keep your share of the money you earn. Learn more about what to expect going forward in Chapter 4.

How Much Do I Really Need to Know About Business?

Okay, maybe I've marginally convinced you that there's some value in developing some degree of business skill. But how much do you really need to know about business?

First, know that you don't need to graduate from business school to be successful in the music business. Now and for always, it's the music that matters most; business skills should supplement your musical skills

That said, you do need to develop a head for business—even if you don't master all the details. That means having a nose for what's a good deal and what's a bad one; if it smells bad, it probably is bad. It also means learning standard industry practices, and knowing where scams are likely to occur. That means looking out for more than just dollar and sense; you need to pay attention to copyrights, royalties, and ownership of everything you create.

Do you need to do all your marketing yourself? Do you have to run your own website? Do you have to write your own contracts? Of course not; you can farm out any or all these tasks to others. That does mean you have to *pay* these folks to do the work, and you have to find people you trust—another essential skill you might not yet possess.

What's important is to know how things work, but not necessarily how to do every-thing yourself. So you need to know how to read a contract, but not necessarily how to write one; you can hire a lawyer for that. You need to know what you expect out of your website, but not how to code it. You need to know what you want your recording to sound like, not how to engineer it. You need to know where you want your music sold, not how to upload it or transcode the files. You get the picture.

Equally important, you need to know what you're good at and feel comfortable with, and what you don't like or just can't do. If you're good with the online stuff and like working with HTML, then by all means develop your own website. But if you don't know JavaScript from a java bean, you should farm out that task. Same thing with marketing, promotion, booking, negotiating—everything business-related that needs to be done. If you're good at and have time for it, then you can and perhaps should do it yourself; it costs less that way. If you don't have the skills, interest, or time, hire someone else to do it.

But even if you parcel out the work, keep your hand in; anyone at any level can scam you if they work unobserved. And *that's* why business skills are important—to keep everybody honest. The more you know, the less likely you are to be taken advantage of. It's better to know a little bit about the business end of things than nothing at all.

The Least You Need to Know

- Business skills protect you from being taken advantage of.
- Business skills enable you to run your own music business.
- Business skills help you negotiate better terms.
- You need to develop marketing, merchandising, online, negotiating, and con-tractual skills.
- If you don't have the necessary skills to do something yourself, hire someone you trust who does.

How the Music Business Works

In This Chapter

- How music becomes a product that is bought and sold
- The major players in the music industry
- How big the music industry is—and who makes the big bucks
- How the music industry is changing—and how it affects the major players

As you learned in the previous chapter, developing some key business skills is important to finding success in the music business. But just what is this "music business"—and how does it work?

The music business is a large, mostly thriving (there's some disagreement about this), ever-changing industry. It is comprised of everything from individual songwriters to massive corporations. At its most basic, however, it's a business concerned with making music—and making money.

What Is Music?

This sounds like a simple question: What is music? Of course, we all know what music is—it's notes and chords strung together into a song. Or is it the performance of that song? And does it matter if that performance is recorded or live? Or is it enough to write it down as sheet music?

Okay, so maybe the answer isn't quite as simple as the question. And maybe the answer depends a lot on the technology available and existing social customs.

In the several centuries before the advent of recording technology, music was something you heard and experienced. In many ways, music was as much a social event (attending a concert or listening to a performance) as it was a musical one. In fact, music of the past was quite often tied to specific social functions—dances, church services, pub singalongs, and various other ceremonies. Music wasn't something you could buy and take home; it was a singular and public experience.

Twentieth-century technology changed how we perceived music. With the advent of printed sheet music and recorded songs and albums, music became a thing that could be bought and sold—a product that you then listened to in the privacy of your own home. Of course, the social aspect of music remained in the form of live performances, but now there was something you could buy and take home, as well.

The form of this music product evolved throughout the twentieth century, and continues to evolve today. To some degree the medium of distribution influenced the final product (the fancy album covers and liner notes common in the vinyl LP age), but the core product was the music itself—the songs or collections of songs that people purchased to listen to.

Who Is the Music Industry?

In general, the music industry consists of those individuals and companies involved with making and selling music, in whatever form that takes. The music industry includes the songwriters and musicians who create the music, as well as the companies who produce and sell the music—both for live performance and on whatever media is in favor at the time.

The People Who Make the Music

Music is both song and performance. A song can be played by any number of performers; conversely, a performer can play any number of songs. While a single person can both write and perform a song, those two functions can also be filled by two different musicians.

The individual who writes the music is a *songwriter* or *composer*. The music this person writes consists of a melody and set of chords, often accompanied by words written by a *lyricist*. This music can be written on paper, using standard music notation, for others to read and play. This written music then becomes a product that others can purchase, typically as sheet music.

def•i•ni•tion

Technically, a **composer** is someone who writes music, not words, while a **lyricist** is the individual who supplies the words or lyrics. A **songwriter** typically writes both words and music.

When he writes a song, the songwriter owns the copyright to the song. Technically, it's this copyright that is sold—or, more accurately, licensed. That is, another entity (either a performing musician or another company) pays money for the right to record the copyrighted material, or to play the song in public. It's the use of the copyright that becomes the product.

You see, a songwriter can play his own songs, or he can sell his songs (or, more accurately, license the copyright) to other musicians for them to perform. When an artist records a song written by another songwriter, the artist pays the songwriter a percentage of all money made from recording that song. And when that song is played in public, the owner of the venue where the song is played also pays the songwriter a royalty.

Behind the Music

The money owed by performers who play or record another musician's songs are collected by an organization called a public performing rights organization. These organizations, such as ASCAP and BMI, track the use of copyrighted songs and act as yet another middleman between the performer or licensor and the songwriter or copyright holder.

A musician can perform a song before a live audience or record a performance of that song. When he performs live, that performance is a product that audience members purchase by buying tickets.

When a musician makes a recording, that recording can then be sold as a product. Today, that product can be sold as a physical product, typically in the form of a CD, or as a digital file containing that recording, which can be sold via online download.

The Companies Who Sell the Music

During the better part of the twentieth century, a musician did not sell his or her music directly. Instead, musicians engaged—and, in many cases, continue to engage—the services of middlemen to handle the sales and distribution of their products.

To sell a song, a songwriter partners with a music publishing company, which arranges for the creation, distribution, and sale of their sheet music. This company also arranges for the licensing of the song itself to other musicians to record, and for use in television shows, movies, commercials, and the like. For its services, the music publishing company takes a percentage of all revenues generated, sometimes as much as half of the monies earned.

To sell a live performance, a musician can partner with a variety of different middlemen. If you're playing a local club, the club owner essentially sells your performance, typically by selling tickets at the door. For larger venues, a booking agent or talent agent might be involved, serving as the middleman between the musician and the venue. And, in many instances, a ticket agency, such as Ticketmaster, is contracted to sell tickets directly to the audience. In any case, the musician seldom stages his own concerts and sells his own tickets.

To sell a recording, a musician typically partners with a record label. The label provides some financing for the recording itself, then arranges distribution of the physical product around the country. Distributors purchase their inventory from the record label; local retail stores purchase their inventory from nearby distributors; and consumers purchase the physical CD from their local retail stores. All these companies take a cut of the money paid by the consumer.

Behind the Music
In many instances, the record company owns the distributor—thus taking two cuts of the pie.

When selling a digital product, there is typically one less middleman. A musician still might sign with a record label, which then sells the digital recording directly to an online music store, no distributor involved. The consumer downloads the music from the online store, of course.

In addition, a musician might employ additional middlemen to perform specific functions. For example, a musician might hire a personal manager to manage various career-related activities, or a business manager to manage his finances. These middlemen also must be paid, either on an hourly basis for services rendered, or by receiving a percentage of all the money the musician earns.

How It Works

Let's work through an example of how an individual song becomes a product, and how that product gets distributed and sold.

It all starts with the songwriter, of course. When the songwriter writes the song, a copyright is automatically created (although official registration isn't a bad idea). So now the songwriter owns a copyright.

The songwriter then signs a contract with a music publishing company, which agrees to handle the licensing of the song for 50 percent of the proceeds. (That's a fairly common deal.)

The publishing company has a staff of people who "push" songs handled by the company. This staff contacts a particular rock group and plays them the song. They like the song, and agree to record it for their upcoming album. This group, of course, is signed with a major record label.

The group records the song and the label releases the album, in the form of a compact disc (CD). The CD is shipped to the label's distributors, who then ship inventory to retail stores across the country. When consumers purchase the CD from a record store, the store pays the distributor for the items sold—keeping a bit of the proceeds as its own profit, of course. The distributor then pays the record label for those same items, also keeping a cut of the proceeds for its own profit. Then, of the money that flows back to the label, a percentage is paid to the recording artist as a royalty.

A percentage of those proceeds are also paid to the songwriter's publishing company, typically facilitated by one of the public performance rights organizations. The publishing company takes the royalty from the record label, keeps half for itself, and sends the balance on to the songwriter in the form of songwriting royalties.

By the way, the songwriter (and his publishing company) also receive a royalty whenever that song is played on the radio or used in a TV show or commercial. The group that recorded the song, however, is not paid when their song plays on the radio; they only get paid when a CD is sold. (Don't ask why this is; we'll get into the whys and wherefores of royalties in Chapter 24.)

In addition, there is money earned from sales of the album online—or, more likely, sales of individual tracks. Whenever the song in question is purchased and down-loaded, the online music store takes a cut and passes the remainder back to the record label. From these proceeds, the label pays the performing musicians a royalty, as well as paying a royalty to the publishing company—which then takes their cut and passes the rest on to the songwriter.

> **Behind the Music**
>
> Most online sales are of individual tracks, not complete albums.

And what of live performances? Well, the band that recorded the album goes out on tour. They sign with a booking agency to arrange the tour and contract with indi-vidual venues along the way. They also sign with a ticketing agency, which sells the tickets. When a fan buys a ticket, the ticketing agency takes a cut, the booking agent takes a cut, and the venue and the performing artist split the rest.

> **Behind the Music**
>
> Songwriting royalties are due for any public performance of a recorded song—on the radio, on TV, even as background music in your local coffeehouse. In addition, royalties are due for any live performance of the song, whether by a cover band in a bar or a high school marching band. Learn more in Chapter 24.

Somewhere in there, the public performing rights organizations keep track of the songs that are played in concert. They then collect a fee, typically from the venue, for the songs performed, and send that fee back to the songwriter's publishing com-pany. Naturally, the publishing company takes their cut, and the songwriter receives the rest.

As you can see, the songwriter gets a pretty good deal, collecting a royalty every time his song is recorded, played on the radio, or performed live. The recording musicians don't make out as well, receiving money only when a CD or digital track is sold, or when tickets are sold to their performance. And, of course, all the middlemen at every stage of the game take their cut.

Regarding those middlemen—they're not always necessary. One of the big changes in the music industry of late is the shift to independent distribution. Instead of signing with a major label, many performing artists are now signing with smaller labels or distributing their music themselves. Likewise, many songwriters form their own publishing companies. By eliminating the middlemen, these musicians keep more of their profits—but have to do more of the work themselves. It's a tradeoff, but one that is changing the dynamics of the industry.

How Big Is the Music Industry?

A lot of music-related products are sold every year, in the form of licenses for copyrighted works, physical CDs, digital downloads, and concert tickets. In addition, kind of circling on the periphery, there are sales of related merchandise, such as T-shirts, hats, and the like.

It's really a big industry. According to industry trade group International Federation of the Phonographic Industry (IFPI), in 2008 the global market for music products totaled $18.4 billion. That's right, more than *eighteen billion dollars.* Of that figure, $4.9 billion was done in the United States.

> **Behind the Music**
>
> Learn more about the IFPI (and view a lot more statistics) at their website, www.ifpi.org.

How do those numbers break down? As a percentage basis, the biggest share of the market (75 percent, globally) continues to come from the sales of physical product. Digital sales accounted for 20 percent of sales, while publishing rights were 5 percent of the total.

Now, these numbers aren't complete. Since the IFPI does not count concert or ticket revenues, nor does it count sales of music-related merchandise, the total size of the music industry is considerably larger than that reported. The IFPI also doesn't factor the profitability of any of these sales, or the percentage that flows through major record labels versus those going directly to independent labels and artists.

But, as big as these numbers are, the industry is in turmoil—because the total numbers are shrinking. That $18.4 billion figure is 8.3 percent lower than the prior year (2007), which isn't necessarily a good thing. It's even worse for physical product sales, which are down 15.4 percent. It's all shifting to digital, which is up 24.1 percent. (Publishing rights are also up 16.2 percent worldwide—which speaks to things being better than they might appear.)

Where Is the Money Made?

Nonetheless, with $18.4 billion or more in play, the music business is a *big* business; there's a lot of money to go around. And as with any big business, there are some big players with a vested interest in their own profits. These are, no surprise, the middlemen we discussed throughout this chapter. The big money goes to the big record labels, publishing houses, concert promoters, and ticketing firms. Fair or not, these companies—the labels, in particular—take the lion's share of music industry revenues and profits.

Take physical product sales which, while shrinking slightly, still account for 75 percent of total industry revenues. Who profits from the distribution of CDs? The big record labels, of course. They profit less from digital downloads, and hardly any at all from publishing rights. So when you hear tales of doom and gloom, it's the big labels (represented in the United States by the Recording Industry Association of America [RIAA]) fearing the demise of the CD cash cow.

You'd think, of course, that musicians would also be concerned by shrinking industry sales. That's not generally the case, however, for a number of reasons. First, many musicians never see a profit from their CD sales anyway; the record labels do a good job of keeping all the profits to themselves. So if there are no profits for musicians in CD sales to begin with, what does it matter to them if sales shrink a little?

Second, artists theoretically should benefit from the shift from physical to digital distribution. Not if they stay with a major label, of course; with a major-label contract, digital downloads earn the same percentage for musicians as do CD sales, but on a much lower average sales price. No, the benefit comes from dumping the major labels and going independent. With no need to manufacture and distribute physical product (a need ably fulfilled by the major labels), musicians can distribute their music on their own websites, or deal directly with online music stores. There is less need for the label when you don't have physical product to distribute; by going direct, musicians can keep a much larger percentage of all revenues generated.

In addition, songwriters benefit from any unit increase in music sales, no matter how that music is distributed. Which gets us back to that year-to-year increase in publishing rights sales; songwriters get their cut of all sales, whether that's a physical CD or a digital download. Owning copyrighted intellectual property is a good thing.

And what of the other big companies in the industry—the publishing houses, concert promoters, and ticket agencies? Publishing companies benefit the same as songwriters, although there is some movement away from big publishing houses to self-publishing. The concert and ticket firms also seem to be doing very well, thanks to an uptick in live performances—although there's an indication that some independent artists are evaluating self-booking, at least for smaller venues.

In general, then, there is a trend away from the big companies to artists doing more and more things themselves. While this probably won't affect the overall numbers, it will affect the distribution of revenues and profits. More money should flow to songwriters and performers, with less money flowing to the middlemen. And, unless you're a middleman, that's probably a good thing. (Learn more about how the music industry is changing in Chapter 4.)

Is the Music Industry in Trouble?

If you listen to the RIAA and the big record labels, you might think that the music industry as we know it is disintegrating before our eyes. Forget the $18.4 billion generated in 2008; the industry is imploding!

And just why is this happening? According to the RIAA, it's all due to illegal music downloads. Nobody's buying music anymore because everyone is downloading it for free. Again, forget that $18.4 billion in industry sales—of which $3.8 billion comes from *legal* music downloads. No, the industry is doomed because of those nefarious music pirates.

You can't always believe the big corporations and their trade-group lackeys, of course. In fact, if one looks at unit sales instead of dollar sales, the music industry picture is much more rosy. More and more fans are buying individual tracks online, at about a dollar apiece, rather than buying expensive CDs at $15 a pop. There is every evidence that the music industry continues to grow, but with a much different mix of product.

And this new product mix should be a more profitable mix—especially for musicians. Sales of online downloads come with zero physical cost. It costs zero dollars to make a song available on the iTunes Store or other online music service; the 99¢ paid to download a track from iTunes doesn't have any associated costs to it.

Compare this to the sale of a CD. The disc has to be manufactured, which involves a fair amount of materials and labor. It then has to be packaged (more materials and labor) and physically shipped from the manufacturing plant to the distributor's warehouse to the retail store. Even though the CD sells for $15 or so, a decent chunk of that price has to pay for all the materials and labor involved to make and move the thing.

An online download, then, should be more profitable than the sale of a corresponding CD. Even though the sale price is less (and even though sales are typically of individual songs rather than complete albums), since you don't have to subtract all those physical costs, everybody involved—the online store, the label, and the artist—should make higher profits.

Now, for the label, that might be a higher profit margin on lower revenues, which could result in lower overall profit dollars. Fair enough. But the musicians in the industry can look to grab both a higher percentage of the profit and more profit dollars—especially if they can cut out the middlemen.

So even though the activities remain the same—musicians still write and perform songs—the way musicians profit from those activities is changing considerably. It's not so much an industry in danger as an industry in flux. How you handle these changes will determine how successful you are in the music industry of the twenty-first century.

The Least You Need to Know

♦ The music industry is built around the sale of music as a product; that product may be a song or a recording or a performance.

♦ When a songwriter writes a song, it becomes a copyrighted intellectual property that can then be licensed for additional use.

♦ When a musician records a song, he receives a payment for each unit sold.

♦ When a musician performs live, he receives payment in the form of ticket sales—or a cut thereof.

♦ For just about every type of music-related product, there is a middleman facilitating the sale—and taking a cut of the proceeds.

♦ In 2008, the global music industry was $18.4 billion in size—although sales are shifting from physical products to digital downloads.

3

Essential Business Skills Every Musician Needs to Know

In This Chapter

- ◆ Understanding key business skills: planning, marketing, and merchandising
- ◆ Learning how to negotiate
- ◆ Expanding your legal and accounting skills
- ◆ Learning important technical skills
- ◆ Gaining business savvy

If you've purchased this book and made it through the first two chapters, you're probably convinced that obtaining some business skills will help you make more money as a musician—and get ripped-off less. But what kinds of business skills do you need?

As anyone who's ever looked at a business-school catalog can tell you, business skills run the gamut from A (accounting) to W (website management). Which of these skills are most important for you to learn? Let's take a look.

Essential Planning Skills

When talking about business skills it helps to start at the beginning—with the plans you need to make for your career. In business terms, we're talking about putting together a serious *business plan*, which requires—you guessed it—planning skills.

def•i•ni•tion

A **business plan** is a tool, in the form of a written document, used to develop, grow, and manage a business—in this instance, your music career.

Business plans? For musicians? Aren't they just for big corporations and such? While big corporations do their share of business planning, so do smaller companies and other organizations. In this respect, think of you or your band as a company; you need to do things similar to what a traditional company does to ensure your success in the music business. And that means putting together a well thought out business plan.

Like it or not, success is most often planned, not a matter of luck or circumstance. The biggest artists plan their careers step by step, so that they know what they need to do to reach specific levels of success. Yes, it's possible to stumble into success, but you can't depend on luck. It wouldn't be smart to depend on winning the lottery to balance your personal budget, and it's no smarter to hope for that lucky break to achieve your musical goals. You need to set specific goals that you want to accomplish, and then figure out how to accomplish those goals. That's planning, plain and simple.

In terms of the music business, planning involves determining what you or your band want to be doing a year from now, and then outlining what you need to do to reach that level. If you want to have a CD on the market, then you put together a plan for recording and distributing that CD. If you want to be playing bigger venues, then you put together a plan for graduating from smaller rooms to larger ones. If you want to get your songs published, then you put together a plan for writing viable songs and signing with a publishing house. Your plan becomes the roadmap you follow to achieve your career goals.

How hard is it to write a business plan? Not that hard, really. You basically need to set one or more goals, detail what you need to do to accomplish those goals, and then figure out how much money you need to spend to do it. It's basically a step-by-step set of instructions, accomplished by a few supporting numbers. It doesn't have to be fancy and it doesn't have to be overly detailed. It just needs to point the way. I explain all about business plans in Chapter 5; turn there to learn more.

Essential Marketing Skills

Marketing is all about getting noticed—in a good way. As such, marketing is necessary for musicians of all types and at all levels. You need to market yourself to other musicians, in order to form a band. You need to market yourself to club owners and booking agents, in order to get a gig. You need to market yourself to your audience, in order to draw customers to your gigs and develop a fan base. You need to market your music to record labels, in order to get a contract. And you need to market your songs to publishing houses and other performers, in order to get them published and recorded.

So marketing is one of the most important business skills you need to master. With that in mind, let's look at the different aspects of marketing that matter most.

Marketing Research

When you think of marketing research, you probably think of filling out surveys or sitting in focus groups or reporting Arbitron radio ratings. While these activities all involve market research, they're more about research on a corporate level.

For you as a musician, research is a lot more immediate and a lot more hands on. Basically, your market research will involve getting to know more about the things you do and the people you work with. You need to research the following questions: What are other musicians earning for playing local clubs? Where are other bands like yours playing? How are artists like you distributing their music? How much do similar artists charge for tickets? Where are competing songwriters selling their songs? What labels are competing bands signing with? How are similar musicians interacting with their fans online and off?

You can most often find out what you want to know simply by observing what others are doing, or by asking a few pointed questions of your fans and fellow artists. You don't need fancy surveys and focus groups; you can get a lot smarter just by keeping your eyes and your ears open. And the smarter you are, the fewer mistakes you'll make—and the bigger the head start you'll have on everybody else.

Marketing Plans

We've already talked about general business planning, but planning is also important for your marketing activities. You need to plan in advance what you need to do marketing-wise, and then determine how to execute those plans.

A good marketing plan lays out all the marketing activities you want to undertake, then details who does what and how you pay for everything. There's no benefit to casually throwing money at all manner of marketing activity; develop a thoughtful plan so that each marketing activity you do achieves the best results.

Marketing Budgets

Part and parcel of developing a marketing plan is developing a marketing *budget*. It's not unusual to have champagne tastes and a beer budget when it comes to promoting yourself and your music; without a realistic budget in hand, you may end up over-reaching or digging yourself into a financial hole. You need to know upfront how much money you have to spend, then develop a plan on how best to spend those marketing funds.

def•i•ni•tion

In business terms, a **budget** is an estimate of expected income and expenditures for a future period of time. Most budgets are done yearly.

As you might suspect, developing a budget requires some degree of accounting or math skills. If nothing else, you need to know a debit (money you spend) from a credit (money you receive), and know how to make sure your outlays don't exceed your income. (In simpler terms, you can't spend more money than you make.) You don't have to create detailed profit-and-loss statements and balance sheets, but you do need to be able to create and work from a basic budget.

Promotion

When most people think of marketing, it's the promotion aspect that comes to mind. Promotion is the act of getting the word out, and encompasses a lot of different activities—PR, advertising, website development, mailing list management, you name it. Whatever you do to make yourself known is promotion.

Promotion requires a blend of creativity, media savvy, and hard work. A creative message is necessary to cut through the clutter; knowing how different media work helps you choose the right one and get the most out of it; and hard work is—well, hard work is necessary to achieve any level of success, period.

Smart promotion harnesses the potential of lots of different media—business cards and demo CDs, posters and flyers, press releases and advertisements, blogs and social networks, mailing lists and message forums. A promotional effort might involve creating band-inspired gifts to hand out to reviewers and DJs, designing flyers to post on neighborhood bulletin boards and lampposts, sending e-mail messages to loyal fans, creating radio and magazine ads, arranging interviews with newspapers and radio stations, putting free download samples on your website, and trying to line up all manner of reviews and press coverage. As you can see, it's a lot of different stuff.

As you can probably tell, you need to do a lot of promotion to get yourself and your music noticed. Promotional skills—all of them—are key to your success, even if you don't possess them yourself. A lot of artists outsource this type of marketing and promotion, sometimes to more than one person or firm. You might have one person doing public relations (PR); another running your website; a third handling your snail mail and e-mail mailing lists; and yet another doing brochures, posters, and ads. There's a lot to be done, and it's all important. (Learn more about promotion in Chapter 12.)

Public Relations

One important part of the promotion mix is public relations—what everyone calls PR. PR involves getting important people to notice what you're doing. It's not about creating brochures or buying advertising space, it's a matter of talking people into talking about you.

A good publicist knows a lot of important people. We're talking newspaper and magazine reporters and columnists, music reviewers, influential bloggers, anyone who has the ear of the listening public. The goal is to get these people to mention you or your latest release; the assumption is that a mention in a newspaper article or blog post will inspire the readers of that newspaper or blog to come out to your upcoming gig, download your latest song, or buy your most recent CD. At the very least, you want media mentions to drive interested listeners to your website, where they can learn more about you and check out your music.

A publicist accomplishes all this without purchasing a single advertisement. It's all about having influence with people who have influence; it's a personal thing. A good publicist can pick up the phone or send an e-mail and get results; they know who to contact and what to say to them.

As such, good publicity generates word-of-mouth excitement. A plug from an influential columnist or blogger is worth much more than a paid ad in the same newspaper or website; it's a personal recommendation that readers take to heart. And the best thing is, publicity—while not free—costs a whole lot less than buying an ad or creating a fancy brochure.

Now some musicians are natural publicists; they like to talk to other people (about themselves, of course) and know a lot of influential folks. Other musicians are more reticent and don't necessarily know people in the media. That's okay, publicity is something you can easily outsource. If you don't have natural PR skills, think about adding a professional publicist or PR firm to your team.

Advertising

Knowing how to put together an effective print, radio, television, or online ad is a skill that not everyone possesses. This is why ad agencies make the big bucks; they have the creative staff necessary to fashion ads that work.

Ad agencies also know where to place these ads for best effect. That's exceedingly difficult these days, with various websites and blogs competing with traditional print and electronic media for ad space. Is an ad for your upcoming CD best placed on music-related websites, music review blogs, in the music section of local newspapers, on college radio stations, on late-night television, or on some combination of the above? That's something that a neophyte won't know; it's a skill (or, perhaps, an art) that comes with experience and training.

To that end, few musicians handle their own advertising. They either leave it up to their record labels or, if they're independent, to ad agencies or freelance media specialists. Don't think you know advertising just because you've read a lot of advertisements; this is one skill that's not easily mastered.

Marketing Analysis

The final marketing skill is that of analysis—tracking the results of everything you've done and determining what worked best and why. This sort of thing is second nature to professional marketers, but is most likely something that inexperienced musicians won't even think of. It's human nature to do something and then move on; reflecting on its success (or lack of) requires forethought and dedication beyond what you or I might possess.

This is, of course, a good reason to create a marketing plan—so that you have something to measure results against. If your goal was to sell 10,000 CDs, did sales reach that level? Equally important, what activities had the most impact on those sales?

It's important to know what worked and what didn't, so you'll be smarter about what to do or not do next time around. If you got a large number of website hits and downloads from reviews in independent blogs, then you know to keep up your PR efforts on your next release. If you didn't sell a lot of product from the website banner-ads you placed, then you know not to spend that money next time around. You get the picture; you have to get smart about what you did so you can be more successful with what you do next.

That's marketing analysis, my friends, and it's a very, very important skill to possess.

Essential Merchandising Skills

How do musicians make money these days? There's always CD and digital download sales, of course, and if you're performing live, you can make a decent living from ticket sales. But more and more musicians are making big bucks from merchandise sales—all those little things you sell at your gigs and on your website.

Successful merchandising requires knowledge of what people want to buy, how much they want to spend for it, and where they want to buy it. It also requires skills in creating and producing that merchandise, and negotiating the lowest costs. And then there's the art of selling; you need to be a good salesperson to get your fans to buy all your stuff.

 Smart Business _____

Many musicians are exceedingly creative in what they offer for sale. Some artists sell off visits to recording sessions, backstage visits to big gigs, and even special weekends with the band. It's all a matter of figuring out what your fans want to buy, and then offering them what they want—at the right price, of course.

If you're successful, you can make a lot of money selling everything from hats and T-shirts to autographed pictures and CDs. For that reason, merchandising should be treated quite seriously. If you're not comfortable ordering gross loads of T-shirts from Taiwan and taking credit card orders, you might want to hire someone who knows what they're doing. It's potential revenue you don't want to pass up. (Learn more about merchandising in Chapter 14.)

Essential Negotiating Skills

There are lots of different ways to make money in the music business. Most of them involve dealing with other people in some way or other. Maybe it's working out terms with your local club owner; maybe it's negotiating costs with a T-shirt manufacturer; maybe it's deciding what's a good publishing deal. In every instance, you need to agree on terms of some sort, which involves the skill of negotiation.

Negotiating Contracts

Perhaps the most important negotiations you'll undertake involve contracts. There are a lot of contracts in the music business, as you'll find out soon enough.

If you're a working musician, you encounter contracts every time you book a gig. You need a contract with the local club, a contract with the tour promoter, a contract with the bride who's booking your band for her wedding. Contracts set down in very precise legal language how much you're supposed to be paid, what you're supposed to do in return, and what the other party has to do for you (in addition to writing the check, of course). It's all very necessary—and completely negotiable.

If you're not a good negotiator, expect to be taken advantage of. If you can't hold your ground, the club owner will try to pay you less than the going rate. If you're not a good negotiator, the record label will expect you to pay all sorts of costs that you don't want or need to pay. If you're not a good negotiator, the bride will have you playing music you really don't like at her wedding reception.

Smart Business

Negotiating is a skill. Some people are better at it than others; some just can't do it at all, caving in at the slightest pushback. If you're a good negotiator, bully for you. But if you're not a good negotiator, then you need to find someone to do your negotiating for you. That might be someone else in the band, a good friend, or an agent or manager. Whoever does your negotiating, make sure they're looking out for your best interests, and that they know what you will and won't accept in all situations.

On the other hand, if you can drive a hard bargain, you'll benefit. It doesn't matter what the "standard" deal is, you can often negotiate something better. You can negotiate higher rates for a club date. You can negotiate lower costs on the merchandise you sell. You can negotiate what you play and for how long. It's all a matter of asking for what you want, and then standing firm.

Mediating Disputes

Negotiating isn't just something you do with others; it's sometimes something you do amongst yourselves. That's right, you will eventually need to negotiate with the other members of your band and your extended musical organization. You can't assume that all of you will always have the same opinions and want to do the same things. Heck, you can't even assume that all of you will always be playing together in the same band.

That's right, bands sometimes break up. In fact, bands break up every day; it's a fact of the music business. I defy you to name one band that has survived with its membership roles (including management) intact from day one. Heck, the Beatles lasted less than 10 years; is your band likely to last longer?

And even if it's just one guy leaving or being replaced, that can cause some significant issues for the remaining band members. Take, for example, the issue of equipment ownership. Maybe everybody in the band went together to buy a P.A. system. What do you do when the bass player leaves—or, even worse, when the entire band breaks up? Who takes ownership of the equipment? Does everybody else have to pay the departing member for his share? Or does the guy leaving have to buy his way out of the band?

It gets even more complicated when there's real income involved. Let's say you recorded a CD and it's actually selling. Do you keep paying departed band members for continuing CD sales? What if they wrote some of the songs on the CD; they're technically owed royalties for their work. What's a fair share?

Smart Business _____

Even if you're a solo artist, you still have to work with others, which requires a fair share of day-to-day negotiations. Maybe you hire backing musicians, maybe you hire studio musicians, maybe you hire roadies and a manager and a publicist. These are all folks who could end up in disputes with you over any and every detail. Being a solo artist doesn't mean you're always alone, after all.

In an ideal world, everybody would agree on what's right and leave on friendly terms. But we don't live in an ideal world, and disputes within a band will happen. When disputes arise, it helps if you've worked out all the details in advance, and have them in a contract somewhere. In the event of a lack of contractual terms, you then have to move into dispute management or mediation—a very special form of negotiation. Someone has to step in and work things out between the members—and that someone may need to be you.

Don't think your band is immune. Musicians get better offers every day, or sometimes they just get bored. Sometimes they change day jobs and have to move away; sometimes they get married and start a family and decide that playing is no longer in their future. And the girlfriend who breaks up the band is no urban legend; if it happened to the Beatles, it can happen to you.

Developing People Skills

Working with other people, in whatever capacity, requires you to develop people skills. If you get along with other people, you'll have fewer disputes, and you'll be better able to work through the disputes that arise.

In addition, the better you get along, the more work you'll get. It's a fact; nice people get hired more often. I've known lots of instances where the more talented musician got skipped over in favor of a lesser-skilled (but still capable) musician, because the more talented guy was difficult to work with. With all the tensions involved in playing live and in the studio, you don't want to make things worse by being a prima donna. People don't want to work with jerks—it's that simple.

> **Smart Business** _____
>
> It's a fact; the better you get along with people, the more work you'll get. The legendary Hal Blaine, session drummer extraordinaire, used to function as a contractor for many of the Wrecking Crew sessions in the L.A. studios. He told me he had one motto for his musicians: "If you pout, you're out; if you grin, you're in." Guys that were easy to work with got the gigs, while the troublemakers didn't get a repeat performance.

It's the same whether you're talking live gigs or recording dates, rock 'n' roll or jazz or blues. Your musical talent will get you in the door, but your people skills will keep the gigs coming—and help you work out any differences that might come up, as well.

Essential Legal and Accounting Skills

Negotiating terms should lead to putting something in writing in the form of a contract. And when we get to contracts, we're now talking legal skills—which, like it or not, every musician needs to learn.

Reading and Writing Contracts

The primary legal skill you need, of course, regards reading and writing contracts. Now you don't have to be a licensed attorney to deal with contracts; all of us deal with contracts all the time in our personal lives. If you've ever bought a car, you've dealt with a contract. If you've ever rented an apartment, you've dealt with a contract. If you've ever signed up for a credit card, you've dealt with a contract.

Contracts are everywhere, especially in the music business. When you book a gig at a club, you sign a contract. When you agree to play a wedding reception or similar event, you sign a contract. When you order a bunch of band merchandise to sell, you sign a contract. When you hire a guy to manage your website, you sign a contract. When you book a recording studio, you sign a contract. When you get a song published, you sign a contract. And when you work with a record label, you sign a very big, very important contract. As I said, contracts are everywhere. (Just like vultures. Coincidence?)

With so many contracts crossing your path, you need to learn how to read the darned things. You can't skip over the legalese and fine print and assume that everything is kosher. You need to read all the details to make sure that you agree with what's there, that the things you negotiated (such as your pay) are there as promised, that nobody has tried to sneak in something you didn't negotiate, that somebody accidentally left something important out, and that you aren't being screwed. Yeah, that's a lot of reading and a lot of fine print, but it's necessary.

Smart Business

Don't think that contracts are only for use with outside parties. You may want to draw up a contract for the members of your band, in order to deal with the eventuality of someone leaving or the band breaking up. Put down in writing who's responsible for what, who gets paid how much, and what happens to common property in the event of a breakup. If you work it out in advance, there will be much less trouble when the end finally comes.

And here's the thing. If you don't read your contracts, sooner or later you *will* be taken advantage of. It happens, either on purpose or by accident, but something will pop up that works against you. Not reading the contract isn't a defense; if you sign it, you agree to what's there, whether you read it or not.

Some musicians are good enough with contracts that they write their own, or at least have their own boilerplate contracts that they can edit for specific circumstances. Other musicians depend on the other parties to write the contracts for them. Equally common, and perhaps most recommended, is having an attorney on call to either write or review all your contracts. After all, few musicians are trained lawyers; having a pro handle the legal stuff makes a lot of sense. Just make sure, of course, that you hire an attorney with music-industry experience; there's a lot of unique stuff in our industry that an inexperienced lawyer might not immediately get. (Learn more about contracts and negotiating in Chapter 23.)

Dealing with Copyrights and Royalties

Contracts aren't the only legal issues you have to deal with as a musician. If you do any recording at all, you need to understand and work with copyrights and royalties. When you sell a CD or digital download, the performing artist is owed a specific royalty for that sale. You need to understand just what you own and what it's worth.

The same thing if you're a songwriter. Every time your song is played or recorded, you're owed a specific royalty. The copyright on your song is your currency; knowing your legal rights and the value of what you write is key to your financial well-being.

For that matter, recording somebody else's song also requires knowledge of copyrights and royalties. Even sampling another song in one of your songs brings up these issues. You can't use someone else's music without paying for it—but how much do you have to pay, and how do you make the payments? That's where royalty skills come into play.

And then there's the issue of licensing your songs for use in commercials, TV shows, and movies. What's it worth to you to get this sort of broad publicity for your work? What are you legally owed, what can you negotiate, and what should you accept? Music licensing is a whole other legal world—which you'll learn about in Chapter 16.

Bottom line, it pays to know about copyrights and royalties, and to engage a music industry lawyer who is experienced in these fields. There's big money involved, especially if you're a songwriter. (Learn more about copyrights and royalties in Chapter 24.)

Essential Accounting Skills

Hiring a legal professional is a good idea; it's also a good idea to hire an accounting professional. That's because managing your money is both important and difficult. It's something you need to do, even if you can't balance a checkbook yourself.

To this end, it's important to learn the art of budgeting. We've talked budgets previously in this chapter, but it's worth repeating. You have to budget how much money you need to spend making and promoting your music, versus how much money you expect to make from your music. Ideally, the difference between the two is a positive number, the bigger the better. But if you don't know how to plan your finances, don't be surprised if you always come up a little short every month.

Then there's the issue of taxes. This seems to be a difficult area for some musicians, probably because you don't always get taxes taken out of your paychecks, as you do with most day jobs. Sometimes you get a single check for the entire band, sometimes you get paid in cash, sometimes you might not even get paid at all. (No taxes due on that last one, fortunately!) This kind of *laissez-faire* approach to monetary matters makes it even more difficult to deal with an issue that most of us don't want to deal with at all.

Smart Business

As a freelance worker (which is what you are, as a musician), you probably don't have a lot of withholding taxes withheld. Instead, you're expected to pay quarterly estimated taxes to the government. It takes some financial discipline to both calculate these estimated taxes and budget for them. Ideally, you want to put a piece of each check you receive in a savings account just for these quarterly payments.

You also need to calculate the taxes you owe the state and the feds, which is a skill unto itself. As a business (which you also are), you're entitled to deduct some business expenses from your total business income. Can you deduct the cost of your instrument as a business expense? (Yes.) What about the mileage you incur driving to and from gigs? (Also yes.) What about the beer you consume between sets? (Probably no, unfortunately.)

These are all answers that you might struggle with on your own, but a trained professional can answer. And when it comes to paying the government what they think they're owed, you don't want to guess at it or make any mistakes. A trained accountant is your best friend come tax time. (Learn more about accounting and taxes in Chapter 8.)

Essential Technical Skills

With the advent of the Internet, you need to develop more than just basic business skills. You now need an assortment of technical skills, in order to develop your online presence.

Why technical skills? Because you need a website. You need a blog. You need an e-mail mailing list for your fans. You need your songs to be downloadable from your website. You need to sell merchandise on your website. You may even need to sell tickets to your gigs on your website. And you definitely need to keep a constant presence on all the social networks—Facebook, MySpace, Twitter, and the like.

So it's a brave, new, technologically complex world out there. You may be technically astute enough to do everything you need to do online; after all, posting a few blog posts a week isn't brain surgery. But maintaining a website is a lot of work, and a lot of it is somewhat technical and you might not be comfortable with that. Heck, you just might not have the time to blog and e-mail and access Facebook and Twitter and do everything else you need to do online in the twenty-first century. You could spend so much time online you don't have any time left over to actually play your music.

So you may honestly want to manage your own online activities, but don't have the time or the necessary technical skills. Just because you know how to navigate the B-flat major scale doesn't mean you also know HTML and JavaScript, after all. Maybe you decide to divvy up the chores, doing your own blog posts and tweets while leaving the heavy lifting of website management to a consultant or third-party firm. However you do it, the technical details do have to be managed—you can't be successful today without a significant online presence. (Learn more about using the Internet in Chapter 17.)

Beyond Skills: Developing Business Savvy

Finally, you need to know that learning these and other business skills isn't the whole picture. Skills are nice, even essential, but even more important is being business *savvy*. That means making good business decisions, knowing the difference between a good deal and a bad one, knowing when to push a little harder and when to walk away from a deal. That's business savvy.

Some people have a natural business savvy; they have a good nose for sniffing out what smells and what doesn't. Other people develop business savvy over time; experience teaches them what works and what doesn't. Still other people never develop business savvy; it's just something that continually eludes them.

Let's hope you're not in the latter group, because whether or not you learn every single relevant business skill, you need to develop your business savvy. If you're not savvy, you'll be taken advantage of by people who are. If you're not savvy, you'll miss out on some opportunities. If you're not savvy, you'll work a lot harder than you might need to.

If you are business savvy, however, you'll know when to walk away from a bad deal. You'll know when someone is trying to take advantage of you. You'll know when you have a sweet deal, and when you lay back and take it a little easy.

In short, business savvy is as important to a working musician as is a sense of rhythm or pitch. It won't manage all the details, but it will get you in the ballpark. And that's often the biggest part of it.

How Do I Develop My Business Skills?

Marketing skills, negotiating skills, legal skills, accounting skills—all are important, but not all are second nature to most musicians. Given that you view these business skills as important, just how do you develop them?

Well, you've already taken the first step by buying this book. Now I can't pretend to teach you every last thing you need to know, but I hope that by the time you reach the last page in this book, you'll at least be on the right track.

Beyond that, it helps to work with professionals. If you don't know how to do something, ask someone who does. Maybe you have to pay for their services (in fact, you probably will have to pay for their services), but you can also learn from what they're doing. Maybe the first time you launch your website you let a pro do the design, but when you redesign the site a few years later, you've learned enough to do more of the work yourself. You don't have to reinvent any wheels; let the pros do their job and then learn from what they do.

You may also want to consider taking a few business courses in your spare time. Maybe it's a basic accounting class at your local community college, or maybe it's a full raft of music business courses at a nearby music school. Whatever the case, formal study can help you master those tricky subjects you have trouble learning on your own.

Finally, learn from those around you. If you want to learn how to book your band, talk to someone who books a band similar to yours. If you want to get your songs published, talk to an established songwriter. The folks in our business are, more often than not, quite helpful and willing to share their knowledge with others. We musicians are a family—and family helps each other out.

The Least You Need to Know

- All musicians need essential planning, marketing, and merchandising skills.

- It's also important to learn how to negotiate—and to develop strong people skills.

- Beyond business skills, you also need to gain some degree of legal and accounting skills.

- In today's digital world, technical skills are also important.

- While skills are important, you also need to develop business savvy—a sense of what's a good deal and what's not.

Chapter 4

The History and Future of the Music Business

In This Chapter

- Understanding the history of the music business

- Examining the music business today—including digital distribution and the Internet

- Predicting future changes in the music business—and preparing for those changes

The music business has always been one of constant change. Business practices that were common back in the 1950s are much less common today; a lot of the stuff happening today wasn't even possible back in the 1950s (or the 1990s, for that matter). Although the same business skills remain important, in spite of all the business changes, you still have to adapt those skills to the changing industry.

Some of the older players in the business are having trouble adapting in this fashion. Unfortunately, doing things the same way you did 5 or 10 or 20 years ago just doesn't cut it in today's digital world. If you can stay on top of the changes, you'll have a real advantage over the slow-moving dinosaurs who still roam the halls of the major labels.

> **Behind the Music**
>
> Learn more about the history of music in general in my companion book, *The Complete Idiot's Guide to Music History* (Michael Miller, Alpha Books, 2008).

So what are these major changes in the music industry—and how do they affect you and your music? That's what we'll examine in this chapter, along with a quick glimpse into the crystal ball to see what the future might bring.

A Brief History of the Music Business

The music business has a long and interesting history. In fact, if you peg the beginnings of the music industry as when musicians first got paid for playing or writing their music, then we're looking at the start of things being somewhere in the medieval period.

Church Gigs

The first exchange of money for music occurred back in the Middle Ages. Musicians of the day—composers, mainly—were employed by local churches. The musicians most often held the title of choir master or musical director, and were directly compensated for their efforts. There was no musician's union around to dictate pay scale, of course, but the bigger the church, the more prestigious the job and the higher the pay.

As terms of employment, these composers were expected to produce work that would be sung or played at church services. It was pay for play, just as it is today—but without any sense of copyright and absolutely no notion of royalties. You got paid your weekly salary and you wrote whatever music the church needed.

The Patronage System

This arrangement stayed pretty much the same through the Renaissance, but things changed substantially during the Baroque era. Starting in the 1600s, musicians moved away from the church into private employment, as part of what was known as the *patronage* system.

In this system, a composer would be employed by a patron—typically a member of a royal court or a wealthy family. The composer was employed to provide music for the court or family; he typically performed himself, accompanied other musicians, and conducted both small and large ensembles. Of course, the composer was also expected to provide original works for his employer's various functions, which led to a move away from church music to secular music.

def•i•ni•tion

Patronage is the support, often financial, that one individual or organization bestows on another.

Playing for Money

The patronage system continued through the beginning of the Classical period, but died out by the mid-1700s or so, around the time that Wolfgang Amadeus Mozart was making a name for himself. Without wealthy employers paying the bills, composers had to pay their own way, essentially becoming self-employed freelancers.

Unfortunately, with no copyright or royalty system in place, there was little money to be made from one's compositions. Instead, most composers paid the bills by performing either their own works or works of others. Then like today, there was big money to be made on the concert circuit, which favored those composers who were also popular and prolific performers. (It's telling that Mozart's fortunes hit the skids when he cut back on his concert work—even though he kept composing right up until his death.)

Behind the Music

The most famous composers of the time made a good living performing or conducting their own works. Ludwig van Beethoven, for example, made money by arranging subscription concerts, where concert goers bought tickets for a series of performances; in essence, he functioned as his own concert promoter. Beethoven also was able to sell his works to music publishers, which supplemented his concert income. Those music publishers, in turn, sold sheet music of Beethoven's works.

The Birth of Music Publishing

By the turn of the nineteenth century, just about every middle-class household had a piano; pianos were a sign of status, as ubiquitous then as iPods are today. If you wanted to hear new music, you played it yourself on your own piano from sheet music you purchased at your local music store.

This big demand for new music was filled by a growing number of music publishing companies. These companies purchased from songwriters the rights to their songs, and then published printed versions of those songs as sheet music. This sheet music was then sold to consumers via music stores, department stores, and the like. The most popular sheet music of the day sold millions of copies—not unlike what a hit song sells today.

The Rise of Copyright

With the boom in music publishing came the need for songwriters to be fairly compensated for their work. In the early days of music publishing, that compensation was typically a one-time fee; a songwriter sold his song to a publishing house for a few hundred dollars (or less), and the publisher could sell as many copies of the resulting sheet music as they wanted to. It didn't matter whether the song sold a hundred copies or a hundred thousand; the songwriter got his flat fee and nothing more.

This all changed (in the United States, at least) with the passage of the Copyright Act of 1909. This law allowed for original works (including musical works) to be copyrighted for a period of 28 years, renewable for a second 28-year term.

Key to the Copyright Act was the creation of a compulsory mechanical license, to account for the mechanical reproduction of musical works. This mechanical reproduction was initially intended to cover piano rolls, popular at the time, but was later applied to phonograph records, CDs, and the like.

The concept of copyright transformed the music industry. No longer were songwriters compensated on a flat-fee or work-for-hire basis; now they owned copyrights that retained value for decades after their songs were written. While a songwriter could still make a one-time sale of a song to a music publisher, it became more common for the songwriter to retain the copyright and be compensated from royalties collected on a per-performance or per-sale basis. If you wrote a hit song that sold a million records, you'd earn more money than if you wrote a flop that only sold a thousand copies. And if your song was used in a Broadway play, Hollywood musical, or television show—well, that just meant more royalties coming your way.

Behind the Music

Music publishers were still essential to the process, as they not only promoted the song-writer's songs to other performers, but they also collected all the royalty payments due. As such, the publisher typically shared in the royalties, taking for their services a percentage of all royalties due to the songwriter.

The collection of royalties was made easier with the formation in 1914 of the American Society of Composers, Authors, and Publishers (ASCAP). ASCAP was founded as a nonprofit organization to protect the copyrighted musical works of its members, both songwriters and publishers; some of its earliest members include John Philip Sousa, Irving Berlin, and Jerome Kern. ASCAP—along with its later-day rival, Broadcast Music International (BMI)—tasked itself with collecting royalties due from all media, from sheet music sales to radio play.

Songwriters for Hire

From approximately 1880 to 1940 or so, the American music publishing industry—in fact, the entire music industry—was concentrated in that area of New York City on West 28th Street between Broadway and Sixth Avenue. This publishing center came to be known as *Tin Pan Alley*, and the lyricists and composers who worked in Tin Pan Alley during this period are remembered for creating some of the most popular songs of the day.

> **Behind the Music**
>
> The term *Tin Pan Alley* was coined by writer Monroe Rosenfield, who likened the cacophony of so many songwriters pounding on so many pianos to the sound of beating on tin pans.

Tin Pan Alley was an interesting environment; songwriters, together and in teams, churned out their compositions in factory-like style. The best of these songs were sold to music publishing companies and issued as sheet music or piano rolls (before the explosion of the record business), or picked up by one of the major singers of the day. Sometimes these Tin Pan Alley tunes ended up in vaudeville productions, Broadway plays, or Hollywood movies. The best of the best endured, and became classics.

> **Behind the Music**
>
> All the major music publishing companies of the day had offices in the creaking brownstones and small commercial buildings of Tin Pan Alley. These included T. B. Harms Company, M. Witmark & Sons, E. B. Marks Music Company, and Irving Berlin, Inc. (Mr. Berlin was a pioneer in self-publishing.) Most of these companies published music instruction books, church music, and classical music, in addition to the popular sheet music of the day.

The most talented songwriters of a generation filtered through Tin Pan Alley. Irving Berlin, Cole Porter, Jerome Kern, George and Ira Gershwin, and their contemporaries were all professional songwriters for hire, and they made money from their music from a number of different sources, including sheet music and piano roll sales, placement in Broadway musicals and Hollywood movies, record sales, and (to a degree) radio play.

By the mid-1950s, the New York music publishing industry moved uptown from Tin Pan Alley to that stretch of Broadway between 49th and 53rd streets. The hub of this activity was the Brill Building, located at 1619 Broadway, along with a neighboring building at 1650 Broadway.

Behind the Music

The 1650 Broadway building was home to Aldon Music, founded by famed publisher/ producer Don Kirshner and his partner Al Nevins. Aldon's stable of songwriters included Neal Sedaka and Howard Greenfield, Carole King and Gerry Goffin, and Barry Mann and Cynthia Weil, who wrote some of the biggest hits of the 1960s.

From the start, the Brill Building had a number of music publishers as tenants, including Famous Music, Mills Music, and Southern Music. By 1962, the building was home to more than 150 music companies, and this concentration of companies made the Brill Building (and its across-the-street companion) a kind of "one-stop shop" for aspiring musicians in the early rock era.

Enter the Record Business

When examining the source of musician's income in the Tin Pan Alley and Brill Building eras, it's important to know that some of these revenue streams developed later than others. The biggest of these were recording royalties, which didn't become a big thing until after the turn of the century.

The record industry grew by leaps and bounds after Thomas Edison invented the phonograph in 1877; by 1920, more than 150 companies were making records or record players. And thanks to the Copyright Act of 1909 and the efforts of ASCAP, songwriters received a fair shake from these record sales, receiving the agreed-upon mechanical royalty rate for all copies sold.

As could be expected, the record industry evolved over time. The original 78 RPM wax discs gave way by the late 1940s and early 1950s to long playing (LP) vinyl records and shorter-playing 45 RPM "singles." In the late 1960s and 1970s, the 8-track tape format had a brief flirtation with consumer success, as did higher-quality audio cassette tapes. But the big change in format didn't happen until the 1980s, with the advent of digital CDs. This switch to CDs spurred music sales to record highs, with many record collectors replacing their analog collections with new digital copies.

> **Behind the Music**
>
> Performers didn't initially receive royalties for the music they recorded, getting only a flat fee for their work at the recording session. That changed over time, however, with recording performers eventually receiving a similar mechanical royalty to that paid to songwriters on each copy sold.

The Rise of Radio

Commercial radio developed after the record industry, rising to prominence in the early 1920s. Early radio programming consisted of a lot of staged dramas and comedies along with a plethora of live music shows. The radio stations and networks eventually supplemented their live programming with the playing of recorded music—literally, playing records over the air.

The music industry viewed this airplay as necessary promotion that spurred record sales, and did not pay performance royalties when records were played. (They did pay performance royalties for live music performances, however.) Songwriters, of course, received royalties whenever their songs were played on the air, but not the recording musicians, which made radio a dubious source of income—loved by songwriters and tolerated (mostly) by the performers.

That didn't stop the American Federation of Musicians (AFM) from striking against the big record labels in 1942. The AFM argued that radio and jukebox play took away opportunities for live performers, and demanded compensation for musicians whose work was played on radio and jukeboxes. While the AFM won the battle, they lost the war; that strike backfired, keeping union musicians out of the studio for more than a year and effectively killing the big band era. Small-group music, played by nonunion musicians, moved in to fill the gap and led to a much different post-war musical environment.

The Rock Era

By the mid-1960s, traditional New York–based music publishing had come to an end. The movie and stage musical had long been in decline, short-playing 45 RPM singles became the major means of selling songs, and individual performers became more important than the songwriters—all of which led to a sharp decline in sheet music sales.

Behind the Music

Music has also become more portable over time. During the first part of the twentieth century, most people listened to music in their homes, either on their own pianos, on phonograph records, or over the radio. In the second half of the century, however, new technology enabled people to listen to music in their cars, on portable transistor radios, on their Sony Walkman portable audio cassette players, and now on their iPod digital music players.

Perhaps even more important, the British Invasion, led by groups like the Beatles, who wrote all of their own songs, dramatically impacted the market for professional songwriters. With all the latest rock groups emulating Bob Dylan and the Beatles by writing their own songs, it became less common for music publishers to hire their own stables of songwriters. For a songwriter to survive, he had to be able to perform his own songs.

Of course, any performing musician who wrote his own songs now saw an additional revenue stream from songwriting royalties. Instead of relying solely on performing royalties from record sales, a performer/songwriter now added songwriting royalties from both record sales and radio play. It was a sweet deal that earned musicians of the rock era more money than the big singers of the 1940s and 1950s, who didn't write any of their songs.

The Music Business Today

The music business today is much like the music business of the past, but with more complicating factors. Sheet music, records (in the form of CDs), and radio still exist—although piano rolls are long gone. But added to the mix are digital music and the Internet, which provide both challenges and opportunities for the musicians of today.

Who Writes the Songs?

The days of the Tin Pan Alley and Brill Building professional songwriter are long gone. Most musicians today write their own songs, and most songwriters sing their own songs; there isn't a lot of writing for others taking place.

Behind the Music

Songwriting for hire still exists in a few niches—on Broadway, for Hollywood movie soundtracks, for the country music industry in Nashville, and in some forms of vocal pop music. While there appear to be no new Gershwins or Bacharachs, there are still a number of freelance songwriters who make a living writing music on spec for these specific markets.

That means that most songwriting royalties today are collected by performers who write their own songs. These new-generation songwriters still sign with music publishing companies, and still have their royalties collected by either ASCAP or its more contemporary competitor, BMI. Royalty rates have risen over the years, of course, but are still collected whenever a composition is sold (via record or digital download) or played (on terrestrial AM/FM radio, satellite radio, Internet radio, and the like).

The Digital Era

The song remains the same, but its delivery evolves with new technology. Songs used to be sold on wax 78 RPM discs, then on vinyl LPs and singles, then on 8-tracks and audio cassettes, then on digital CDs. Today, however, the CD business is shrinking as more and more listeners get their music via digital download from the Internet— either legally, via a music download store or service, or illegally, via a file-sharing service.

Behind the Music

The digital era affects more than just the way consumers purchase music; it also affects how music is recorded. Digital recording made its way into studios in the 1990s, replacing older analog tape recorders, changing the whole nature of the recording industry. Today, virtually any musician can create high-quality recordings in the comfort of their own home studios without racking up huge studio bills; this, as much as anything, has led to the rise of the indie music movement—and to the decline in major recording labels.

With the rise of the Internet in the late 1990s, listeners found they could download the songs they wanted from a variety of legitimate and illegitimate websites. The original Napster was one of the first of the free file-sharing websites, encouraging listeners to "rip" music from their CDs and upload the tracks to the web where they could then be downloaded (for free) by others. Napster was eventually shut down for illegal file sharing, but the public developed a taste for downloading single tracks (not complete albums) over the Internet in MP3 format.

> **Behind the Music**
>
> Even though some listeners like file sharing as a source of free music, it's illegal. This practice infringes on the artists' copyright and deprives artists (and their labels) from royalties earned.

This digital music boom got a big boost when Apple released its iPod portable music player. There were other digital music players before, but Apple got everything right and encouraged a new generation of listeners to take their music with them in digital format.

The iPod is supported by Apple's iTunes Store, which legitimized music downloads. At an initial cost of just 99¢ per track, iTunes enabled listeners to load up their iPods with all their favorite songs—and effectively contributed to the death of the $20 CD album. Why purchase an entire album (at a high price) when you can get just the songs you like (for a low price)? This per-song thinking brings the industry full circle to the Top 40 days of the 1960s, where singles, not albums, ruled.

Music Online

Of course, Apple doesn't have a monopoly on digital music. There are a number of competing online music stores, as well as subscription services and Internet radio stations. In addition, many artists offer their songs for free or paid download from their own websites—which acts as a new source of independent promotion.

In short, the Internet provides several new models for music distribution. These include:

- ◆ Online music stores, selling individual tracks for about a buck apiece
- ◆ Music label and artist websites, offering either featured tracks for free streaming or full albums offered for paid download
- ◆ Online subscription services, which let listeners subscribe to all the music they can listen to for a monthly fee

♦ Internet radio stations that stream specific genres of music to listeners, typically for free

♦ File-sharing sites that offer illegal music downloads—for free, of course

While the online music store model, exemplified by the iTunes Store, is probably the most successful model to-date, there's no guarantee that it will be the dominant model going forward. This is still a market in flux, and where it ends up is anybody's guess right now.

The Independent Movement

In the old days, signing with a major label was the holy grail for most musicians; you hit the big time when you signed with RCA, Atlantic, Columbia, or Motown. In fact, artists pretty much had to sign with a major record label if they wanted to become more than a regional performing act. If you wanted your music recorded, the label would advance you the money for the studio time. If you wanted your recordings distributed, the label would have the discs pressed and shipped to all major record stores. If you wanted your music heard, the label would promote the records with DJs at radio stations across the country. Everything revolved around the label.

All this came at a cost, however. While artists most often received some sort of initial payment from the label, typically in the form of a signing bonus or advance, they also signed over to the label most of their rights to the music they wrote and recorded. The label could take a cut of performance royalties, and sometimes acted as music publisher, dipping also into songwriting royalties. Even worse, artists found that their labels billed them for all possible (and often impossible) expenses, from studio time to legal fees to promotional expenses to limousines. Yes, the label got you recorded and played, but the expenses they billed more often than not exceeded any royalties due. Most artists never saw a dime beyond the initial advance.

These practices eventually led to a backlash against the major labels. With digital technologies enabling lower-cost home recording, artists no longer needed a label to finance their records. Artists could make their own recordings, press their own CDs, and even distribute their own discs (via mail or at performances). With the rise of the Internet, artists had another source of promotion; by establishing a website or Facebook/MySpace page, artists could communicate directly with their fans, further obviating the need for major label promotion.

Thus the 1990s and 2000s saw a rise in small, independent record labels, many of which existing solely to distribute a single artist's recordings. By doing everything themselves, artists could save themselves the expenses charged by the major labels and take home a much larger share of the revenues they generated. Artists were increasingly operating on their own—and benefiting from it.

Segmenting—and Oversegmenting—the Music

There's something else different about the music industry today. The industry is a lot less monolithic, and a lot more segmented. Some of this results, of course, from the decline of the major labels. With lots of little independent labels doing their own thing, the majors have less and less control over what radio stations play and what regular people listen to.

But it goes well beyond that. Back in the heyday of Top 40 radio (the 1960s and early 1970s), AM radio stations played pretty much everything. Listeners could be exposed to the Beatles one minute, followed by a Bob Dylan track, followed by the country sounds of Roger Miller, followed by a little crooning from Frank Sinatra. That kind of variety helped promote all musical genres—everybody heard a little bit of everything.

That's not the case today. Over the past several decades, radio programming has become much more segmented. Instead of one station playing everything, you now have multiple stations, each playing a narrow slice of music. You have hip hop stations, heavy metal stations, alternative stations, R&B stations, country stations—and there's no cross-breeding between them. A listener picks his station of choice and never gets exposed to anything else.

> ### Behind the Music
>
> The radio industry has also become more concentrated in recent years. Today, a handful of large corporations (such as Clear Channel) control the majority of top stations in most major markets. Unlike the old days when local DJs chose the songs they played on their shows, the playlists for today's radio stations are set at the corporate level, making it increasingly difficult for new artists to break into the mix.

This blinders-on programming is even worse in the worlds of satellite and Internet radio, where segments get further subsegmented. You want a station that plays only gangster rap? You got it. How about an outlaw country-only station? It's there. What about a station that plays only Elvis Presley tunes? Yep, there's one of those, too.

Then there's the iPod. When you can program your own music, you need not even be exposed to anything new, let alone anything different. How do you hear the latest and the greatest when all you have playlisted are old hair-metal tracks from the 1980s? We're all listening to our own private stations, everything else be damned.

The effects of this oversegmentation are many. First, there's no such thing as a big act any more. In the old days, a hit single could sell tens of millions of copies, because people from all walks of life were exposed to it. Not the case today, where a "big" single only sells a hundred thousand copies or so, and isn't even recognizable by most listeners—who happen not to listen to that particular format. That means, of course, that even if you hit it big, you won't be as big as you could have been back in the day.

But while oversegmentation makes it difficult to break out of your own particular niche, it makes it easier to reach your fan base. You don't have to spend money promoting to the masses; instead, you can use the Internet to go directly to people who've bought your music in the past. Artists today are more likely to have a smaller but more dedicated fan base than in the past, which isn't necessarily a bad thing. It's harder to make it big, but it might be easier to make a living.

Money from the Road

All this adds up to a much different revenue stream for most artists today. In the past, musicians (songwriters, especially) could rake in big bucks from record sales—especially when those sales were in the millions, and of high-priced LPs. Today, however, sales are in the tens or maybe the hundreds of thousands, but are likely to be primarily 99¢ downloads. That's a lot less money earned from the sales of music.

Of course, you can still make money selling your music—if you don't have to deal with the big labels. Yes, you might sell fewer copies, but if you're an independent artist, you get to keep a much larger piece of the pie. It can more than balance out in your favor.

Beyond music sales, then, where do musicians make money today? Believe it or not, many musicians make more money from touring and performing live than they do from selling CDs and digital downloads. It used to be that touring was at best a break-even proposition, sometimes a losing one. But in recent years ticket prices have gotten sufficiently higher and artists have gotten correspondingly smarter in how they do things, to the point where even a regional tour can be a big money maker. Add to ticket sales the revenues generated from selling band-related merchandise, and you can see why many artists now consider their albums promotion for their tours, rather than the other way around.

Behind the Music
There's also less money to be made from the creation of music. Back in the day, almost all major cities had a lively studio scene, and studio musicians were in constant demand to create the music that got played on Top 40 radio. Today, however, with most recordings being made in home or smaller studios by the musicians themselves, there's little or no call for high-priced studio pros.

Tomorrow's Music Business

So that's where we stand today. The music industry is both larger in terms of number of players, and smaller in terms of the size of those players. Music is now recorded and distributed digitally over the Internet. Artists connect directly with their fans, again using the Internet, and make more money from touring than they do from music sales.

It's a much different music business than it used to be—and likely to be even more different in the future. Just what sorts of changes should we look forward to in the years to come, and how will they affect the way we make music and do business?

More Digital Music

Here's the easy prediction: The move to digital recording and distribution will continue at a rapid pace. The harder part is predicting just how the digital movement will eventually shake out, particularly on the distribution side.

The facts are clear. Physical CD sales continue to decline (down 20 percent from 2007 to 2008, according to SoundScan), while digital downloads continue to rise (up 27 percent from 2007 to 2008). In fact, it's likely that physical music distribution will fade away completely at some point—maybe not next year, but possibly within a decade.

Today, most online music is sold on a per-track basis by online music stores. But that may not be the model for the future, especially as more and more listeners want their music on the go—which doesn't necessarily mean from iPods and other portable music players.

To that end, I'm placing my bets on music delivered over smartphones, such as the Apple iPhone, Google Android, and BlackBerry Storm. Not that these devices will have tons of digital files stored locally, of course. It's more likely that music will be streamed in real time over the accompanying cellular phone network.

I can envision a scenario where you speak into your phone, "Play the Beatle's White Album" or "Play 'Louie, Louie,'" and the requested music will be sent over the cell network to your phone. It's not that farfetched. In fact, you get similar streaming music today with the Pandora and Last.fm iPhone applications. Just imagine a giant music server out there in the clouds, with every track ever recorded available for immediate streaming to anyone's cell phone, the entirety of music history just a voice command away. Trust me, it's coming.

With this in mind, how do you prepare for this streaming digital-music future? At this point, it's difficult to say. You'll definitely need to have all your music in digital format, of course, although it's unclear which file format will eventually become the standard. Then we're faced with the issue of who (or rather, which entity) runs the music streaming service. Will it be an existing player, such as Apple? Will each cellular provider run their own services? And whichever service dominates, how will you work with them—Will they dictate terms, and will those terms be fair? Or will the cellular providers offer streaming from multiple sites, enabling labels and artists to continue to manage their own music?

You see the issue. Even if you think you know what direction things are headed, you don't know exactly how they're going to get there—or how all the details will shake out. All you know is that things are going to change, and you have to be flexible in how you deal with that.

More Independence

It's possible that all music downloading or streaming will be consolidated in a single provider or database, but it's just as likely that multiple providers will exist, and that they may even pull content from a multitude of smaller providers, such as individual artists and labels.

One nice thing about technology is that it levels the playing field. For example, advances in recording technology make it possible for artists to record great-sounding music on a shoestring budget, without the need for expensive recording studios. You put together an album in your own home, complete with string and horn samples that sound pretty much like the real thing, for less than $1,000. Every artist, large or small, can get the full orchestral sound; an artist with a large label budget has no inherent advantage in this respect.

It's the same thing with distribution. In the old days, you needed the muscle of a major label to get your music out and heard. That's not the case today; you can burn and sell your own CDs after your performances, distribute your music digitally from your own website, and negotiate your own deals for digital downloading with online music stores.

In short, there's little need to partner with a major record label today, and that independence will only grow in the future. The Internet is not only helping to link artists with their listeners, it's also connecting artists with individuals and firms that provide the services they need. Web-based booking services abound, as do web-based marketers, web-based PR firms, and the like. Anyone you need to work with is only a click or two away.

And you may not even have to hire an outside firm. Given the proliferation of online message boards and blogs for musicians, it's becoming increasingly easy to get questions answered and share vital information. You don't need to reinvent the bicycle; some other musician out there has gone through the same thing you're going through and can share his experience and advice.

The Internet, in short, is turning the old music industry into a new music community. It's the difference between working for a big company and working with your family; the family way is almost always better.

More Direct Connection

As you can probably sense, the Internet has been the driving force behind many of the big changes in the music business. That's also true when it comes to marketing yourself and communicating with your fans. Instead of relying on expensive radio, magazine, and newspaper ads, you can now notify your fans of upcoming gigs and new albums via the web, blogs, e-mail, and social networking. Not only is Internet promotion lower cost than traditional advertising, it's also more targeted; there's less waste in online communications.

Even better, the Internet enables a degree of connection between you and your fans that didn't exist in any previous media, except perhaps written fan mail. Manage your website or blog correctly, and your audience will feel like they're included in everything you do and become extremely loyal. In essence, you can build a new family or community of followers online.

Gazing Into the Crystal Ball ...

In any case, you need to be prepared for a world where musicians are no longer sequestered in their rooms or the studio. Tomorrow's listeners will expect more direct connection with their favorite artists, which means you need to more frequently communicate with them. You need to develop not only your musical skills, but also your communication skills.

You see, the nature of being a musician is changing. You have to do more; you need to not just play but also record and distribute and promote and interact directly with listeners. All of a sudden you're not just a musician, you're a recording engineer, a digital distributor, a blogger, and anything else that anyone needs you to be. You're going to have to become more involved in all facets of your career, not just the playing.

And in doing so, you need to figure out new ways to make money. It will no longer be just about selling records; it will be about selling tickets and selling merchandise, calculating download payments, and monetizing your website and blog. Maybe you make money from selling advertising on your website; maybe you use the web to find patrons to subsidize your recording activities. Heck, maybe you forgo recording completely to focus on live performances. It's going to be different—and different for different artists.

Going forward, you have to apply the same creativity to your business affairs as you do to your music. That's the brave new future of the music business; everything is subject to change, and the better you adapt to that change, the more successful you will be.

What Still Works—and What Doesn't?

With all the changes happening and upcoming in the music business, just how valuable are the business skills of the past? You'd be surprised.

You see, the key business skills will always be important. Whether you distribute your music on vinyl records or via digital downloads, you still need to negotiate contracts, promote yourself and your music, and manage your finances. That's right, negotiating and contract skills, marketing skills, and accounting skills still matter. I can't imagine anything happening in the future that will change that.

If anything, the old skills become more important. While you may have been able to rely on your record company to do some of the business stuff, the move to independent distribution and promotion puts more of that responsibility on your lap.

Instead of the record company promoting your new release, you have to do it yourself. Instead of a management agency booking your gigs, you have to do it yourself. Instead of a label's promotion person managing your fan club, you have to do it yourself. You get the idea.

Going forward, it will be those musicians who have the strongest business skills who will be the most successful. The musician of tomorrow will need to be a multiple-threat performer/businessperson. And that means getting the most out of those business skills that we all should have had, anyway.

The Least You Need to Know

♦ While early musicians were supported by wealthy patrons (or the church), the concept of ownership and copyright led to the payment of royalties to both songwriters and performers.

♦ During the twentieth century, musicians generated income from the distribution of their music via piano rolls, sheet music, vinyl records, CDs, and digital downloads—as well as their music being played on the radio, on TV, and in movies.

♦ Over the past decade or so, distribution has shifted from physical recordings (records and CDs) to digital recordings (Internet downloads and streaming audio).

♦ Today, an increasing number of musicians are making more money from touring (and associated activities) than from traditional music sales.

♦ Advancing technology has enabled a growing independence from major record label control—and a more direct connection with fans.

Part 2

Becoming a Business-Oriented Musician

How much do you know about the business part of the music business? These chapters show you how to plan your career, assemble your team, manage your career, and manage your money. (Assuming you actually make any money, that is!)

Chapter 5

The Business of Planning Your Career

In This Chapter

- Why you need a business plan
- Setting goals and developing a roadmap—the key parts of a business plan
- Writing an effective business plan
- Following your plan—and evaluating your success

In today's music business, you have to plan for success. You just can't expect a major label A&R guy to be in the crowd at your local club and sign you up for a recording contract on the spot—the music world's equivalent of winning the lottery.

Now I'm not sure that kind of Hollywoodesque rags-to-riches story ever really existed, but it certainly has no place in the music industry of the twenty-first century. In today's music business, smart musicians plan every step of their careers, and then work hard to accomplish their goals. Yes, I'm talking about creating a bona fide, words-on-paper business plan, a blueprint for your future success. Like it or not, this sort of plan is essential for guiding your career.

Planning for Success

You probably don't want to hear about business plans. They sound so … well, so *corporate*—big binders full of charts and graphs and lots and lots of numbers and fine print. Bo-ring.

The thing is, planning isn't the exclusive province of the corporate world. Lots of people make plans—heck, you probably do, too, at least on a small scale. When you look at your income and outflow and put together a budget so you can buy that new keyboard or guitar, you're making plans. When you look at your schedule and try to figure out when you can get a whole two weeks off for a vacation, you're making plans. When you put together a recording schedule for the musicians you want to play on your next album, you're making plans.

Okay, everybody makes plans. But that's not the same thing as writing a formal business plan.

Or is it? Ask yourself this question: Why do you make plans? For most of us, we make plans so we can figure out how and when to do something. Put slightly differently, we're putting together a set of instructions to help us accomplish a goal. The goal comes first, of course, but then we plan how we're going to get from here to there.

Goals, of course, are important. Without a goal, you're likely to wander aimlessly in your musical career. And without a plan on how to accomplish that objective, your goal is nothing more than a pipedream. You see, a plan is like a roadmap. You follow the route and you get to where you want to go. Put more succinctly, you'll never get anywhere as a musician unless you know where you want to go, and how you want to get there. That's planning.

Setting Your Goals

So if you need goals to be successful, what should those goals be? Naturally, every musician has his or her own specific goals. Goals are personal; they're what you want to accomplish in your career, and everyone's career is different. That said, there are some common goals shared by many musicians:

Form a band. Hey, everybody has to start somewhere. When you're first starting out, finding a group of musicians to play with is a big deal; forming or joining a band is a good goal to start out with. And if you're a solo artist, you can translate this goal into the equally important goal of "find backing musicians."

Get a gig. Now that you have a band and have (hopefully) learned a bunch of songs, the next logical goal is to get a gig. That may be a freebie, if you're doing this for fun, or your goal may be to get a paying gig. What kind of gig you get should also be part of your goal—do you want to play casuals and wedding receptions, or do you want to play the local clubs? Specify what kinds of gigs you want to play to better target your goals.

Get a better gig. If you're already a working musician, your goal may be to better your lot in life—that is, to upgrade the gigs you play. Maybe you want to move from wedding receptions to clubs, or from small clubs to large clubs, or from clubs to concert halls. Develop a vision of where you want to be playing 12 months from now, and make that your goal.

Write a song. If songwriting is your forte, or just your desire, make that one of your goals. You can't become a songwriter until you write a song, one with real chord changes, a melody, and lyrics and such. Your first song doesn't have to be good (and it probably won't be), but it does have to get written.

Get your songs published. Once you get a few songs under your belt, what do you do with them? For a songwriter, a good goal is to get your songs published—and, after that, get them played or recorded by other musicians. It's all about achieving an even longer-term goal of making money from your songs.

Record your music. For many musicians, a big goal is that of making a recording. That may mean recording a track or two or recording an entire album. Recording your music is a worthwhile goal, and one that can lead to other goals beyond that.

Sell your music. Here's a goal that is kin to the recording thing—selling the music you record. That may be via CDs you sell at your gigs, from tracks that fans can download from your website, from songs that get downloaded from iTunes and other online music stores, or from honest-to-goodness physical product sold through major music retailers. Getting your product distributed is the goal, and how you get that done is part of the plan.

Create a website, blog, or Facebook or MySpace page. Creating an online presence is an important goal if you want to promote your music and connect with your fans.

Sign with a record label. This used to be the ultimate goal for a lot of musicians. It may still be a legitimate goal for you, once you evaluate all the alternatives. Just make sure this isn't one of those pie-in-the-sky things, where the *image* of being a major-label artist is more appealing than the reality.

Generate a livable income. Now here's a goal you can sink your teeth into. You're playing music because you love music, of course, and because you're an artist. But even artists have to eat and pay the rent, which means either keeping a day job or generating some income from your music. How much money do you want to make? That's the goal. Maybe all you need is to supplement your day income; maybe you want to live full time from your music career. Whatever the case, figure out how much money you want to take home from your music, and then plan on how to generate that income.

As you can see, your goals don't have to be big-picture, life goals. They can include short-term goals, things you want to accomplish within the next six months or a year. Whatever the time span, however, your goals should be both *measurable* and *achievable*.

By measurable, I mean that your goals have to be specific. A vague goal, such as "I want to be successful," is practically useless, because you can't measure something fuzzy like "success." A better goal would be "I want to join a working band," "I want to record a CD," or "I want to play the biggest club in town." All of these goals are measurable; you know whether you've joined a band or not, recorded a CD or not, or played that club or not. There's nothing arguable about what constitutes those achievements.

Achievable means that your goals should be realistic. If your goal is to become the next Michael Jackson or Elvis Presley, well, best of luck to you, but that's probably not going to happen. If your goal is to go from playing in your basement to making a million dollars within a year, well, that's a bit pie-in-the-sky, too, don't you think? Set smaller goals, even if they're short term, that you know can be accomplished. There's nothing wrong with dreaming big, but your plans should be a bit more down to earth.

Smart Business

Your goals can and probably should shift over time. When you accomplish one set of goals, you should then come up with new goals going forward. If you don't accomplish a given goal, figure out why and set a new goal that is achievable. Or maybe things just change, and you realize that you're better at one thing than another, or you discover you don't like what you're doing. In these instances, it's okay to revise your goals. Life is all about change, and everyone modifies their life goals at one time or another.

Preparing a Roadmap

Once you set your goals—either singular or plural—the next step is to figure out how to accomplish them. In other words, create a roadmap to your goals.

A goal roadmap is just like those roadmaps you use when driving to a vacation destination. It tells you, turn by turn, how to get from where you are now to where you want to go. It's a set of step-by-step directions that help you accomplish a specific goal.

What might a roadmap look like? Let's say your goal is to generate enough money from your music to quit your day job—a common goal for many musicians. Your roadmap would include all the things you need to do to generate that income, such as playing X amount of gigs each month that pay Y number of dollars each, or selling Z amount of CDs or merchandise each month. Each step in your roadmap brings you closer to your goal.

Ideally, once you've prepared your roadmap, all you have to do is follow the steps you laid out. If your goal is to get your songs published and your roadmap includes (1) writing a song, (2) making a demo recording, (3) putting together some sort of proposal or promotional kit, and (4) contacting a variety of music publishing houses, that's what you have to do. Follow the instructions in your plan, step by step, and you'll move toward your goal.

Writing a Music Business Plan

I know, I know. You really, *really* don't want to sit down and write a formal business plan. So let's not call it a "business plan." Let's call it a "career plan," "career guidelines," or something similar. That might help a little.

Smart Business _____

Your business plan doesn't have to be formal, nor does it have to be long or overly detailed. In fact, there aren't any rules for creating such a plan; the only rule is that you need to do something in the way of planning. Your own personal plan need only reflect the way that you personally do things.

In essence, a music business plan is a set of goals accompanied by instructions on how to accomplish those goals. The goals, as we've discussed, should be specific and quantifiable—which means, assuming that some goals are financial, you'll need to put a few round numbers into your plan. Beyond that, however, what you write down can be fairly general.

Here's the way I like to approach this sort of thing. Instead of sitting down in front of the computer, I envision sitting down with a friend over a beer or cup of coffee. I then tell my friend what I plan to do with my career over the next year or so, in a casual fashion. What I tell my friend becomes my business plan.

Here's an example. Just imagine yourself sitting in a comfy chair, beverage in hand, shooting the bull:

Okay, you know I've been playing in this band, and we've been doing a couple of small gigs a month. Well, I'd like to turn this into a bigger thing, and I've been thinking about what I want to accomplish over the next year or so.

First, I'd like to see us play more often, get it up to once a week, maybe a couple of nights each weekend. We should develop some steady gigs at some of the local clubs, maybe even branch out regionally—you know, big clubs within driving distance. That's going to take some work, of course; we'll need a longer set list, work up some new songs.

We'll also need to promote ourselves, both to the club owners and in the community. To help us get the gigs, I want to work up a promo kit, with a CD, publicity photos, bios, and stuff. We'll need to record some songs for that, but we can do that with Pro Tools on my computer in my basement; since I already have the equipment, that shouldn't cost a lot.

Once we get the gigs, we can do the normal posters and flyers and stuff. But I also want to set up a website for the band, something that fans can follow. Tell them where we're playing next, if we're recording, that sort of thing. Maybe even have some of our songs for download from the site, once we get them recorded.

If all this works out, maybe we can think about recording a whole album, and then selling the tracks online or at our gigs or whatever. But I'm not focusing on that yet. I just want to get to the point where we're playing regularly, and bringing in at least $1,000 per night for the band. Split between the five of us and playing two nights a week, that could give me $2,000 a month of income—heck, that's $24,000 a year. That would really help to pay the bills.

Let's look at what we just did. In that brief little conversation we laid out everything we need for a successful music business plan. Here's what we did:

◆ **Established a goal.** It's right there at the very beginning. We want our band to play more often—at least one gig a week, ideally two nights on a weekend. That goal is numerically quantifiable—you either play once a week or you don't. And there were dollars associated with the goal; we want the band to take home at least $1,000 a night.

◆ **Laid out a roadmap.** How do we achieve our goal of playing at least one gig a week? By putting together a promotion kit to hand out to club owners. By recording a demo CD and shooting publicity photos to put into the promotion kit. By looking for gigs at big local clubs and expanding the market to include clubs within a reasonable driving distance. And by launching a website to promote gigs to the band's fan base. That's a pretty extensive to-do list, and one that should be effective in achieving the stated goals.

But wait, you say, that isn't a business plan—it's just a conversation. Right you are, but also wrong. This simple little conversation *is* your business plan. Just put everything important you said down in writing, and you have your plan. Voilà! It's that simple.

How long does your business plan need to be? Well, our conversation was a whole five paragraphs long. The plan doesn't have to be any longer than that—and can be shorter. In fact, you don't even have to write it out in complete paragraphs and sentences. It's okay to use major headings and bullet points, like this:

GOALS:

◆ Play at least one night a week, preferably two nights over a weekend.

◆ Generate a minimum of $1,000 for the band per gig.

ROADMAP:

◆ Record some of our best songs and burn a demo CD.

◆ Take publicity photos of the band.

◆ Create a publicity kit to give to club owners and booking agents, containing the demo CD and publicity photos.

◆ Target large clubs in town and within a reasonable driving distance of town.

◆ Create a website to promote the band and our gigs to our fans.

And that's your business plan. You know what you want to achieve, and what you need to do to achieve it.

Following the Plan—and Evaluating Your Success

Writing a business plan is one thing; what you do with it is another. It goes without saying that if you lay out a series of steps you want to follow, you need to follow them. That puts some reality into the planning process—and gets you up and running.

Your roadmap in hand, you now have to figure out how to do the things you said you'd do. You need to figure out who does what, and when they need to do it. That's right, you need to assign specific tasks to members of your team; give them each a goal and a deadline.

Everybody is responsible for the tasks assigned, but you also need a leader (probably you—you're the one who bought this book, aren't you?) to make sure everybody does what they're supposed to. You don't want your band to fail because the bass player didn't get the demo CDs burned, or because your manager wasn't aggressive enough with local booking agents. You have to monitor everyone's performance, and be prepared to crack the whip if somebody isn't pulling their weight.

At the end of the plan period—a year from now—you can judge whether you've achieved your goals. If your goal was to be playing gigs on a weekly basis, you've achieved that goal if you are indeed playing weekly. If you're only averaging one or two gigs a month, however, you fell short of your goal—and you need to reevaluate what you hope to achieve in the future.

Smart Business

It's a good strategy to do some mid-period evaluation of your plan. You don't want to wait an entire year to see if you're making progress toward your goals; by then it's too late if you discover you're on the wrong path. Instead, look at your plan three or six months down the road and see how far along you are. If you're well on your way, good for you. If you find that you're not keeping pace, then you may need to reevaluate your roadmap or even the goals you set out. Be realistic. If you've bitten off more than you can chew, redo your plan.

In any case, the one-year mark is time to write *another* business plan—this one for the next 12 months. And that's how you manage your career, one year—and one business plan—at a time. Your career is a series of steps, after all; making plans along the way helps guide your direction.

When Does Your Music Become a Business?

Most musicians I know like to think of their music as art. It's hard to make the switch and think of it as a business.

Indeed, if all you do is write and play music for yourself in your own home, your music probably isn't a business. It only becomes a business when you start trying to make money from it.

Even then, working a few gigs a year does not a music career make. While there are no set rules, below a certain dollar amount, playing for money is more of a hobby than a job.

Above a certain income, however, your music definitely—and legally—becomes a job. And as a job, you have to report to the government all the income you earn. Income is income after all, whether it comes in the form of a weekly paycheck or some crumpled bills you get handed at the end of a night at the local club.

When the money you make from playing music becomes substantial enough to be treated as income, you have to think of your music as a business. That means tracking not just income but expenses, which can be deducted from the taxes you owe. And you will owe taxes—which you probably should pay quarterly, in the form of estimated tax payments.

If your music income gets large enough, you need to start thinking about what type of business you are. Are you a sole proprietorship, or should you incorporate? There are tax ramifications in either case.

And here's the thing. If you're a professional musician, you need to think of your music as a real business. You're not just Joe Guitar, you're Joe Guitar Music, Inc. You have to manage your affairs as any business would, and that means availing yourself of the services of a professional business manager or accountant, someone who knows all the financial ins and outs. If money is important to you—and if you have rent to pay, it is—then you have to treat all this money stuff very seriously. Your music *is* your business.

The Least You Need to Know

- A business plan is necessary for any musician who wants to make a living in the music business.

- A good music business plan consists of two primary sections—your goals and the steps you need to take to achieve them.

- Your business plan doesn't have to be long or complicated; it can be short and bulleted.

- Once you write your business plan, you need to follow the steps you outlined.

- Evaluate your progress after three to six months, and again after a year—and revise your plan as necessary.

Chapter 6

The Business of Assembling Your Team

In This Chapter

- ♦ Why you need to surround yourself with a team of business professionals
- ♦ The key members of your team—your personal manager, business manager, booking agent, publicist, webmaster, and attorney
- ♦ Which tasks you can do yourself—and which you can't

Accomplishing your goals is easier when you don't have to do it alone. In fact, in today's music business, you probably *can't* do it all yourself; you need a team of skilled professionals to ensure your success.

Who should be part of your team—and why? That's what this chapter is about: learning how to surround yourself with the right business professionals to enhance your music career.

Why You Need a Team

To become a successful musical artist, you surround yourself with a team of skilled musicians—your band. Well, think of your business team as your "business band," the men and women who back you up and help you do all the things you want and need to do.

What kind of team do you need to assemble? Well, every artist is different, and it's different at different stages of your career, but in general you want to consider the following people, on either a full- or part-time basis:

- Personal manager

- Business manager/accountant

- Booking agent

- Publicist

- Webmaster

- Attorney

We'll discuss each of these team members separately.

Smart Business

In addition to the full-time members of your team, you'll probably also need to bring in "hired guns" to do some specific one-time tasks. For example, if you want to record your music, you may need to bring in a producer and engineer to help with the recording process. Or, if you're launching your website, you probably need a website designer. But these are one-time things; you don't need either a recording engineer or website designer on staff full time.

Your Personal Manager

A *personal manager* may be the most important member of your team. This is the person who takes responsibility for your career and helps you interface with the other members of your team, other musicians, and third parties (club owners, label execs, and so on). Think of him as your coach; you follow his direction.

Your relationship with your manager is like a marriage. Your manager is your spouse, looking after you, giving you advice, pushing you forward (or pulling you back) when needed. It's an intimate relationship.

Your manager helps you develop your career plans. He should be closely involved with the creation of your business plan, the setting of goals, and the drawing up of your roadmap. He should also be involved with the execution of the plan.

def•i•ni•tion

A **personal manager,** called an *artist manager* or just plain *manager,* guides the professional career of an artist in the entertainment business.

For some artists, the manager is their driving force. For other artists, the manager is a facilitator, helping to execute the strategies laid out by the artist. Some managers are very hands-on, orchestrating all aspects of the artist's career, including creative issues; other managers limit themselves strictly to business issues.

Smart Business

If you're a solo artist, you have a one-on-one relationship with your manager. If you're in a band, the manager typically represents the entire band; the individual band members generally don't have their own individual managers.

Some managers will function as your *de facto* attorney. At the very least, expect your manager to ask for a limited power of attorney, so that he can easily deal with your day-to-day business affairs, such as endorsing checks, signing contracts, and the like. Be cautious, however, of giving your manager too much autonomy; you don't want him signing contracts in your name that you're not aware of.

When I said that a personal manager is like a spouse, that also applies to your financial arrangements. Most managers provide their services in return for a percentage of your gross earnings—typically somewhere in the 15 to 25 percent range. That's a big chunk of your earnings that comes off the top to your manager; he needs to do a bang-up job to justify that expense.

Scam Alert

Your relationship with your manager is a long-term one. Beware of managers who only want a short-term relationship; they're probably in it just for the immediate money.

While personal managers have been essential in the past, in today's environment you may not need all the services a manager has to offer. Evaluate what duties you can perform on your own, and consider signing a limited management agreement to fill the gaps. (Learn more about personal managers in Chapter 7.)

Your Business Manager

In addition to a personal manager, many artists employ a *business manager*. This person functions as your accountant and financial advisor, handling all the financial affairs related to your music career.

Now some artists, especially those with low incomes or uncomplicated finances, may be able to make do with just an accountant to handle the inflows and outflows and make sure your taxes are paid. However, a true business manager goes well beyond simple accounting services, offering financial advice and consulting on the terms of the contracts you sign.

def•i•ni•tion

A **business manager** is an individual who helps an artist with financial planning, investment decisions, tax matters, monitoring of income from contracts, and other financial matters.

Most business managers are paid on an hourly basis, so you use them only as much as you need (or can afford). Some higher-powered business managers may insist on being paid on a percentage basis (taking a cut of your income), but that's rare for beginning artists. You may, however, be asked to pay a monthly retainer for the business manager's services; this is a common practice. (Learn more about business managers and accountants in Chapter 8.)

Your Booking Agent

When you're a performing musician, you can hustle gigs yourself or you can employ the services of a *booking agent*. An agent is an individual or, in some cases, an entire firm whose job is finding you employment. (Learn more about booking in Chapter 13.)

If you're a big-name artist, you probably sign with a big-name agency, such as CAA or ICM. If you're a local musician, you're better off with an independent agent, someone who knows the local scene. In other words, you want to size your agency representation to your own goals.

Getting an agent to represent you is sometimes a challenge, especially when you're first starting out. Most agents handle a roster of clients, and don't want to bog themselves down finding work for an unknown artist. It helps if you have a bit of history on the scene, so that the agent knows you're bookable.

def•i•ni•tion

A **booking agent**, called a *talent agent*, *booker*, or just plain *agent*, is an individual or firm who finds jobs for people and groups in the entertainment business.

While an agent typically represents more than one client, he will want to represent you exclusively. That is, you probably can't sign with multiple agents; you have to give your business to a single agency. Expect to sign an exclusive contract from one to three years in duration.

Your agent gets paid a commission on the income you earn, typically 10 to 20 percent. (And remember, you're giving a similar percent to your personal manager.) Make sure that your agent's commissions are limited to gigs he gets you, and don't slop over into any recording or publishing income you generate separately.

Your Publicist

When it comes to developing public awareness of you and your music, you need a *publicist*. This is a person, or sometimes an agency, who gets the word out about where you're playing, what you're selling, and in general just how great you are.

It's the publicist's job to make the media aware of you and what you're doing. That means establishing relationships with writers for newspapers and magazines, the guys who run or write for blogs and websites, and on-air personalities who work in radio and television. These relationships, ideally, translate into favorable reviews, stories, and mentions in the desired media.

def•i•ni•tion

A **publicist** is responsible for generating and managing publicity for an individual, group, or organization.

When you want your latest CD reviewed, you call on your publicist. When you want your gig featured in the local newspaper, you call on your publicist. When you want a feature story in a big music magazine or website, you call on your publicist. That's what they do.

Publicists or publicity firms may charge an hourly rate, a monthly fee, or even a per-project fee. That is, you may get billed for the time they actually work, or they may charge you a flat fee for a specific project, such as launching a new CD. (Learn more about publicists and publicity in Chapter 12.)

Your Webmaster

These days, a big part of your public presence comes from your website, your blog, your Facebook and MySpace pages, and your Twitter account. You don't think that your favorite big-time artists do all those blog posts and tweets themselves, do you? Of course not; they're too busy making music. They leave all the online stuff to their *webmaster*.

def•i•ni•tion

A **webmaster** is an individual who creates and manages the content and organization of a website.

Technically, a webmaster is responsible for managing the day-to-day workings of a website. In the music world, a webmaster is probably also responsible for all of your online presence, including blogs, social networks, and even e-mail lists. And that means updating the content on each site, from the artist bios to the latest news. (Learn more about webmasters and websites in Chapter 17.)

Note that the webmaster is not the person who actually creates your website. You'll have to hire a web-design firm for that. You'll also have to contract with a web-hosting firm to host your web pages, which is an additional cost. But your webmaster does what needs to be done on a daily basis across all your online properties, which makes him a very important person of your team, indeed.

You can hire professional firms who specialize in webmastering (if that's really a word), in which case a single firm will have multiple clients. You can also hire a full- or (more likely) part-time person to handle the webmaster chores; in fact, you may already know someone in your organization or have a fan who would be ideal for this task. You'll probably pay this person an hourly rate, or perhaps a flat salary.

Your Attorney

The last, but certainly not least, member of your team is your *attorney*. You're going to be signing a lot of contracts during your career, and you need a legal expert to make sure you sign everything you should, and nothing you shouldn't.

A good lawyer not only makes sure that all the contractual i's are dotted and t's are crossed, but also offers ongoing legal advice. It's not just that you need a contract to be legally sound, you also need it to be a good thing for your career—and in this aspect, your attorney is key.

def•i•ni•tion

An **attorney** is an individual licensed to practice law who represents his or her clients in various legal matters.

It's important that you use an attorney who is familiar with or ideally specializes in the music business. You'll need your attorney to represent you in negotiations with club owners, promoters, music publishing companies, and record labels. Your lawyer needs to be fluent in copyrights and royalties, and work hand-in-hand with your business manager in these affairs. And if worse comes to worse, your attorney has to work on your behalf in any litigation that arises.

Naturally, your attorney will have many other clients; in this regard, your lawyer is only a part-time member of your team. As such, expect to be billed by the hour, and expect that hourly rate to be anywhere from $200 or so on up plus expenses. Some lawyers will require you to pay an upfront retainer before they take you on.

In addition, some entertainment lawyers in big cities like to charge a percentage of all deals they negotiate, typically in the 5 percent range. (Yes, that's another percent off the top of what you earn.) That last bit isn't a given, especially for beginning artists, but once you reach the big time, expect to see it. (Learn more about entertainment attorneys in Chapter 23.)

How Much Can You Do Yourself?

Reading through this chapter, you should now be familiar with the basic business activities that are necessary to advance your career. We're talking career planning (personal manager), accounting and financial planning (business manager), booking (booking agent), publicity (publicist), online management (webmaster), and contracts and legal matters (attorney).

The bigger question is, do you really need to outsource all of these tasks, or can you do some of them yourself?

In the old days, you definitely outsourced these activities, either to individuals or to your record label. That's just the way it was; few artists had the skills or training to do anything other than write and play their music.

Today, however, you *can* do some of these tasks yourself—if you're prepared to handle them. It all depends on your training and abilities, and how much time you want to devote to nonmusical activities.

For example, many working musicians are taking advantage of various online resources (relatively new in the business) to book their own gigs. Other musicians are sufficiently comfortable with the online world to function as their own webmasters. And it's not unthinkable to imagine a musician who's taken an accounting class using QuickBooks to manage his finances.

Some artists today are extremely self-sufficient, managing several of these business functions themselves. It's certainly a more cost-conscious way to go; you don't have to pay all those points off the top to the professional help. In addition, you end up with more control over your career and your music, which isn't a bad thing.

That said, it's always a good idea to have outside input on your career; doing *every-thing* yourself can lead to narrow self-centered thinking. To that end, I think it's a good idea for most musicians to have a personal manager—although, again, some well-rounded artists can probably do this themselves, too.

More important, I think, is the issue of where your time is best spent. Yes, some artists can do some or all of these essential business-related tasks, but you could end up spending more time on business than you do on making music. No matter what other skills you may possess, your unique talent lies in your music. It's easy to find a lawyer or an accountant; it's much, much more difficult to replicate the musical talent you possess. Focus on your music first, then add in those business activities that don't detract from your music.

The Least You Need to Know

- You need to surround yourself with a team of professionals who provide the business skills you either don't have or don't have the time to provide.

- Your personal manager is kind of like a coach who helps guide all aspects of your career.

- Your business manager handles all your finances—from accounting to financial planning.

- Your booking agent finds you gigs to play.

- Your publicist gets the word out about you and your music.

- Your webmaster manages all your day-to-day online activities.

- Your attorney takes care of all the legal details of your career, including overseeing all your contracts.

Chapter 7

The Business of Managing Your Career

In This Chapter

- ◆ Understanding what a personal manager does
- ◆ Discovering how the role of management has changed in recent years
- ◆ Learning where to find a manager
- ◆ Understanding the terms of a management agreement
- ◆ Finding out how to manage your own career

One of the most important members of your business team is the personal manager. Yet many artists, especially newer ones, don't have managers. Without a professional manager, just how do you manage your career? And what do you need to manage, anyway?

Understanding Personal Management

As you learned in Chapter 6, a personal manager—sometimes called an artist's manager, or just plain manager—is like the coach of your team. Your manager not only helps decide the direction you should go, he calls a lot of the shots on the way there.

Behind the Music

One of the best examples of the importance of artist management is Brian Epstein's work with the Beatles. Before Epstein signed the band, the Beatles were just a semi-popular club band. Epstein had the vision that they could be something more, and strove to land them a very important record deal, established the band's early image, worked tirelessly to promote their music, and helped make them the legendary band that they eventually became.

Not all artist/management relationships are the same, however. Some artists rely more on their managers than do others; some artists treat managers more like employees, while others treat their managers as partners. It's all a matter of how you, the artist, like to do things and what you're comfortable with. Some artists rely on their managers to guide them in all aspects of their careers; others assign only the nitty-gritty details to their managers, while they deal more with the big picture themselves. There's no one best way to do things.

Behind the Music

Don't confuse a personal manager with a business manager. The former guides all aspects of your career, while the latter handles just your financial affairs.

In general, however, there are a set of activities that managers typically deal with. In any case, these are activities that have to be dealt with, whether it's the manager or the artist doing the dealing. Here are a few of the management tasks most artists face:

- **Help develop your career business plan.** As you learned in Chapter 5, you need to develop a plan for your short-term and long-term music career; your business manager can, and should be, a part of that process.

- **Find other musicians for your band.** If your band isn't yet complete, or if you're a solo artist needing a backing band, your manager can help with this task.

- **Find other members of your business team.** As you learned in Chapter 6, you need to surround yourself with a team of business professionals—a business manager/accountant, booking agent, publicist, webmaster, and attorney. Your business manager can help assemble this team and then help lead the team on a day-to-day basis.

- **Set up your music business.** Your career is a business and you should set it up as such. That means deciding what type of business to create, filing the proper forms, dealing with taxes, and the like. While the day-to-day management of the business will fall to your business manager or accountant, your personal manager can help with a lot of the initial decisions.

◆ **Arrange funding.** Funding? That's right; many artists need a little investment to get their careers on track. That might mean money for new instruments or the financial backing to fund recording or CD replication. In any case, a good personal manager knows the financial angles—and some financial angels—and can work with your business manager to find the funds you need.

◆ **Devise a promotional plan.** How you present yourself as an artist is important to getting gigs and filling seats at those gigs. While you can rely on a publicist and promotional staff to do much of this work, your manager can help develop the creative direction for your promotional activities. In fact, your manager can do a lot of the work here, especially if he has contacts with the right players; I'm talking about sending out demos and promo kits to radio stations, local print media, online media, record labels, and the like—in general, networking with industry pros to help advance your career.

◆ **Manage practice sessions.** It sounds like a little thing, but a manager can really help to focus a band through its practice sessions. A manager can find and book practice space, schedule practice sessions, and be a taskmaster when the band's attention starts to flag.

◆ **Book important gigs.** Yes, the task of booking you or your band typically falls on your booking agent, but a good manager will also have some connections that might help land a few big gigs. He can also get record industry pros and media representatives to the gigs—and work them while they're there.

◆ **Arrange recording sessions.** Recording is an important part of any artist's career, whether you record in a major studio or in your own basement. Your manager can help arrange recording sessions: booking studio space, scheduling musicians into the sessions, hiring producers and engineers, and just generally supervising the recording.

◆ **Negotiate contracts.** Whatever deals you do throughout your career, whether it's a gig at a local club or a big-time contract with a major record label, your personal manager should be there. He's the one with the business experience, and should be a part of all major negotiations.

That's a lot of work, which, if you don't have a manager, you'll have to do yourself. You can have your manager do some or all of these functions; it all depends on what you're comfortable with. But as you can see, these are all things that need to be done—whether you have a manager or not.

And remember, whatever the relationship you have with your manager, keep in mind that you're the artist and your manager is working *for* you. Your relationship may be more like a partnership, but you're still the boss—you're the one whose affairs are being managed. (If you're interested in becoming a personal manager in the music business, learn more in Chapter 18.)

The Next Generation of Artist Management

The previous section discussed what a personal manager has traditionally done for artists. Moving into the twenty-first century, how has the manager's role changed?

First, know that thanks to the Internet, you have a lot more resources available to you than you did just ten years ago. I'm talking both services and information.

The Internet is a great source of third parties offering all sorts of services for working musicians. If it needs to be done, chances are somebody has made a business of doing it. For this reason, it's a lot easier to outsource parts of your business than it used to be. Maybe you can do some things yourself, and hire out the rest—and not have to rely on a single manager to do everything.

 Smart Business _____

> The Internet is also a great way to learn things you need to know. Not sure whether a given deal is a good one or not? Consult one of the many web-based musician's message forums or groups; chances are, somebody there has the knowledge you seek. You don't always have to rely on a manager to help you make good decisions.

That said, managers need to do a lot more today than they used to. There's the whole online thing, of course, which has to be managed; a savvy manager should be able to do this for you, either directly or by hiring out the pieces and parts. In addition, if you decide to forgo a major-label contract, your manager can help you do all the things a label used to do—schedule recording sessions, manufacture physical product, arrange CD distribution, work with online download services, and the like.

In fact, I'd argue that without major-label support, the role of a personal manager becomes even more important for most artists. There's a lot more to do, and a good manager can help you do it.

This presumes, of course, that your manager is experienced with and skilled in the new tasks that need to be completed. I wouldn't rely on a 60-year-old guy who managed '60s-era psychedelic rock bands to grasp all the nuances of social networking and online promotion, for example. You need a manager who's hip to all the changes in today's digital marketplace to guide your career going forward. Twentieth-century management won't cut it in the twenty-first century music business.

Finding a Manager

So where do you find a twenty-first century business manager? You have several options.

Nonprofessional Management

First, you may have a friend, fellow musician, or fan who has management skills and experience—and who is willing and eager to take on some or all of your management duties. This is often a good choice when you're just starting out and don't have the budget for a big-name manager.

Managers like this are trying to make a name for themselves, and will likely work very hard on your behalf. In essence, you'll be growing your careers together; your success is important to your manager's success.

Professional Management

As you achieve more and more success, however, you may find that your friend/colleague/fan doesn't have quite the skills or experience necessary to move you to the next stage in your career. When this happens, you can hire someone to handle additional parts of your management needs, allowing your original manager to focus on only certain tasks, or you can replace this person with a more experienced professional manager.

An experienced manager brings a lot to the table. Not only has this person been there and done that, he also knows lots of people in the business. These contacts are extremely important, as they can lead to future bookings, reviews, airplay—you name it.

Behind the Music

Many managers work for larger artist-management companies. Contracting with a manager from an agency often provides access to other resources offered by the agency, which can be a good thing.

Where do you find a professional manager? The first place to look is within your own circle of musical friends. Ask around, see who other musicians know and recommend. In fact, it's a good strategy to find another artist similar to you and see if their manager will also represent you; if he's doing a good job for them, chances are he'll do a good job for you, too.

You can also find lists of managers and management firms in the following online directories:

◆ Artist Management and Music Management (www.artistmanagementonline.com)

◆ Artist Management Resource (www.artistmanagementresource.com)

◆ band-me-up.com (www.band-me-up.com/FIND/management/)

◆ HitQuarters (www.hitquarters.com)

◆ Music Socket.com (www.musicsocket.com/managers/)

Signing a Management Agreement

Amateur managers aside, when you contract with professional artist management, you'll need to sign a management contract and pay for your manager's services. Professionals earn a living by taking a percentage of your earnings in the form of a commission. The percentage is often negotiable, and typically falls in the 10 to 25 percent range.

Management commission is typically earned on all income from live performances, publishing, record sales and royalties, publishing advances and royalties, sponsorship, merchandising, and so on. In fact, some management contracts insist that the manager continues to earn commissions on these activities for some period after the expiration of the contract, on the basis that the manager's prior work set the stage, so to speak, for that future income.

To earn this commission, your manager should agree to perform specific duties with the goal of meeting certain objectives: booking a certain number of performances, getting a publishing deal, signing with a record label, and so forth. As with the goals in your own career business plan, the goals in your management contract should be both quantifiable and achievable. (And the contract should set out what happens if the manager doesn't achieve these objectives.)

Scam Alert

You don't want to be saddled with an underperforming personal manager. Consider placing a provision in your management contract that enables you to terminate the agreement if you fail to earn a minimum level of income during the first two years, or if certain identified milestones are not met. For example, you might have a clause that gets you out of the contract if your manager doesn't get you a recording contract within 12 months.

Most management agreements are for a three- to five-year period, which gives both you and your manager enough time to accomplish some significant goals. Of course, you may not want to be locked into a management contract for that long; a shorter contract, or one with some sort of escape clause, may be to your benefit.

Remember, your personal manager is just part of your business team. Your personal manager should not assume attorney or business management/accounting duties. In fact, it's wise to keep these functions separate on the off chance that one team member decides to cheat the rest of the team. If you have all your business eggs in one basket, the guy managing that basket can walk away with all your eggs. In particular, keep the financial and contractual functions separate from your manager; that's just smart business.

Smart Business

When you sign a management agreement, you should run that agreement past your attorney. It is, after all, a contract, and you have to examine all the details and fine print. (And it should go without saying, don't use your manager's attorney; the same guy can't represent both sides of the table.)

Managing Your Own Business

What if you don't want to sign with a personal manager just yet? How do you do all the things that you might otherwise rely on a manager for?

Let's start with the basics. Any artist starting out needs to do a few basic things, business-wise. Normally, your personal manager would help you do these chores; without a manager, you have to do them yourself. Fortunately, it's all stuff that's doable, with a little effort.

So as a professional musician or band, here are the essential business tasks you need to do, more or less in the following order.

1. **Create a band agreement.** Obviously, this is only necessary if you're in a band; if you're a solo artist, you deal with your backing musicians as employees or freelance contractors. However, it's important to set out in writing how the band is organized, who is responsible for what, how each member is to be compensated, and the like. You need to set out each member's contribution to the band (financially and otherwise), as well as each member's share of the band's profits (or losses). You also need to trademark your band's name and determine who owns the trademark if the band breaks up; you want to ensure against members using the name if they leave. And with regards to leaving the band, you should set out just what it takes to fire a nonperforming member, and who has a say in hiring new members. Basically, you need to consider every eventuality and detail how the band will deal with it.

2. **Hire the other members of your business team.** As discussed in Chapter 6, you need to surround yourself with a strong team of business professionals. The time to do that is early, when you're first starting out. You want your team on the ground so they're ready when you first start generating income.

3. **Set up your business.** You need to literally treat your career as a business. Whether you're a solo artist or a band, you need to set up your business to represent your artistic endeavors. That means deciding what type of business to create—a sole proprietorship, partnership, or corporation—each of which have specific legal and tax implications. (Learn more about different types of businesses in Chapter 8.)

4. **Obtain the necessary business licenses.** Once you settle on the type of business you want, you need to do all the legal paperwork to make it official. That includes obtaining the proper business licenses from both your state and the federal government.

5. **Open a bank account for your business.** With your business set up, you need to open a bank account for your business. All your income (from gigs, CD sales, merchandise sales, you name it) should flow into this bank account; you should then write checks to each band member (or member of your business team) from this account. Even if you're a solo artist, it's important that you open a business account separate from your normal personal account; keep your business affairs separate from your personal ones.

6. **Write a business plan.** With the basic business stuff out of the way, you can now focus on big-picture thinking. Follow the advice set forth in Chapter 5 and set out your goals and a roadmap on how to accomplish those goals. It's the best way to both envision and plan your career success.

7. **Record demo tracks.** These days, you need to do a little recording before you get your first gig. I'm not talking about a big studio production, just a couple of tracks you can include on a demo CD for your booking agent to hand out to potential employers. You can probably do this on the cheap using your personal computer and home recording software, but it has to be done. (And make sure the recording does a good job representing how you actually sound today—not how you'd like to sound tomorrow.)

8. **Create promotional materials.** The demo tracks you record should go into a promotional kit that you or your booking agent can hand to potential clients, club owners, concert promoters, and the like. In addition to the demo CD, you need a publicity photo, a one-sheet bio, and probably a set list or list of music in your repertoire. Once you get some gigs, include them in the kit, as well as any (good) reviews you inspire.

9. **Sign with an existing publishing company or form your own.** This matters if you write your own songs, of course; if you don't, you can skip this step. Securing publishing rights is important for getting your songs copyrighted, getting them recorded by other artists, and collecting any royalties due. (Learn more about music publishing in Chapter 15.)

10. **Join a performing rights organization**. Finally, you want to join one of the major performing rights organizations—ASCAP, BMI, or SESAC. These organizations collect and distribute the income generated from the use of the music you write and record, and are essential to your future income flow.

Sound like a lot to do? Well, even without a personal manager, you can still hire out a lot of the work. In particular, your business manager or accountant can help with a lot of the financial and even legal issues, such as setting up your business and filing all the necessary registrations. For that matter, your lawyer can also help with a lot of these details.

But if the thought of all this work boggles your mind, then reconsider the use of a personal manager. It's nice to be able to hand off a lot of these business details to someone else and keep your focus on your music.

Ongoing Career Management

Beyond the initial setting up of your business, a personal manager handles a lot of the day-to-day aspects of your music career. A good manager will help you find gigs, direct your publicity and promotional efforts, arrange your schedule, and just generally keep you on track. That's in addition to the career advice and planning that happens on a continuous basis, of course.

If you don't have a personal manager, who manages your career on an ongoing basis? That would be you. That's right, even without a manager, your career still needs to be managed. Everything a manager normally does—including focusing on the big picture—still needs to be done. And if there's not a manager there to do it, you have to do it yourself.

It's quite possible that your needs differ in different stages of your career. Many artists do just fine without a manager in their early years, but find a need for one as they become more successful. Let's face it; a busy and successful artist has more to manage than one just starting out. So you might want to try going without formal management for awhile, but be amenable to hiring a manager when things get busier.

Do I Really Need a Manager?

Are you capable of managing your own career? Is this something you like to do, or is it something that bores you to tears? Are you good at it, or are you hopeless at managing things like this? These are all issues to consider.

Some artists, after all, do a great job of managing themselves—a better job, in fact, than most professional managers might do. These folks think with both sides of their brain and have no trouble switching from creative mode to management mode and back again. They also probably have a little bit of the control freak about them; they wouldn't think of turning something as important as their own career over to someone else.

Other artists are … well, they're artists, not managers. These folks couldn't manage themselves out of a paper sack; they lack not only organizational skills, but also the ability to look at their career in a big-picture kind of way. It's one thing to write a compelling melody or play an electrifying solo; quite another to envision merchandising opportunities for a West Coast tour.

So whether you *need* a manager or not depends a lot on you: what you're comfortable with, what you're good at, and what you have time for. It also depends on just what you need managed; as we just discussed, your needs get more complex the more successful you become. If you're just starting out playing a few wedding receptions, you may not need a manager. But if you have a CD out and are trying to get distribution, airplay, and reviews, a hard-working manager will more than earn his cut of the money. (In fact, if you're seeking a record deal, many labels won't even talk to an artist unless they have professional management in place.)

More important, a good manager lets you focus on what's really important—your music. When you leave the business stuff to your manager, you can keep your full attention on the music part of your music career.

The Least You Need to Know

◆ A personal manager, sometimes called an artist's manager, is responsible for managing both the big picture and the business details of your career.

◆ A manager helps you develop your business plan, find other musicians to work with, assemble your business team, set up your business, develop a promotional plan, arrange practices and recording sessions, and negotiate contracts.

◆ Not every artist needs the same type or level of management; some artists are more reliant on managers than are others.

◆ Most professional managers charge a 10 to 25 percent commission on your earnings, as stipulated in a formal management contract.

◆ If you don't contract with a manager, you still have to do all the things the manager would do—either yourself or by contracting with one or more third parties.

Chapter 8

The Business of Managing Your Money

In This Chapter

- ◆ Why you need to create a business for your music

- ◆ Choosing the right type of business

- ◆ Setting up a business bank account

- ◆ Discovering why you need a business manager   and how to find one

- ◆ Learning more about taxes

Even if you only play for fun, you're likely to make a little money playing now and then. But when you receive that first paycheck, you're now a professional—and your music is no longer a hobby, but a business.

Dealing with your music as a business is challenging. Let's face it, few musicians are numbers savvy; if you had bean-counting in your blood, you'd be taking the CPA test right now. So you need someone in your corner to help you deal with all the money issues you're likely to encounter. That means hiring an accountant or a business manager—and treating your music as a business.

Treating Your Music as a Business

Here's something you just have to accept: If you're a professional musician, you're also a businessperson. In effect, you're running your own business, and you—or your band—needs to be treated as a business entity.

Why Your Music Is a Business

Here's the way to think of it: You want to keep your personal and professional lives separate, as much as possible. Your life as a professional musician is your "work"; what you do outside of work is personal. Your work, then—your professional life—is your business.

Actually, it's quite easy to see why your professional music activities form the core of a freestanding business. First, like any business, you have revenues coming in—the money you make from playing gigs, selling CDs and downloads, and the like. You also have expenses going out—purchasing your instrument; buying sticks, strings, picks, and such; buying sheet music; paying for hotel rooms and meals when you're on the road, and that sort of thing. And at the end of the day, you have a profit—or a loss. It doesn't matter whether we're talking about you individually or several people joined together as a band; all of these professional activities—revenues, expenses, and profits—are what you find in any type of business.

Treating your music as a business means taking the money seriously. It means keeping track of all the money you make and all the money you spend. It means budgeting for future expenses. And it means paying the appropriate taxes, when they're due. Like I said, it's serious professional stuff.

If you *don't* treat your music as a business, bad things can happen. First, you probably won't know whether you're really making money or not, because you won't be tracking all the inflows and outflows. And if you don't know if you're making money, you probably *won't* be making money; it's way too easy to spend more than you bring in, especially in our business.

In addition, unless you think like a businessperson, you probably won't budget properly for all the taxes you owe. In fact, you may not even *know* all the taxes you owe, which means you might not pay what you owe when you owe it. And if you don't get the tax thing right, the government won't look kindly on you.

Now all this might not add up to much if you only play one wedding reception every few months; the money involved might not be enough to worry about. But when you're gigging regularly, selling CDs and other merchandise, and spending a lot on your music, the pennies start to add up real fast. As a general rule of thumb, the more you depend on the money you make from your music, the more important it is to establish your business credentials.

So if you regard yourself as a professional musician, you have to think of your profession as a business and organize accordingly.

Your Band as a Business

The music-as-a-business thing becomes even more important if you're in a band. As a solo artist, it may be difficult to distinguish between you the individual and you the business. But when you're a member of a band, the band is the business—and this band/business is infinitely more complex than a solo business.

Who do club owners pay at the end of the gig? Who pays the individual band members? Who pays for the band's expenses? Who tracks the money coming in and the money going out? Who has say-so over what gets spent where? For that matter, where exactly does the band's money go?

You can answer all those questions by organizing your band as a business, complete with a president, a set of owners, or whatever. In interpersonal relationships, money troubles often lead to relationship troubles. It's the same thing in a band; unless you treat the band as a separate business, money issues will entangle the band, and could lead to its premature demise.

Even worse, it's easy for one band member to take advantage of the others; money is a great temptation, after all. However, if the band is a business—and is treated as a entity separate from each of the individuals—then it's a lot harder for any one member to cheat the others out of their money.

Choosing a Type of Business

When it comes to setting up a business for yourself or for your band, you have some choices to make. That's because there are different types or classes of business, each of which works a little differently. You have to choose which type of business is best for you.

In the United States, there are three primary types of businesses: sole proprietorship, partnership, and corporation. Each type of business has its pros and cons, as we'll learn.

Behind the Music

You can learn more about the legalities of starting a small business at Business.gov (www.business.gov), the U.S. government's guide for businesses. Also good are the Business & Human Resources section of the Nolo website (www.nolo.com) and the Entrepreneur's Help Page (www.tannedfeet.com).

Another good source of information is your local secretary of state's website, which should have all the forms you need to get started. Naturally, if you live outside the United States, you should consult with local authorities (or an attorney) to find out which types of businesses are best in your area.

Sole Proprietorship

With a *sole proprietorship*, you are your business. It's not a bad way to go if you're a solo artist, but not really an option if you're in a band. (Unless, of course, each band member creates his or her own sole proprietorship; in this instance, you don't have a business for the band, but rather several individual businesses.)

On the plus side, a sole proprietorship is the easiest type of business to form and manage. You don't have to file any papers of incorporation, nor do you need to withhold and pay monthly payroll taxes and the

def•i•ni•tion

A **sole proprietorship** is a business entity owned by a single person that legally has no separate existence from its owner.

like. You file income tax for the business under your own name, using your Social Security number as your tax identification number. You'll file and pay this tax in quarterly estimates, but the paperwork burden is minimal compared to other forms of businesses.

On the downside, a sole proprietorship doesn't do a great job in legally separating you, the individual, from your business. The owner of a sole proprietorship is personally responsible for the debts and legal obligations of the business, which means if the business owes money, you're personally on the hook for it. And if your business gets sued, you end up in court.

Registering as a sole proprietorship is relatively easy and relatively cheap. You can probably handle all the paperwork yourself, although using an accountant or attorney is never a bad idea.

Partnership

A *partnership* is like a sole proprietorship, but with more than one owner. This is a good option if you have multiple members in a band; each band member becomes a partner in the business.

Of course, the two or more partners have to contractually agree as to who is responsible for what, and how to share the business's profits or losses. You'll definitely want to draw up formal partnership papers, which means bringing in a lawyer. Setting up a partnership is relatively easy, similar to setting up a sole proprietorship.

def•i•ni•tion

A **partnership** is a business entity formed by a contract between two or more co-owners.

Legally, a partnership is similar to a sole proprietorship in that all partners are held personally liable for losses and other obligations. This also means that one partner is liable for the other's actions; if one member of the band runs up a huge debt or is sued, you can also be held responsible.

In addition, breaking up or selling a partnership is often problematic. If one member wants to quit the band, the other members have to buy out his or her share—and valuing a band (or any business, for that matter) at the breaking point is seldom quick or easy.

In terms of paperwork and such, a partnership has to file a tax return for itself and must have a Federal Employer Identification Number (EIN), although the business itself pays no income tax. The individual partners report the company's income on their personal tax returns.

Smart Business

When you form a business for yourself or your band, you probably have to register this new business with your local government. You may also need to obtain a permit or license for your business. As the rules differ from state to state (and sometimes from county to county!), you'll probably need an attorney to sort out the details and do the necessary paperwork. You should also check with the staff at your county clerk's office or chamber of commerce, or on your state's official website; they'll tell you what you need to do.

Corporation

If you want to go hard-core on the business side, forget sole proprietorships and partnerships and instead incorporate. That's right, you or your band can become a *corporation*—although for many the effort is more trouble than it's worth.

def•i•ni•tion

A **corporation** is a business entity legally separate from the persons that formed the business. The corporation is typically owned by one or more shareholders, who own stock in the company.

When you incorporate, your business becomes a separate entity and you become an employee of that business. (As well as one of the shareholders, of course.) As such, all monies from gigs, CD sales, and such go directly to the business, and you get paid a salary. Nothing flows directly to you; it all goes through the business.

One of the main advantages of incorporating is that it separates you personally from the business entity. That means your personal liability is reduced if the business falls into debt or gets sued—in theory.

Another advantage of incorporating is that you may be able to set up health insurance and retirement plans for you and your bandmates. And depending on the amount of revenue your business generates, you may pay fewer taxes as a corporation than you would as an individual.

These benefits come at a cost, however, in the form of increased fees and paperwork. At the very least, a corporation must have a Federal EIN and withhold and pay monthly employment taxes for each of its employees. (That's you again.) This is a bit complicated, so you'll probably need an attorney or accountant to handle the details for you.

You can form several types of corporations. The most popular is the *subchapter S corporation*, which is simple to set up and isn't subject to corporate taxes. Also popular is the *limited liability corporation (LLC)*, where business income and losses are shared by all investors (band members), although investors are subject to limited liability (hence the name) for the corporation's debts and obligations. Ask your lawyer which type of corporation is best for you or your band. (You do have a lawyer, don't you?)

Smart Business

Although it's always good to work with a local attorney, you can complete your incorporation papers online with LegalZoom (www.legalzoom. com). This website lets you create all manner of simple legal documents—typically for a lower cost than you would otherwise pay an attorney.

Setting Up a Business Bank Account

When you form a business to handle your music affairs, your banking needs are likely to be different from your previous personal needs. You *can* make do by running your band's checks through your personal savings and checking accounts, but it's much cleaner to establish a separate banking identity for your business. This way it's clear which funds are personal and which are business-related.

The best business practice is to set up a business checking account separate from your personal accounts. You don't have to do this, but it will make your record-keeping easier.

You may also want to get a credit card in your business's name. This will make it easier to track all your music-related expenses.

Smart Business

If your business is a partnership, the partnership's bank account should be separate from all the partners' accounts and should require more than one name to be signed on the checks. That's to protect against any one band member from running off with all the funds.

New bank account and credit card in hand, you now have to use them. Deposit all the income you earn from your music into your business bank account. Pay all your music-related expenses using checks drawn on that same account. Alternately, you can pay for your music-related expenses using your business credit card, and then pay that card off every month from your business checking account. And it goes without saying, use your business credit card and checking account to pay for music-related expenses only—not for any personal expenses.

Working with an Accountant

When you're running a business, you need to keep track of what you're doing. That means keeping records about the money you bring in from your musical activities and the money you spend to support them. These records not only help you determine how much profit you're making with your music, they also help you prepare your yearly taxes.

Smart Business

Good recordkeeping is really just a matter of tracking every penny you earn and every penny you spend. That sounds simple, but it requires a lot of discipline—especially if you're tracking expenses for all the members of your band. Establishing separate business bank accounts and credit cards is a good start. You should also buy an expense log at your local office supply store and get used to writing things down.

Keeping good records is just part of it, however. You also need to employ the services of a professional accountant—at least to prepare your year-end taxes. That's because an accountant is likely to be more experienced and qualified than you to manage your business's tax obligations.

Of course, you can also use an accountant to handle *all* of your financial activities. You'll pay for this service, of course, but it may be necessary, and is a particularly good idea if …

1. You're generating a high income from your music.

2. Your income comes from a variety of sources.

3. You're in a band.

4. You aren't particularly interested in or good at handling the books.

Working with a Business Manager

An accountant keeps your books and figures your taxes. A business manager, on the other hand, handles *all* your financial affairs. He functions much like a personal financial advisor, but for your entire band or business—as well as acting as an accountant for your business.

What Does a Business Manager Manage?

Your business manager will not only handle your business's accounting duties, he will also offer advice regarding the business direction of you or your band. He will help evaluate and negotiate contracts, provide investment and tax-planning advice, and assist you in developing your business plan and financial budget.

Some business managers literally manage all of an artist's money; all the paychecks come to the business manager, and he pays all the artist's expenses. Other business managers function more like an accountant, expanding to other duties only when required. How you use a business manager depends on your particular situation.

Smart Business

A good business manager will help you make more money than you would have otherwise. That might mean helping to negotiate better terms on a contract, or avoiding contractual terms that reduce your actual take-home. It might mean auditing a record label or music publishing firm to recover unpaid royalties. It may also mean investing the money you make to earn a better return.

Finding a Business Manager

Remember, a business manager is more than just an accountant. In addition to the requisite standing as a certified public accountant (CPA), your business manager will also likely be a certified financial planner (CFP); many also have degrees in business administration or something similar. For your purposes, you also want a business manager with some prior experience in the entertainment business.

What you *don't* want is someone who doesn't have this type of financial background, training, and accreditation. Your business manager will be handling your money, and you don't want to hand your money over to someone who doesn't have the proper training and—dare I say it—accountability.

So where do you find a reputable business manager? The first thing to do is ask your other team members. Your personal manager or attorney will probably know someone who fits the bill. If you already have an attorney, he might have some thoughts. For that matter, other artists in your area might also know potential candidates. Working by reference is always a good idea.

Scam Alert _____

You should *never* look for a business manager within the band or within your circle of friends or family. Asking one member of the band to handle the finances for all of you is just asking for trouble. Same thing with recruiting family members or friends; it's never a good idea to mix your personal and professional lives in this fashion. Trust me on this one; you want to keep your business affairs in the business.

Beyond that, you can check with the various professional organizations in your area. Remember, you're looking for someone to manage your business finances. Check with your local chamber of commerce or SBA office, as well as other local small business organizations for business managers in your area. In addition, the National Association of Personal Financial Advisors (www.napfa.org) has lists of advisors by region on their website.

By the way, when you think you've found a business manager, don't sign on the spot. Do a little investigation, make sure the guy's legit. Again, this is your money we're talking about: you don't want to hand it over to a total stranger without doing a little homework first. And make sure you also set up some form of periodic audit, so that you can make sure your money is where it's supposed to be. There is an untold number of horror stories, even among major artists, regarding the business manager who ran off with the money. It can happen to you, so you need to apply the appropriate caution.

Paying for Business Management

There is no hard and fast method of compensation used by all business managers. Some charge an hourly rate; some charge a flat monthly or yearly fee; some charge a percentage of the revenues you generate. (That's revenues, not profits; they take their cut off the top, whether you actually make a profit or not.)

If you're not sure how badly you need a business manager, look for one that charges by the hour. This way you only pay for the work done. Know, however, that some business managers will want to be guaranteed a minimum amount per month; this amounts to a flat monthly fee, called a *retainer*, toward which the hourly bills apply.

You're also likely to pay a flat monthly fee if you sign a percentage deal with a business manager. Again, the business manager wants to be guaranteed a minimum amount for his work; he doesn't know whether you really will generate the revenues you say you will. In this instance, the percentage is really an upside payment, so that the business manager shares in the riches if you make it big—but still receives that minimum fee if your career tanks.

These monthly fees are all over the place, but will probably set you back between $1,000 and $5,000—more if you're a name artist. Percentage deals are typically in the 5 percent range, but may have a cap—a maximum amount the business manager can earn. Now that cap may be $200,000 or so per year (which means you'd be bringing in $4 million or so yourself, which would be nice), but they do prevent gross overpayment for the business manager's services.

In any case, you will need to sign a contract with your business manager. The contract will be for a fixed period of time (two to three years, typically) and include descriptions of the services the business manager will provide. Make sure your attorney reviews this contract, of course.

> **Behind the Music**
>
> Until you reach near-superstar status, you're unlikely to employ your own business manager full time. You'll have to share your business manager with other clients.

Dealing with Taxes—and Deductions

Taxes are confusing, especially in the entertainment business. Did you know that you need to pay taxes on the money you earn from playing—even if you're paid in cash? Did you know that different types of businesses pay different tax rates? Did you know that the money you spend on your music—your instruments, accessories, sheet music, even the gas you buy to drive to gigs—can be taken as tax deductions?

Because you don't have all the answers, you need a financial professional to help you with the tax situation. It doesn't matter if you only play a few gigs a year. You owe

> **Smart Business**
>
> The tax thing is another good reason to keep detailed records of not only what you make but also what you spend. A lot of what you spend can be deducted from the taxes you owe, reducing your tax liability.

taxes on the money you earn, no matter how little (or how much) that might be. Again, a good attorney or business manager will help you deal with this, but you do need to deal with it.

Do I Really Need a Business Manager?

Does every musician need a business manager? No, probably not. There are a lot of factors in play.

First, bands need business managers more than do solo artists. A band of any size at any level will benefit from forming a business entity and hiring a business manager to manage that entity's financial affairs. Solo artists can probably hold off longer before needing a business manager; it's a less-complex situation.

The amount of money you make is also a factor. Let's face it, if you're only playing a few wedding receptions during the season, a business manager adds little value. You still need the services of an accountant, of course, to handle your taxes and such, but a business manager won't have a lot to manage.

Once you start generating larger and more consistent revenues—a few gigs a month, let's say—then business management becomes more important. Business management is also key when your revenue comes from multiple sources, such as performances, merchandise sales, CD sales, digital downloads, and the like. Your business manager can help to keep everything straight.

The need for business management also increases when you *want* to become bigger. A business manager can help you manage your financial affairs in a way consistent with your goals. As with a traditional business, you need to plan for growth, and these plans may include taking out loans to purchase equipment, buy an equipment truck, and such. This is business management on a scale beyond simple accounting.

Of course, if you yourself have business management training or skills, then perhaps you can act as your own business manager. Again, this makes more sense if you're a solo act; my previous advice against hiring a band member to manage your money still stands, even if that band member is you. If you're comfortable with the financial stuff, good at it, and have the time for it, then you may be able to do it yourself. Otherwise, hire a pro.

The Least You Need to Know

- ◆ If you consider yourself a professional musician, you need to organize your professional affairs into a formal business entity.

- ◆ You can form one of three basic types of businesses: sole proprietorship, partnership, or corporation.

- ◆ Whatever type of business you form, you need the services of an accountant to help you manage taxes and other items.

- ◆ Alternately, consider hiring a business manager to plan and manage all your business's financial affairs.

- ◆ If you hire a business manager, expect to pay a monthly retainer against either an hourly fee or percentage of revenues.

Part 3

The Music Business for Musicians

There's a lot you need to know about how to make money from your music: recording, distribution, promotion, touring, merchandising, publishing, licensing—you name it. Then there's the question of whether you should sign with a major label, or stay an independent artist. And don't forget the Internet! (I told you there was a lot you need to know ....)

Chapter 9

The Business of Recording Your Music

In This Chapter

♦ The recording process from preproduction to postproduction

♦ Understanding today's recording options

♦ Using a professional recording studio

♦ Recording at home

♦ Making a live recording

For many musicians, making a record is kind of a holy grail; it's what they've always been working towards. But record-making is just another part of the music business, with its accordant challenges, hassles, and (hopefully) benefits. How you go about it depends on what you want to get out of it—and what you can put into it.

Understanding the Recording Process

There are lots of different ways to record music today. You can go the old-school route and rent a professional recording studio; you can record yourself in a home studio; or you can use portable recording gear to record a gig live. Whichever way you choose to record, however, there are four definite steps in the process. From pre-production through recording and mixing, all the way to the final step of mastering, it's important to know what needs to be done—and how to do it.

Preproduction

The first step of the recording process occurs before you do any recording. Pre-production is essentially the planning you need to do for your recording; it's the master plan you'll follow throughout the rest of the process. Since everything follows from this initial planning, preproduction is one of the most important steps in the recording process.

The goal of preproduction is to make sure everything else in the recording process goes as smoothly as possible. This means planning what you want to record, how you want to record it, who you want to record it, and what end result you want to achieve. Follow the steps you lay out in preproduction and your recording will be a success.

Finally, work out all the details in advance with the recording studio. Know how many tracks you're recording, approximately how much studio time you'll need, and the final output format for the recordings. (For example, if you're recording for downloading only, the studio will want to mix into the MP3 format.) Determine who's doing what—is the studio supplying the engineer, or do you have to arrange one? One nice benefit of a thorough preproduction process is that you should have no surprises once the sessions start. You want things to go smooth as silk.

Smart Business

When you make your track selection beforehand, you end up with much more efficient recording sessions because you know exactly what you want to record and how. Remember, you don't have to record tracks in the order in which they will appear on an album; it may be more efficient to record all the tracks featuring a specific group of musicians together, while those musicians are available.

Recording

Once everything is planned out and arranged, it's time to start recording. This is where everything comes together—the songs, the musicians, the engineers, and everything else.

Recording can be fun, but it's also a lot of hard work. Whether you're recording in a studio or in your home, don't expect a bunch of one-take wonders. Expect to do multiple takes for each song—along with the necessary overdubs.

Smart Business

One thing that surprises newcomers to the studio is just how long the process takes. You'll spend hours—that's right, *hours*—setting up your equipment, tuning up, setting up the microphones, and getting just the right sounds. Yes, playing music can and should be fun, but the recording process itself is *work*—whether you're recording at home or in the studio.

Mixing

The recording process is where you lay down the multiple individual tracks for each song. Those tracks then need to be edited and mixed together to create the final recording.

Mixing, then, is when you assemble all the individual tracks, adjust volume levels, add effects, and the like. It's also where you can edit your songs—cut a superfluous verse, for example, or copy a cookin' chorus to make a longer play-out at the end. And that editing process can be exceedingly fine; it's not unusual for an engineer to slice out unwanted notes, adjust a singer's pitch, or take one measure from one take and graft it into the whole of another take.

As you can imagine, then, mixing is a tedious, arduous process. It also doesn't necessarily involve all the musicians who made the recording. It's quite common for only the engineer and producer to attend mixing sessions, maybe with a representative member of the band in tow. If you're a hired gun for a recording, chances are you won't be involved in the mixing at all.

Mixing is necessary, however, whatever type of recording you're doing. Even if you've recorded a live club date, you still have to adjust volume levels between the instruments. And smart mixing can save an otherwise questionable project.

Behind the Music

If you have any doubts about how important mixing is, compare the Beatle's original *Let It Be* album with the *Let It Be: Naked* re-issue. The *Naked* album reflects the recording sessions more or less as they were, warts and all; the original *Let It Be* album, produced by the legendary Phil Spector, was substantially remixed to produce the album most of us remember. In his role as producer, Spector changed the entire complexion of several songs, most notably the title track, to which he added strings, inserted extra choruses, and otherwise "sweetened" for a mass audience. Paul McCartney didn't like Spector's fiddling, but that's what happens in the mixing process; the final album is carefully and deliberately shaped.

Mastering

The final part of the recording process is mastering. This is where you put the final touches on your mixes and make sure everything fits together as a whole.

The goal of mastering is to prepare your recording for final release—whether that be CD duplication or digital downloading. This involves setting EQ and volume levels for entire songs (not for the individual instrument tracks that comprise the song), equalizing for the desired output format, matching sound and volume levels between songs, adding compression and other overall effects, and the like.

When you're done mastering the songs, knit them together and send them on their way—the CD duplicator or to your website or online download service. The recording is now complete!

The Changing Industry: Different Recording Options

In the old days, recording was left to the professionals. A singer came into a recording studio, surrounded by hired studio musicians, and ran down two or three tracks in a three-hour session. Recording in a professional recording studio used to be the only way to make a recording; today it's just one of several options.

You see, the changing nature of the music business has dramatically affected recording studios. Fewer and fewer musicians record in expensive professional studios, opting instead for the lower cost and increased convenience of home studios. This is especially true of new artists, those handling their own distribution, and those signed to smaller, independent labels. (Major-label artists still tend to go the studio route, however.) Today, not only can you record in a studio (and in different sizes of studios, from small and intimate to large and cavernous), but you can also record in your own home or live at a gig, using a standard-issue personal computer.

For many musicians—first-timers, especially—home-based recording is probably the way to go, as it can be done on a very small budget. And a small budget means you don't have to rely on a major label recording contract; you can retain more control over your music and your career.

So where should you record? There are a lot of different factors to consider. If you're on a tight budget, home recording is the cost-effective way to go. With a minimal investment in recording software (and using your existing personal computer), even the most poverty-stricken artists can produce professional-sounding recordings.

If you're working at your leisure, home recording is also the best choice. Recording in a studio means adjusting your schedule to the time you've booked; recording at home means recording whenever you have free time and inspiration. Plus, there's no charge for the time you use; spend as much time as you want on your album and it won't cost you a penny more than your initial investment.

If you give killer live performances, consider making a live recording at one of your gigs. You can use the same equipment as you would when making a home recording—assuming you have a notebook PC, that is. You can set up a bunch of mics or just capture the output from your sound board. It's inexpensive and you can capture a lot of energy along with your music.

If you have a major-label deal, chances are you're headed into a big-time professional studio. The big labels are getting more comfortable with home-based recordings, but they still tend to default to the pro studio route. (It also gives them more control over the recording; chances are you'll see the label's guy in the engineering booth during the date.)

If you have a large band or use a lot of backing musicians, a big studio is probably the only place they'll all fit. Let's face it, you can't record an orchestra or a big band in your bedroom. The bigger the session, the better a pro studio looks.

> **Behind the Music**
>
> A pro studio is probably the only place you're going to find a big grand piano to record, if that's an important part of your sound.

If you want the utmost quality, a professional studio is still the best place to go. This is especially true when recording acoustic instruments and vocals, where room ambi-ence contributes a lot to the sound. Most home studios just don't have the space and surfaces to create great-sounding, natural reverb; they're good for "dead" sounds but not "live" ones. And a pro studio is going to have the best equipment possible, including the best-sounding, most expensive ribbon microphones. Most home recordists don't have this type of high-end professional equipment.

In addition to the size of the group, you have to factor in the complexity of the recording. The more complex the recording, as with a lot of pop music with orchestral sweetening, the more likely you are to choose a pro studio. Home studios are better for projects where you add one track at a time, not for those where lots of musicians play together; it's difficult to capture a live band performance in a home studio. And where true live performance matters, as with jazz, recording live at a gig may be the best way to go.

> ### Behind the Music
>
> The type of music you record will also influence where you record it; different types of music are better suited for different types of recording spaces. Many hip hop and techno musicians do all their work in home studios, as do many singer/songwriters. On the other hand, big rock bands, country superstars, and big orchestras record in pro studios. Jazz musicians, just to be different, often like to record live in clubs. And so it goes.

All that said, there are no hard and fast rules. For example, lots of great jazz recordings have been made in the studio, and there are more than a few great live rock albums. You should record where you feel most comfortable, where you think you'll get the best results—and where you can afford to.

Recording in a Professional Recording Studio

Let's start with traditional studio recording.

Using a pro studio still makes sense for many types of music—especially music that utilizes a lot of orchestral instruments. You're also likely to get a better sound (especially on vocals) at a pro studio than you can accomplish at home, so if audio quality matters, this is still the way to go. And many artists simply prefer the studio atmosphere; it's nice to work with professionals who know how to get the job done, and can do so quickly. That way you can really focus on what *you* do: creating and performing the music.

Inside a Recording Studio

If you've never been in one before, your first visit to a big recording studio might be overwhelming. There are two main rooms to any studio—the studio part, where the recording is made, and the engineering booth, where the sounds are recorded on tape or (more likely, these days) hard disk.

The studio room can be a very big room or a very small one. Larger rooms are often equipped with movable baffles, so that groups of musicians can be isolated. Both larger and smaller rooms are filled with lots of different microphones on stands, with mic cables snaking everywhere across the floor.

> **Behind the Music**
>
> Some larger studio rooms have side rooms—booths, actually—where individual musicians can be isolated. These booths are typically used for drums and sometimes vocals, and usually feature a glass window that overlooks the main recording room.

There is typically a large glass window between the recording room and the engineering booth. Inside the engineering booth you'll find a large mixing board; all the microphones from the main studio are connected to this board and operated by sliding controls called faders. The engineer sits in this room and listens to the recording over a set of monitor speakers, adjusting levels, panning from left to right, equalization, and whatnot as the recording goes down. He can also hear the musicians talk via their microphones; he has his own talkback microphone to communicate with the musicians.

In addition, many studios offer a choice of different recording spaces. For example, you might find a studio offering three different types of rooms—a large room that can hold entire orchestras, a medium-size space with ample room for most groups, and a small room best suited for playing solo keyboards. The different rooms will rent for different rates, so you can choose the size that meets your need and the price that meets your budget.

Of course, the recording space is only part of the entire studio space. Most studios have some sort of recreational space—a room you can rest and relax in, sometimes fitted with TVs, DVD players, and video games. Since you'll be spending a lot of time in the studio between takes, be sure to find out everything that's offered.

Renting the Studio

To use a studio, you have to book a block of time. You can rent studios either by the hour or by the day, but when your time is up, your recording is over.

When you record in a pro studio, you can take advantage of everything that studio has to offer. That means all the professional recording equipment—microphones, mixing board, tape decks, hard disk setups, you name it. You can also choose to use the studio's own engineers, or supply your own freelance engineer.

Most studios also offer a variety of instruments you can use if necessary. For example, most studios have their own grand pianos, so you don't have to haul your own piano in—or use a poor electronic copy. Expect to find keyboards (pianos and sometimes organs), drums, amps, and the like. Sometimes these instruments are included in the basic studio rental rate; sometimes you have to pay extra. Ask before you sign the contract.

Meet the Staff

A recording studio is more than just an empty room. It's a business that employs a number of different people, all of which are essential to your recording. You can use as many members of the staff as you need, or you can bring in your own people to fill crucial positions. (If you're interesting in pursuing a career in the recording business, check out Chapter 20.)

One of the most important people behind a professional recording is the record producer. The producer is essentially the "coach" for the recording sessions, controlling every aspect of the recording. The producer helps decide what songs to record, how to perform them, where to record, and who should play on each track. He schedules the recording sessions, supervises the sessions, and guides the musicians during recording. If outside musicians are necessary, he contracts them. The producer is also responsible for the mixing and mastering processes, working with the engineer to get the best possible final result.

> **Behind the Music**
>
> Producers are seldom provided by the studio. Artists arrange for their own producers for their sessions.

Even more important, the producer provides a vital set of independent ears during the session. Artists hear things their way, which is fine, but the producer hears things the way the ultimate listener will. It's the producer's job to tell the artist that one more take is necessary, or that the guitar part isn't cutting it, or that a track really needs some sweetening. Without a producer, artists can sometimes tend to get a little self-indulgent. Producers keep things on-track and focused.

If the producer runs the session, the recording engineer (sometimes just called the engineer) sits behind the controls in the recording booth and makes sure the recording gets made. This guy does more than just punch the "record" button, however. The engineer helps set up the instruments in the studio, if necessary, and positions the mics to get the sounds he wants. He adjusts the levels for each track, and determines what EQ and effects are necessary. A good engineer will also provide feedback to the musicians, letting them know when a track wasn't up to par or when something else is needed.

Most often, the same person engineers the recording session and does the mixing and mastering. In some instances, however, a different engineer might be brought in for the postproduction work in order to lend a new set of ears to the project. Studios typically have their own staff engineers they provide for recording projects. Some studios, however, will allow artists to hire their own outside engineers, if they want.

A big recording studio also has a lot of other people running around: various assistants who help set up instruments, position mics, move baffles around, the like. There are gofers who bring in lunch and coffee and such. And of course, there's the office staff who answer the phones, handle billing, and the like. Few studios are one-man shops; it takes a lot of people to produce a lot of different recordings.

Playing a Session

Once you're in the studio, it's time to step up your game. Since you're paying for the time, you need to pack the most productivity into each minute you spend there. Get there early, so you're not spending expensive studio time unloading and unpacking.

As to what a typical studio session entails—well, there's no such thing as a typical session. One session might see the individual musicians laying down a song track by individual track. Another session might find a band playing the instrumental parts together, but then overdubbing the vocals. Another session might find a solo artist doing the track-by-track thing. Still another session might find a vocalist singing live with an entire orchestra. Each session is different.

As to how much time to allot, some performers take their time when recording, spending days or weeks on a single track. Other performers work much faster (either by choice or budgetary necessity), recording several tracks in a single day. There's no one right way to do it.

Pricing Studio Time

What is common, however, is the money. Renting a recording studio is a major expense, and the longer the project, the bigger the budget. While rates differ from city to city and studio to studio, expect to pay between $50 and $150 per hour; a little more for larger rooms, a little less for smaller rooms. Most studios include their own engineer in that per-hour price; if you want a third-party engineer, you'll have to pay extra for him, of course. You may also have to pay more if you use additional equipment beyond what's normally included. You'll also have to pay for all materials, be that recording tape, blank discs, or whatever—and maybe soft drinks and meals depending on what the studio offers.

If you're pricing out a project, then, multiply the number of hours you expect to spend per track by the number of tracks by the studio's cost per hour. So for example, if you think you can lay down one track in an 8-hour day and you have 10 tracks to record, and you're using a studio that charges $150 per hour, the math goes like this:

Hours per track:	8
Total tracks:	10
Studio cost per hour:	$150
Total cost:	**$12,000**

That total cost, by the way, is before you pay for the incidentals, equipment rental, catering, and the cost to hire any studio musicians you might need. So you might want to factor in an additional 10 to 20 percent above the base studio price—for a possible total budget of $15,000, or so.

Smart Business

You don't have to use the same recording studio for postproduction as you do for recording. Many artists record at one facility and mix/master at another—either for convenience or due to the nature of the different studios.

And that's *if* you can do a track a day. You have to have all your songs written, arranged, and practiced for this to happen as planned. If you tend to do things more on the fly, you'll spend a lot longer in the studio.

One more thing: This budget is for recording only. You'll also need to budget separately for mixing and mastering. That might be an hour or two per track, or more if you or your music is especially demanding. Most studios charge a little less for postproduction, and you probably don't need to rent the largest studio room for this task. Still, budgeting an additional $2,000 or so for mixing/mastering makes sense.

Recording in a Home Studio

Not every artist can afford professional studio recording. If your budget is a concern, or if you want more control over the whole process, you can record yourself in a home studio using your own personal computer.

Home recording has been around forever, and many artists have overdubbed their way to chart-topping success. In the old days, that meant either investing in lots of expensive tape machines and such, or going the lo-fi route and recording with consumer-grade mics and recording equipment.

Today, however, you can make high-quality recordings in the convenience of your own home. Computer processing has advanced to the point where you have all the power you need to make high-resolution recordings at an affordable price point. And that goes for both hardware and software; there are plenty of affordable recording programs that run on just about any relatively new PC.

Assembling the Equipment

What do you need to make a home recording? Here's a list of essential equipment—some of which you probably already have:

- Personal computer
- Recording software
- Headphones
- Monitor speakers
- Audio interface
- Microphones
- Instruments

You'll need a relatively new, relatively fast computer to handle all the necessary digital audio processing. Lots of memory and a big hard disk are also essential. Either a notebook or desktop model will work; likewise, either a Windows or Mac model will do the job.

To monitor your recordings while you're making them, invest in a good pair of headphones. Go with the full-ear type, so that you hear only what's coming through the system, not the live sound from the room. You'll also need headphones for each musician you're recording.

To best evaluate the resulting recording, you'll need a pair of quality speakers for playback use. I'm not talking typical, low-end computer speakers; you'll want to invest a few hundred dollars on a pair of powered studio monitor speakers, just like those used in the big studios.

Unless you plan on recording only one instrument at a time, you need an audio interface unit that provides multiple inputs for microphones, guitars, and keyboards. This is an outboard box to which you connect all your mics and instruments; the box then connects to your PC, via either USB or Firewire. Expect to spend from $200 to $500 for an audio interface unit.

To record your performances, you use a software program that functions as a digital audio workstation (DAW). This software lets you record your music to a digital file, and then mix and process the individual tracks you record.

Smart Business

When it comes to DAW software, the gold standard is DigiDesign Pro Tools; this program is the one used by most pro studios. Pro Tools runs on any Mac or PC and can do everything necessary for the recording process, from basic audio and MIDI recording to digital editing and processing to mixing and mastering.

Smart Business

If you're recording just one track at a time, you may be able to get by with a single low-cost USB microphone, which connects to your PC via a USB connection. With this type of mic, you don't need a separate audio interface box.

If you perform live, you probably already have a few microphones lying around. You may be able to use these for recording, although more professional results are possible with higher-end mics designed especially for recording.

Naturally, you'll need to assemble all the instruments you need for a given recording, even if you're doing so in your bedroom. Of all the instruments, probably the most crucial is a good keyboard synthesizer, something you can use to drive a variety of different digitally sampled sounds.

Budgeting Your Recording

How much money you spend on a home-based recording depends on how much equipment you already have and how much you need to purchase new. The good news is that most of these purchases are one-time expenses; you don't have to buy a new version of Pro Tools every time you record, for example.

Let's work through a worst-case-scenario budget that assumes you don't have anything at your disposal:

Personal computer (Windows or Mac)	$700
Monitor speakers	$200
Pro Tools software	$250
Audio interface box	$200
Quality microphone	$100
Microphone stand and cable	$50
Studio headphones	$50
Total cost	**$1,550**

That's not bad, especially when compared to renting a big studio, but the cost could be even lower, so let's revise this budget and assume you already have some of the necessary items on hand. In particular, we'll assume you have an adequate home computer, a decent quality microphone and stand, your own headphones, and can do without a set of studio monitor speakers. Now the budget looks much more affordable:

Pro Tools software	$250
Audio interface box	$200
Total cost	**$450**

Now that's affordable! And remember, even this is a one-time expense; the next time you record, your cost will be zero.

Making the Recording

DIY recording means doing everything yourself. You probably don't have the budget or the desire to hire a separate engineer, so you'll be both playing and manning the controls. This combination of tasks takes a particular skill, so you may need to practice a bit before you get it down.

Smart Business

Because it's physically tricky to play and engineer at the same time, you might want to recruit a friend or fellow musician to work the controls while you're playing.

First, you'll have to get sound levels on each of the instruments on this particular track. This sounds easy enough, but try both playing and fiddling with the controls at the same time!

Then comes the recording itself, which is actually easier. Just click the "record" button, pick up your instrument, and start playing; click the "stop" button when you're done. You can edit out the empty space before and after the actual playing later.

Postrecording, you use the DAW software to stitch together the best takes and tracks into a cohesive whole; adjust and balance sound levels among the tracks; add various EQ, processing, and effects (such as reverb); and then create a final mix. That mix then gets mastered, using either the same software or special mastering software, and then gets output to the desired file format for either CD duplication or digital downloading.

Recording a Live Performance

Not all recordings are done in the controlled environment of a pro or home recording studio. Live recordings have long been an important part of the music scene, although in the old days that meant trundling expensive tape recorders and mixing consoles out to a club or auditorium (or at least to a van parked outside). Today, any notebook computer can function as a self-contained portable recording studio; just make sure your DAW software is installed and you carry an audio interface box with you to the gig.

In many ways, then, live recoding is just like home recording, except you're doing it all in one take in a club or concert hall. When recording live, prep work is especially important; you need to have everything set up and ready to go when the first note drops. That probably means recording a sound-check or preshow run-through, so you can position all the mics and set all the levels. Then it's a matter of pressing the "record" button when the set starts and monitoring the levels for each track during the performance.

Naturally, you'll still have to mix and master the recording when the performance is over. Fortunately, you can do that at your leisure in the comfort of your own home studio, or by using the facilities of a pro studio. Mixing a live album is sometimes challenging, as you may need to edit together different performances of the same song, to work around any bad notes during a given performance. Still, it's basic post-production work.

The cost should be similar to making a home recording. (You use the same equipment, after all.) So budget around $1,500 if you're starting from scratch and need to buy a new laptop PC, or around $500 if you already have a laptop and only need to buy Pro Tools and an audio interface box.

Do I Need to Use a Professional Recording Studio?

With all the options available today, the big question remains: Do you need to use a professional recording studio? The answer isn't as clear as you might think.

Back in the '50s, '60s, '70s, and '80s, using a professional studio was pretty much the only option available when you wanted to make a record. Starting in the '90s, however, advances in home computing technology have made home recording a viable option for more and more musicians.

Here's the deal: If you have an unlimited budget—that is, if your label is paying for it—by all means, book a pro studio. Recording in a big studio is a wonderful experience—the highlight of many musician's professional careers. For many folks, it signifies that they've hit the big time.

That said, you can achieve similar results today with a quality DIY recording. If your music is such that you assemble it track by track, and you use primarily close-micing or direct-injection techniques (that is, plugging your guitar or keyboard directly into the board), the sound you get from a home studio can be identical to what you can achieve in a pro studio. Today's DAW software, such as Pro Tools, includes all manner of processing and effects, from simple reverb to advanced pitch shifting (great for wobbly vocalists), so there's little a pro studio can do that you can't. Why spend big bucks for what you can do for pennies—or for free?

Of course, a pro studio has the edge when it comes to recording acoustic instruments and vocals, especially for pop music and jazz. And if you're recording a big group, you may just need the space that a big studio provides. I also appreciate the skills that a talented engineer brings to the game; they can do a lot of finessing behind the board.

But for many musicians, especially independent artists or those just starting out, DIY recording is the way to go. It's not just about budget; there's also a matter of control and freedom—control of your own music and freedom from label interference and the tyranny of the clock. Recording yourself isn't as easy as it sounds, of course (you're doing the studio staff's work yourself), but the extra effort may be worth the musical rewards.

The Least You Need to Know

- ◆ Making a recording involves four separate processes: preproduction, recording, mixing, and mastering.

- ◆ Professional recording studios offer large recording spaces and professional equipment and staff.

- ◆ PC-based home recording enables you to record yourself without spending a lot of money, and to record on your own schedule.

- ◆ You can make live recordings at a club or concert hall with a notebook computer and home recording software.

10

The Business of Working with a Major Record Label

In This Chapter

- ◆ Discovering the Big Four major record labels
- ◆ Uncovering what a major label does
- ◆ Finding out how to get signed to a major label
- ◆ Learning the details and the economics behind a major-label deal

Sure, recording your music is an ego boost. All musicians would like a CD with their name on it. But beyond the obvious strokes, most performers make recordings in order to make money from their music. That means generating revenue from physical CD sales, as well as from digital downloads.

In the old days, there was really only one way to sell your music—by signing a deal with a major record label. Today, more options exist, but many artists still prefer to sign with a label. Why is that—and what benefits do you get with a major-label deal? That's what we'll discuss in this chapter.

Getting to Know the Major Labels

A handful of major record labels dominate the commercial music business today. These companies handle everything from recording to pressing (actually "burning," when it comes to CDs) to distribution to promotion. Think of a major record label as a one-stop shop that handles the entire music-making process—and earns a healthy profit doing so.

There used to be a large number of major labels, but the industry has consolidated over time to the point that today there are only four major players, collectively known as the Big Four:

◆ **EMI Group:** A British company and the fourth largest of the Big Four, it owns and distributes the following labels: 10 Records, Angel Music, Apple Records, Astralwerks Records, Blue Note Records, Capitol Records, Caroline Records, EMI Classics, Fuel Records, Manhattan Records, S-Curve Records, Sparrow Records, and Virgin Records.

◆ **Sony BMG Entertainment:** The second-largest music company, it owns and distributes the following labels: Arista Records, Bluebird Records, BNA Records, Brentwood Records, Columbia Records, Daylight Records, Epic Records, J Records, Jive Records, Legacy Recordings, Praise Hymn Music Group, RCA Records, Reunion Records, Ruffhouse Records, Sonic Wave America, Sony Classical, and Sony Music Japan.

◆ **Universal Music Group (UMG):** The largest music company in the world, it owns and distributes the following labels: A&M Records, Casablanca Records, Commodore Records, Decca Records, Def Jam Records, Deutsche Grammophon, ECM, Geffen Records, GRP Records, Hip-O Records, Interscope Records, Island Records, Lost Highway Records, MCA Nashville Records, Mercury Nashville Records, Roc-a-Fella Records, Sanctuary Records, SRC Records, Universal Motown, Universal Records, V2 Music, and Verve Forecast Records.

◆ **Warner Music Group (WMG):** The third-largest music company, it owns and distributes the following labels: Asylum Records, Atco Records, Atlantic Records, Bad Boy Records, Elektra Records, Maverick, Nonesuch Records, Reprise Records, Rhino Records, Rykodisc Records, Sire Records, Teldec, Warner Bros. Records, and Word Records.

> **Behind the Music**
>
> Until recently, the Big Four were the Big Five—until Sony Music bought Bertelsmann Music Group (BMG) in 2008. (Which means the Big Four could become the Big Three—or Big Two—should further consolidation happen.)

What a Major Label Does

Here's the main thing a major record label brings to the table: Money, and lots of it.

First off, the label pays you a big advance when you sign your contract. That's cash in your pocket, and it's mighty attractive.

Next, the label bankrolls your recording. Or rather, it loans you the money for your recording. That typically means lots of expensive studio time in a big-name studio, accompanied by a big-name producer, big-name engineer, and all the big-name studio musicians and guest artists you want. The label pays these bills, but charges them against your account. (More on this in a minute ….)

The label then pays to get your CD pressed in bulk, and pays for all the fancy design and packaging. It also pays to distribute your CD to record stores around the world; it owns all the necessary distribution centers (warehouses) and such.

Next, the label pays to promote your CD. It takes out ads in music magazines and newspapers, runs commercials on radio stations, you name it. And if payola existed (and I'm sure it doesn't), the payoffs would be paid by the label's people.

> **Behind the Music**
>
> The label also pays to produce those fancy music videos you make to promote your music. This can be an expensive promotion, when you consider the cost for a multiday shoot with an expensive director and big crew. But the label picks up the bill (and charges it against your account).

In some instances, the label may pay to create a website or a MySpace page for you, may bankroll the production of various merchandise, and may even help finance your next tour—all for a cut of the proceeds, of course.

In other words, the label has its fingers in just about everything you do musically. As such, it also wants some say in what you do—the songs you include on your next album, the musicians you use on the recording, the places you tour, even the image you project. The label owns you, after all, and wants to control its property. That's the deal you make; the label's financial support for your musical soul. That may be a good deal for some artists, but not for all.

Beware the 360-Degree Deal

Because of the way the music business is changing, labels are making less money from traditional CD sales than they used to. Perhaps understandably, labels are looking to make up those lost revenues in any way possible. The result is what's called the *360-degree deal*—and it's something you need to beware of.

In this sort of deal, the label takes a cut of virtually everything the artist does. Labels are looking to get a 10 percent to 20 percent cut from your touring and live performances, merchandise sales, endorsements and corporate sponsorships, and music publishing. (That's right—labels are now trying to take a cut of songwriting royalties!)

Now just because the label *asks* for a 360-deal doesn't mean you have to agree to it. (Of course, the label can refuse to sign you without it, too.) And not all 360-degree deals are created equal. For example, you may be able to negotiate whether the label finances some or all of your tour expenses in return for their cut of the tour proceeds. It's certainly worth talking about.

> **Scam Alert**
>
> The worst kind of 360-degree deal is one with "passive participation." That is, the label gets a cut from more activities without doing anything more themselves. Money for nothing is what this is, and it's not a good thing for artists.

Getting Signed by a Major Label

All objections aside, let's say you like the idea of having the backing of a major label. Just how do you go about getting signed?

One approach is to just hunker down and do what you do. Hone your music and play the local club circuit; build up a loyal following. You do your job well—and produce unique and marketable music—and a hungry record label will hear about you and send an A&R guy your way.

A&R, by the way, stands for Artists and Repertoire, and is the department of the music label responsible for finding and grooming new artists. A&R guys are essentially talent scouts, always looking for the next big thing. In this scenario, the A&R guy will catch your act and, if he likes what he hears, make you an offer. Hey—you've just been discovered!

If you'd rather take things into your own hands, you can put together a demo package and send it to the A&R department of a major label. Or rather, send it to one of the individual labels owned by a Big Four music company. Your demo package should include a CD of your best stuff, personal bios, publicity pictures, a nice history of you or your band, and the like.

How do you know where to send your demo package? Well, you should be familiar enough with today's music scene to know which labels focus on the type of music that you make, and then target those labels. The best source of A&R contacts for both major and indie labels is the *A&R Registry*, available on CD-ROM at www.musicregistry.com. You'll pay $75 for this list, but it's worth it. (One popular alternative to signing with a major label is to sign with a smaller independent label. Learn more in Chapter 11.)

The Details Behind the Deal

When you're offered a deal from a major label, that deal comes in the form of a contract—a very long, very detailed contract with lots and lots of fine print.

It goes without saying that you should have your personal manager, your business manager, and your attorney look over this contract in excruciating detail. In fact, you should probably have your manager and your attorney do some of the negotiating for you. (That's right, everything the label offers you is negotiable.)

Smart Business

Many artists prefer to let their managers handle all dealings with the label. This lets the businesspeople focus on the business stuff so you can focus on the music.

What are some of the details you'll find in a label contract? Let's look at a few of the key points.

Term

Most labels sign artists for a given number of records, not for a specific length of time. So your contract might be for five or six albums, and isn't fulfilled until you've had this many releases. Make sure that the number of releases specified in your contract is realistic—and figure out how many years it will take you to release that many albums.

Exclusivity

You can only sign with one label at a time. That is, you can't release an album for Sony if you're signed with EMI. Make sure you're comfortable with the extent of exclusivity in the contract.

Smart Business _____

If you like or want to play on other recordings, insist on some sort of "sideman exclusion" that lets you perform as a credited sideman (not as a featured artist) for other recording artists.

Creative Control

This is a big one. Who decides what you record? Who chooses the producer and engineer? Who decides what is acceptable—and what isn't? In other words, who calls the creative shots?

Don't be surprised to see the first draft of the contract say that the label has final creative say. If you can't live with that, try negotiating something different—or sign with a smaller label.

Advance

The record label may not want you to get rich off their dime, but they don't want you to starve. To that end, the label typically will pay you a certain amount of money in advance—called, not surprisingly, an *advance*. This advance may be a one-time payment or it may be a monthly check.

def•i•ni•tion _____

An **advance** is technically an advance against royalties. That is, the record company advances or loans you a sum that will theoretically be repaid from your future royalty stream.

Is the advance big enough for you to live on? If you're in a band, are all members paid equally? How much of the advance goes to your personal manager, business manager, attorney, and such?

In most instances, this advance is technically an advance against royalties—that is, you have to earn more in royalties than you are paid as an advance before you see a single royalty check. Let's say you get paid a $10,000 advance and you generate $12,000 in royalties from CD sales. You take the $12,000 in royalties and subtract the $10,000 advance, and you get to take home the $2,000 remaining. On the other hand, if you only generate $8,000 in royalties, you take that $8,000, subtract the $10,000 advance, and you're left with a negative number: that's $2,000 you owe the record company!

Signing Bonus

Some labels will pay some artists a tidy sum just for signing the contract. In some instances this is merely an advance against royalties; in other instances, this is a dollar figure free and clear of any advances and royalties. Obviously, a true bonus is more valuable than one where the label just advances you some of your own money.

Royalties

Ah, now we come to the real money—or what should be the real money. The record label pays you, the artist, a certain percentage of all monies it makes from selling physical recordings (CDs) and digital recordings. This is a negotiable rate, typically between 6 and 10 percent, based on the list price of the final product.

For example, if you negotiate a deal to earn 10 percent royalties on a $14.99 CD, you would receive $1.49 for each CD sold. Note that that's 10 percent for the entire band, if you're in a band; each member would receive a portion of that 10 percent. So if you're in a five-piece band and your band agreement states that you share these things equally, then each of you earns a 2 percent royalty (one fifth of the band's 10 percent).

> **Behind the Music**
>
> Don't confuse artist royalties with songwriter's mechanical royalties; if you write your own songs, you earn a songwriter's royalty in addition to the royalty paid by the record label to you as an artist. Learn more about royalties in Chapter 24.

Royalty Reductions

The royalty rate you theoretically earn is typically not the final royalty you receive. That's because all labels include what are called *royalty reductions*—lower rates for specific types of sales.

For example, foreign sales (those made outside the United States) typically are paid at half the U.S. royalty rate; if you have a normal 10 percent royalty, you earn 5 percent on sales in Europe, Japan, and other countries. Sales made to record clubs are also at a lower royalty; products given for free, such as for promotional purposes, earn no royalty.

Controlled Composition

You may not be able to exactly double your income if you write all the songs you record. Many contracts include a controlled composition clause, which states that the label will pay mechanical songwriting royalties for a maximum of 10 songs per album and at 75 percent (or less) of the current mechanical royalty rate.

This clause is an attempt to either reduce artist payments or force nonoriginal material on a label's artists. (Don't be surprised if you're asked to include a song or two from one of the label's favored songwriters.) If faced with this clause, you can try to negotiate out of it—although you may not be successful.

Returns Reserve

Here's a good one. The label will try to reserve a certain amount of royalties earned against any future product returns.

For example, the label might anticipate having a 20 percent return rate from stores with unsold merchandise. Since these are sales that become nonsales (due to being returned), the label doesn't want to pay royalties on them, so they hold back ("reserve") 20 percent of your royalties in anticipation of said returns. If your CD has a lower actual return rate, you should get some of these reserves reversed—but that's something for your business manager to manage.

Recording Costs

This is a big one. In most contracts, most if not all of the costs incurred in making a recording are billed back to the artist—which go against any royalties you might earn. The amount you're on the hook for is negotiable, however, so pay attention to this clause—and try to keep your recording costs under control.

Video Costs

Guess who pays for the promotional videos you make? You do! Yes, the label handles all the costs up front, but then bills them to your account—where, like recording costs, they're deducted from any royalties you earn.

Promotional Costs

First off, make sure that the label is responsible for specific marketing activities; get it spelled out in writing. But keep in mind that the label will bill you back for the costs of this promotion—and, you guessed it, deduct some or all of those costs from royalties owed. (How much is recoupable may be negotiable.)

Merchandising

Some labels want a cut of any merchandising sales you may make, either on your website or at gigs. Try to wriggle out of this one if you can.

Tours

In the old days, record labels didn't want anything to do with your touring activities. That's changing, however, and some labels will either want to help manage your tours (for a fee, of course) or just want a cut of tour revenues. Again, try to negotiate your way out of this sort of thing.

Accounting and Auditing

The label is responsible for providing you with regular accounting reports. Most labels make such reports every six months, and pay royalties on the same six-month schedule. You should insist on a right to audit the company's books, just to keep them honest.

Assignment

You might not like it, but most big companies reserve the right to sell your contract to other companies. The label can also move you to other labels within its corporate umbrella. This is called "assignment of contract," and it's fairly standard.

Smart Business

Most of these contract details are designed to work in the label's favor. That's why you need to have all the members of your team—personal manager, business manager, and attorney—involved in the negotiations. You'll have to work hard to get the terms even close to equitable.

Termination

All contracts can be cancelled if one side doesn't live up to what they promised to do. Don't be surprised if your contract includes all sorts of "outs" for the label, but fewer such escape clauses for you. And beware of clauses that say you can't record for a certain amount of time after the termination of a contract.

The Economics of the Deal

Let's look at the practical economics of a typical major-label deal. As you'll see, you can sell a lot of CDs and make very little money—or even end up in debt to the record company.

For our example, say you've just recorded an album that you hope to sell on CD for $15. (Round numbers are best for this example.) If you, the artist, make a 10 percent royalty on all copies sold, that's $1.50 in your pocket every time somebody buys a CD.

Other People's Money

A buck and a half doesn't sound like that much money for all your effort, does it? So just where does the rest of the money go?

First of all, major record labels sell their products through record stores, and the retailer has to take his cut. Most retailers make a 30 to 40 percent margin on the CDs they sell, based on the product's list price. For a $15 CD, this means that the retailer probably pays the label (or its designated distributor) $9—and pockets the $6 difference. (If the CD sells for full list price, that is.)

So the label gets paid $9 for a $15 CD. From that $9, the producer of the record takes a cut, in the form of *points*. In plain English, if a producer gets "three points," he gets paid 3 percent of what the label generates for that recording—27¢ per CD from the label's $9 revenue.

Behind the Music

Producers typically get paid an upfront advance; they get this fee even if the CD sells zero copies. The advance is subtracted from the money owed from the producer's points, until the advance is paid out. So if a producer got a $20,000 advance and the CD sold 10,000 copies, that $20,000 is subtracted from the $27,000 generated by points and the producer takes home $7,000 from CD sales.

Another percentage is paid to the writers of the songs on the CD, in the form of mechanical royalties. Now if you wrote all the songs you recorded, that's a good thing; that royalty money flows to you, via either ASCAP or BMI, the major music publishing organizations. (If you're not the songwriter, it's just more money going to somebody else.) This royalty is a flat rate per song, with no advances or holdbacks, or anything else withheld. The money is calculated on a per-song basis; the current rate for a song less than five minutes long is 9.1¢ per copy sold. So if you have 10 songs on your CD, that's another 91¢ that goes elsewhere. (Learn more about songwriting royalties in Chapter 15.)

Of course, it costs money to physically manufacture and distribute each CD. Costs vary, but figure about $0.50 per unit in manufacturing/duplication/distribution costs.

Your Money—or What's Left of It

But that's all about money going to other parties. What about the money you, the artist, earn? That's the $1.50 we discussed previously, based on a 10 percent royalty rate.

As I said before, making a buck and a half per CD doesn't sound like much—unless you have a million-copy seller, of course. But it gets worse. That's because most major-label deals require artists to pay off all recording, marketing, and promotion costs before they see a penny of revenue from CD sales. Depending on how much money you (and the label) spend, that payoff may never come.

To demonstrate how this works, let's continue working through our example. We'll say that your CD sells 100,000 copies in the United States—a good number for a new artist these days.

Of course, the label fronts a bit of money to make the CD. You'll see the itemization on the following page, but the upfront costs include recording (studio rental, equipment rental, paying the engineer, and so forth), producing (in this instance, the producer gets a $40,000 advance), marketing and promotion, and the like.

> **Behind the Music**
>
> To keep the example simple, I'm not going to throw in the costs of making a video to support the CD, although this is a real expense for many performers. I'm also not going to factor in what the band might pay their manager, although again that can be a real cost.

Running the Numbers

So doing some rough calculations, here's how the numbers break down for this typical major-label recording:

Revenues

CD sales (100,000 × $15.00)	$1,500,000
Minus retailer profit (100,000 × $6.00)	($600,000)
Net label revenues	**$900,000**

Variable Expenses

Manufacturing/distribution (100,000 × $0.50)	$50,000
Songwriting royalties (100,000 × 10 songs × $.091)	$91,000
Artist royalties (10 percent of $1,500,000)	$150,000
Total variable expenses	**$291,000**
Gross label profit (revenues minus expenses)	**$609,000**

Fixed Expenses (Paid by the label but charged to the artist)

Recording (including studio fees)	$75,000
Producer's advance	$40,000
Equipment rental	$5,000
Mastering	$5,000
Album artwork	$5,000
Marketing/promotion	$50,000
Total fixed expenses	**$180,000**

Artist Profit

Artist royalties earned	$150,000
Minus fixed expenses charged to the artist	($180,000)
Artist profit (loss)	**($30,000)**

So in our little example, the artist sells 100,000 CDs but ends up $30,000 in the hole. The label, on the other hand, ends up making $609,000 (before paying staff, utilities, and such, of course). Hardly seems fair, does it? (Which is why many artists today choose to forgo a major-label contract.)

Recouping Advances

Of course, there's one more factor we didn't take into account—the artist's advance. Remember, this is an advance against royalties and since there aren't any royalties to be paid (we're at a $30,000 loss), the advance obviously won't earn out. But the artist does get the advance and does get to keep it.

So if, in this example, the artist got a $50,000 advance, that's $50,000 in the artist's pocket—which is better than being $30,000 in the hole. Of course, the artist *is* still in the hole—actually now he's $80,000 in the hole, because he technically owes the label both the $50,000 advance and the $30,000 loss on the CD project. But labels normally don't come after artists for the unearned difference; you get to keep whatever advance you negotiated … sort of.

Remember, you're still $80,000 in debt to the label (your advance plus the loss on the CD project). This goes on your account, in the form of something called *cross-collateralization*. What this means, basically, is that if you don't pay off all the costs incurred for one project, those costs can be applied to your next project. You don't start each project with a fresh slate.

def•i•ni•tion

A contract is **cross-collateralized** when the terms of that contract—specifically the financial terms—are applied across more than one project. This is typically structured to ensure that costs incurred on one project can be recouped from the profits made on another project.

So in our example, when it's time to record album number two, you start out $80,000 in the hole. So even if you sell more copies on your second go round, enough to actually turn a profit, that profit is eaten by the negative $80,000 balance on your account. No royalty payments for you!

How does this scenario change if your album makes money? It depends on how much money it makes. Remember, you still have to earn through the advance before you receive any royalty payments. So let's say your album made a $30,000 profit, instead of a loss, after all label expenses have been deducted. That $30,000 profit is less than the $50,000 advance you were paid, which means you still owe the company $20,000.

So when do you actually see a royalty check? Only if your album makes enough money to earn through your advance. Let's say this particular album sold enough copies to make a $60,000 profit for the artist. That's $10,000 more than was paid for the advance, so the advance earns out. The artist gets to keep the $10,000 difference as a royalty. Yippee!

Other Pros and Cons of Signing with a Major Label

That's the thing with major-label deals. Due to the creative accounting most labels employ, most albums do not make a profit, most artists don't earn out their advance, and most artists never see a penny in royalty payments. The label, of course, makes a big profit; the artist, however, gets an advance but not much in the way of ongoing royalties. And that's not a good thing.

It gets worse. Given the huge number of albums released each month by most major labels, it's easy to get lost in the shuffle. When it comes to allocating promotional resources, you may end up at the bottom of the bag—and the less attention you get from the label, the lower your sales will be.

On the plus side, if you do get the attention of your label's promotion department, the resources of a major label can really make an impact. Let's face it, Sony or Warner can make a big splash when they decide to really get behind an artist. No indie label—and no artist promoting himself—has these kinds of promotional resources, in terms of both people and money.

And that may be the biggest benefit of signing with a major label. If you want to be a really big name in the business, a major label can take you places that you can't reach otherwise.

Why Would I Want to Sign with a Major Label?

You might think from reading this chapter that signing with a major label is making a deal with the devil. I admit, there's a lot to dislike about dealing with a major label; even big-name artists are apt to come out on the short end more often than not.

All that said, a lot of artists are signed to the Big Four labels and their affiliates. If life with a major label were so bad, where do they get all their artists—and how?

First, there's the prestige. Musicians are artists, and artists have egos. Signing a contract with Sony or Warner (or one of their perhaps better-known affiliate labels, such as Atlantic or Columbia) is a huge ego boost. I mean, if you sign with Atlantic, you're on the same label that released Ruth Brown and the Drifters, Ray Charles and Aretha Franklin, Led Zeppelin and Genesis, Gnarls Barkley and Rob Thomas. That's the big league, man—who can resist that?

Prestige aside, a major label can do major things for your career. The Big Four have big bucks to back big efforts; if you're one of their favorites, they'll provide a lot of promotion, publicity, and everything else it takes to get your music heard. Every record store in the land will stock your CD, you'll be featured on Amazon and the iTunes Store, and your record will get reviewed in *Rolling Stone* and most of the other major music rags. Big labels mean big presence, much more than you could accomplish as an independent artist.

Then there are all those things that a label does that you would have to do yourself if you didn't sign with a label, big or small. Don't like making phone calls to journalists? Don't like answering e-mail messages from fans? Don't have any idea how to put together a marketing plan? Not sure how or where to distribute your music? Then going without a major-label contract could put you in the lurch. Somebody has to do all these things—and more. If your label doesn't do them, then you have to. (Or you could hire somebody else to do them—but that's more money out of your pocket, and you still have to manage the people doing the work.) Record labels do add some value, you know.

And financial issues aside, many artists have very good relationships with their labels. Once you get inside the machine and establish the right relationships with the right people, a major label can be very supportive. It helps, of course, if you have a good track record; the more successful you are, the more creative clout the label will let you have. Deliver the goods and you'll be able to do just about anything you want.

As to those financial issues, they, too, diminish as you gain success. Cut a million-seller and you can pretty much call the shots when it's time to renew your contract. In fact, you'll likely have multiple labels bidding for your services—which means you don't have to accept any of the normal B.S. that labels impose on newer, less-proven artists.

But if you're not a household name or a proven hitmaker, your relationship with the label is likely to be a little more one-sided—with the label having the most weight. I admit, however, it would be difficult to turn down a deal from one of the Big Four; just make it as good a deal as you can.

The Least You Need to Know

♦ A major record label pays you an advance, finances your recording project, and then presses and distributes the resulting CDs. It also provides marketing and promotional support for your release.

♦ You sign with a major label via the efforts of the A&R department, either being discovered by an A&R person or sending the label a demo kit.

◆ Signing with a major label is complex and often confusing; there are a lot of questionable clauses to look out for.

◆ Most major labels charge a bunch of expenses to your account, making it unlikely that your album will make an actual profit—or that you'll see royalty payment.

◆ On the plus side, major labels have a lot of clout—and big pocketbooks—to put behind your product.

Chapter 11

The Business of Independent Distribution

In This Chapter

- Understanding what exactly you're selling
- Appraising independent distribution
- Learning how to distribute your own music
- Discovering how to sell music online

For the better part of the past century, getting a record deal was the holy grail sought by every working musician; the record label financed your recording, distributed your records, and promoted your music to radio stations and other media. And while the record company was obviously in it to make a profit, most artists hoped to make a killing, too.

Unfortunately, that isn't how it turned out. Most artists don't make much money from their record deals—not even artists with huge million-sellers. That's because most record deals are structured in such a way that all the profits accrue to the record label and most of the expenses are charged to the artist.

Today, however, signing with a major label isn't your only option. You also have the option of signing with a smaller, independent label, which might offer better terms. You can also distribute your own music, either physically or digitally, or even form your own record label. All these options offer potentially more money in your pocket—but might require more work on your end.

What Are You Selling?

Being an independent artist means you're not aligned with a major record deal. In one way or another, you're selling your own music. But what does "selling your music" really mean? It all depends on when you ask.

Singles vs. Albums

In the early days of the twentieth century, selling music meant selling individual songs via either sheet music or piano rolls. That had changed by the 1930s, when you sold your music on 78 RPM records. Each side of a record could hold a single song or so, so you were still selling singles, more or less.

This notion of selling individual songs continued in the 1950s and 1960s, via the newer vinyl 45 RPM records. Starting in the mid-1950s, however, and becoming even more important a decade later, long-playing 33⅓ RPM records ushered in the era of the album; all of a sudden you weren't selling a single song, but rather a collection of them. This album mentality continued into the compact disc age of the 1980s and 1990s, with single releases becoming less and less important.

Smart Business _____

Artists of a few decades ago learned to think of their music in terms of albums—10 to 15 songs collected together—but that's not how people are buying music today. It's less important to go into a studio and record an entire album's worth of songs; one strong song available digitally may be enough to make your career—and generate serious income.

Moving into the twenty-first century, we see a return to selling single songs. That's due to digital downloading, of course, where listeners have the option of downloading single tracks instead of complete albums. It's a single-song mentality again, just the way it was a century earlier.

Physical vs. Digital Media

Let's return to that short history of music distribution. It's easy to see that the medium in which music is distributed is in constant flux; each distribution medium only lasts for a few decades until it's replaced by newer technology.

We started out, a hundred years ago, distributing music via piano rolls. In the 1930s, piano rolls got supplanted by 78 RPM records. In the 1950s, 78 RPM records were replaced by 33⅓ LPs—and, in a bit of a sideline, by 45 RPM singles. Then in the 1980s, LPs (and singles) got replaced by CDs. Finally, at the dawn of the twenty-first century, CDs are being replaced by digital downloads.

So to some extent, the medium doesn't matter. Consumers buy music in whatever form it is available at the time. Back in the 1900s, everybody had a piano in the household, so they either bought sheet music or (if they had a player piano) piano rolls. In the 1930s, everybody had a gramophone, so people bought records that played on that technology. In the 1980s, everybody bought CD players, so they then purchased their music on CDs. And today we all have fast Internet connections and iPods, so digital downloading is the medium du jour.

The important lesson here is to not get caught up in the way music is distributed; what we did yesterday isn't what we do today, and what we do today is bound to change tomorrow. No, the important thing is to recognize changing media and make your music available on the appropriate media for the times.

> **Smart Business**
>
> What is always important, no matter the year or the medium is the music itself. You still need strong songs and strong performances, recorded well. That argues for basic musical talent and mastery of the current recording environment. Write a great tune and make a great record, and then you can distribute it appropriately.

Of course, it also means tailoring your music to the medium. When single-song piano rolls were in vogue, you sold one song at a time. When the long-playing record became popular, you collected a dozen or so songs together to sell as an album. And now that we're back to single-song distribution over the Internet, you need to dump the album mentality and focus on individual songs again. In this regard, the medium shapes the music, to a small degree.

Signing with an Independent Label

For the better part of the twentieth century, the only practical way to get your music distributed was via a major record label. After reading the previous chapter of this book, you should know the pros and (mainly) cons of signing with a major record label—which probably gets you thinking of other options. (Learn more about major record labels in Chapter 10.)

One popular option for many artists today is to sign with a smaller *independent label*. You're still using a label to do most of the business and distribution stuff, but indie labels typically give you more creative control—and take less of your money in the bargain.

Indie labels do most of the same things the major labels do, but on a much smaller scale. For example, indie labels tend to not own their own *distributors* for physical product, instead using independent distributors to get their products into stores. (This is less important in the digital age, of course.) They also may contract out other functions, such as publicity and promotion. There is less of an in-house staff to do these things—but also less in-house bureaucracy to deal with and pay for.

def•i•ni•tion

An **independent label** is any record label that is not affiliated in any way with one of the Big Four major labels.

A **distributor** is a company that serves as a middleman between the label or artist and the retail store. Distributors purchase CDs from the labels and then sell them to retailers, handling all the paperwork, financing, and such. Most distributors handle product from multiple labels, becoming a one-stop-shop for retailers in need of product.

Indie Label vs. Major Label: Similarities

In many ways, a contract with an indie label is similar to a contract you'd sign with a major label. Business stuff is business stuff; you're going to have the same clauses for advances, royalties, expenses, holdbacks, and the like. The accounting will also be similar, in that any royalties you make will have appropriate expenses charged against them, and you'll still need to earn out any advance you're paid before you see a royalty check. Remember, you're still dealing with a record label, even if it's a smaller, more personal one.

As to the terms of a contract, expect the royalty rate to be similar to that paid by a major label—something in the 10 percent range. The length of the contract, however, might be shorter—one or two records as opposed to five or six.

And in general, expect everything to be a little easier to negotiate with an indie label. If you really want a particular clause in the contract, you can probably get it.

Indie Label vs. Major Label: Differences

When talking about indie-label deals, the personal relationship makes the difference. You see, instead of dealing with a big bureaucracy, you're dealing with a handful of people. You're likely to deal with the head of the label personally, which isn't going to happen if you sign with Warner or Universal. If you have an issue, you can pick up the phone and talk to the head guy. That's a good thing.

And here's another good thing about working with a smaller company: you get more of their promotional attention. Your CD isn't one of dozens coming out this month, it's one of just a handful of releases. That means you get more face time with the sales reps and distributors, and you get the full force of the label's promotional efforts. It's highly unlikely that you'll get lost in any kind of shuffle.

On the other hand, the smaller scale of an indie label has its drawbacks. Whereas Sony or EMI can throw really big bucks and lots of people-power behind a favored release, an indie label has neither the budget nor the staff to make that kind of splash. The promotion is going to be more guerilla-like in nature. Don't expect to see big magazine ads, radio commercials, and the like. You may also be asked to do more of the promotional work yourself, and pick up some of the recording costs. (Although indie labels are more acceptable of home-based recordings, which help to lower everyone's costs.)

In addition, don't expect to see six-figure advances or signing bonuses with an indie contract. In fact, you may not see *any* advance, which means you'll be living off royalty payments. It's a totally different financial situation.

That said, you'll likely find the finances working a little more in your favor. Indie labels are less likely to sock you for every conceivable expense like the major labels do. Yes, you'll be

Behind the Music
Most smaller labels depend on artists to do their own self-promotion. A lot of this can be done online, of course, but you may have to pony up some of your own money to promote a new release.

on the hook for *some* expenses, but don't expect to be billed for the company's legal and accounting staff—guys that sometimes work against you. (Yes, this happens at the major labels.)

The bottom line is that signing with an indie label is a much more personal experience. A big part of why they're signing you, and you're signing with them, is probably that you all like each other and see eye-to-eye about music *and* business. You'll probably get less money upfront but might make more money in the long term.

Distributing Your Own Music

Moving into the twenty-first century, there's a viable third option for distributing your music, beyond major and indie labels. Thanks to digital downloads and the various resources available on the Internet, you can now distribute your music yourself—no record label necessary.

Distributing CDs

Let's start with the simplest form of self-distribution—selling your own physical CDs. These days you can burn CDs for just pennies per disc, using your own personal computer. You can then sell your CDs at your live performances and on your own website, for anywhere from $10 to $20 apiece.

In this instance, self-distribution means not giving any cut to a label; all the revenue you generate flows back to you. All you have to do is subtract the costs of producing the CDs—as well as the sunk costs of the recording itself, of course.

The Economics of Self-Distribution

Let's look at the math. For our example, I'm going to assume that you cut the CD in your home studio without hiring a professional producer or engineer. I'm also going to assume that you didn't have to buy or rent any recording equipment; that is, you used your regular instruments and mics from your stage sound system. I'll also assume that you recorded on your existing computer, and that the only recording expense you had was purchasing the recording software, an audio interface box, and a few extra cables.

As to the CDs themselves, let's assume that you burn them in batches on that same PC, so there's no professional duplication involved. I'll toss in $500 to have a friend of yours create and print the CD artwork, but beyond that you do everything yourself.

Doing everything yourself also means selling the CDs yourself. I'm not factoring in any traditional retail sales. Instead, you hand-sell the CDs at your performances, on your website, via your fan club, or whatever. Each CD sells for $15 apiece. If there's any shipping/handling involved, the customer will pay it.

All that said, here's how the profits look if you sell just 1,000 CDs.

Revenues	
CD sales (1,000 × $15.00)	$15,000
Expenses	
Recording budget	$1,000
CD artwork	$500
Disc cost (1,000 × $0.50)	$500
Total expenses	**$1,750**
Total profit (revenues minus expenses)	**$13,000**

That's right, if you sell just 1,000 CDs (not a large number, really), you take home $13,000. That profit gets lower if you spend more money on recording—for example, if you have to buy a couple of microphones or pay somebody to handle the engineering chores. But you see how this can be a significant revenue stream for independent artists—if you don't mind doing all the work yourself.

> **Behind the Music**
>
> Compare this $13,000 profit from self-distributing 1,000 CDs versus the $30,000 *loss* from selling 100,000 CDs on a major label, as detailed in Chapter 10.

Finding a Distributor

If you want to release on a grander scale, you can look to have your CDs sold at retail in traditional record stores. To do this, you have to find and sign a deal with one or more record distributors.

Types of Distributors

There are several types of record distributors in the United States:

- ◆ **One-stop distributors** carry a wide selection of products from both major and indie labels, and sell to chain stores, independent record shops, and other types of outlets that sell CDs.

- ◆ **Rackjobbers** rent or lease space in other retail stores, such as department stores and mass merchandisers. They usually carry only best-selling products—the top 100 or 1,000 CDs—concentrating on items from the major labels.

- ◆ **Independent distributors** are probably your best bet. These companies distribute CDs from indie labels and individual artists, either on a regional or national basis.

Behind the Music
What the distributor doesn't do is promote individual releases. They're a stocking service only; the business of promotion falls on the label or the artist.

What all these distributors have in common is that they work to get CDs placed into retail outlets. Most distributors publish print or online catalogs of the labels they carry and the titles available. The distributor functions as a middleman; the retail store pays the distributor for the product, and the distributor then pays the record label.

Details of the Deal

To get picked up by a distributor, your CD must be released on a record label, even if it's a label you create solely for this release. The CD must also have a catalog number ("00001" is fine), a suggested list price, and a Universal Product Code (UPC) on the physical product. The UPC is located on the back of the product; retailers scan this barcode when they sell an item, as it contains necessary inventory information.

When a distributor agrees to distribute your CD, you'll sell them the physical product for approximately 50 percent of the suggested list price. For example, if you have a $14.99 price on your CD, the distributor will pay you in the neighborhood of $7.50.

And don't expect to get paid when you ship the product to the distributor. Most distributors pay you only when they sell an item to a retailer. So if a distributor orders 1,000 CDs but sells just 600 of them the first month, you'll receive a check for those 600 units.

Behind the Music

The music industry operates on a practice of 100 percent returns. This means that a retailer can return to its supplier 100 percent of any goods that don't sell to consumers. Accordingly, a distributor will pass these returned goods back to the label (you), and expect full credit.

Finding a Distributor

Who are these independent distributors? Here's a list of some of the larger distributors in the United States, along with their websites, where you can find the necessary contact information:

◆ Alternative Distribution Alliance (ADA) (www.ada-music.com)

◆ Caroline Distribution (www.carolinedist.com)

◆ Fontana Distribution (www.fontanadistribution.com)

◆ E1 Entertainment Distribution (www.e1distribution.com)

◆ Navarre Distribution Services (www.navarre.com)

◆ RED (www.redmusic.com)

◆ Redeye Distribution (www.redeyeusa.com)

Smart Business

Not all distributors will be amenable to stocking individual items direct from artists. They are amenable, however, to stocking items from independent record labels. For this reason, it may be in your best interest to sign with an indie label that already has independent distribution contracts in place.

By the way, many of these big independent distributors are actually owned by major record labels. For example, ADA is owned by Warner Music Group, Caroline is owned by EMI, Fontana is owned by Universal, and RED is owned by Sony BMG. You just can't get away from the big guys!

Selling CDs Online

Independent distributors are necessary to place physical products in traditional brick-and-mortar retail stores. Selling CDs online, however, is a completely different and, potentially, much easier process.

The big dog of online CD sellers is Amazon (www.amazon.com). Amazon stocks products from both major and independent labels. In addition, you could establish your own Amazon merchant account to sell your own products on their site, although this is a bit of work.

The problem with selling on Amazon is that you still have a distributor working as a middleman, taking his cut. If you want to cut out the middleman—and put more money in your pocket—consider signing with a site like CD Baby (www.cdbaby.com).

CD Baby specializes in selling CDs from independent labels and independent artists. You can sell your CD directly to CD Baby, no distributor necessary, and make more money per CD sold. There are some small startup fees to get started and to set up your own page on the CD Baby site, but this site is set up to do what you need them to do. You pay CD Baby just $4 for each CD sold; the rest of the money paid goes directly to you. That's a sweet deal.

Selling Digital Downloads

As you're well aware, the CD business is quickly being supplanted by digital downloads. Not that CD sales are unimportant, but digital downloads are becoming increasingly bigger. To this end, online music download services should be an important part of your online distribution mix.

Getting Listed with Online Music Stores

If you're not yet aware, the biggest online download service today is Apple's iTunes Store (www.apple.com/itunes/). To reach the biggest potential market, you need to get your music listed with and uploaded to the iTunes Store—as well as to other music download sites. But how do you do this?

> **Behind the Music**
>
> You can also sell digital music directly from your own website. Learn more about the different ways to sell music over the Internet in Chapter 17.

While you could try to get your music placed yourself with iTunes (which is a lot of work, especially if you don't have a label affiliation), there are services that will do all the necessary work for you. Take, for example, our old friend CD Baby. In addition to selling physical CDs, CD Baby can also handle the digital distribution of your music at the iTunes Store, the Amazon MP3 Store, and other online services. CD Baby will take your physical CD, rip the tracks in the appropriate formats, and upload the digital tracks to the stores you choose. You pay 9 percent of your net earnings from these sites to CD Baby for this service, but all the work is done for you.

TuneCore (www.tunecore.com) is another service that handles online digital distribution for independent artists. TuneCore charges a flat fee of 99¢ per store per track you want to sell, but then doesn't charge a percentage of sales. So for example, if you want to sell a track in five different online stores, you pay TuneCore $4.95 upfront, and then get to keep all the revenues you earn at each store.

Both of these services—and several others—do all the work necessary to get your music listed with iTunes, Amazon, and other music download services. This includes ripping the tracks from your physical CD to the digital file format used by each online store, so you don't have to worry about a lot of technical details.

Smart Business

Before you list your music with any online store or service, you need to do a little work in advance. You'll need to supply the listing service with album artwork in JPG format, as well as information about the track and album. And as with physical product, you'll need a UPC number for each item you want to sell—although both CD Baby and TuneCore can obtain UPCs for you.

Making Money from Digital Downloads

How much money can you expect to make from online downloads? It differs from site to site, but it's a much larger percentage than you typically earn with CD sales. For example, Apple is currently paying artists 70¢ per each 99¢ track sold in its iTunes Store. Sell 1,000 tracks (that's 1,000 individual songs, not 1,000 albums) at the iTunes Store and you take home a cool $700—less any fees to CD Baby or TuneCore, of course. That's a good deal for not a lot of work on your part.

You can compare this rate to what you'd earn from digital sales if you were signed to a major label. First of all, the label would get that 70¢ per-track payment, not you. Your share, as a major-label artist, is 10 percent of that—or a measly 7¢. So if you sell 1,000 downloads, you make a whole $70, which is hardly worth talking about.

Behind the Music

The 70¢ per-song rate is for Apple's U.S. iTunes Store; this rate differs in other countries. Apple also pays $7 for each digital album sold online.

So there's a huge difference between selling your music yourself and selling through a major label. Given how easy it is to do the whole online thing yourself, why bother with a major label?

Forming Your Own Record Label

If you're really ambitious about distributing your own music, another option is available. Many musicians are forming their own record labels, to distribute not only their own music but also releases from other musicians.

Owning your own label has many advantages. First, with your own label you get taken more seriously by independent distributors, who might not otherwise stock a single release by a nonlabeled artist. Second, when you're pressing and distributing several releases, you can negotiate lower prices, which, in the end, will increase your profits.

On the downside, running a record label is work—real work. All of a sudden you have an honest-to-goodness business to manage, and other people (the label's other artists) whom you're responsible to and for. That might be more work and more responsibility than you want. Or you might find that the business stuff is actually kind of fun. You never know.

The business of forming your own independent record label is much too involved to cover in this book. It's a little like distributing your own music, only more so. Know that you have to arrange CD pressing/duplication, forge deals with independent distributors, do publicity and promotion, and spend some money on advertising. You'll also want to build a website for your label, and arrange for all the major download services to offer your label's products for sale.

As you can see, running your own label can take up a lot of your time. And the more artists you have on your label, the more work is involved. So enter into this one carefully; it's not for everyone.

Can You Do Everything a Major Label Does?

Major record labels serve a lot of functions. The label functions as a bank, financing your recording and paying your advance. The label functions as a distributor, making sure your CDs end up in record stores across the nation. The label also functions as a marketing firm, P.R. agency, advertising broker, and everything else necessary to get your music promoted.

If you don't have a label, none of these functions gets done. You don't get any financing. You don't get your music distributed. And you don't get your music promoted.

Fine, you say. You can do a little work, especially if it means you get a (much) bigger cut of the proceeds. But do you really want to play public relations person? Do you really want to work the phones and contact the media? Do you really want to deal directly with thousands of fans via e-mail and your website? Do you really want to think about (and pay for) placing print advertisements, radio commercials, and so on?

Some artists are comfortable doing some or all of these activities. Many are not. A few years back I talked to a big-name artist who was debating whether to renew her major-label contract or go out on her own as an independent artist. The independent route had a lot of appeal, both financially and creatively. But I asked, "What is it you *really* like to do? Do you like cold-calling people? Do you like dealing directly with your fans? Do you like dealing directly with retailers? Or do you just like sitting in your room writing songs?"

This particular artist didn't like any of the business stuff; she wanted to sit in her room with her guitar and write songs. For her, the major-label option held a lot of appeal. Realizing that all the business and marketing stuff still had to get done was a big challenge to overcome.

You see, not all artists are social creatures. Many artists like to sit by themselves writing and playing music. Some artists don't even like performing; that's not when they're at their best. These artists appreciate the fact that somebody else—in most cases, somebody at the record label—does all the dirty work, all the social contacts, and all the public stuff for them. They're not salespeople or publicists by nature, aren't comfortable doing this sort of thing, and aren't even good at it. These artists see value in having the label provide these services; for them, it's worth giving up some bucks to have the label do all this.

Like I said, all these things need to be done, whether you have a major-label contract or not. You can't just record an album and expect it to sell itself. The album has to be promoted, which means a lot of selling to a lot of different people. Your fans have to be dealt with, the distributors have to be lined up, and the radio people have to be prepped. Normally, these are activities that the record label does. If you don't have a label contract, you have to do them yourself.

Alternately, you can hire someone to do some or all of these activities. A publicist can be hired, a webmaster can be brought on board, and you can contract with a firm to handle your physical and digital distribution. But if you bring in third parties, you have to pay them; those services aren't free, whether it's the label or a third party providing them. And then you have to manage the people you hire, which will take some of your time as well.

My point is, the money you might save by not going with a major label isn't all free and clear cash in your pocket. A record label provides a lot of valuable and necessary services, services that you'll have to pay for or do yourself if you go it alone. For many artists, it's worth paying the label to do these things—or arranging with other companies or individuals to take over those responsibilities.

The Least You Need to Know

♦ Independent labels offer a more personal experience than you get with the majors—and the possibility of taking home more of the proceeds.

♦ You can make even more money by distributing your music yourself—either at your shows or via your website.

♦ Self-distribution is even easier when you're selling digital music online; there are several services that ease the process of listing and uploading tracks to the iTunes Store and other online music stores.

♦ Know, however, that if you decide to distribute your music yourself, all the things the label normally does still need to be done—whether you do them yourself or hire others to do them.

Chapter 12

The Business of Promoting Your Music

In This Chapter

- ◆ Discovering how to promote local gigs
- ◆ Learning all about advertising
- ◆ Uncovering the secrets of radio promotion
- ◆ Discussing the merits of promotional music videos
- ◆ Finding out how to publicize your music
- ◆ Discovering the many ways to promote your music online—and in other media

Whether you're playing live gigs or have a new album for sale, you need to make people aware of you and your music. This is what promotion is all about: promoting what you do.

There are lots of different ways to promote your music. The traditional methods of generating radio airplay and other publicity still have value, but the Internet offers many more ways to get the word out.

Read on, then, to learn how best to promote your music—whether you're an independent artist or working with a label.

Promoting via Flyers and Handouts

Even if you're a local band playing small clubs, you still need promotion—in this instance, to promote your gigs and bring a bigger crowd through the doors. Fortunately, this type of promotion doesn't require a big expenditure.

What's the best way to promote local gigs? The tried and trusted method of distributing flyers, handouts, and handbills is surprisingly effective. You know what I'm talking about—printing up single sheets of paper announcing your band and your gig, and then putting the things in as many places as you can. You can post handbills on neighborhood bulletin boards, in the windows of local businesses, even (and especially) on light poles and power poles. The point is to get as much visibility as possible, so that potential audiences literally stumble over your message.

Smart Business

Make sure you place your handouts where music fans are known to gather. You'll garner the most attention by placing your handouts on the bulletin boards or front windows of local music stores, record stores, coffeehouses, and the like.

You can print up a few hundred single-sheet handouts for 10 or 20 bucks. It helps, of course, if they have a catchy design and look somewhat professional; this may mean contracting with an artist or designer friend ahead of time. Once you have them printed, it's nothing but manual labor to post them around town or in the appropriate neighborhood. That's something you and the rest of your bandmates should be able to do without incurring additional costs.

Advertising Your Music

Putting up handbills is a crude (but often effective) means of advertising. There are other ways to advertise your music, however—and you can spend a pretty penny doing so, if you have the budget.

The big problem with advertising is the cost. It's common to pay thousands or even tens of thousands of dollars for a single print ad; you'll spend much more than that to produce a radio or television commercial and purchase the necessary airtime. Given these costs, few independent artists have the funds to conduct a national advertising campaign.

This tends to leave most advertising to the big boys. That is, you find most national ad campaigns placed by major labels to promote their largest artists. That's one of the benefits of signing with a major label, of course; they have very deep pockets when it comes to promotion of all types.

If you're not signed to a major label, you have to be smarter and choosier about what types of advertising you do. Weekly alternative papers are fairly cost effective and do a good job of hitting your target audience. Ditto with college newspapers and radio stations. Unless you have a Beyoncé or Tim McGraw–size budget, however, you probably want to stay away from television and national print advertising—it's just too expensive.

Smart Business

You need to coordinate all your different marketing activities. You want to send a single message from everything you do, which means making your online promotions look and feel the same as your print and radio promotions. You need to send out a single message, whatever media you use.

Print Advertising

One of the oldest and most traditional forms of advertising is print media. This includes running ads in local newspapers, weekly alternative papers, music magazines, and, if you have the budget, even national newspapers and magazines.

Local papers—both dailies and weeklies—are good places to advertise upcoming performances. You can also use these media to advertise CD releases. National music magazines are also good places to advertise your latest CD, if you have a larger budget.

I like local and college print advertising; it's perhaps the most affordable advertising you can do. You may be able to purchase a small ad in your local weekly or college paper for a few hundred bucks, or a bit more than that for a similar ad in a larger daily paper. While that's not nothing, it's considerably less expensive than placing an ad in a national publication, which will run you tens of thousands of dollars.

Smart Business

Assuming that your music appeals to a younger demographic, advertising in college newspapers may be particularly cost effective. These papers reach a prime music-buying audience and ad space isn't that terribly expensive.

Radio Advertising

It makes sense to advertise your music on radio stations that play similar music. If you're a country artist, that means advertising on country stations; if you're a hip hop artist, advertising on urban stations makes sense.

Know, however, that buying time on large radio stations can be quite expensive—several hundred or even thousands of dollars for a typical 30-second commercial. And you don't just buy one spot; you have to purchase a minimum number of spots, set to run within a specified period of time.

> ### Behind the Music
>
> Many commercial radio stations are owned by a handful of large corporate parents. As such, you'll be encouraged to make national ad buys across multiple stations around the country. While you might receive a decent discount for buying across the network in this fashion, it takes a large budget to participate in this type of national advertising.

In addition, you have to produce the commercial. Now that may involve nothing more than hiring a voice-over artist to read some narration over a catchy track from your album. But radio commercials do need to be professionally produced, and that's an expense beyond the purchase of radio time.

As with newspaper advertising, running commercials on college radio stations may be the most cost-effective approach. Ad time on these stations is typically cheaper than with big-city stations, and you reach a very targeted audience.

Television Advertising

If you think radio advertising is expensive, wait until you try to buy television time. Television advertising is, without a doubt, the most expensive advertising you can do. Even if you stick to local stations, you'll still pay tens of thousands of dollars for a single 30-second spot; advertising on a national broadcast or cable network will cost much more than that. And then there's the cost of producing the commercial, which is probably another five-figure expense.

As you can imagine, then, television advertising is not for the faint of heart or short of budget; it's really something only the big labels can afford, and even then only for their biggest artists. That said, if you're a mid-tier artist, you might want to consider advertising on local cable channels or even on specialty cable networks, both of which cost much less than you might think. You still have to produce the commercial, of course, but the actual ad time might be within your reach.

Online Advertising

These days, the Internet is another essential piece of the advertising puzzle. You can use Internet advertising—either pay-per-click ads or banner ads—to drive traffic to your website, or to promote your latest CD release. Online advertising can be surprisingly affordable and, when done correctly, quite effective; that's because it's easier to target a specific audience online than it is with traditional forms of advertising.

We'll discuss online advertising in more depth in the "Promoting Your Music Online" section, later in this chapter. Read ahead to learn more.

Smart Business

You need to *always* be promoting your music; your promotion should be continual. Remember, when you're not promoting your music, someone else is promoting *theirs*. Music promotion today is a 24/7 business; you have to have something going all the time to please your fans and attract new listeners.

Generating Radio Play

Perhaps the most traditional form of music promotion is via radio play. Since the advent of radio, musicians have used radio to gain exposure for their music and drive record or CD sales. Listeners hear your song on the radio and then, if they like it, head to their local record store to buy a copy.

That said, radio promotion is not cheap. It costs real money to get radio programmers to listen to and decide to play your music. It takes a lot of work and a big budget to get your music played.

And you can't guarantee results. In fact, if you're an independent artist, I can almost guarantee that you won't get results—at least on commercial radio. The twenty-first century radio landscape is such that a small number of big corporations own and control the biggest radio stations across the country. Unless you're signed to a major label or have some really big bucks to toss around, promoting your music to these networks of corporate stations is prohibitively expensive.

That doesn't mean that you should rule out radio promotion. Aside from the big corporate stations in most major cities, there are still independent stations and—more importantly—college stations. In fact, college stations are more important than ever for breaking new music.

Then there's satellite radio. Satellite radio in the United States used to be a two-player game, but became a monopoly when Sirius acquired XM. While the new Sirius XM satellite radio does have close to a hundred different music channels, including some with very narrow niches, these channels have the same short playlists that you find on commercial terrestrial stations, and, with some exceptions, are very difficult to break into.

Internet radio, however, shows more promise. There are hundreds if not thousands of genre-specific stations narrowcasting over the Internet, and these stations are gaining in popularity, especially with younger, more tech-savvy listeners. It's kind of like college radio, but with a lot more variety.

Identifying Key Stations

One of the big challenges to generating radio play is identifying the individual stations—traditional AM and FM, satellite, and Internet-based—that will play your music. It's a lot of work.

With terrestrial stations, you have to identify individual stations in each city in every state across the country. We're talking literally thousands of stations, all of which need to be contacted individually.

Behind the Music

Alternately, you can research radio stations yourself online—for free. Use Google or another search engine to search for radio stations in major market areas, then go to each station's web page to get the name of the music director and the appropriate contact info.

Internet radio is no easier, with thousands of stations online, and more being added daily. Just finding what's available is a major task; identifying and contacting the ones most likely to play your music is even harder.

It's easier with satellite radio, since you only have one player in the United States (Sirius XM). That said, you still have to identify the appropriate channel and contact the programming directors for those channels.

Assuming that you can't personally travel the country from coast to coast, twiddling the radio dial as you go, how do you find all these stations? The best approach is to subscribe to the CMJ Directory, either in print or online. This is a database of contact information for radio stations and other music industry companies; it will tell you what stations are where and who to contact at each station. Learn more at www.cmj.com.

Of course, generating a huge list of radio stations isn't the goal. The real goal is identifying those stations that are likely to play your music. You should start by sorting stations by genre, then sifting out those college, independent, noncommercial, and public stations that are more amenable to individual submissions than the big commercial giants. This smaller list, then, is the one you want to target.

Getting Your Music Heard

Once you've targeted a list of sympathetic radio stations, you need to get your music in the hands of the right people at these stations. Be forewarned—this is a large to-do list that will take up a lot of your (or someone else's) time.

What should you send to the stations? Here's a basic checklist:

♦ **Your CD:** It's best to send the finished product with full artwork, if you have it. If you're soliciting stations in advance of the final product, make sure the CD you send is accompanied by the track list, album title, record label info, and the like. Obviously, the CD should be in a standard jewel case or cardboard pack.

♦ **A "one-sheet" cover letter:** This sheet—literally, a single page, never longer—should summarize what you're sending and why it should be listened to.

♦ **Other promotional items:** If you have a band T-shirt or other interesting merchandise, include that. It's not a bribe, it's just to get the programming director's attention.

Your one-sheet should be folded and inserted inside the CD case. It should include a CD song list, including a shorter list of any songs not suitable for airplay, such as those with obscene language. You should also point out the key or "go-to" tracks on the album—three to five of the strongest songs. If you have them, include a handful of favorable reviews or press quotes. Also include a short comparison to other artists that the station gives heavy play to. And don't forget your contact information—e-mail address, phone number, postal address.

In addition, if you have resources online—a MySpace page, for example, or videos on the YouTube site—you should mention these items in your kit. Include the URLs for all appropriate pages, videos, and blogs on the chance that radio programmers will give them a whirl.

Behind the Music

Given the ubiquity of digital music and the Internet, you might think you can send all this information (including your CD in MP3 format) to stations electronically, via e-mail or the program director's MySpace page. This may not be a good idea, however, as it's all too easy for programming directors to delete unsolicited e-mails and ignore MySpace postings. While you might want to send out a feeler via e-mail, it's probably best to include physical product in your official solicitation—it's harder to ignore.

Once you've sent your kit to a station, you need to personally follow up to make sure it's been received. You can e-mail the programming director or call him on the phone; if you call, make sure you do so during office hours. Wait about two weeks after you've sent the package, then e-mail or call the programming director once a week until you've heard back from him.

Smart Business

If the station has started playing your album, offer up some free CDs, tickets to an upcoming show, a few T-shirts, and/or anything they can give away to their listeners. Also offer to do on-air interviews, promo messages, or whatever else the station may be interested in.

When you talk to or exchange messages with the programming director, thank him for his time and ask if he received your CD. If so, then ask if he was able to review it. If so, ask if he plans to add it to the station's rotation. If so, ask where in the rotation it's being added (light, medium, or heavy). Finally, ask if there's anything else he needs. And whatever the answers, remember to thank the programming director for his time and efforts.

If you're getting airplay on a station, call back in a week or so to see where you're charting. Follow up for about 6 to 8 weeks, which is the typical life of a new release in rotation.

Promoting Your Music—Professionally

Sending out your CD and calling a programming director doesn't sound like a lot of work, but multiply that by hundreds or thousands of stations, and you see how all-consuming this activity can be. This is why many artists sign with major labels, which have the staff to do all this work for you. If you prefer to remain independent, however, you can hire a firm to push your albums for you.

An independent record promoter will do everything we just discussed, as well as use his own contacts at key stations to get your music heard. Chances are a veteran promoter will know a lot more people in the industry than you do, which is a good thing.

Naturally, you have to pay for a promoter's services. A promoter will typically charge anywhere from a few hundred to a few thousand dollars per week, depending on his reputation and the number of stations you want him to target. You may want to start with a smaller, targeted list of stations and see how it goes before ramping up to (and paying for) a full list.

> **Behind the Music**
>
> Many of these firms also offer other marketing and promotional services for musicians.

Who does this type of promotion? Here's a list of some of the more popular companies:

- Advanced Alternative Media (www.aampromo.com)
- Fanatic Promotion, Inc. (www.fanaticpromotion.com)
- Heavy Hitter Inc. (www.heavyhitterinc.com)
- musicSUBMIT (www.musicsubmit.com)
- Nice Promotion (www.nicepromo.com)
- Pirate! Promotion and Management (www.piratepirate.com)
- Planetary Group (www.planetarygroup.com)
- Spectre Music Inc. (www.spectremusic.com)

Promoting with Music Videos

Another way to promote your music is via a promotional music video—the kind that MTV used to run all day long, back in ancient times. These videos can cost big bucks, however, so this may only be an option if you're signed to a major label.

If you have the budget—and I'm talking tens of thousands of dollars here—a catchy music video can draw attention to your latest single release, and thus help spur CD sales. The problem, though, is getting your video viewed. After all, MTV no longer plays a lot of music videos; video apparently did not kill the radio star.

So where can you get your video played? On the Internet. That's right, several venues on the web provide the perfect exposure for music videos, especially from up-and-coming artists. YouTube (www.youtube.com) is one of these sites. You're familiar with YouTube as a video-sharing community; well, you can also share your music videos on the site. The nice thing about YouTube is that it doesn't cost anything to upload a video, or to serve it to millions of viewers. You still have to spend the bucks to produce the thing, of course, but after that, promotion via YouTube is completely free.

Smart Business

You can get double duty from your music video by pulling footage to create a television commercial—thus saving on your production costs.

And if your video is particularly appealing, you'll find fans sharing it with each other. If enough fans share it, your video can go viral—and that's great promotion for your music.

You can also upload your video to your MySpace page and to your own website or blog. In addition, the MTV (www.mtv.com) and VH1 (www.vh1.com.) websites host a plethora of music videos, much more than their broadcast counterparts play these days; other sites, such as AOL Music (music.aol.com), are also good to target.

Generating Publicity

One of the most popular and effective forms of promotion is publicity. Unlike advertising, where you buy your space, publicity is all about influencing the influencers—getting key people in the media to pay attention to and mention or review your music.

How to Publicize Your Music

Publicity is typically handled by an individual publicist or public relations firm. The publicist ideally has a database of contacts within the entertainment industry, including music reviewers, arts editors, journalists, bloggers, and the like. When you have something to promote, the publicist uses all the tools at her disposal to get the word out to these key individuals. If all works well, some or all of the people contacted will give you exposure in the newspapers, magazines, blogs, websites, and such they write for or manage.

Now you could obtain a list of these individuals and contact them yourself, thus saving you the expense of a freelance publicist. But you probably don't know any of these folks firsthand, which means you'd be cold calling—which may or may not be successful. A good publicist knows many of these people personally, which means they'll answer her calls and open her e-mails. In other words, a good publicist won't be ignored.

Creating a Press Kit

If you do choose to do your own publicity, you need to start by preparing a press kit. This kit should include the following:

- **Your CD:** The finished product with full artwork, if you have it, or a pre-release version if that's all you have.

- **Track list:** Include all song titles, songwriter info, artist name, and other important credits.

- **Cover letter:** This is your welcome to the reviewer. It should briefly introduce you and your CD, and point out (subtly) why your music is worthy of review.

- **Bio:** This should be a one-page background of you or your band, with information about your current CD at the very top.

- **Fact sheet:** Separate from everything else, this is a short bulleted list of important information culled from your bio and cover letter.

- **Photograph:** The typical publicity photo of you or your band. It should be an 8" × 10" black and white glossy, of course.

All the contents should be placed within an attractive, well-designed folder of some sort. And make sure that every element in your kit—including your CD—includes your e-mail address and other contact information. The worst thing in the world would be for a reviewer to like your CD but have no way to contact you for more information.

Contacting the Press

You should send this press kit to key national and local reviewers, music journalists, bloggers, and the like. You can get the names with a targeted Internet search or by subscribing to CMJ, as described earlier in this chapter.

Once you've sent out your press kits, follow up personally. Wait a week or two then phone or e-mail the reviewer and ask if he received your CD. If so, ask if he's listened to the CD yet. If so, then ask if he plans to write about it. If so, ask when the review will appear, and if you can get a copy of it (or a link to it, if it's online).

Smart Business

If you're not sure who to target, start by looking for reviews of artists similar to yourself, then target the reviewers who liked that artist. Avoid those reviewers who dislike similar artists—or who don't write about your type of music in general.

And remember, it's not just about getting reviews. It's even better if you can score an interview or feature article. To that end, include any interesting information about yourself in the press release—anything that might be worthy of journalistic interest. Maybe you're the relative of someone famous, or worked with a well-known artist on the album; if so, mention it. Try to think of anything that gives you or your music a hook that a magazine or newspaper can grab on to.

Promoting Your Music Online

So far all the promotional activities we've discussed are rather traditional; they're tried-and-true activities that have been used by artists for a half century or more.

Today, however, a whole range of additional promotion is available via the Internet. That's right, you can do lots of things online to promote your music—many of them both lower cost and more effective than traditional promotional activities. These include the following:

- ◆ **E-mail:** Sign up your fans to an e-mail mailing list and then send out e-mail bulletins and newsletters when you have something you want to announce, such as a new CD release, upcoming tour, and so forth.

- ◆ **Website or blog:** Use your website or blog to keep your fans informed of your latest news, including CD releases and tour dates. You can also use your website to promote a CD release by offering free tracks for downloading.

- ◆ **Social networks:** Most artists today have their own MySpace (www.myspace.com) page, which offers news, streaming music, and the like. You can also use Facebook (www.facebook.com) and Twitter (www.twitter.com) to disseminate important information about new releases, tours, and the like.

- ◆ **Online publicity:** Thanks to the Internet, you no longer need to send out physical press kits, instead, you can send out virtual press kits via e-mail. In addition, you need to target bloggers and online music journalists as part of your PR efforts.

♦ **Online advertising:** Internet-based advertising, especially of the pay-per-click variety, is a lot less expensive and a lot more effective than traditional print, radio, or television advertising. It's affordable enough that even new and struggling artists can include it as part of their promotional mix.

Online promotion is well suited for the independent musician. The Internet does a good job of leveling the playing field; the little guys can do the same things online that a major label does, and in fact look more important than they might be. That's because online promotion is also much less expensive than traditional promotion; you can reach a lot of people for little expense, which is a good thing.

In addition, the Internet facilitates direct contact between an artist and his fans. Whether you're talking an e-mail newsletter, blog, MySpace page, or whatever, you're communicating directly with the people who care most about you and your music. It's the type of one-to-one relationship that just isn't possible with traditional media. (For more detailed information on online promotion, turn to Chapter 17.)

Promoting via Nontraditional Media

You know how radio play can help promote your music. Unfortunately, in this age of iPods and the Internet, fewer and fewer listeners are listening to traditional radio. This makes it difficult for them to hear new music; all they listen to is what they've always listened to.

So where do people hear new music these days? Believe it or not, many listeners get exposed to new songs by hearing them in TV shows, movie soundtracks, and even television and radio commercials. That's right, placing a song in any of these musically nontraditional media can have a big impact. In fact, this is how many bands of late have made a name for themselves.

To this end, you need to work with your music publisher to get your music considered for placement in these media. It's not easy, and you probably won't receive a big payment for the placement (typically a few thousand dollars), but the impact comes when listeners like what they hear and want to hear more. For this placement to be most effective, make sure you negotiate a mention of you and your music (and a link to your website) on the show or movie's web page; you want to make it easy for people to find out who's playing that song they liked. (Learn more about nontraditional media placement in Chapter 16.)

The Big Question: Who Should Promote Your Music?

Okay, by now you're probably overwhelmed with the number of different promotional activities you can and perhaps should be engaging in. They all make sense, but do you really have the time or budget to do them all?

This isn't an issue, of course, if you're signed with a major record label. That's one of the benefits of being a major-label artist: the labels have big pockets and big staffs to do all these different kinds of promotions. As a major-label artist, you can just sit back and let the label people do all the work.

If you're with a smaller label, however, or if you're an independent artist, you don't have anybody doing this stuff for you. Which means you either have to do it yourself or hire someone else to do it.

Doing it yourself might sound attractive from a monetary perspective (you work for free, don't you?), but prohibitive from a time or talent perspective. That is, doing publicity, radio promotion, online promotion, and all the rest takes a tremendous amount of time. Maybe you have a lot of free time on your hands, but you probably don't—you're busy writing or playing or touring or whatever. Promotion is a full-time job (actually, several full-time jobs), and you already have a full-time job as a musician.

To that end, lots of freelance promotion firms are eager to have your business. These companies can handle some or all of these promotional activities for you; most have a menu of services available. Maybe you want to do publicity yourself but farm out the radio promotion; maybe you just want to do online stuff and have someone else do traditional promotion. Most music promotion firms can work with you to do what you want or need them to do.

For that matter, you may want to contract with multiple firms. Maybe you contract with a freelance publicist for the PR stuff and a promotion firm for radio promotion. You're not limited to using just one firm; you can pick and choose which firms you want to provide which services.

Know, however, that you'll pay for any third-party services you use. If you're signed to an independent label, maybe you can get them to kick in to cover some of the costs, but in general these are going to be out of pocket expenses for you. To that end, budget wisely—and contract only for those services that best serve your immediate and long-term needs.

The Least You Need to Know

- You can promote local gigs by using low-cost flyers and handouts.

- If you have a big-enough budget, you can advertise a new album in print, on the radio, and on television.

- One of the most effective forms of promotion is to garner radio play—assuming you can convince program directors to play your music.

- If you have a big budget, you can produce your own music video—and upload it to a number of music video websites.

- To generate reviews and interviews, send out press kits and personally contact journalists and reviewers.

- The most popular forms of online promotion include e-mail mailing lists and newsletters, websites and blogs, MySpace and other social networks, and pay-per-click advertising.

- Many listeners get exposed to new artists from hearing their songs on TV and movie soundtracks, and in commercials; licensing music to nontraditional media has become a significant form of promotion for many artists.

Chapter 13

The Business of Live Performance and Touring

In This Chapter

- Understanding the steps—and the players—behind a booking
- Discovering where the gigs are
- Learning how to find and work with a booking agent
- Understanding the parts of a performance contract
- Learning how to put together a regional or national tour

For most musicians, playing live is an integral part of their musical activities. Yes, making a recording is exciting and selling CDs can be quite profitable. But music is all about the performance—which can also be a big revenue generator.

Know, however, that playing a gig is a business transaction. Whether you're playing a wedding reception, a local club, or a big concert hall, your performance is part of a contract with the person doing the booking. In order to get paid, you have to fulfill your contractual obligations. Club owners and promoters are businesspeople who have to make a living at their profession, too. You're just a means to their business success.

Dealing with these businesspeople can be trying, especially if you're more a musician and less a businessperson. To that end, many musicians engage the services of talent agents to find gigs for them; other musicians, especially in this Internet age, take on this task themselves.

Booking a Gig

Before you take on the task of finding a gig, it's important to know who does what in the booking chain. You essentially have four players in the process—the artist, the booking agent, the promoter, and the venue.

The Artist

This is the person or band who will play the gig. The artist agrees to play on a specified date at a specified time, for an agreed-upon amount of time. You may also agree to play a specific type of music, or even a particular list of songs.

In most instances, the artist is paid by the venue, typically the club or concert hall. However, if you're playing for an individual or company, then that entity will pay you. For example, when you play a wedding reception the happy couple pays you, not the country club where you play.

Artists may receive a negotiated fee, or a percentage of the ticket sales or cover charge. In some instances, the artist also receives other perks—meals, drinks, accommodations, and such.

The Booking Agent

A *booking agent* is hired by the artist to find and book paying gigs. The agent contacts promoters, clubs, and other venues on his client's behalf, working as a middleman to arrange the gig and negotiate the contract. He often also puts together some sort of promotional kit that he sends to potential customers.

def•i•ni•tion

A **booking agent,** sometimes called a *talent agent,* is an individual who finds paid performances for his artist clients. Some agents work alone; others work as part of a larger talent agency. A booking agent typically has multiple clients, while artists most often have a single agent.

In return for his efforts, the booking agent (sometimes just called the *agent*) receives 10 to 20 percent of the artist's performance fee. So if your band is being paid $1,000 for a weekend gig, your agent will receive $100 to $200 of that total. (The venue or contractor typically pays the agent, who takes his cut and then pays the artist the remainder.)

The Promoter

Where the booking agent represents the artist, the *promoter* represents the venue that the artist plays. The promoter identifies and signs artists (through their agents) to play a specific venue, and then works to promote those appearances.

def•i•ni•tion

A **promoter** contracts with artists for a given venue, and then promotes the artists' shows.

As the name implies, the promoter is responsible for promoting a show. He will send out press releases to the local media, put up flyers and the like, and sometimes even purchase advertising or commercial time. The promoter coordinates with local retailers for event sponsorships, as well as in-store appearances and other promotional efforts.

As noted, the promoter is hired by the venue, and is paid by the venue. He typically receives a negotiated fee for his work. In smaller venues, such as most local clubs, the promoter is actually the club owner himself. By acting as his own promoter, the club owner saves himself the fee of hiring a separate promoter.

Smart Business

You can't depend on a promoter to fully promote your appearance at a club or other venue; his job is to promote the venue, not to promote you, the artist. As such, you'll still need to engage in your own promotion for your gigs, as discussed in Chapter 12.

The Venue

The *venue* is where the artist plays. This could be a club, a concert hall, or a big stadium. There is typically a venue operator, sometimes employed by the venue and sometimes a third-party contractor. In the case of clubs, the club owner typically handles the functions of the *venue operator*.

def•i•ni•tion

A **venue** is a facility for the performance of live music. A **venue operator** is an individual who manages the venue and coordinates with artists, promoters, and booking agents.

The venue operator coordinates with the promoter and the booking agent to arrange the artist's booking. He works with the promoter to promote the show; he also manages the venue's facilities and staff. For larger venues, this means providing security, ticket sales, merchandising space, stagehands, sound and lights, and the like.

Freelance operators receive a negotiated fee for their services. Operators employed by a venue do this as part of their normal salary.

Behind the Music

For big shows and tours there's a fifth player: the ticket agency. This firm handles the selling of tickets for the venue; customers purchase tickets from the ticket agency, which then reimburses the venue (minus a hefty fee, of course). In the United States, the dominant ticket agency is Ticketmaster (www.ticketmaster.com), although many venues and artists are moving toward handling their own ticket sales.

Putting It All Together

So here's how it works, at least in theory:

1. The artist signs with a booking agent.

2. On behalf of the artist, the booking agent sends out promo kits to appropriate venues and promoters.

3. The promoter and booking agent agree on the details for the artist to perform at a given venue.

4. The promoter publicizes the upcoming performance.

5. The venue readies its facilities for the performance.

6. The venue or its representative ticket agency sells tickets to the performance.

7. The artist performs at the venue.

8. The venue pays the promoter a flat fee for his efforts.

9. The venue pays the booking agent for the artist's services.

10. From this payment, the booking agent extracts his percentage and then pays the artist the balance.

As you've probably noticed, there are several middlemen in this scenario. It's possible to eliminate the booking agent and have the artist represent himself. It's also possible for the venue to eliminate the promoter and contract with bands and promote performances itself. In the most efficient scenario, the artist deals directly with the venue, bypassing all middlemen.

Putting Together a Promo Kit

If you want to forgo the cost of a booking agent, it's possible to represent yourself. This means contacting promoters and club owners and venue operators yourself, which can be a lot of work.

If you represent yourself, you need to put together the same sort of promo kit that an agent would. You then send this kit to prospective customers—that is, to those promoters and venues you'd like to work with.

Here's what to include in your promo kit:

- **Cover letter:** This should summarize you or your band, the kind of music you play, and why you'd be a good fit with this particular venue.

- **Music CD:** This can be a studio recording on a commercial CD, although it's better to send a live recording you've burned on your own computer. Sending a few live tracks (no more than a half dozen) is always a good idea, as it lets the promoter or club owner hear what you sound like in a live situation.

- **Track list:** This is the standard list of the tracks on the CD, so the promoter or club owner knows what he's listening to.

- **Bio:** This is the standard bio of you or your band. Include a list of similar gigs you've played, and any press clips or reviews you've received.

- **Publicity photo:** This is the typical 8" × 10" black and white glossy, so they'll know what you look like.

Smart Business

If you have some videos of you performing live, you may also want to add them to the kit. You could include these videos on a DVD, or simply upload them to YouTube and then reference their URLs in your promo kit.

Package the whole thing up in a nice folder and mail it away to the selected promoters, club owners, or venue operators. Wait a week or two then call the person to see if they've received the kit. Ask for their response and see if you can arrange a booking.

Smart Business _____

Just because you think you're ready for prime time doesn't mean you really are. Whether you're playing a local club or a wedding reception, you need at least three hours of prepared material that you can perform live. If you only have a CD's worth of songs (or less), you don't even have enough music to fill up multiple sets.

Finding Gigs

Just where should you be looking to play? It all depends on what you want to do and where you want to go, career-wise; it also depends on where you're at in your career.

Whether you're first starting out or are a regular working musician, here are some of the places you can look at for paying gigs:

- Local nightclubs
- Concert halls
- Music festivals
- Local events, such as town festivals, fish fries, and the like
- School dances and events
- Fraternity and sorority parties
- Record store events
- Restaurants and lounges
- Coffeehouses
- Bookstores (typically weekend evening events)
- Wedding receptions
- Private parties
- Conventions
- Corporate events
- Charity functions
- Church events

Smart Business _____

It also pays to do your homework, especially when you're looking for gigs outside your normal area. Find an artist who plays music similar to yours and then look at where that artist has played recently. Chances are that a club or concert hall that did well for that artist will do well for you, too.

Some of these venues and events are easy to target. For example, it's easy to look up the address of a local club on the Internet. You can also find a list of venues in the Pollstar Concert Venue Directory (www.pollstar.com).

It's more difficult to find some of the "hidden" gigs, such as corporate events and private parties. For these types of gigs, it's probably best to sign with a booking agent who specializes in this sort of gig and has the contacts necessary for success.

Smart Business

A lot of musicians make big bucks from playing corporate events, such as sales conferences and company parties. These gigs may be relatively invisible to your public fan base, but pay much better than the average wedding reception or club date.

Behind the Music

The toughest gigs to get are your first ones. For understandable reasons, promoters and club owners are reticent to hire artists who have little or no live performance experience; it's the old Catch-22 that you can't get a gig unless you've already gotten a gig. For that reason, be ready to perform for free, if necessary, and for whatever venue will hire you—until you establish your credentials, that is.

Working with a Booking Agent

If all you're doing is playing local clubs and events, you probably don't need a booking agent. Agents become necessary when you want to play so-called "hidden" gigs (corporate events, wedding receptions, and the like) or expand your performances beyond your local region. They're especially important when you start putting together a regional or national tour.

You can find a list of booking agents and agencies in the Pollstar Booking Agency Directory (store.pollstar.com). Otherwise, search online for booking agents near you.

Before you sign, of course, you need to check out the agent in question. There are a fair number of unscrupulous agents out there, so it's good to be cautious. Ask for a list of other acts that the agent represents, then get on the phone and start talking to them. You might also check on the other end by talking to club owners, venue promoters, and such to see how they like dealing with this particular agent. If you hear too many horror stories, run away!

Scam Alert _____

Make sure that your contract stipulates exactly what the agent will be paid for—specifically, those gigs that the agent arranges. You don't want to pay your agent for gigs that you arrange or for nonperformance activities, such as CD sales, merchandising sales, and the like.

You sign with a booking agent in much the same fashion as you sign with a personal manager. You'll negotiate and sign a contract with the agent; the contract will detail the agent's territory (local, national, or worldwide), the types of gigs the agent is responsible for, the term of the contract (at least a year, typically), and the percentage that the agent will be paid (in the 10 to 20 percent range). Try to include a clause that terminates the contract if the agent doesn't find you work within a specified period of time—90 days or so.

Negotiating and Signing the Contract

Whether you book yourself or use an agent, you'll be negotiating and signing a lot of contracts. While you can do a gig with a verbal contract, it's not recommended; you need something legal in hand just in case the promoter or club owner doesn't hold up his end of the deal.

Contract Details

The contract needs to detail the terms of the deal—in other words, how much you're going to be paid and for doing what. Here's some of what you need to include in any contract you negotiate:

◆ The name of the artist (you or your band).

◆ The name of the client (the promoter, club owner, or venue).

◆ Date of the event.

◆ Number of sets to be played, and the length of each set.

◆ Deposit—the amount paid to you in advance of the performance. (Not all contracts include a deposit.)

◆ When you'll be paid.

◆ How much you'll be paid.

- For club and concert dates, the ticket price and capacity of the venue.

- What type of music you'll play. In some instances (wedding receptions, corporate events, for example), the client may specify particular songs for you to play.

- What happens if the unexpected causes the event's cancellation. This would include any fees due to you if the event is cancelled.

- Whether audio recording, video recording, or photography is allowed.

- Merchandise sales—that is, whether you're allowed to sell your own merchandise at the gig, and whether the venue takes a cut of your merchandise sales. (Some do.)

- Promotional commitment. This specifies the minimum amount of money the venue is expected to invest in advertising and publicizing the show.

You can negotiate each of these points separately.

Payment Details

In terms of how you get paid, there are several options:

- **Flat fee:** Also called a guarantee, this is the simplest and most common form of payment; you get a set amount, no matter how many people show up for the gig. For example, the contract might specify that the artist receives $1,000 for playing the gig.

- **Percentage:** Some contracts detail a percentage of the door—that is, of ticket sales or cover charges collected. For example, the contract might specify that the artist receives 30 percent of the door; if the club sells $5,000 worth of tickets, you would receive $1,500.

- **Flat fee versus percentage:** In this scenario, you receive either a flat fee *or* a percentage of the door, whichever is higher. For example, if the contract stipulates $1,000 versus 30 percent of the door, and the club sells $5,000 worth of tickets, you'd receive $1,500 (30 percent of the door, which is the higher amount).

- **Flat fee plus percentage:** In this scenario, you receive a flat fee *plus* a percentage. For example, if the contract stipulates $1,000 plus 30 percent of the door, and the club sells $5,000 worth of tickets, you'd receive $2,500 (the $1,000 flat fee plus $1,500 from the door).

These are just the most common payment plans; there are even more complicated forms of payment. For example, some venues like a scenario where the artist gets a guaranteed fee plus a percentage of the door after the venue reaches a break-even point. So you might not get a simple 30 percent of the door; your 30 percent might not kick in until the venue sells a certain number of tickets.

Scam Alert

Beware percentage-only plans with no upfront guarantee or minimum. In these plans, the club owner will typically pay you a percentage of the cover charges collected—which, on a slow night, might be next to nothing. You need a guaranteed minimum (or a flat-versus-percentage deal) to protect yourself in this sort of situation.

Obviously, the better the deal you can negotiate, the more money you make. When you're just starting out, expect simple flat-fee deals—or, in smaller clubs, percentage-only plans.

As you build a fan following, however, you should be able to negotiate a percentage of ticket sales—and have a say in the ticket price. When you can consistently fill the major clubs, you can make some decent money. (And that's before you start selling CDs, T-shirts, and the like between sets ....)

Putting Together a Tour

As your fan base grows, especially after a CD release, it's time to start thinking about expanding your performance area. This may mean scheduling a small regional tour, or going big-time and touring nationally.

In many ways, going on tour is just like playing a series of local gigs. It's just one club or hall after another, after all; you set up, you do a sound check, and you play.

But when you're on the road, you're away from the comforts of home. Heck, you're away from home, period. That means arranging all the things you normally do when you're at home, like eating, sleeping, bathing, doing laundry .... Plus getting from place to place, of course.

For all these reasons, putting together a tour is much more complex than scheduling a series of local gigs. It's also potentially more rewarding; presumably, you're getting a good share of ticket sales and filling some larger venues.

To put together a successful tour, you need a good supporting team. In particular, assemble the following players.

- **Booking agent:** You need an agent or agency to determine which venues to play in various cities, and to negotiate all the separate agreements. Make sure your agent has strong regional or national contacts; don't expect a local agent to know where to play halfway across the country.

- **Tour manager:** This individual is in charge of making sure everything goes smoothly on the road. The tour manager books hotel reservations and airline tickets, arranges for tour buses and local transportation, and makes sure everything is copacetic at the venue itself. This person also manages *you*, making sure you and your bandmates show up at the gig on time, get on the bus when you're supposed to, stay out of jail, and all the rest. In addition, the tour manager is your interface to the individual promoters and venues on the tour; he's responsible for collecting the money you're owed.

- **Personal manager:** Your manager should be intimately involved in all aspects of your tour—planning the thing, deciding what cities and dates to play, negotiating deals—you name it.

- **Promoter:** On a smaller scale, promoters work for the individual venues you play. But if your tour is big enough, you can hire a national promoter who handles entire tours. That is, they promote every date on your tour, and often manage the individual venues you play. There are two big national promoters: Live Nation (www.livenation.com) and AEG Worldwide (www.aegworldwide. com); if you're at this level, have your manager negotiate a deal with the promotion firm.

- **Ticket agency:** When you're touring smaller venues and clubs, the venue is responsible for selling tickets. If you're putting together a larger tour, however, you or your promoter may engage the services of Ticketmaster or another national ticketing agency to handle all your ticket sales.

In addition, you may want to take a few roadies with you to help schlep the equipment. And depending on how you do things, you may also want to bring your own sound and light crew with you on tour; you can't always rely on good sound and lighting when you're on the road.

Behind the Music

Your manager may or may not accompany you on the road. His work is mainly done in advance, leaving the day-to-day running of the tour to the tour manager.

Do I Need Professional Management to Book My Gigs?

This isn't an easy question to answer. Unlike promotion and distribution, which are both made easier by the Internet, booking and touring doesn't necessarily take advantage of online resources. As such, it's still a people-intensive part of the business; there's a lot of work that has to be done.

That said, many artists today are doing at least some of their booking themselves. Certainly you don't need a booking agent to book local clubs and such; once you get established, you can establish the proper contacts and negotiate your own deals. But beyond local gigs, it's possible to book smaller tours on your own—if you have the time and inclination. Just know, however, that any issues you encounter are yours to solve.

As a good rule of thumb, the less comfortable you feel doing something, the more you should call in professional assistance. If you're fine with making your own airline reservations and booking hotel rooms online, and if you feel good about the venues you're playing, then doing a small tour is probably within your grasp. If, however, you're not that terribly organized and you have no clue about where you'll be performing, then hiring a tour manager makes a lot of sense.

Perhaps the biggest stumbling block for most musicians is determining where to play on tour. Here is where it pays to be a little savvy; as mentioned previously, one approach is simply to contact the same clubs and venues that similar musicians play. No sense in reinventing the wheel, after all. But if you're not comfortable doing this, then by all means contract with a booking agent; just know that you'll pay for his services.

The Least You Need to Know

- The key entities involved with any booking include the artist, the booking agent, the promoter, and the venue (typically represented by the venue operator).

- There are lots of places to look for gigs, from local nightclubs and coffeehouses to public festivals and corporate events; if you don't know where you should be looking, you can hire a booking agent to do the work for you.

- You should sign a contract for every gig you play. This contract should specify how much you're going to be paid and for doing what.

- Typical payment deals include flat fee or guarantee, a percentage of the door, a flat fee versus a percentage, and a flat fee plus a percentage.

- When you put together a tour, consider hiring not only a booking agent but also a tour manager, to make sure everything goes smoothly when you're on the road.

Chapter 14

The Business of Merchandising

In This Chapter

- Discovering how to make money by selling nonmusic items
- Learning what types of merchandise to sell
- Finding out where to source your merchandise
- Discovering where and how to sell these items

The music business of the twenty-first century is evolving in many ways, not the least of which is where you generate your income. In the old days (that is, up until a few years ago), musicians generated income from performing and selling their music. There's still money to be made in performing, but increasingly the music itself is being viewed as a commodity, in many cases being given away or shared for free (legally or illegally).

If music itself is losing value, then how does a musician make money? One way is to sell things other than music—in a word, to merchandise nonmusic goods and, in some cases, services. Merchandising can bring in decent money for even small artists, as you'll soon learn.

Augment Your Income by Selling Merchandise

Here's something that all successful businesspeople know: Once you have a customer, it's easy to sell that customer additional merchandise. In the music world, simply substitute "fan" for "customer," and you can see how it works. Once you've attracted a paying fan—someone who purchases your CD or a ticket to your performance—you now have direct contact with someone who is willing to buy more things from you. That's right, a fan is a valued customer who has already proven that he or she will spend money on your stuff.

Knowing this, you now have a new way to generate money from your musical career. It's not just selling your music, per se (although you can sell CDs to your fans), it's selling items related to your music to people who love your music. If you do it right, you can make as much as if not more money from merchandise than you do from playing live. It's a simple matter of setting up a merchandise table and having the right stuff for sale. Even if you play a gig for free, you can walk away with money in your pocket by selling items from your merchandise table.

And here's the other thing: You don't have to be a major artist to sell artist-related merchandise. Anyone spending money to hear you play live is a potential customer for the merchandise you have for sale. Fans *will* buy your merchandise; it's a fun and cool thing to do. Just make sure you have an attractive assortment of items your fans want, and that they're reasonably priced. You'll be surprised how many people will plunk down a few dollars to bring home a piece of you or your band.

What Types of Merchandise Can You Sell?

Many artists are finding that their fans will buy all sorts of related merchandise from them. CDs, of course, but also various nonmusic items—posters, T-shirts, and such. And the nice thing about selling this type of merchandise is that you get to keep all the profits; unless you're under some sort of onerous 360-degree contract with a major record label, you don't have to share any of the money you earn with anybody else.

So what can you sell to your fans? Here's just a small list:

- CDs
- DVDs
- Clothing
- Collectables
- Appearances

If you have one or more CDs available for sale, then you might as well sell them. If fans like what they hear when you perform, some percentage of them will want to purchase your CD to listen to you at home.

If you've put together a few music videos or shot a live performance, put together your video clips into a DVD that fans can watch at home. This DVD doesn't even have to be commercially available; it can be a special offer just for fans of your live shows.

Clothing includes all manner of wearable items, including long- and short-sleeved T-shirts, sweatshirts, hoodies, skullies, baseball hats—you name it. If you have a particularly enthusiastic and prosperous fan base, you can even add high-end tour jackets and the like. The reality for most artists is that clothing sells better than any other type of merchandise, except physical CDs; fans just like to display their love of their favorite artists. Just make sure that each item of clothing includes either your band's logo or a photograph of you or the band.

Smart Business

Increase your CD sales by offering to autograph all CDs purchased at a gig. You can even offer signed CDs from your website—often at a premium!

By collectibles I mean any item that fans will want to collect. This includes pins (those large buttons with your band's name or logo or likeness on the front), posters, stickers, coffee mugs, bobble-head dolls, you name it. Just go on eBay and see what people collect; maybe you produce a limited run of drinking glasses with your band's logo on the side, or yo-yo's with your picture on them. The sky's the limit with this one.

Okay, appearances aren't really a product, but rather a service. Believe it or not, some fans will pay money to spend a day hanging out with their favorite band. Maybe you can sell (or perhaps auction?) a day in the studio making your next recording, or a backstage pass at a big gig, or even a fancy dinner with you and your bandmates. This is where you can get really creative—and tap the resources of your more affluent fan base.

Smart Business

Don't fly blind. Take the time to ask your fans—either at your gigs or via an online form—what types of items they're interested in purchasing. A little market research goes a long way!

Bottom line, you can sell just about anything your fans want to buy. Don't limit yourself to CDs and T-shirts; there's a lot of other stuff that's viable—and profitable.

Purchasing Merchandise to Sell

It's fine and dandy to say you want to sell these types of items—but just where do you *get* them? After all, you're a musician, not a manufacturer.

First, you *could* be a manufacturer—of your own CDs and DVDs. You don't have to have a commercial CD release to offer CDs at your gigs. Fans are more than willing to purchase CDs you burn on your own computer, as long as they sound okay and are relatively professionally packaged. Fortunately, there's a lot of commercial software out there that lets you produce professional-looking and -sounding CDs (and DVDs, if you're into that), so you don't have to source CD replication to offer CDs for sale.

> **Smart Business** _____
>
> Burning one CD at a time on your computer is fine if your needs are small, but when you need larger volumes, consider purchasing a freestanding CD/DVD duplicator machine. These machines run as little as $200 and let you burn 15 or more CDs per hour, automatically. For more information, see the Copystars (www.copystars.com) or Disc Makers (www.discmakers.com) websites.

When it comes to other merchandise, however, you need to find a vendor to produce what you want to sell. In the case of clothing and most collectibles, you choose a stock item (such as a plain white T-shirt) and then have your logo or photograph silk-screened on it.

To place an order, you need to specify a few things in advance:

♦ The particular item you want to purchase—that is, the specific item number of the T-shirt or hat or whatever.

> **Smart Business** _____
>
> The simpler and bolder the design, the better the results will be when silk-screened onto most items—especially clothing.

♦ You'll probably want to order a variety of sizes, from S to XXL. If an item is available in different colors, you have to decide whether you want to offer it in a single color or a variety of colors.

♦ You'll have to supply the design you want silk screened on the items, typically in a JPG graphics file.

◆ Make sure the ink color goes well with the background color of the item. Unlike printing on paper, silk screening isn't four-color, it's typically just one or two colors.

◆ How many do you want? The more you order, the more you have to pay in total. That said, you can typically get a lower per-unit price by ordering larger quantities. It's a balancing act.

You also have to pony up the cost of the items in advance. So if you think you can sell 100 T-shirts, you have to purchase 100 T-shirts; that's money out of your own pocket. Of course, you purchase items at dealer cost (wholesale) and sell at a higher price (retail); the difference between what you pay and what you sell it for is your profit.

Where can you find this type of custom merchandise? There are lots of vendors out there, but here are a few that are popular with the indie music crowd:

◆ Anger Epidemic Extreme Merchandising (www.metalheadmerch.com)

◆ Branders.com (www.branders.com)

◆ CustomInk (www.customink.com)

◆ Disc Makers (www.discmakers.com/merch/)

◆ Fishhead (www.fishhead.net)

You may even have one or more local sources of merchandise. Search the Internet or consult your local yellow pages to see what's available. And if your needs are small, you can purchase plain white T-shirts at your local Wal-Mart or Target store and have them silk-screened at a local printing shop.

Where Can You Sell Your Merchandise?

Now the $64,000 question: Where can you sell your merchandise? There are two main sources of sales—at your gigs and on your website.

Smart Business

You can even sell your CDs at other artists' gigs. Find an artist who has a similar sound and fan base, and then agree to cross-promote your CDs at each others' gigs. This means you'll put some of that artist's CDs on your sales table at your gigs, and they'll put some of your CDs on their sales table. It's a great way to expand your reach— and make new fans!

Selling Merchandise at Your Gigs

Let's start with the obvious. You can sell your CDs, shirts, and other merchandise at any gig you play. It doesn't matter whether you're playing a small club or a large hall, a wedding reception or outdoor festival—anywhere your fans gather is a perfect place for merchandise sales.

Of course, you have to do it right. The best approach is to set up a merchandise table, either at the back of the room or just outside the venue; a high-traffic location, near an entrance or exit, is best. Hire someone (a roadie, maybe?) to man the table, and stack your merchandise high and wide. (Make sure the person manning your table is wearing your merchandise, too; that's good exposure.)

Smart Business

Don't limit merchandise sales to before or after your shows. Keep your merchandise table manned between sets and even during sets, for those fans who wander out for a drink or bathroom break.

You should also draw the crowd's attention to your merchandise. Several times during your set, mention that you have merchandise for sale. Heck, mention the *specific* merchandise you have for sale—your latest CD, cool new T-shirts, whatever—and how affordable it is ("only 10 dollars!"). Also mention if you'll be available after the show to sign the items you sell. This type of personal pitch can be quite effective.

Some customers will want to pay in cash, so make sure you start out with a fair amount of small bills and coins for change. It's also a good idea to accept credit card payments, which can really increase the volume of sales.

Smart Business

Several companies offer low-cost credit card services for sales at live shows. For example, CD Baby offers a program where you get your own portable credit card terminal for live processing; check it out at members.cdbaby.com.

And here's the bottom line. For some musicians at some gigs, you can make more money selling merchandise than you can from the gig itself. This is particularly the case for newer or independent artists. I have a nephew who's in a group with some of his high school friends, and he's played several gigs for free, but made money on merchandise sales—not a bad deal.

Selling Merchandise on Your Website

You can and should also sell your merchandise on your website and MySpace page. Pretty much everything you sell at live shows can also be sold online; you just need to set up the mechanism to take orders and ship the merchandise.

To this end, enlist your webmaster to set up a merchandise page on your site. This page should be enabled for real-time sales, complete with a shopping cart and check-out. All the merchandise you have for sale (including CDs) should be displayed on this page, and the page should be updated constantly as your inventory changes.

To accept credit card payments, consider signing up for PayPal (www.paypal.com), or contracting with a commercial credit card processing service. To be honest, PayPal is probably the easiest and most accepted way to go; your customers will be familiar with it.

Then you have to put together a back-end operation to manage the sales you make. That means depositing the funds collected, communicating with customers, and, most important, packing and shipping the items sold. This can be a bit of work, especially if you're on the road a lot. You might want to offload this activity to your webmaster, or hire a third-party fulfillment firm to do the dirty work.

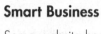 **Smart Business**

Some website hosting services offer what they call e-commerce hosting packages, which include everything you need to sell merchandise on your site—a shopping cart, checkout system, and credit card processing.

Once you get it set up, make sure you promote your merchandise by including links to the merchandise page from your site's home page. You can also promote your merchandise page in your e-mails to fans, blog postings, and the like—and don't forget to mention your site's URL at all your gigs!

Do I Really Need to Sell Merchandise?

I know what some of you are thinking—you're a musician, not a salesperson. It may even be a little distasteful for you to hawk trinkets and doodads when you're playing onstage. Do you really need to do it?

No, you don't. Lots of musicians over the years have never sold a penny of merchandise of their own. It's okay to stay artistically pure if that's what you want to do.

Of course, that means you don't benefit from your fans' desire to purchase a souvenir of their concert experience. It doesn't matter whether you're Frank Sinatra or the Grateful Dead, you will have fans who are more than willing, if not eager, to shell out their hard-earned bucks on everything from baseball hats to posters to coffee mugs. If you don't sell these items, you're kissing off a lot of potential revenue in the name of artistic purity.

But if you want to make the most you can from the music you play, you have to pay attention to these alternative revenue streams. For many fans, the musical experience goes well beyond the music itself; if you think of your business in this sort of three-dimensional fashion, you'll realize that there are lots of different ways to make money. That doesn't mean you're selling out, just that you're helping your fans realize the full experience—and profiting from doing so.

Here's the reality: There's a lot of money to be made from merchandise sales, both at your shows and on your website. Smart musicians know they need to maximize *all* potential revenue streams, no matter how unlikely. Ignore this revenue at your own financial peril—especially in today's changing market.

The Least You Need to Know

♦ Many artists generate substantial revenues from selling a variety of merchandise to their fans.

♦ You can sell CDs and DVDs, T-shirts and other items of clothing, posters and other collectibles, and even private time with you or your band—anything fans are willing to pay for.

♦ There are lots of wholesale sources for this type of custom merchandise; you'll typically have to pay in advance for a quantity order.

♦ You can sell your merchandise at your live shows (via a merchandise table) or on your website.

The Business of Songwriting and Publishing

In This Chapter

◆ Understanding how the songwriting business works

◆ Learning how to find a music publisher and get your songs published

◆ Discovering how to copyright your songs

◆ Understanding all about ASCAP, BMI, and other performing rights organizations

Beyond performing and recording, many musicians make money from songwriting. If you're a songwriter, you can perform your own songs or "sell" your songs for others to perform and record. When someone else uses one of your songs, you earn royalties for each performance or for each recording sold. If you're good at it, you can make a nice income.

The first challenge, of course, is writing a great song. After that, you have to get the song copyrighted, published, and then picked up by other performers. If that sounds like an important part of the music business, you're right; music publishing is a very big deal, on both sides of the table.

Understanding the Business of Songwriting

Songs are the driving force of popular music. Without songs, musicians would have nothing to perform, radio would have nothing to play, and record labels would have nothing to sell. Even the best band in the world would be just four guys standing around on stage, if they didn't have any songs to play.

To that end, some of the most famous musicians of the twentieth century are songwriters, from Irving Berlin and George Gershwin to Paul McCartney and John Lennon. Yes, many of these musicians performed their own songs, but that doesn't diminish their accomplishments as songwriters. Songs make the music industry go round and round.

This is why, perhaps, songwriters are so valued and so well compensated—relative to performing musicians, that is. Performers get paid for live performances, yes, and receive a royalty for each record they sell, but they don't get paid for radio play or use of their recordings on TV shows and commercials. Songwriters, on the other hand, get paid whenever their songs are played on the radio, used as background music in a store or coffeehouse, or placed in a TV show or commercial. That's in addition to being paid whenever someone sells a record that contains their songs, or performs their songs live. (Learn more about licensing your work to television, movies, and commercials in Chapter 16.)

> ### Behind the Music
>
> The current royalty rate for mechanical licenses—that is, for music sold via CD or digital download—is 9.1¢ per song. So for example, if your song is recorded by an artist who then sells 100,000 copies of that CD, you earn $9,100—split 50/50 between you and your publishing company.

Here's how it works, in general:

1. The songwriter writes a song.

2. The songwriter copyrights that song.

3. The songwriter contracts with a music publishing company to handle the licensing and royalty collections for the song. The contract typically states that royalties will be split 50/50 between the artist and publishing company.

4. Another artist records the songwriter's song.

5. The songwriter earns a royalty for each copy of that artist's record that is sold.

6. The songwriter earns a royalty for each time that artist's record is played on the radio or over the Internet.

7. Sales and airplay of that artist's record are tracked by one of several performing rights organizations. (In the United States, that's ASCAP, BMI, or SESAC.)

8. The music publishing company collects all royalties due.

9. The music publishing company pays the artist his share of collected royalties—typically 50 percent.

And repeat. If a song has legs, a songwriter can collect royalties for many years after writing the song. A really big song, in terms of sales and airplay, can generate more than enough money for an artist to live on.

As a songwriter, you also earn royalties if you perform or record your own song. That is, you receive a royalty for each record sold or played on the radio, even if you also receive payment as a performer. Better yet, this songwriting royalty is not part of any deal you make with your record label; you're owed songwriting royalties even if you don't earn out your advance from the label. Sweet.

Throughout all of this process, you own the song—that is, you own the copyright on the intellectual property you create. As the copyright owner, then, you are owed royalties for the use of your property. It's a nice concept.

Behind the Music

While songwriters typically do not "sell" a song (as noted, they sign with a music publisher), there is an exception to this, in that it's possible that a company or organization may commission a songwriter to write a song for a particular use or event. In this instance, the company buys the song outright as a work for hire. With this sort of work-for-hire arrangement, the songwriter receives a single payment for the song (actually, for the work's copyright) and does not receive any future royalties of any type.

Getting Your Songs Published

If you're in the business of selling your songs for others to perform, one of the first orders of business is to sign a deal with a music publishing company. The music publisher will handle all the dirty work associated with getting your song placed, collecting royalties due, and the like. Of course, you pay a price for this service—in most instances, 50 percent of all royalties due.

What a Music Publishing Company Does

A music publishing company does many things, all of them in service to the songs created by their songwriting clients. Naturally, the publishing company benefits from performing these services, in the form of taking half the royalties earned. But without a music publisher, most songwriters would have no means of getting their songs placed with other performers.

> **Behind the Music**
>
> Before you pitch to a publishing company, you need to have a great song to pitch. To improve your songwriting craft, check out my companion book, *The Complete Idiot's Guide to Music Composition* (Michael Miller, Alpha Books, 2005).

So what is it exactly that a music publisher does? Here's a short list:

- Submits all necessary copyright forms.

- Places your songs with other artists.

- Places your songs for use with television shows, movie soundtracks, and radio/ TV commercials.

- Handles all necessary contracts when placing your songs with third parties.

- Collects royalties when your song is performed, recorded, or sold.

- Handles all necessary accounting and paperwork regarding song usage.

- Takes legal action against infringing parties who are not paying appropriate royalties.

- Publishes your songs as sheet music.

- Pays you half of all royalties collected.

> **Behind the Music**
>
> Some publishing companies also help pair aspiring composers with lyricists, as well as help their songwriters work to improve their craft.

If that sounds like a lot of work, you're right—assuming that you're writing songs you want performed by other artists. If all you do is write songs that you perform yourself, there's a lot less work for a publishing company to do—although, to be fair, tracking and collecting royalties due is still a very big deal.

Finding a Music Publishing Company

If you're a songwriter and you see the value of signing with a music publishing company, just how do you go about finding and signing with one?

First, know that there are several different types of music publishers. At the very top of the industry are the big players, typically arms of the major record labels, who control the publishing rights for that label's artists (as well as for other songwriters, of course). These companies include the following:

◆ EMI Music Publishing (www.emimusicpub.com)

◆ Sony/ATV Music Publishing (www.sonyatv.com)

◆ Universal Music Publishing Group (www.umusicpub.com)

◆ Warner/Chappell Music (www.warnerchappell.com)

Then there are the large independent music publishers, such as Bug Music (www.bugmusic.com) and peermusic (www.peermusic.com). These are large firms, often as large as the label-based publishers, who cater to independent songwriters rather than those performing songwriters signed to major labels.

Finally, there are a number of smaller publishing companies. These companies typically handle a smaller number of songwriters and are always on the lookout for new clients. You can find a list of smaller publishers at the Music Publisher's Association website (www.mpa.org).

As to which type of publishing company is best for you, it all depends. The big, label-based publishers naturally want your business if you're a performer signed to the master label, but they also actively seek nonlabel talent. These big companies have a lot of power and contacts, which can help get your songs placed—but they handle so many clients that your relationship with them will probably be a tad impersonal; it's easy to get lost in the crowd.

 Smart Business

Try to sign with a publishing house that does a good job with songs in a similar style to yours. One good approach is to find out which companies are publishing hit songs in your particular style, then contact those companies. (*Billboard* magazine will have this info.)

For that matter, the big independent publishers have similar pros and cons. They're big enough to have a lot of contacts, but also big enough to feel overwhelming to newer artists.

That's why many songwriters just starting out prefer to sign with a smaller independent label. You'll get a lot more handholding at a smaller publishing house, but they may not have the contacts or resources necessary to make really big placements.

All publishing companies, fortunately, should have the back end apparatus necessary to track and administer all royalties due. So don't feel as if you have to sign with a big company just to have your royalties properly tracked; all the companies will do a good job at this. (Learn more about working for a music publishing company in Chapter 22.)

Pitching Your Songs to a Music Publisher

Getting signed to a big music publishing company is every bit as challenging as getting signed to a major record label. The big publishing companies are inundated with solicitations, in addition to staying busy managing their existing clients.

For that reason, it's always good if you can somehow establish a connection with someone in the publisher's creative or A&R department. If you have a friend of a friend of a friend in the business, that's great. If you know a songwriter who has a contract with a given company, use that person's references, if you can. It also doesn't hurt to attend various music industry functions and showcases to make some personal contacts; it's harder to ignore you in person than it is via an unsolicited letter or e-mail.

Your first contact with a publishing company should be a letter or e-mail message—*not* a full demo or manuscript. Many publishers automatically return or destroy unsolicited music, so that they won't be accused of stealing someone else's ideas. So you need to contact the publisher first and get their permission to send in some of your music for review.

This initial letter or e-mail is essentially your pitch to the company. You want to point out any pertinent experience you've had, any previous songs you've had performed by others, anything that would make them think you're capable of writing a successful song. This is the place to drop any names they may recognize, as well.

Once you get permission to send a further submission, put together a handful of your best songs. You want to include a manuscript, in proper music notation, for each song, as well as a recorded demo on CD. The manuscript can be handwritten (neatly, of course), but it's better if you can use a music-notation program to make it look more professional.

As to the demo, it doesn't have to be fancy. It can be just you and a piano or guitar, or you can put together some backing musicians to flesh things out. There's no need to go overboard; you're pushing the song, not the production. But make sure it doesn't suck; if you're not a strong singer yourself, hire a professional singer to do the duties on the recording.

Smart Business

Don't push any songs that have been previously recorded. A music publisher wants songs that are unencumbered by any legal contracts—not songs that it won't have full rights to.

You can send this submission either via postal mail or e-mail, as directed by the publishing company. Make sure you include an informative cover letter with your submission, a bio of yourself, and all pertinent contact information.

Follow up with the company about two weeks after your submission. Keep following up until you get a response, positive or negative—and, if the response is negative, move on to the next publisher on your list.

Signing a Publishing Deal

In the formative years of the music publishing industry, back in the early twentieth century, songwriters sold their songs outright to music publishers for a flat fee. The publisher kept all the money generated by the song; the songwriter received no royalties.

That's different today. In today's industry, the songwriter doesn't sell his songs, he contracts with the music publisher to promote his songs and collect all royalties due. The publisher then keeps half of the royalties collected and sends the rest on to the songwriter.

That's the basic deal, anyway. There are actually eight different variations you may encounter, which vary according to which party owns the copyright, how the publishing income is split, what functions the publisher performs, and how long the agreement lasts. The different agreements are as follows:

◆ **Traditional publishing agreement:** This is the most common arrangement. In this type of contract, the songwriter agrees to a one-year (renewable) deal for all songs written during that period, assigns 100 percent of the copyright to the publisher, and in return receives 50 percent of all royalties collected. The publisher may pay the songwriter an advance on future royalties.

◆ **Single-song agreement:** In this type of contract, the deal is to publish just a single song or specified group of songs—not all of the songwriter's output. As with the traditional deal, the songwriter assigns 100 percent of the copyright for those songs to the publisher, and in return receives 50 percent of all royalties collected. There is seldom an advance paid to the songwriter.

◆ **Co-publishing deal:** This type of contract is often offered by label-related publishers to musicians already signed to the record label. This type of deal typically covers all the original songs on the artist's records, sometimes with options for several follow-up records. The songwriter transfers one half of the copyright ownership to the publisher, and retains the balance for himself. The publishing company keeps 25 percent of all royalties collected and pays the songwriter 75 percent. There may or may not be an advance associated with this type of contract.

◆ **Administrative agreement:** This type of deal is typically used when a song-writer only needs a publisher to collect royalties and handle paperwork, not to promote the song to other artists. An administrative agreement most often covers all material written by the songwriter during a specified period (typi-cally three to five years); the songwriter retains all copyright. The publishing company takes 10 to 20 percent of all royalties collected, returning the balance to the songwriter. There is seldom an advance paid for this type of agreement.

◆ **Income-participation agreement:** This type of deal is used to cut another party (such as the band's manager) into the publishing revenues. In this type of agreement, no copyright is transferred, and only a small share of the revenue (10 to 15 percent) is paid to the other participant.

◆ **Catalog-representation agreement:** This type of deal is used when trying to place a song with TV shows, movies, and other media; the publishing company in this instance specializes in representing songs to the nonmusic part of the entertainment industry. No copyright is transferred, and the publishing com-pany takes 25 to 50 percent of any deals made.

◆ **Self-publishing agreement:** If you want to act as your own publisher, you can sign this type of deal with foreign publishers to represent your songs in other countries. No copyright is transferred, and the foreign subpublisher typically takes 25 percent or so of publishing income generated in that territory.

Which type of publishing deal should you sign? If you want a company to represent your entire catalog, the traditional publishing agreement is most common. If you're only selling a single song, however, then you should go with a single-song agreement. The other types of deals are more suited for specific situations. (Learn more about copyright and royalties in Chapter 24.)

Copyrighting Your Songs

Whether you sign with a music publishing company or form your own publishing company, you still need to copyright all the songs you write. This protects you from anyone stealing your intellectual property and making money off of your song, and provides the legal basis for the collection of royalties due.

Now if you are signed with a publishing company, most companies will handle the copyright registration for you. That's a good deal; no paperwork to handle on your end. If you're not yet signed to a publishing company, or if you publish your own songs, you have to handle the copyright process yourself. Fortunately, it's not that difficult.

The easiest way to copyright a song is go to the U.S. Copyright Office website (www. copyright.gov) and click the Register Online link. Follow the onscreen instructions and be prepared to pay the $35 registration fee, and you're good to go.

If you prefer to file via mail, go to the same website and request Form PA. (Use Form SR if you're submitting your work on CD or tape instead of on paper.) You'll pay a $65 fee for this type of manual submission. Mail the completed form and a nonreturnable copy of your song to the following address:

Library of Congress
U.S. Copyright Office
101 Independence Avenue SE
Washington, DC 20559

Scam Alert

Technically, you have a copyright on your song the moment you finished writing it. To protect your rights, however, you need to officially register the song with the U.S. Copyright Office. Some people think they can get a "poor man's copyright" by mailing a copy of the song to themselves, thus proving (by means of postmark) that the song was written on such and such a date. This type of nonregistration is not legally binding, however; it's better to go through the official registration process.

Understanding ASCAP, BMI, and SESAC

The dirty work of monitoring performances of songs falls into the hands of what is known as a performing rights organization. In the United States, there are three such organizations: The American Society of Composers, Authors, and Publishers (ASCAP); Broadcast Music, Inc. (BMI); and the Society of European Stage Authors and Composers (SESAC).

ASCAP, BMI, and SESAC work with music publishing companies to issue licenses to users of music. They then collect monies due from performances of licensed works (both live performances and the playback of recordings) and distribute the income generated from mechanical and performance royalties.

Each publishing company is associated with one of the three performing rights organizations. So if you're a songwriter who signs with a given publishing company, you'll use the organization that the publishing company is affiliated with. If you form your own publishing company, you'll need to partner with one of these three organizations directly.

> **Behind the Music**
>
> ASCAP, BMI, and SESAC are U.S.-based performing rights organizations. Additional organizations exist to monitor royalty collection in other countries.

Here is how to contact these organizations:

- ◆ ASCAP (www.ascap.com)
- ◆ BMI (www.bmi.com)
- ◆ SESAC (www.sesac.com)

Do I Need to Sign with a Music Publishing Company?

You understand how music publishing works. What you don't understand is why you want to give away half of your songwriting royalties to a music publishing company.

Do you really need to sign with a music publisher? It all depends. If you're a song-writer only in the sense that you write songs that you or your band record, and you're not at all interested in placing those songs with other artists, then there's little reason to forfeit half your songwriting royalties to a publishing company. In this instance, you're better off forming your own publishing company, letting ASCAP or BMI do their thing, and keeping all the royalties yourself.

If you want to place your songs with other artists, however—that is, if you truly are a professional songwriter—then signing with a music publishing company makes a lot of sense. The music publisher will work on your behalf to promote your songs to other performers; in fact, most of the bigger publishers have a lot of contacts in the industry just to this end. Without a publisher, you're left to push your songs yourself, which, unless you have a lot of contacts, may prove fruitless.

So paying a publisher half of royalties earned makes sense if the publisher helps to get your songs recorded. Earning 50 percent of potentially significant revenues is much preferable to owning 100 percent of nothing.

The same goes if you want to place your songs on TV shows, movie soundtracks, radio and TV commercials, and the like. Music publishing companies have contacts throughout the entertainment industry; you probably don't. You're paying the publisher to get your songs placed, which is money well spent.

Remember, a music publisher does more than just administer copyrights and royalties; it's also an agent or promoter for your songs. If you hope to make a living from your songwriting, this is the service you're paying for.

The Least You Need to Know

- Songwriters earn royalties when their songs are recorded by other artists and sold on their CDs, as well as when they're played on the radio or Internet.

- Music publishing companies administer copyrights, collect royalties, and help promote songs to other performers.

- Most publishing contracts split songwriting revenue 50/50 between the music publishing company and the songwriter.

- Whether you sign with a big music publishing company or publish your songs yourself, you need to formally register your songs with the U.S. Copyright Office.

- In the United States, the monitoring and collection of performance royalties is handled by one of the three major performing rights organizations—ASCAP, BMI, or SESAC.

16

The Business of Music for Other Media

In This Chapter

- ◆ Licensing your songs to television, film, and commercials
- ◆ Pursuing and negotiating a licensing deal
- ◆ How stock music libraries work
- ◆ Writing original music for films and TV
- ◆ Breaking into the commercial jingle business

As you learned in the previous chapter, the music business can be quite profitable for a successful songwriter. It gets even better if you can license your music for use in TV shows, movie soundtracks, commercials, or video games.

This sort of licensing not only brings in much-needed income, it's also great promotion for your music. People hear your song on a TV show and want to hear more, which results in increased downloads and CD sales. In fact, many industry people think that licensing is the best way to promote your music in today's market.

Licensing Your Songs in Other Media

It used to be that selling a song for use in a commercial or TV show was a sign of selling out. I remember, when I was younger, hearing Carly Simon's "Anticipation" used for a ketchup commercial and thinking that I liked her and her song a little bit less for it. But that's not the case today; licensing has become a big deal for both songwriters and performers.

Understanding Music Licensing

Put simply, licensing is selling the rights to use a song or recording in another medium. As a performer, you can *license* a recording you've made; as a songwriter, you can license your song as recorded or to be performed by another artist in that medium. When a recording is licensed, both the original performer and the songwriter are compensated. When a song alone is licensed, only the songwriter is compensated; a new performer makes a new recording for the TV show, movie, or commercial.

def•i•ni•tion

A **license** is the transfer of a copyright that does not amount to an assignment; the party that owns the copyright is the *licensor,* while the party obtaining the license is the *licensee.* A license does not give the licensee the legal right to the copyright.

You can license your music to a variety of different media. The following media, in particular, license a lot of music:

- **Television shows:** This includes shows on the major networks, of course, but also original productions on the hundreds of different cable and satellite channels out there.

Behind the Music

If you license your song for use in a commercial, don't be surprised if you're asked to okay revisions to your lyrics to be more friendly to the sponsor's product.

- **Films:** Existing songs are often used as background music in movie scenes, as well as played over opening or closing credits.

- **Radio and television commercials:** Commercial producers will often license a song—not an existing recording—to be shortened and otherwise altered for use in a 30-second commercial.

A licensing deal can be quite complex because of all the variables involved. First, there's the issue of whether they're licensing just the song or the song and an existing recording; that's potentially two different entities the licensee has to deal with. In addition, there are all the different ways a film or TV show can be viewed; you have to consider licensing for broadcast rights, release on DVD, Internet rights, you name it. Plus there's the issue of release in different countries. As I said, it can get quite complex.

That said, getting a song placed in a TV show, film, or commercial not only generates immediate income in the form of a licensing fee, but also serves to promote your music. Millions of people will hear your song, even if just for 30 seconds, and some of them will like it enough to want to hear more. That means an increase in CD sales and downloads, which for many artists is the real reason they license their music in this fashion.

> **Behind the Music**
>
> Technically, when you strike a licensing deal, you're granting what is called synchronization rights to your music. Learn more about synch rights in Chapter 24.

How to Pursue a Licensing Deal

Not surprisingly, music licensing has become quite the thing. In fact, the field of music licensing is highly competitive. Looking just at licensing to TV shows, you have tens of thousands of artists trying to get their songs on just 100 or so shows. How do you break through the clutter and into the licensing business?

Like other aspects of the music business, it helps if you have contacts. Let's face it, if the producer of a given TV show happens to be your bass player's uncle, or if you went to high school with a famous movie director, you have an advantage. Good for you. But everybody else not related to anyone in the business has to rely on their record label and music publishing company.

Your record label is important if you're a performing artist trying to get a recording placed. Your label, naturally, has an interest in generating more revenue for its recordings, and this is a great way to do so. In fact, all the major labels and many of the larger independent labels have people in Hollywood specifically dogging these types of licensing deals. They're out there working on your behalf.

If you're a songwriter, your music publishing company's job is to get your songs placed, and they're out there pushing on all sorts of fronts. Like the major labels, major publishing houses have people in Hollywood pushing their clients' songs. They do well when you do well.

Beyond that, if you happen to know somebody in the business, or feel that a particular song is well suited for a particular show or film, there's no harm in sending a copy of the song, along with accompanying press kit, to the show's or film's producer or music director. You can typically find names and addresses on the web, often at the network's or producing company's websites. If you send a full CD, make sure your cover letter flags the song you're targeting; otherwise, cut a special CD that contains only the song in question.

Negotiating a Licensing Deal

As we've discussed, licensing your music for TV and film is a great way to gain exposure, although it's not necessarily lucrative. Here's why: The average fee for licensing a song to a TV show is in the $4,000 to $6,000 range; payments are a little higher for songs licensed for film use. That's not nothing, but won't let you live in luxury for the rest of your life, either.

Smart Business _____

Your odds of cutting a licensing deal often turn on how fast you can make a deal. Both theatrical films and television shows work on very tight schedules; the music person on a TV show might only have a few days to find and clear rights for the songs he wants to use. The easier you are to work with and the faster you can approve a deal, the more likely you are to find work.

Of course, the actual amount you get paid depends on a number of factors, including the music budget for the show or film, how much of the song is used and how, whether it's a new song or a library track, and how big an artist you are. If you're just starting out and only a few seconds of your song is used, you'll probably be paid at the low end of the scale. If you're a major artist licensing a hit song to be played over a movie's closing credits, however, bigger bucks can be expected.

The actual terms of the licensing deal will likely be negotiated by your record label (for existing recordings) or your music publishing company (if you wrote the song). All sorts of details have to be worked out, including the following:

◆ **Territories:** Where in the world do you grant rights to use your song? Rights can be U.S.-only, worldwide, or for specific countries only.

◆ **Media:** In what media will your song be used? This could be radio, television, theatrical, DVD, Internet—you name it.

◆ **Length of license:** How long are rights granted? This could be for the life of the copyright, or for a specified number of years only.

◆ **Usage:** How is your song used in the film or show? Is it featured on camera, used in the background, sung by a character onscreen, or what?

◆ **Length:** How much of the song is used? Is it the entire song, or just a snippet?

◆ **Version:** Is the film/show using the original recording, or a rerecording?

Okay, that's a lot of details. Let your label/publisher deal with these things, unless you have a particular bugaboo about how you want your music used. Be aware, however, that any spanners you throw in the works can quickly sink the deal.

Behind the Music

Because of how fast the TV business works, chances are the actual contract won't be signed until after the first broadcast of the program. Naturally, all negotiations and permissions will be finalized *before* the program's broadcast. Movie licensing isn't quite so last-minute, but still works at a relatively fast pace.

Licensing to a Stock Music Library

So far we've discussed one-time licenses, where your song is used in a single TV show or movie. There's another kind of licensing, however, where your music can be used in any number of programs or films. This licensing is to a *stock music library* (SML), which then offers your music for repeated use in any number of third-party projects.

Here's how an SML works. A musician sells his work to the SML, either for a flat fee or for a cut (typically 50/50) of all future usage fees. The SML then sells that music to third parties who pay a flat fee for the use. The SML does not charge its clients royalty payments for the use of its music, which is why many music directors like using stock music. (Also attractive is that the usage rates

def•i•ni•tion

A **stock music library,** or SML, is a firm that offers royalty-free music for use in television, film, commercials, and other media. Library music is sometimes known as *production music.*

are lower than with traditional licensed music.) If the songwriter signed a split deal, he then receives 50 percent of the usage fees collected by the SML.

Of course, the third party doesn't get exclusive rights to the music; it's common to hear the same stock music used in many different projects. Clients for stock music include not just TV shows and movies, but also radio stations, video game manufacturers, websites, and corporations (for in-house videos).

> **Behind the Music**
>
> Stock music is used in a lot of lower-budget films and TV shows. For example, all the incidental music in *Monty Python and the Holy Grail* was stock music.

In most cases, SMLs purchase complete recordings, not individual songs. In fact, some SMLs commission recordings from musicians, typically based on a given style or mood that they feel has good sales potential.

If you sell a song to most SMLs, you're giving that SML (but not its clients) exclusive rights to that song. You cannot sell it to another SML, nor release it yourself. It's a strict deal, but potentially profitable. In fact, many musicians specialize in creating this sort of generic music for stock use, and make a good living at it.

Who are the major stock music libraries? Here's a short list:

- Killer Tracks (www.killertracks.com)
- NEO Sounds (www.neosounds.com)
- Premiumbeat.com (www.premiumbeat.com)
- RoyaltyFreeMusic.com (www.royaltyfreemusic.com)
- Shockwave-Sound.com (www.shockwave-sound.com)
- Stockmusic.net (www.stockmusic.net)

Writing Original Music for Other Media

Beyond licensing existing music, there is also a call for original music composed specifically for TV, film, and other media. There's less call for this original music than there used to be (more and more producers and directors want to use known music in the productions, for whatever reason), but countless composers still make a good living composing movie and TV soundtracks.

Becoming a movie or TV composer is a whole other subject; only the truly talented and well-schooled should apply. You need to be versatile, you need to be fast, and you need to be at the top of your form. But there are few professional moments more thrilling than hearing your music played on the big screen.

Most film composing is done on a flat-fee basis; that is, the composer receives a negotiated one-time fee for his or her work. That's a little different than with some Hollywood films, where a name composer might get a flat fee plus a percentage of the film's profits. When you're just starting out, however, expect to see flat-fee offers.

What kind of fees can you expect to earn? It depends on your experience and on the scale of the production. An A-list composer, such as a John Williams or James Horner, working on a big-budget film can make upward of $750,000 per project, while a newbie composer on a low-budget film might be lucky to see a $20,000 paycheck. TV projects pay even less. Still, assuming you can score several projects in a year, it's not a bad way to make money from your music.

Composing for Film

A film composer creates soundtracks for motion pictures and television films. Today's film composers must be able to create both memorable theme songs and appropriate background music to play underneath the entire film. The film's score should also comment on particular passages of the movie. As you might expect, strong arranging and orchestration skills are also necessary, as many movie scores involve large orchestras, as well as other smaller combinations of instruments.

In most cases, the scoring of a film takes place in a short period of time after the filming and editing have been completed, which means that the ability to write quickly and efficiently is necessary. While the rise of independent films has somewhat decentralized the industry, most major films are still produced in Hollywood; for this reason, most serious film composers are based on the West Coast.

Composing for Television

A television composer is similar to a film composer, but instead composes music for a weekly television series. This often includes composing both the series theme song and the incidental music for individual episodes. As with film composing, most major players are based in Los Angeles.

When you consider the large amount of original programming produced for the hundred or more broadcast and cable networks today, you realize the potential in this industry for an aggressive composer. It's not just soundtracks for TV movies; every show needs its own theme song. There is plenty of incidental music used on everything from documentaries to reality TV shows, and even local TV news programs need "bumper" music leading into and out of commercials.

Composing for Video Games

One of the newest venues for composers is the video game soundtrack. Many state-of-the-art video games have scores no less sophisticated than what's found in the average film, complete with theme songs and incidental music.

One factor that distinguishes video game composing from film or television composing is that, in many cases, you're working exclusively with digital instruments rather than with live performers. (This isn't unique to video game composing; many television scores today are performed with high-end synthesizers and sequencers, as a cost-cutting measure.) Look for this type of composing to become more important over time.

Writing for Commercials

Then there's the world of commercial *jingles*—the music played on 30-second radio and television commercials. Jingle writing, while not quite as big a business as it used to be, is still a good way for a songwriter to make a living.

That said, jingle writing has become somewhat of a vanishing art form. Many of today's advertising people feel that jingles are old-school, and not in a good way. They prefer licensing existing pop songs to hook the listener to their pitch. By some accounts, fully half of all commercials today use licensed music rather than original jingles, a far cry from the 90 percent of commercials that used jingles a decade or two ago.

def•i•ni•tion

A **jingle** is a simple song about a product or service, used in a commercial message.

But that still leaves lots and lots of commercials out there that use original music. Many of these are commercials for smaller companies that air on local radio and television stations—an ideal environment for a newcomer to break into.

Writing Jingles

How do you get started in the jingle business? By writing catchy jingles, of course.

A jingle is nothing more than a short song—anywhere from 10 to 60 seconds in length. The jingle must have a memorable hook, and in fact may be nothing but the hook. The lyrics should match the musical hook and play up the name of the product or company being plugged; they should be clear and succinct while catchy in their own way.

When you write a jingle, make sure you include some instrumental space—called a "donut"—in the middle. This is where the announcer talks over the music to deliver the sponsor's message. The donut can and probably should be an instrumental reprise of the main melodic hook.

Producing the actual jingle is another matter. Most jingles today are recorded in home studios or in small studios hosted by ad agencies, so you won't be working with large orchestras in a professional studio. That means playing most of the instruments (or sampling them) yourself; you can

Smart Business

The best jingles are the ones that make listeners want to sing along—whether they want to or not.

and probably should work with a professional vocalist, however. You'll probably be asked to create several different versions of the jingle—different lengths (10, 30, and 60 seconds), different mixes, with and without vocals, and so forth. Naturally, you should bill the production/recording work separately from writing the jingle itself.

Finding Work in the Jingle Business

Most jingles are written for and contracted by an advertising agency who works on behalf of the client. In smaller markets, the local radio station serves as the *de facto* ad agency, contracting with local jingle writers. In some rare instances, a local business might contract with a jingle writer directly, but it's more common to go through a middleman.

The best advice for getting started in jingle writing is to start locally. Contact a local radio station that does a lot of original commercials and offer your services. Work up some spec jingles for local businesses that you can use to demonstrate your skills. Make sure the demos are professional; use a pro singer to give them the proper sheen.

Alternately, you can contact one or more local advertising agencies. Use the yellow pages or Google to look up the top agencies in your area, then use their websites to find a list of clients. Look for an agency that produces commercials for local firms—and that is known to use jingles in their ads.

Once a radio station or ad agency knows your work, expect the offers to start coming. As with all work for hire, you'll need to be fast and flexible; the client has to like your work for it be aired.

How lucrative is the jingle business? It all depends on the size of the client and the reach of the ad. Local commercials can pay anywhere from $1,000 on up, while national commercials might earn you $5,000 or more. In most instances you sell the rights to your jingle to the advertiser to use as often as he wants, but some agencies will still cut deals that let you retain the copyright to the jingle. In this later instance, you earn royalties every time the jingle airs, which can amount to some very hefty paychecks.

Is Licensing Replacing Radio for Music Promotion?

Where do you hear new music? In the old days, you heard new music on the radio. Or maybe you heard (or saw) a new song in a music video on MTV. But that was back when radio stations had longer, more diverse playlists and actually broke new music; it was also back when MTV actually played videos (and also broke new music).

That isn't the case today. Radio stations have short and stringent playlists. MTV does long-form programming instead of music videos. And everybody and his brother listens to music they already know on their iPods.

In short, the average listener never gets exposed to anything new. Radio stations play extremely narrow formats with lots of "classic" cuts, iPods play music from the own-ers' collections—it's just more of the same, repeat ad nauseum. It's almost impossible for new music—and new artists—to get heard.

But here's the thing. I'm still hearing new music. It's not on the radio, because I don't listen to the radio much, and when I do it's classic stuff from a narrowcast satellite channel. It's certainly not on my iPod, since I can only play the music I already own. No, I'm hearing new music on TV shows and commercials—good stuff, too, that makes me go out and buy the artists' CDs.

There are untold tales of bands who got their break by placing a song on a TV show like *Grey's Anatomy* or *Ugly Betty*, or having a big advertiser like Apple or Volkswagen pick up their music. I can't tell you how many times I've heard a song on *Scrubs*, one of my favorite shows, then almost immediately went online to purchase that artist's CD. It's how I got turned on to the Fray, Polyphonic Spree, Jon McLaughlin, and more. That's great promotion for those artists.

And that's the point. In a world where no one is being exposed to anything but their own private playlists, how do you break through and get your music heard? Millions of people watch a typical TV series every week; get your song placed and that's millions of potential new listeners and purchasers of your music. The same thing with placement in movies and in TV and radio commercials; you're reaching listeners who you have no way of reaching otherwise.

I truly think that licensing to other media has replaced radio as the most effective means of promoting new music today. I wish that weren't the case, as it kind of feels like selling out, but you have to go with what works. So until something different comes along (and it always does), both songwriters and performers should be pursuing placement in all types of media. It's like getting paid to advertise.

The Least You Need to Know

- ◆ Licensing music to films, TV shows, and commercials is a way to both generate income and promote your music.

- ◆ Songwriters can license the songs they write; performers can license the recordings they make.

- ◆ Another alternative is to license existing music or write new music for stock music libraries—which then license the music, royalty-free, to all manner of productions.

- ◆ For composers, writing for television, movies, and video games can be a lucrative profession.

- ◆ While not as big a business as it used to be, jingle writing for radio and TV commercials is still a good way to break into and make money from the music business.

Chapter 17

The Business of Music Online

In This Chapter

- ◆ How the Internet changed the music business
- ◆ Dealing with illegal downloads
- ◆ Promoting your music online
- ◆ Creating your own website and MySpace pages
- ◆ Selling your music and merchandise online
- ◆ Other creative ways to distribute your music

There is no denying that the Internet has changed the music business forever. The shift from physical CDs to digital downloads (both free and paid), the ability to connect directly with fans, the need to maintain websites, blogs, the creation of MySpace and Facebook pages—it's all part of the Internet effect, and indicative of how the music business works today.

On the plus side, the Internet has made it easier for musicians to forego major-label indentured servitude and pursue independent careers. On the minus side, the Internet has enabled rampant piracy, a decline in total industry revenues, 24/7 tweeting, and a kind of stalker mentality among some fans. Good or bad, however, the Internet has to be dealt with and incorporated into the plan for your musical career.

How the Internet Has Changed the Music Business

Let's recap what the world was like prior to the mid-1990s Internet explosion. Back then, virtually all music was sold on physical media (CDs by then), either in brick-and-mortar stores or in direct-mail record clubs. If a fan wanted to contact an artist, she did so by writing a letter, putting a stamp on it, and dropping it into the nearest Post Office mailbox. And artists had few ways to let their fans know of upcoming releases and appearances, short of advertising in local media or giving newspaper and magazine interviews.

Fast forward about 15 years and almost everything has changed. Most of the big record store chains (and many local independents) are now out of business, as more and more listeners both buy CDs and download individual songs over the Internet. Fans contact their favorite artists via e-mails and messages on online forums. And artists have a number of different ways to interact with fans and promote the latest happenings, from websites and blog postings to messages on Twitter and Facebook.

Changes in Distribution

If you're used to purchasing your music on CDs, here are some surprising statistics. First, the International Federation of the Phonographic Industry (IFPI) estimates that in 2008, fully 20 percent of recorded music sales were in the form of digital downloads. According to Nielsen SoundScan, that meant that there were more than one billion digital tracks legally downloaded in 2008—up 28 percent from the previous year.

The practical impact of this shift from CDs to digital downloads is significant. First, the changes in distribution have shifted the financial dynamics of the industry. No longer are major labels necessary to distribute physical product; instead, smaller labels and independent artists can distribute their own product via online stores and download services. The freedom for independent artists is there for the taking.

Digital downloading has also presaged a change from long-form productions to individual songs. Listeners can now download individual tracks, for about a buck apiece, instead of spending $15 or more for a full CD—on which there's only a song or two they wanted to listen to, anyway. That changes—or should change—the way artists approach their craft, both financially and musically.

Changes in Promotion

The Internet not only makes it easier to distribute product, it also makes it easier to communicate with both existing and potential customers—fans, if you will. Thanks to e-mail and Twitter and blogs and such, the cost of contacting a fan via the Internet is essentially zero (after initial setup costs, anyway). You don't have to take out ads, you don't have to put stamps on envelopes; all you have to do is post a message, electronically. The Internet does the rest.

Along with this lower cost is a greater ease in communication. How hard is it, after all, to post a 140-character message on Twitter? Or to post a slightly longer message to a blog or your MySpace page? You don't have to devote a lot of time to spreading your message; you can do it from your cell phone, if you want.

That said, there is now an expectation of communication that didn't exist before. If you're essentially a private individual, the Internet is not a friendly place. Fans now demand some form of interaction with their favorite artists; if you go more than a week without blogging or tweeting, they'll lose interest. This means that being a musician in the Internet age is about more than just making music—it's also about communicating in a variety of media on an almost-constant basis. Like it or not, that's the way it is.

The Rise of the Independent Artist

All these changes put more power—and responsibility—in the hands of the artist. In the pre-Internet days, artists had to rely on major labels to both distribute their music and communicate to the public. Not anymore; artists can now handle their own distribution and promotion.

This means, of course, that you don't really need a deal with a major record label, at least not in the same way you did a few decades ago. Assuming that you have the time and inclination to handle the details, you can distribute and promote your own music, no middleman necessary. That means you now have the kind of creative and financial control that major labels seldom allow.

But what if you don't want to deal with the dirty details of distribution and the continual demands of online promotion? Well, you could still contract with a major label to do it all for you, or you could hire freelance firms or individuals to handle the various pieces and parts. Just because you're not an online wiz doesn't mean you can't benefit from the Internet; lots of people out there can help you do what needs to be done—for a fee, of course.

Dealing with Illegal Downloads

The Internet has brought both positive and negative changes to the world of music. But one of the most negative effects of the Internet is the significant rise in music piracy, enabled by illegal music downloads.

The Spread of Piracy

Piracy, of course, has been around forever. Back in the 1970s, for example, I did my share of illegal copying. I wasn't able to download pirated tracks, of course, since the Internet didn't exist then. Instead, one guy in our dorm would buy an album and the rest of us would make illegal copies on cassette tapes. Still, that was piracy, just like the type we have today.

> ### Behind the Music
>
> The record industry's obsession with piracy isn't new. Not that I claim any personal responsibility, but a slide in music sales in the late 1970s led the RIAA to campaign for a tax on blank audio cassette tapes, essentially to fund a *de facto* royalty that would compensate record companies for claimed lost sales due to illegal recording.

Today's music piracy, however, is more widespread, in part because it's easier to do. One person somewhere in the world buys a copy of a CD and then rips that CD to his computer's hard drive. He then uploads the digital tracks to a file-sharing service, and anyone anywhere in the world can now download that album for free. One legal purchase results in tens of thousands of illegal downloads, all thanks to the Internet.

The recording industry has tried to crack down on this illegal downloading, of course, through various scare campaigns and legal actions. Many illegal download sites have been shut down, but new ones have just as quickly arisen. The result is that illegal downloading continues to thrive, particularly among cash-strapped high school and college students, to the detriment of the big labels and the musicians who wrote and performed the downloaded songs.

The Impact of Illegal Downloading

The financial impact of this illegal downloading is difficult to ascertain. The RIAA contends that illegal downloading is the cause of the sharp decline in physical CD sales, and has released various studies that purport to prove this. Several independent researchers, however, have released competing studies that show just the opposite.

I tend to side with those who say that illegal downloading has a negligible effect on sales. To support this theory, take a look at the 2004 report "The Effect of File Sharing on Record Sales: An Empirical Analysis," where researchers Felix Oberholzer-Gee of the Harvard Business School and Koleman S. Strumpf of the University of North Carolina at Chapel Hill showed that illegal downloads essentially have zero impact on record sales. According to their analysis, it would take close to 5,000 individual downloads to reduce the sales of an album by a single copy. That's because most downloaders are individuals who would not have bought the album in the absence of downloading; in other words, downloaded tracks are in addition to those that would have been purchased normally.

> **Behind the Music**
>
> The two researchers contrast their study, based on direct data obtained from music downloaders, with the surveys conducted by the music industry. Surveys, voluntarily completed by participants, are inherently less reliable than raw data.

The RIAA countered by noting that total sales of Top 10 albums, according to SoundScan data, declined from 60 million units in 2000 to 33 million units in 2003. (It's dropped even more since then.) The RIAA contended this sales decline is due primarily to illegal downloads, although they had zero evidence of such a causation. You see, there can be other factors for the decline; maybe popular music isn't as good or as popular as it used to be, or maybe consumers are spending their money elsewhere (on video games, for example). I tend to think it's a mix of all these factors.

Is illegal downloading a huge problem? Maybe, maybe not. I know it's difficult for musicians to think kindly when someone obtains their hard-earned work without compensating them. But there is every indication that illegal downloading is this generation's way of sharing music on the cheap, and in fact may help expose more potential purchasers to one's music. As previously noted, there has always been some degree of music piracy; illegal downloading is just the way it's being done today.

One thing that everyone agrees on, however, is that sales of physical CDs continue to rapidly decline. Whether it's caused by illegal downloading, the genre fragmentation of the market, or some other factor, distribution is shifting from physical product to downloadable digital product—both legal and illegal.

Dealing with Illegal Downloads

What can you do to stop the illegal downloading of your music? The answer is: Not a lot.

Assuming you do want to stop it, one approach is to encode all the music you have available for download with some sort of digital rights management (DRM) technology. This is essentially a form of copy protection that inhibits downloaders from copying a legally downloaded music file, and until recently has been a feature of most legal online music stores.

The problem with DRM is that users hate it. It gets in the way of doing perfectly legal stuff, such as making backup copies and transferring music from one computer to another. In fact, users hate DRM so much that most of the online music stores no longer sell DRM-protected tracks. So there.

Of course, there's really no way to keep users from ripping music from one of your CDs and posting those tracks to a file-sharing site. The RIAA does its best to take legal action against these peer-to-peer (P2P) networks, but as soon as they swat one down another pops up in its place. There was even a campaign to sue individual users who uploaded tracks illegally to P2P networks, but that proved relatively pointless and a huge public relations nightmare; there's nothing like suing poor kids and grandmothers to alienate your entire customer base.

So what can you do to stop illegal downloading? As I said, not much. You pretty much have to learn to live with it—or find a way to turn all those new (illegal) listeners into paying customers in the future.

Promoting Your Music Online

One of the great things about the Internet is how it lets you directly connect with current and potential fans—for little or no cost. You can use the Internet to promote music you have for sale, make people aware of upcoming gigs, even just let people know what you're up to. In this fashion, the Internet is a great leveler; there's nothing the big guys can do that you can't do, too.

Promoting via E-Mail

The oldest and most established form of online promotion is the e-mail mailing list or newsletter. This is where you collect your fans' e-mail addresses and then send out bulk e-mail messages announcing stuff you want to announce—a new CD release, upcoming tour, performance in their town, whatever. E-mail promotion like this is easy, and it's free—unless you hire someone to do it for you, of course.

Where do you get the names and addresses for your e-mail mailing list? There are lots of ways to get these names:

Smart Business

Make sure any e-mail list you assemble is an opt-in list, meaning that your fans volunteer their addresses and agree to receive your mailings. You don't want to send out unsolicited spam messages.

- ♦ Have an e-mail sign-up sheet at all your gigs, preferably at your merchandise table, and make sure you mention it during your performances.

- ♦ If you have an existing postal mailing list, encourage all current subscribers to e-mail you with their e-mail addresses.

- ♦ Create an e-mail sign-up form page on your website.

- ♦ Consider people on your MySpace and Facebook friends lists as members of your e-mail mailing list—that is, send your e-mail notices to all your MySpace and Facebook friends, too.

Once you have a list of addresses, you can send out mailings of any sort on your own schedule. Obviously you want to do big mailings when you have a new album to promote, but you can also notify the list of other happenings—new merchandise in your online store, a new website design, your upcoming performance schedule, you name it. It's a great way to maintain your awareness level with your fans.

In addition, sending out e-mail messages is virtually free—a big advantage over traditional postal mailings. I have a friend who maintains a postal mailing list of more than 700 names, to which he sends a schedule of his band's performances once a quarter or so. Between printing and postage, each mailing costs him over $400. By shifting these mailings to e-mail, he can save close to $2,000 a year—which is real money.

Smart Business

Encourage people to submit their e-mail addresses by giving them a kind of "signing bonus." Offer a free download to anyone giving you their e-mail address; you'd be surprised how many people will give up their contact info for a small gift.

Promoting via Your Website or Blog

Every artist today should have their own website or blog—or both. A blog is good for posting the latest news and announcements, while a full website can do that plus a lot more.

To that end, I like the idea of creating a full-service website that includes a blog section. We'll talk more about creating your own website later in this chapter.

Promoting via Social Networks

Social networking is hot; I dare you to show me anyone under the age of 25 or so who doesn't spend at least a few minutes every day on Facebook, MySpace, or Twitter. As such, many musicians today use these social networks to promote themselves and their music.

def•i•ni•tion

A **social network** is a website that enables virtual communities of people who share interests, activities, or other connections. Each user posts his or her own personal profile on the site; users with similar interests connect as "friends."

MySpace (www.myspace.com) is particularly suited for musicians and other entertainers; as we'll discuss later in this chapter, you can use the site's tools to create your own home page on the site. You use MySpace to build a fan following and then sell or give away your music online.

> **Behind the Music**
>
> To learn more about marketing via social networks, read *The Complete Idiot's Guide to Social Media Marketing* (Jennifer Abernathy, Alpha Books, 2010).

In addition, many performers use Twitter (www. twitter.com) to send out bursts of news and information to their fans. It's easy to create a Twitter account and start posting short (140-character) messages; make sure your tweets are informative, however, and not just self-serving blather.

Whatever social networks you use, know that you have to actively participate to make it work. If you open a Twitter account, you can't expect your fans to follow your tweets unless you tweet with some regularity. Same thing with MySpace and Facebook (and with blogs, for that matter); go too long without posting something new and people will quit following you. You have to feed the beast, as it were, which means going online and writing *something* at least once a week.

Smart Business _____

Whatever presence you have online—a website, blog, MySpace page, or Twitter feed—make sure you promote your presence by displaying the appropriate URLs at your gigs, on your CDs, in your e-mail mailings, and on all your promotional material. You have to make your fans aware of what you're doing online; don't rely on them stumbling over you accidentally.

Promoting via Online Publicity

Publicity is publicity is publicity, but the Internet makes it easier to contact the people you want to contact. You no longer have to send out physical press kits; instead, you can send out virtual press kits, containing key tracks in MP3 format, your bio as a Word file, and your publicity photo in JPG format.

In addition, you now have a new group of influencers to target. There are a lot of music-related blogs on the Internet, as well as influential fan sites. Spend the time to find all the websites and blogs that focus on music like yours, and make sure they're part of your online PR efforts.

Promoting via Online Advertising

Print, radio, and television advertising might be beyond the budget of most independent artists, but not so online advertising. That's because most online advertising costs less than traditional advertising—much less, in fact.

The most common approach is to use Google's AdWords service to purchase so-called *pay-per-click* (*PPC*) advertising. With this type of advertising, you create a small text ad that contains a link to your website. You only pay when someone clicks on the ad to go to your website; you're literally paying by the click.

The way it works is that you purchase (actually, bid on) *keywords* that people search for. When someone searches for a keyword you've purchased, your ad then appears on Google's search results page, in the "sponsored links" section. AdWords ads also appear on other websites that are related to the keywords you've purchased.

def•i•ni•tion _____

Pay-per-click (PPC) advertising is so named because you only pay when someone clicks on the link within the ad. Most PPC ads are small text ads that appear on search results pages or on related websites.

def•i•ni•tion

Keywords are words or phrases that people use as part of their queries on Google and other search sites.

You sign up for AdWords online at adwords.google.com. When you sign up, you tell Google what keywords you want to bid on, how much you want to pay for each keyword, and how much money in total you want to spend. You can set as small or as big a budget as you like, and then drive searchers to your website or blog to listen to and hopefully purchase your music.

For example, if you play jazz in the Dayton, Ohio, area, you might want to purchase the keywords "live jazz" and "dayton." If you're a group named the Rhythm Kings and have a new CD titled *Red Hot Mama*, you might want to purchase the key phrases "rhythm kings" and "red hot mama." You see how it goes.

Behind the Music

Learn more about AdWords advertising in my companion book, *Using Google AdWords and AdSense* (Michael Miller, Que, 2010).

Once you've signed up with AdWords, you specify your keywords and create your ad—three short lines of text, one of which is the URL for your website. Google will then put your ad into the rotation for the keywords you've purchased, and your ad will start appearing on Google and other sites.

Google will run as many ads as your budget allows. If you bid $2 per keyword and set a budget of $20 per month, Google will run exactly 10 ads, no more. If you set your budget at $100 per month, Google will run 50 ads. It's all very by-the-book.

Smart Business

Beyond PPC advertising is the category of banner advertising—those obtrusive ads that stretch across the top of many web pages. Banner advertising is much more expensive than PPC advertising, and therefore out of reach for most independent artists. If you want to advertise online, start with Google AdWords and see where it goes from there.

Creating and Running Your Own Website

It's imperative today for any serious musician to have his or her own website; or, if you're in a band, to have a band website. Your website is where your fans find out about your latest releases and performances. It's also a means to solicit new business—new gigs, songwriting contracts, you name it. It's your face on the web.

Sections of a Successful Website

A good website contains everything that a fan, reviewer, or potential employer might want to know. To that end, consider including the following sections or pages:

◆ **Home page:** Functions as an introduction to you, the artist. Most home pages include a picture of the artist, a blurb about the latest CD release, and some of the artist's music automatically streaming in the background.

◆ **About:** A page that tells people who you are.

◆ **News/announcements:** A page that details the latest happenings—record releases, performance dates, media appearances, you name it.

◆ **Blog:** Different from news and announcements, a place where you, the artist, get to talk directly to your fans via periodic postings.

◆ **Downloads:** A page full of music for fans to download. Some artists like to include a mix of free downloads with paid downloads—the free ones serving to promote the ones you charge for.

◆ **CDs:** A page detailing all your CD releases, with links to purchase the physical CDs online—either on your site or on other online music sites.

◆ **Merchandise:** A page where fans can buy artist merchandise—T-shirts, hats, you name it.

◆ **Performances:** A page listing your upcoming performances.

◆ **Videos:** A page with all the music videos you're produced—if you have any music videos, that is.

◆ **Photos:** Where fans can see pictures of you.

Smart Business

To keep fans coming back to your website, make sure that you keep it updated with fresh content on a regular basis. That means posting updated news, announcements, and blog posts at least once a week.

◆ **Community:** An online message forum where fans can talk about you and your music. (You may even want to participate yourself.)

◆ **Reviews:** A page with the most favorable reviews you've garnered, as well as favorable articles written about you.

◆ **Press:** A page for the working press; this page should contain downloadable pictures, a bio, maybe a few sample tracks.

Of course, these sections aren't set in stone. Some artists like to combine the Downloads, CDs, and Merchandise pages into a single Store page; others put the Blog and News sections right on the home page. Your site should reflect your own personality—and feature an attractive design.

Designing Your Website

Unless you just happen to be an HTML wizard and have lots of free time on your hands, you probably want to contract out for site design and management. The design is typically handled by a freelance web designer or design firm. You can find many such firms in any city or town; there are a lot of website designers out there. Just make sure that the designer knows exactly what you're looking for—and can deliver what you want on the budget you specify.

How much should you spend to design your website? A good design for a decent-size site will run anywhere from $2,000 to $5,000. The more fancy stuff you include— Flash animations, merchandise store, and the like—the higher the cost. Expect to pay extra if you need a logo or artwork designed.

That sounds like a lot of money, and it is, but it's also a one-time cost. Once you get a design you like, let it ride for a year or two. You want your fans to find something familiar when they visit.

Optimizing Your Website for Search

Creating a website is only part of the process. You also need to attract visitors to your website. You want your fans to be able to find your site, as well as to attract new listeners who might become fans.

Most people find websites by searching for them, using Google, Yahoo!, Bing, or some other search engine. As such, you need your site to appear high in the search results when someone searches for you or your type of music.

Behind the Music
Learn more about SEO in my companion book, *The Complete Idiot's Guide to Search Engine Optimization* (Michael Miller, Alpha Books, 2009).

You do this by optimizing your site for search. This is called *search engine optimization*, or SEO for short. It's kind of a technical thing, but it involves making sure that the keywords that people search for appear prominently on your site's key pages. There's more to it than that, of course, so you probably want to engage a third party—such as your website designer—to perform these SEO duties.

Proper SEO is every bit as important as basic site design. Just remember—if your site isn't properly optimized, nobody will be able to find it!

Managing Your Website

The day-to-day management of your website is handled by a webmaster, whom you hire to post news and announcements, add information about your schedule and CD releases, monitor messages on your community forum, just generally keep the content fresh and up-to-date.

Now being a webmaster for a musician's website probably isn't a full-time job. In fact, you may have someone on your team—someone associated with your band, or a friend of a friend—who has the technical expertise to handle webmaster chores. Alternatively, you can look for a webmaster among your fans; many fans will jump at the chance to manage your site—for free!

If you can't find someone to manage your website for free, you'll have to pay for a professional webmaster. You'll probably pay an hourly rate; most experienced webmasters earn from $10 to $15 per hour. For most musician's websites, you're talking about a half dozen or so hours per week, so expect to pay between $50 and $100 a week for the webmaster chores.

In addition, you'll need to pay a monthly or yearly fee for web hosting. Web hosting is just what it sounds like, the physical hosting of all your web page files on a web server somewhere. Web hosting firms charge anywhere from $50 to $100 a year, depending on the plan you pick.

Smart Business

If you're not particularly tech-savvy, you may want your webmaster to manage *all* your online activities—your own web page, of course, but also your MySpace page, e-mail mailing list, even your AdWords advertising. Expect to pay more for these additional services, of course.

Managing Your MySpace Page

Of all the social networks, MySpace is the most artist-friendly. Most musicians keep some sort of presence on MySpace; in fact, many use MySpace as their home base rather than a dedicated website.

Creating a MySpace Page

Here's the great thing about MySpace—it's totally free to use. Once you sign up for the site you're prompted to create your profile page. This is your home page on MySpace, the page that all your friends will see.

You can customize your profile page in any number of ways. In addition to choosing your own custom background (called a *theme*), you can include any or all of the following elements on your page:

- ◆ **Blurbs:** Tell visitors a little about you, the artist.

- ◆ **Interests:** Lists your favorite music, movies, television shows, books, and so on.

- ◆ **Details:** Displays more detailed information about you—your marital status, location, astrological sign, and so on.

- ◆ **Contact Info:** Contains links to send e-mail and instant messages. You need to include this section for others to add you to their friends list.

- ◆ **Blog:** A place for you to write your own blog postings.

- ◆ **Images:** Post pictures of yourself or your band.

- ◆ **Music Player:** Upload your music for visitors to listen to while they're viewing your page.

- ◆ **Videos:** Where you can post any music videos for users to view.

- ◆ **Calendar:** A great way to post your upcoming performance schedule.

- ◆ **Friend Space:** Lists all your friends on the MySpace site.

- ◆ **Comments:** Displays comments made by your friends for you and all other visitors to read.

To customize your MySpace profile page, simply click the Profile link on the main menu and select Customize Profile. All your options will now be available.

Smart Business

Facebook (www.facebook.com) is also becoming more music-friendly. You can create what Facebook calls a "fan page" that functions essentially like an online fan club, and then promote your music and appearances to all your fans (friends) on the site.

Selling Your Music on MySpace

You can also sell your music on MySpace, as downloadable MP3 files. MySpace uses a company called Snocap to handle its music sales. Go to www.snocap.com to learn more.

When you sign up for the service, Snocap places a store module on your profile page. You determine which tracks you want to sell, and for how much per track. Visitors can then preview your tracks and, if they like them, purchase and download them. It's a no-muss solution for you; all you have to do is fill out a few forms and upload the files you want to sell.

Selling Music and Merchandise Online

Given that a fifth of all legal music sales are via online downloads, it's imperative that you have your music available for downloading online. That means placing your tracks for sale on your MySpace page, as we just discussed, as well as on your own website and at the iTunes Store and other online music stores.

We discussed how to distribute your music online back in Chapter 11, so I won't go into those details again here. Suffice to say that you need to turn your website into an e-commerce site, complete with a shopping cart and checkout system. You also need to set up some sort of payment system, typically via PayPal or Google Checkout. Some website hosting firms offer these e-commerce services; your website design firm can also put these pages together for you, and your webmaster can manage the day-to-day sales.

Your website should also include all the nonmusic merchandise you offer for sale. This argues for having a unified "store" section that sells physical merchandise—CDs, T-shirts, baseball caps, posters, you name it. Any item ordered should go directly into the visitor's shopping cart, so that the checkout is a one-stop-shop experience.

Equally important is having your music available for download from the iTunes Store, Amazon MP3 Store, and other online stores. This is actually a fairly easy process, facilitated by firms such as CD Baby, as we've previously discussed. Again, this may be something you want your webmaster to handle; in any case, it's imperative that you place your music everywhere online that users may want to find it.

Other Creative Ways to Distribute Your Music

This last bit kind of falls outside this chapter's focus on the Internet, but there are some other interesting ways to distribute your music that bear examination.

Enhanced Albums

When I say "enhanced albums," I'm not talking about those bastardized "Enhanced CDs" released in the late 1990s that included music videos, computer wallpaper, screensavers, and the like, accessible when you inserted the CD into a computer. Those things went over like a lead zeppelin; listeners wanted to listen to music, not fiddle with unwanted junk stuck on their CDs.

No, today's enhanced albums refer to material added to digital downloads. This is a relatively new thing at the iTunes Store, a way for artists to push complete albums rather than individual tracks. The goal is to include enough valuable material to make it worth the customer's while to pony up the price of a complete album. It may or may not be successful, but it's certainly worth evaluating.

What kinds of extras are we talking about? Apple calls these enhanced albums "iTunes LPs," and they typically come with animated lyrics and liner notes, artist photos, performance videos, and other bonus materials. Yeah, I know, kind of the same thing as those Enhanced CDs that flopped big time. But still, it's worth thinking about.

Ringtones

Here's a way to make money from your music that you may not have thought about. Many artists bring home some big bucks by selling their tunes (or parts of their tunes) as ringtones. Yeah, that's right, ringtones.

Behind the Music
You'll need to edit your original music track to the typical ringtone length of 30 seconds or less. You can use your own audio mixing software to do this, or the tools on the Myxer website.

Probably the best place to start is with a service like Myxer (www.myxer.com) that lets you sell your original music as ringtones. Just sign up for an Artist Account, fill in the appropriate online forms, and then upload the ringtones you want to sell. You can then place modules on your MySpace page and your own website that lets visitors purchase your ringtones from you.

How much money can you make selling your ringtones? A typical ringtone sells for $1.99; if you use Myxer or some similar service, you take home 30 percent of that, or about 60¢ per ringtone purchased. That's about the same amount of money you take home for selling a complete track on iTunes, which isn't a bad deal. It certainly adds up.

Cell Phone Apps

Beyond simple ringtones are cell phone applications—in particular, apps for smartphones like the Apple iPhone. This is a whole other thing, as you'll need to come up with some sort of concept for the application, then find a developer to create the thing, but it certainly bodes well for innovative artists going forward.

For example, Alice in Chains developed an iPhone App that serves as a direct connection between the band and their fans. The "Black Gives Way to Blue" app includes songs, videos, news, social networking, and more, right from the iPhone interface.

You can opt to make money from the app itself, by charging for downloads, or view the app as a new medium for the sale of your music and merchandise. There's little precedent at this point as to which approach is best; this is one you'll have to watch for future developments.

> **Behind the Music**
>
> To learn more about developing applications for the iPhone, check out *The Complete Idiot's Guide to iPad & iPhone App Development* (Troy Brant, Alpha Books, 2010).

Cell Phone Streaming

Then there's the concept of the cell phone as a distribution medium for your music. It's not there yet, but I certainly foresee the day when listeners will get their music over their cell phones, rather than from the Internet or their iPods. This will require completely new streaming audio applications and services, but it's a development I'm sure is coming.

And after all, why should you care how your music is distributed—as long as it *is* distributed? As a musician, you just want people to hear your music, and to be fairly compensated in return. It shouldn't matter whether your music is distributed on vinyl records, compact discs, digital downloads, or streaming audio over a cell phone. Just keep abreast of the latest technological developments and make sure you're playing in all of them. It'll shake out how it shakes out.

Should I Give My Music Away Online?

So far we've focused on the various ways you can sell your music online. But there's something else to consider—giving your music away for free. That's right, I said for *free*. Let me tell you what I mean.

Let's start by recognizing that you're already giving away some of your music for free. That is, some listeners are getting it for free, thanks to illegal downloading, music sharing, and the like. For that matter, you may be giving away some tunes via streaming audio on your website or MySpace page. And let us not forget, when a song of yours gets played on the radio, the audience is listening to that song for free.

The concept behind giving away your music is the same as that behind the radio business. When a radio station plays your song (for free, remember), that serves as exposure and promotion for you and your music. Some percentage of the listening audience will like what they hear and want to buy more, thus leading to increased album sales for you.

With that in mind, why not give away some of your own music in order to spur other sales? Maybe you offer a track or two from your latest album for free downloading from your website, as kind of a teaser for the full CD. Listeners who like the free tunes can then download the rest of the album, or purchase the physical CD online.

Let's go a step further. Consider giving away a complete album—an older album from your catalog—to anyone purchasing a newer album. Or you can do like Prince did, and give away a copy of your latest CD to anyone purchasing a concert ticket; this could spur ticket sales and perhaps enable you to charge a higher ticket price.

Or maybe you give away *all* your music. This is a radical approach, I know, but perhaps there's more money to be made in personal appearances and merchandise sales than there is in traditional music sales. Hook listeners on your music and let that drive sales of tickets, T-shirts, you name it.

I'm not necessarily advocating any or all of these approaches, mind you. All I'm suggesting is that you need to rethink the traditional models of generating revenue. One thing is for sure; if you rely solely on physical CD sales, the future looks bleak. New things are happening, and you need to both be aware of them and take advantage of them. That will require some experimentation on your part, and not a small amount of creativity. But then, as a musician, you should be used to experimentation and creativity. Just apply the same outside-the-box thinking to your business affairs as you do to your music, and you should be fine.

The Least You Need to Know

◆ The Internet has changed virtually every aspect of the music business, from the way music is sold to the way artists connect with their fans.

◆ One negative aspect of the Internet is illegal downloading—the digital generation's way of sharing music without paying for it.

◆ You can use the Internet to promote your music via e-mail mailing lists, websites, blogs, social networks, online publicity, and online advertising.

◆ It's imperative to have your own artist website—as well as your own MySpace page.

◆ You can sell your music from your own website or MySpace page, as well as via online music stores such as Apple's iTunes Store.

◆ Beyond basic Internet downloading, other ways to potentially sell your music include enhanced digital albums, ringtones, cell phone applications, and cell phone streaming.

Part 4

The Music Business for Nonmusicians

There are a lot of nonmusicians in the music business—running the business side of things. If you love music and want a career in the business, you have a lot of choices, from being a manager or agent to working in a studio to working for a major label or publishing company.

Chapter 18

The Business of Managing Musicians

In This Chapter

- ◆ What a personal manager does
- ◆ How to become an artist's manager
- ◆ Careers in business management for musicians

Throughout the first half of this book I dealt directly with helping musicians improve their business skills. But the music business includes more than just musicians; there are a fair number of nonmusicians who support the musicians in the business.

In this chapter, we address some of these nonmusic jobs, focusing on those positions that directly support working musicians. I'm talking about personal management and business management—an artist's manager and financial consultant.

The Business of Artist Management

One of the most significant nonmusic jobs in the music business is that of the personal manager or artist's manager. A personal manager is the manager for a band or solo artist; he directs the artist's career from start to finish.

What a Manager Does

Artist management is important because not all artists are good at managing their careers. Musicians are great at being creative, but not so great at promoting themselves, booking their gigs, negotiating deals, or even planning out where they want to go in the future. That's where the manager steps in, handling the business aspects so that the artist can focus on the creative things.

> **Behind the Music**
>
> Think of the manager as the brains and mouthpiece of the artist. The manager is the guiding light and, needless to say, *the guy who manages things.* The manager's true goal should be the success of the artist, whatever that means and whatever that takes.

What a manager does depends to a degree on what the artist needs him to do and on the stage of the artist's career. An artist just starting out needs slightly different management than one who is ready to sign with a major label.

For a newer artist, one not yet with a major-label contract, expect to do some or all of the following:

◆ Plan out the artist's career path for the next 12 months or so.

◆ Book gigs or instruct a talent agent about the kinds of gigs to book.

◆ Invite members of the media, reviewers, and industry people to key gigs.

◆ Send out music demos to interested labels, radio stations, local media, and online media.

◆ Network with other musicians and club owners to help advance the artist's career.

◆ Help the artist schedule and manage practice sessions.

◆ Arrange and manage recording sessions.

◆ Explore funding opportunities.

At a later state in the artist's career, a manager should step it up a notch, adding the following activities:

◆ Negotiate all deals—with club owners, booking agencies, even record labels.

◆ If the artist stays independent, help arrange distribution deals.

◆ Help decide upon and arrange manufacturing of artist merchandise for sale.

◆ Help assemble and manage the other members of the artist's business team.

Learn more about artist management from the artist's point of view in Chapter 7.

How to Become a Manager

Many managers start out as friends or fans of the artist. The manager, after all, must have the complete trust of the artist; recruiting from close circles is quite common.

I've found that, when it comes to establishing a management relationship, the would-be manager often makes the first move. You find an artist you like, someone you think you can do something with, and you make a proposal. You want there to be a good fit between you and the artist; you also want the artist to have a degree of potential that you think you can help realize.

In this scenario, you may start out doing smaller, more specific things for the artist and work your way in from there. Maybe you start out by offering to manage the artist's website, or organize his live shows. Maybe you do some of this work for free on a volunteer basis, so that the artist can get a feel for you and your work. Then after a period of time, you offer to make the relationship more formal.

Another way into the field is to look for employment with a larger management company. Maybe you start as a lower-level staffer, maybe you start as a junior member, maybe you start as an unpaid intern. The point is to get your foot in the door, work with a few lower-profile clients, and then eventually manage more important clients in the agency's list. The ultimate goal is to wrangle some big-name clients for yourself.

Smart Business

A manager can and often does manage more than one artist. An artist, however, can only have one manager. If you decide to manage multiple artists, it helps if they have something in common; it's difficult for one person to manage a rap artist, a country artist, and a jazz artist, for example. Think of your stable of artists as a portfolio, with all your assets working in concert.

Signing a Management Contract

Whether you work for a large management agency or are the artist's best friend, you need a contract with the artist. You simply can't work without a contract. Fortunately, the contract doesn't have to be fancy, but it does need to spell out what you're obligated to do for the artist and how you will be compensated for your work. The contract also needs a termination date; most management contracts are for two or three years, with some sort of escape clause if either the artist or manager isn't doing (or paying) what they said they would.

Most managers receive a percentage of the revenues that the artist generates. Most managers work on somewhere between 10 and 25 percent of the artist's total revenues, including income from music sales, touring, and merchandising; the exact percentage is negotiable.

Some management contracts also specify some sort of minimum monthly payment, so that the manager is guaranteed some income while the band is making its way up the ladder—but be realistic. If the band isn't making any money yet, it won't have any money to pay the manager. It's better for the manager to be compensated based on the artist's success; the more money the artist makes, the more money the manager makes.

Behind the Music

In addition to the manager's normal compensation, all expenses he incurs on the behalf of the artist should be paid for by the artist. For example, if you take a local DJ out to lunch to talk about the artist's latest release, that lunch is a business expense that should be paid for by the artist. Keep detailed records of all the money you spend, so you can be properly reimbursed.

The Business of Business Management

It's interesting. The personal manager is the high-profile, high-paying gig (assuming the artist hits the big time, that is), but it doesn't require much in the way of training or prerequisites. The business manager is a much lower-profile, lower-paying gig (even if the artist hits the big time), but it requires a lot of education and skills and even certification. So goes the life of a professional bean-counter.

That's right, the business manager is the numbers person on the artist's team; he handles all the financial affairs for the artist. A business manager is part accountant, part financial consultant, and part enforcer when it comes to money matters. But he's also a vital component in an artist's path to success—an artist really can't do without a talented business manager.

What a Business Manager Does

What exactly does a business manager do? While the actual tasks vary somewhat depending on the stage of the artist's career (and how much money is coming in), in general a business manager is expected to …

- ◆ Handle all the bookkeeping and accounting for the artist.

- ◆ Manage an artist's tax obligations and provide tax-planning advice.

- ◆ Accept all payment for the artist's services, then write paychecks to the artist or band members.

- ◆ Evaluate and often help negotiate contracts.

- ◆ Provide financial-planning advice; in some instances, manage an artist's investments.

- ◆ Help the artist prepare and manage an ongoing budget.

> **Behind the Music**
>
> Unless you're dealing with an A-list celeb, you'll likely not have an exclusive relationship with your musician clients. That is, you'll probably have more than one client—although each client will have only one business manager.

In other words, a business manager functions as an accountant, a financial planner, and a contract advisor/negotiator. It's all about the numbers side of the music business. (Learn more about business management, from the artist's point of view, in Chapter 8.)

How to Become a Business Manager

Because of the financial demands, most business managers come from the business world rather than the music world. That's okay; you don't have to know chord progressions to prepare an income statement.

What you do have to know are numbers, inside and out. Most business managers have a degree in accounting or business administration; some even have MBAs. It definitely helps to be a certified public accountant (CPA) or even a certified financial planner (CFP). And any experience you have in managing the financial affairs for entertainers or entertainment-related enterprises is always good.

Assuming the proper training and credentials, the best way to get a gig as a business manager is to contact the artist directly. Not surprisingly, many local bands and musicians just starting out don't yet have business management; they may not even have accountants. You'll need to sell the artist on the services you offer and the benefits you can provide. Point out how you can make the artist more money and you'll likely have a new client.

Getting Paid

Naturally, you should sign contracts with all your clients. You'll want some sort of guarantee of stability, typically in the form of a two- or three-year contract. The contract should specify your exact duties as well as your compensation.

When you first sign a new client, you'll probably charge the artist by the hour, at your going hourly rates. As you step up your involvement with the artist, however, you may want to negotiate something more binding, such as a retainer, a monthly salary, or even a percentage of the revenues the artist brings in. What you charge is directly related to the value you bring your clients; if you're aggressive about pursuing things like underreported royalties, you can probably ask for a bigger slice of the pie.

Do You Need to Be a Musician to Manage Musicians?

Managing musicians is a little like herding cats; it's tough to control people who are by nature resistant to control. But that's what personal managers and business managers try to do: control various aspects of an artist's career. It's a tough job, but somebody has to do it.

The question, though, is whether you need to be a musician to manage musicians. The answer, of course, is no; in fact, musicians often need a clear outside voice to help them deal with their music-related matters. If you try to impose your own musical opinions on an already opinionated group of musicians, fireworks are sure to result.

That said, the best personal managers (we'll exempt business managers from the rest of this discussion; numbers is numbers, after all) do have a musical or cultural viewpoint and vision for their artists. I don't think someone totally disinterested in all things musical would make a good manager for musical artists; not that you have to know how the Aeolian mode works, but it does help if you can talk the talk and generally follow how things are going. That calls for some background in or experience with the world of music, no matter how minor. You are a member of the artist's team, after all—but not a member of the band.

The Least You Need to Know

♦ A personal manager provides direction to an artist.

♦ There's no formal training to become an artist's manager, but it helps if you know a little bit about music—and have a vision for the artist's career.

♦ A business manager handles all the artist's financial affairs.

♦ To become a business manager, you need a solid education and training in accounting and financial management.

Chapter 19

The Business of Booking Musicians

In This Chapter

- ◆ What booking agents do
- ◆ Venue booking
- ◆ How to become a concert promoter

If you love music but prefer to work behind the scenes, consider a career in booking. Whether you work as a booking agent, venue operator, or concert promoter, working in booking lets you hang out with real musicians—often famous ones—while earning a somewhat steady salary. What's not to like?

The Business of Being a Booking Agent

A booking agent—also known as a talent agent—books personal appearances for musical artists. An agent typically has a roster of musician clients and works to book those clients into a variety of venues.

What a Booking Agent Does

So what exactly does a booking agent do? Well, it's more than just joining Artist 1 with Venue 2 and collecting a percent of the proceeds. An active agent is expected to do at least some of the following for his clients:

♦ Establish and maintain contacts with venue operators and promoters.

♦ Advertise his clients' availability.

♦ Set up auditions or meetings between artists and venue operators/promoters.

♦ Arrange gigs for his artist clients at a variety of venues.

> **Behind the Music**
>
> Some booking agents work solo. Others work as part of larger talent agencies. The largest talent agencies, such as the Creative Arts Agency (CAA) and the William Morris Agency, handle entertainment industry clients of all types, from musicians to actors to screenwriters.

♦ Negotiate contracts between artists and venues/promoters.

♦ Help coordinate artist tours.

♦ Help promote his clients' gigs.

♦ Collect payment for performances from venues/promoters and distribute those funds to the artists (minus the agent's commission, of course).

♦ Constantly search for new artists to add to his client list.

Yes, some agents just sit behind their desks all day and wait for the phone to ring. These are not successful agents, however—at least, that's not how they got successful. The best agents work hard to promote their musician clients, and benefit from the success the artist achieves. (Read about booking from the musician's standpoint in Chapter 13.)

What's the Pay?

How much can you make as a booking agent? Well, most agents take 10 to 20 percent off the top of all performance revenues. So if you book a band for a $1,000 wedding reception, you make $100 to $200; if you book a band for a $100,000 regional tour, you make $10,000 to $20,000.

Naturally, you should have a signed contract with all your artist clients. Most agents sign at least a one-year contract; longer contracts encourage agents to book their clients further in advance. The contract should have a termination clause in case you fail to do your job or the artist doesn't hold up his end of the deal. (For example, you could terminate the contract if a band broke up.)

Smart Business

Some agents also receive a portion of ticket sales and CD and merchandise sales made at an artist's gigs. An agent should not receive any royalties from CD sales through traditional channels, digital download, songwriting, or music publishing.

How to Become a Booking Agent

Like most careers in the music business, there's no direct path to becoming a booking agent. That said, many agents start off by working entry-level jobs in the industry. You could get a job as an assistant to a local agent, or as a worker in a large talent agency.

A real-world example is industry bigwig David Geffen, who went on to found Asylum Records. He started in the mailroom at the William Morris agency, moved into the company's talent-agent trainee program, and went onward and upward from there. Similarly, big-time agent Max McAndrew started in the mailroom of International Creative Management (ICM). It's a way to get your foot in the door.

Another path into an agent career is to find work at a local club or concert hall. From there you can get involved with the booking activities of the club or venue, especially if they book their own acts.

Finally, you can enter the profession from the musician's side of things. That is, if you have experience booking your own band, why not branch out and book some other local bands, too? Before long, you can develop a stable of artists that you handle, and keep going from there.

Behind the Music

To protect entertainers from fly-by-night con artists, many states require a special license to be a booking agent. In addition, some states regulate the fees an agent can charge; for example, in California a booking agent can charge no more than a 20 percent commission (10 percent if working with union talent).

The Business of Venue Booking

The booking agent works one side of the table; the concert promoter and venue operator sit on the other side. It's two sides of the same coin, of course, but with very different perspectives.

Some venues book their own acts; others rely on concert promoters. We'll discuss promoters in a few pages, but for now let's focus on booking from a venue's point of view.

Booking Acts for a Venue

Lots and lots of venues book their own acts. Think about it; most local clubs have their own bookers, as do many concert halls, theaters, auditoriums, performing arts centers, and the like. These venues have many issues in common. No matter the size or type of venue, the person doing the booking for the venue has to do the following:

♦ Find acts to perform at the venue.

♦ Put together a long-term schedule of performances for the venue.

♦ Maintain relationships with talent agents and promoters, as well as with local artists.

♦ Negotiate contracts with performing artists.

♦ Manage the facility itself.

♦ Provide the agreed-upon equipment for the artist—possibly including a sound system, lighting system, various musical instruments (pianos are common), and the like.

♦ Provide a space (typically called a *green room*) for the artists before and after the show.

♦ Provide merchandising space for artists.

♦ Possibly provide transportation and lodging for the artists.

♦ Work with the artists while they're at the facility; handle all artist requests and problems.

♦ Provide security for events.

♦ Publicize and promote upcoming events at the facility.

♦ Arrange insurance for the facility—and for any events scheduled.

That's a lot of work, no question about it. And as you can see, the actual booking of artists is just a small—but important—part of the job.

Smart Business

Event insurance is especially important when scheduling outdoor events. You need to be protected if your event is rained out.

The interesting thing is that the tasks involved are pretty much the same whether you're booking for a small jazz club or a large concert hall. You still have to find the acts, sign the contracts, provide the facility and equipment, and handhold the artists while they're there. The job doesn't end at 5:00 P.M.; you'll need to be onsite during all performances to make sure everything goes as planned.

Becoming a Venue Booker

How do you become a venue booker or venue operator? There are two popular paths to this position.

The inside path is to get a job within the venue or organization. Maybe you start as a waiter at a local club or an usher at a concert hall, and then work your way up and in from there. Try to arrange things so that you get to work closer with the current venue operator or booker, even if that means volunteering some after-hours time. Get in close, learn the business, and position yourself for advancement.

The outside path is more common with larger venues. Here you start out by managing smaller venues and work your way up to bigger and better things. Maybe you start by booking bands at a local club and then look for work at larger venues either locally or around the country. This is how you get a job booking talent at Lincoln Center or the Meadowlands.

Behind the Music

Not all venues book their own artists. Many venues, especially larger ones, contract with promoters to handle the booking for them.

The Business of Concert Promotion

Then we have the concert promoter, the middleman between middlemen. A concert promoter works with agents on one hand and venues on the other, booking talent and organizing events.

What a Concert Promoter Does

The job description for a concert promoter looks, unsurprisingly, like a mix of talent agent and venue operator, with a little bit of marketing thrown in for good measure. Here's a short list of what you'll be expected to do:

 ◆ Create musical events, often with two or more artists.

 ◆ Create series of events.

 ◆ Book artists to play scheduled events.

 ◆ Book venues to host scheduled events.

 ◆ Arrange event security.

 ◆ Arrange all necessary equipment, decorations, and services at the venue.

 ◆ Sell tickets to the event, or arrange the services of a ticket-selling service.

 ◆ Publicize and promote scheduled events.

That's a short list, but each task is quite involved. In addition, the promoter may put up his own money to finance an event; for example, the promoter may have to pay a deposit to rent a venue, or an advance to secure a given artist.

How Promoters Work

As a middleman, the promoter can market his services to venues, to artists, or to both. I'll explain what I mean.

As an example of marketing to a venue, consider the promoter who is hired by a venue to book acts for that venue. The venue may pay the promoter either a flat fee for services rendered or a cut of the venue's ticket sales.

As an example of marketing to an artist, consider the promoter who works with a booking agent to put together a tour for an artist. Again, the promoter may receive either a flat fee or a cut of tour revenues.

Finally, many promoters operate independently, renting a venue (either for a fixed fee or a cut of the gate) and then booking artists to fill the event. This is the "classic" promoter model, as typified by the late Bill Graham. This type of promoter creates and promotes his own events, and typically takes most of any profits generated.

> **Behind the Music**
>
> Bill Graham was famous for promoting concerts featuring seminal 1960s rock artists such as Janis Joplin, Jefferson Airplane, and Santana. He later operated the Fillmore East and Fillmore West venues, where the best-known acts of the time played.

How to Become a Promoter

There's no formal training available to become a promoter. All you need is a little seed money, a lot of hard work, and a fair amount of ambition.

That said, many successful promoters began their careers working for other successful promoters. Everybody needs an assistant, and that's always a good way to gain real-world experience.

The thing about being a freelance promoter, however, is that you don't have to have any experience to get started. There are tons of stories of kids still in college scraping up the cash to rent a local club or concert hall, booking a few local bands, and putting on a decent event. That's promoting, folks, and those college kids can work their way up to bigger bands, bigger venues, and bigger events. Start small and soon you'll be promoting bigger things.

What's the Worst That Can Happen?

Handling bookings for musicians is a job full of fun and excitement (look at all the talented people you get to meet!), and equally fraught with complications and crises. As you might suspect, dealing with temperamental, egotistical, often neurotic musicians is not always cookies and cream.

Throughout this book I've told a fair number of stories about how the sharks in the business try to take advantage of innocent musicians. It's only fair, then, that I turn the tables and tell a few stories about how musicians make life difficult for agents and bookers.

First, there's the common story about the little perks that musicians demand backstage or in the green room when they play. Now it's not unusual to have a band request something like a deli tray, some soft drinks and bottled water, that sort of thing; nothing wrong with that. But some of these demands border on the ridiculous: Vegan pate for the Pretenders, Hennessy cognac for Lil Wayne, prune juice for Kansas, soy cheese and Flintstones vitamins for Mariah Carey, cough drops and Tootsie rolls for the late Frank Sinatra, and M&Ms—with all the brown ones removed—for Van Halen. All these demands make the "good-quality" peanut butter and jelly that Jay-Z requests look mundane, don't they?

Then there are the issues that arise at the gig. A friend of mine books acts for a major concert hall in a major Midwestern city, and he recounts the time he booked a famous R&B artist, biggest act of the concert season. Comes performance time, and the artist refuses to exit his hotel room, claiming he hasn't been paid. My friend had made the proper payment, of course, to the artist's agent. But nothing could lure Mr. Big Time Artist out of his suite until my friend cut the artist a brand-new check, made out in the artist's name. He never got a refund on his initial payment, so he ended up paying twice just to get the guy on stage. Needless to say, he didn't make any money on that act.

Bottom line, artists are often eccentric types who need to be handled with kid gloves. If that's in your nature, then you're good to go on the booking side of the business. If you're not into coddling musicians both major and minor, then perhaps you need to look into another position in the profession—something not quite so hands-on.

The Least You Need to Know

♦ A booking agent, also known as a talent agent, represents a portfolio of clients to promoters and bookers; his job is to find work for his clients. Most agents receive a percentage of all revenues earned by their clients.

♦ A venue operator or booker books acts for a specific venue, often working directly with agents and promoters. Most venue operators receive a standard salary from the venue.

♦ A promoter works between agents and venues, lining up acts for specific events. Promoters have to put their own money up front to secure the artists and the venue, but then take the profits that remain after all fees have been paid.

Chapter 20

The Business of Recording and Production

In This Chapter

- ◆ What a producer does
- ◆ How to become a recording engineer
- ◆ Evaluating a career as a studio musician

So far we've looked at careers in artist and business management, as well as booking. Well, other careers can be had in the recording part of the music business. Granted, many recording studios are seeing their business migrate to artists with their own home studios, but there's still a lot of recording being done at all levels, and a lot of people continue to work in the recording business.

There are two main careers in the recording industry: producers and engineers. In addition, there remains some work for studio musicians (the guys who play on other people's recordings), arrangers (the guys who orchestrate music for bands and orchestras), and contractors (the guys who contract with studio musicians for recording dates). We'll focus, however, on the major jobs: producers and engineers.

The Business of Production

A producer, by definition, helps to produce recordings. What that means differs from project to project.

What a Producer Produces

In most instances, the producer is in charge of a given recording. He works with the artist to decide which songs will be recorded, helps to work out the songs' arrangements, schedules the recording studio, hires an arranger/orchestrator if necessary, contracts with the necessary studio musicians, hires or approves of the recording engineer, and pretty much manages the recording sessions.

During the recording session, the producer sits in the booth with the engineer and makes suggestions regarding the recording; he often has the final say (with the artist, in some cases) as to when a recording is acceptable. He also works in the studio itself, coaxing the best performances out of the musicians.

Behind the Music
Producers work one project at a time, but often work multiple projects throughout the year. A producer can be hired either by the artist or by the label; in rare instances, the recording studio hires or supplies a producer for its clients.

The producer also sits in on the mixing process, to help create the final version of the recording. He helps pick the final songs that go on the finished album. And if the artist is signed to a major label, the producer reports back to the label regarding the status of the recordings.

As you can tell, a producer has a lot of power and creative control. In some instances, the producer runs the entire show; in others, he works in cooperation with the artist. In either instance, he's the guy in charge; what he says, goes.

Breaking Into the Business

How do you get started in the producing business? Well, it's certainly a position to aspire to, not one you start out at. One becomes a producer only after years and years of training.

That training typically starts by apprenticing with an experienced producer. That might mean working as an assistant or unpaid intern, doing the work of a glorified gofer. You may also be able to break into the biz by working at a recording studio and making contacts that way. In addition, many producers start out as engineers and then progress from one chair in the booth to another.

Behind the Music
As with all recording-industry jobs, there are fewer producers today than there used to be. Thanks to the upswing in home recording, fewer recording sessions are being booked into professional studios. And while all projects can benefit from the hand of an experienced producer, artists recording in their own homes don't always bring in an expensive outside producer. So while the big-name producers will always be in demand, there look to be fewer jobs for producers overall going forward.

Producers get paid for their time and for their success. Their time is paid for by an up-front advance, anywhere in the $10,000 to $50,000 range, with the lower value being the most common; the price depends on the producer's reputation and the length of the project.

In addition, most producers negotiate a percentage of the album's revenues, in terms of "points." One point is worth 1 percent of revenues generated, and producers typically negotiate deals guaranteeing anywhere from one to five points per album. So if a $15 album sells 100,000 copies, generating $1,500,000 in revenues, a producer with a "three-point" deal earns 3 percent of that total, or $45,000.

Smart Business

A producer's points are typically paid only after the advance has been earned out. So if a producer gets a $10,000 advance and then earns $45,000 in points, he'll only receive an additional $35,000—the $45,000 earned minus the $10,000 advance.

The Business of Engineering

It's important to note that the producer does not himself make the recording. That is done by the recording engineer, which is another popular career path in the recording industry.

What an Engineer Does

The recording engineer handles the actual recording of a song or album. He and his staff are responsible for setting up and micing the instruments in the studio, setting the input levels and equalization for each mic and instrument, and mixing everything together to make a completed song. The engineer "works the faders," as the phrase goes, to ensure the best-sounding recording. He isn't responsible for what gets recorded (that's the producer's job), but rather for how the recording sounds.

Behind the Music

Not all engineering projects involve recording individual songs for popular artists. Engineers also record classical pieces for orchestras and choirs, soundtracks for movies and TV shows, and advertising jingles for radio and TV commercials. In short, every recording made in a major studio has to have an engineer behind the board.

A recording engineer can be employed by a major recording studio, in which case he earns a regular weekly salary. These days, however, many experienced engineers work freelance, which means being paid either on a per-project or hourly basis. Rates vary depending on your name and experience; you might start out in your career earning $5 or $10 per hour, but after many years of work end up getting $100/hour or even a few thousand dollars per song.

Pursuing a Recording Career

Some recording engineers get their start running live sound for bands or clubs. Others start as apprentices to more established engineers, or for large recording studios. A select few learn on their own in home studios, but this isn't a very good path to success in professional studios, primarily because you don't make any contacts.

You can get a leg up on the competition by attending recording classes at a qualified music school, or at a school that specializes in audio recording. There's a lot to learn, not only about working the mixing board but also about mic choice, placement, and the like.

Know, however, that engineering jobs tend to be clustered in that handful of major cities that host the largest and most popular recording studios. That means you may need to relocate to Los Angeles, New York, or Nashville—or be happy with whatever opportunities exist in your local studios. (Learn more about recording from the artist's point of view in Chapter 9.)

> **Behind the Music**
>
> As with producing, the move to home recording has dramatically affected the engineering profession. With more and more artists making their own home-based recordings, there is simply less work for even the most talented engineers. Artists who make home recordings seldom if ever employ professional engineers—although they probably should. But that's another story ....

Should I Pursue a Career as a Studio Musician?

Most recording-related jobs are for nonmusicians—producers, engineers, and the like. But there is a way for a performing musician to make a living in the studio: As a professional studio musician.

A studio musician makes his living playing on other people's recordings. A band needs an extra keyboard player for a specific track? They call in a studio musician. An artist wants to sweeten some tracks with a string section? He calls in the appropriate number of studio musicians. A singer needs a backing band for an album? She calls in a bunch of studio musicians.

In the old days (pre-1975 or so), studio musicians were responsible for the bulk of albums recorded in popular music. A singer would come in the studio and sing to the backing tracks recorded by the studio pros; even working bands used studio musicians to lay down quality tracks fast.

But with the rise of self-contained bands in the 1960s, the need for studio musicians decreased. The old studio system was replaced by bands recording as a whole, and later by artists forsaking studios completely for home recording. While the studio system still exists full-bore in country music, aside from Nashville (and, to a lesser degree, New York and Los Angeles), studio musicians have had to find other places to play.

It's a shame that studio playing is on the decline, as experienced studio musicians bring an unparalleled level of professionalism to a recording. I bemoan the quality of playing on most albums produced in the past few decades; I miss the solid playing of studio pros like Hal Blaine, Larry Knechtal, Carol Kaye, and Tommy Tedesco. In the heyday of studio recording, these cats played on two or three dates per day for different artists, and brought home big salaries for their work. Most of today's artists could improve the quality of their recordings by hiring cats like these; there's only so much you can fix with Pro Tools, after all.

But that's the way it used to be; today, studio work is hard to come by and doesn't pay much, unless you're an established star in your own right. There's a small cadre of studio players in select locations—New York, Los Angeles, and Nashville—and it's tough to break into this select group. To get hired at all, you need both stellar contacts and super chops—not only playing but also sight reading. Only the best of the best get work, and there's not much work to go around.

So while playing in a studio might be appealing, it's not a realistic career choice today. Unless you live in one of the major recording centers, there simply won't be much work at all. And even in these cities, you'll have to work long and hard just to get your foot in the door. No, as much as I admire the art of studio musicians, I can't recommend that musicians today pursue this type of career.

The Least You Need to Know

◆ A producer is the driving force behind a recording, helping to pick songs, choose musicians, and ensure the best possible result.

◆ An engineer is the person who actually makes the recording; he is responsible for instrument setup, mic placement, and working the board during the recording.

◆ Studio musicians are used to supplement a band's normal musicians during the making of a recording.

◆ Due to the rise in home recording, there is much less call for producers, engineers, and studio musicians today than in the past.

Chapter 21

The Business of Distributing Music

In This Chapter

- ◆ What the A&R department does
- ◆ Different jobs in marketing and promotion
- ◆ All about the publicity department
- ◆ Comparing jobs at major and minor labels

Some of the biggest employers in the music business are the record companies. There are lots of jobs available at any of the Big Four companies or their associated labels, or with the numerous independent labels. Both types of companies offer a variety of different jobs ideal for the music-loving nonmusician.

The Business of A&R

If you like hanging out and working with musicians, the best label jobs can be found in the A&R department. A&R stands for *artists and repertoire*, and this department is responsible for finding new talent and developing an artist's career. An A&R guy is like a talent scout, scouring local clubs and record stores for independent artists who are ready to break into the big time.

What A&R Does

The A&R department scouts new talent. That means listening to demo CDs and MP3s, visiting clubs, and keeping abreast of the playlists of college and independent radio stations—keeping abreast of those new artists that have the most potential for a label contract.

> **Behind the Music**
>
> It's also normal for an A&R guy to work directly with record producers to manage the artist's recording process, often helping to choose the songs that the artist records.

Once a new artist is targeted, A&R signs and manages the artist, at least within the company. The A&R department interfaces with all the other departments at the company—marketing, publicity, distribution, you name it—to get the most out of the artist. The A&R department, then, shapes the artist's image and guides his career.

Exploring Different A&R Jobs

A&R isn't a single position, at least not at a major record label. In fact, there are three levels of A&R jobs at most major companies:

   ◆ **A&R representatives** (sometimes called *A&R scouts*) are the feet on the street, looking for new talent. Starting salaries are in the $20,000 range, plus expenses, although experienced major-label A&R people can earn $80,000 or more per year.

   ◆ The **A&R manager** (sometimes called the *A&R director*) makes the decision on whether to sign a new artist. He also negotiates contracts and interfaces within the company on the behalf of the artist. Salaries start at $80,000 and go up from there.

   ◆ The **A&R head** runs the entire A&R department. This is a true corporate management job, rather than a hands-on working position. These guys pull down the big bucks.

Obviously, most people start as an A&R rep, then after a fair amount of experience move into an A&R manager job. Only the best of the best become heads of the A&R department; this is something to aspire to long-term only.

> ### Behind the Music
>
> As with many record industry jobs, there is less and less call for traditional A&R today, largely due to the continuing shift from major labels to independent labels and self-distribution. An A&R guy has a lot of selling to do to get an artist to sign with a major label; it's not the slam dunk it used to be.

Pursuing an A&R Job

If you aspire to a career in A&R, there are many ways to start. Many A&R guys start out as musicians, later transitioning to the other side of the table. Others start in radio or retail, or start at the label in another position or even as an intern before moving into A&R. Even with the changes in the industry, competition for A&R jobs is intense.

Because A&R is concentrated with the major labels, most jobs to be had are in (you guessed it) New York, Los Angeles, and Nashville. Once you're in, expect to spend a lot of hours on the road. You'll stay up late visiting a lot of clubs and listening to a lot of bands. It's a lot of work, but it's fun—and, if that's your thing, you get to hang with a lot of different musicians. (Learn more about how record companies work, from the artist's point of view, in Chapter 10.)

Smart Business

An A&R person needs a good ear and a sense for what's hot—what the music-buying public will buy. That's not necessarily the best music out there, but rather the most commercial. Record labels, after all, are in business to sell a lot of records; noncommercial artists, by definition, do not make for good business.

The Business of Marketing and Promotion

A&R isn't the only important department at a major record label. Also key are back-office departments, such as accounting and legal, and the ever-present marketing department.

Marketing is a very important function at any size record label. The marketing department is responsible for promoting new releases, which is done via advertising, publicity, and other similar activities. It's typically a big department with staff performing a variety of marketing-related duties.

Exploring Music Promotion Jobs

Without promotion, no one would ever know about a new artist. No one would ever hear about a new release. No one would learn about a new club or concert venue. People, places, and things need to be promoted to gain the attention of the intended audience.

Promotion involves a lot of different activities. You can promote an artist or event in any or all of the following ways:

◆ Purchasing ad space in traditional print media, like newspapers and magazines

◆ Buying commercial time on radio or television stations

◆ Handing out or tacking up flyers or one-sheets

◆ Putting the word out on the artist's or venue's website or blog

◆ Managing an e-mail or traditional mailing list for the artist's fans or venue's customers or subscribers

This means that there are a lot of different jobs in the marketing and promotion department, especially at major labels. It's typical to start as a "jack of all trades" marketing assistant, and then begin to specialize in a specific aspect of marketing as your career progresses. (Learn more about promotion and publicity from the artist's point of view in Chapter 12.)

Smart Business

Beyond the major labels, there are lots of jobs available in music promotion. Independent artists sometimes hire their own full-time or contract promotions people; concert halls, music clubs, and other venues have promotion staff or hire freelance promotions people; and, of course, radio and television stations have promotions staff, as well. You could choose to work directly with artists as a freelancer, for a major label, or for the places where musicians play.

Exploring Public Relations Jobs

Another important aspect of marketing is publicity—which is its own career path. While a promotions person basically spends money to promote the client, a publicist works a network of contacts to get other people in various media to talk about the client. We're talking public relations here, which isn't about paid placements but rather word of mouth.

Publicists try to get reviewers to review a show or CD. They try to get reporters and columnists to write about an artist or event. They try to get bloggers to blog about musicians and venues. They try to get mentions, however brief, in newspaper and magazine articles, on radio and TV shows, and on websites and blogs.

To get the word out, publicists spend a lot of time on the phone, and even more on their computers, sending out e-mails, instant messages, and such. A key PR tool, of course, is the press release, which these days can be either hard copy or electronic. A publicist will send out a press release to a list of appropriate contacts to get the word out about the artist or event that's being promoted.

> **Smart Business** _____
>
> While most large record labels have in-house publicity departments, many publicists work freelance, either for themselves or for larger PR firms. As such, publicists are often engaged for specific projects—to push a new CD, to publicize an upcoming tour, to get the word out about a concert series at a major venue. Billing can be either by the hour or by the project; better-known publicists bill more than those just starting out.

Pursuing a Career in Music Marketing

In many ways, the marketing department is the easiest way into a record company. You'll need a degree in marketing, of course, but hiring in as a marketing assistant (or unpaid intern) is a lot easier than trying to score a job in the A&R department. Once you're in the marketing side, you may then be able to slide into A&R, if that's where your real interests lie, or you can stay in marketing and work your way up through the department.

Another approach is to join the marketing department of a smaller, independent label, and then, after you've established yourself, make the jump to a major company. In addition, many staffers start out as freelancers before joining with a major label.

Salaries are all over the place, depending on your level and your specialty. If you're looking to get hired, you'll probably have to go through the company's human resources department—although it never hurts to have a contact or two within the company who can vouch for you.

Is It Better to Work for a Major Label or an Independent?

I mentioned it in passing, but it's important to know that both major and independent labels have A&R and marketing departments. These departments function pretty much the same whether you're at a big label or a small one.

You may set your ultimate sights on working for Sony BMG, but it may be more realistic to start at a smaller independent label. For one thing, indie labels are easier to get hired into; the competition is a little less fierce. Equally important is location; while the majors are congregated in New York, Los Angeles, and Nashville, you may very well have an independent record label in your own town.

And here's something else. With the shift from major labels to independents, the indies are in need of more talented people than ever before. In the coming years it's likely that the indie companies will have more openings to fill than the majors will, which means this may be the best place to look for a job of any sort.

The Least You Need to Know

- ◆ The A&R department is charged with scouting, signing, and managing new talent; for many people, this is the "sexy" department within a label.

- ◆ The marketing department is charged with promoting a label's artists, via advertising, publicity, and other activities.

- ◆ The publicity department helps get the word out about new releases.

- ◆ Both major and independent labels have similar jobs—although it's often easier to get in the door of a smaller label.

Chapter

22

The Business of Publishing and Licensing Music

In This Chapter

- ◆ What a music publisher does
- ◆ Different jobs in music publishing: A&R/creative, production/editorial, sales/marketing, rights administration, and accounting/royalty
- ◆ How to get a job at a music publishing company

Music publishing companies do more than just publish sheet music; they also manage the use of those songs that they publish. Put another way, the music publisher is charged with administering, exploiting, and collecting royalties for its copyright properties.

As such, there are a variety of jobs available in the music publishing business. Whether you're an extroverted salesperson type or an introverted numbers person, there's probably a job for you at a big publishing company.

What a Publishing Company Does

So what exactly goes on inside a music publishing company? It's a mix of marketing, sales, and accounting.

It all starts with the songwriters. A publishing company has to sell its services to songwriters, in order to sign them up as clients. This means seeking out new talent, evaluating demos (in both audio and written format), making contacts at clubs and concert halls and music industry events, just generally trolling for songwriters who don't yet have a publishing contract—and then persuading them to sign with your particular publishing house.

Once a songwriter is signed up, the publishing company has to promote that person's songs. That means pairing a song with a performer, placing songs in movie soundtracks and TV shows, just generally seeking exposure for the publisher's catalog of songs. A song, after all, doesn't earn anybody any money by just sitting there. Songs have to be placed in order to be profitable, for both the songwriter and the publishing company.

Once a song is placed, however, then the detail work begins. The administrative work actually begins when a songwriter writes a song; at this point, the publisher has to file a notice of copyright with the U.S. Copyright Office. Then the publishing company works alongside the major performing rights organizations (ASCAP, BMI, and SESAC) to track recordings and performances of each song in its catalog. Royalties are then collected, paperwork is shuffled from one desk to another, and royalty checks are cut to the songwriters. This is actually a very involved process that involves the majority of a publishing company's employee base.

Smart Business

If a publishing company finds that a song has been recorded or performed without proper compensation, then it has to engage its legal staff. In most cases, infringing use is dealt with without going to court; the threat of legal action is most often enough to make the infringing parties pay up. But you still need the lawyers to issue nasty notices and such, so that's a big part of any publishing company, as you might expect.

The final thing a publishing company does is actually publish music, in the form of printed sheet music and music books. This part of the company is charged with putting together sheet music compilations, packaging individual sheet music and compilations, and then selling and distributing these items to music stores around the world. This is traditional packaging, marketing, and sales, applied to the sheet music business.

Exploring A&R/Creative Jobs

Let's start our look at jobs inside a publishing company by focusing on the A&R or Creative department. This department is like the A&R department at a record label; it's responsible for seeking out and signing new songwriting talent. To do this, the staff listens to demos submitted from aspiring songwriters, as well as attends live performances. The goal is to find songwriters whose material will be particularly marketable.

Once a songwriter is signed, the A&R department is charged with getting that client's songs used in as many places as possible. That means submitting songs to performing artists, record labels, you name it. The more exposure for a song, the more income it can generate.

> **Behind the Music**
>
> The A&R department is also charged with working with their songwriters to help them improve their craft, sometimes pairing composers with lyricists to create new songwriting teams.

Exploring Licensing Jobs

While the A&R department is charged with placing songs with performers and record producers, the licensing department is charged with placing songs in other media. That means working with movie and television producers to license songs from the publisher's catalog in films, TV shows, commercials, video games, and the like. Licensing department staff must establish strong relationships with their licensing counterparts in these other entertainment industries, which often means working where movies and TV shows are made—in Hollywood.

Exploring Production/Editorial Jobs

Let's not forget that a music publishing company also publishes sheet music. The production and editorial departments are responsible for getting a client's songs into printable format. That means transcribing any songs submitted in audio format; editing, revising, and even rewriting submitted music; and converting submitted music into proper sheet music format.

These departments are also responsible for putting together sheet music collections. These might be songs performed by a particular artist, songs from a Broadway show or movie, or collections on a theme or for instructional purposes. It's all about creating a product for retail sale—complete with fancy cover.

Exploring Sales and Marketing Jobs

All that sheet music has to be sold, and that's where the sales and marketing departments come in. The sales staff is responsible for getting sheet music placed in major music stores across the nation, while the marketing staff is responsible for promoting those releases. It's standard sales and marketing stuff, geared specifically to the needs of the sheet music market.

Exploring Rights Administration Jobs

The bulk of the jobs in a publishing company, however, are not very sexy. Most of the staff is responsible for monitoring and administering the use of the company's songs.

First up is the rights department, which deals with contractual issue. This includes contracts with songwriters, of course, but also contracts with licensors, foreign sub-publishers, and the like.

This department is also responsible for taking legal action when contracts are infringed. For example, if a rapper uses a sample of a copyrighted song without prior agreement or permission, the rights department steps in and takes the appropriate legal steps to protect its copyright—and obtain all royalties due.

Exploring Accounting and Royalty Jobs

A large number of staff in a music publishing company deals with record keeping. The accounting and royalty departments track the use of all the company's songs and collect royalties owed. They then make the appropriate royalty payments to the company's songwriters. It sounds simple, but it's a lot of work—and is where you'll find the bulk of the company's job openings.

The most common job in the accounting and royalty departments is alternately called an administrator or coordinator. In general terms, this position is charged with tracking and maximizing royalty collections. This person analyzes statements to identify royalties due, and initiates appropriate actions to collect payments in cases of unauthorized use or infringement. This position is also responsible for creating data and reports for company management.

What do you need to get a job in the accounting or royalty departments? Strong organization skills are a must, as is experience with Excel spreadsheets and Access databases. An accounting degree isn't necessary, but some accounting experience is.

Pursuing a Career in Music Publishing

If music publishing interests you, how do you go about breaking into the industry? Well, music publishing is probably the most traditional of all music-industry occupations, and as such a music publishing company functions pretty much like any other large company or corporation.

That means that to get a job with a publishing company, you need to go through that company's human resources department. Look for open positions, submit a resumé, and be prepared to interview. Naturally, if you have music industry experience or contacts, you have a bit of a leg up. But getting a publishing job is little different from scoring a job at any corporate headquarters.

Where Is the Music Industry Located?

So you're interested in a job in the music industry. Where exactly are these jobs, geographically speaking?

If what you want is a job in a club or working for a concert hall or similar venue, then you don't need to look any further than your hometown. The music *performance* industry is highly localized, with lots of places for musicians to play (and nonmusicians to work) in virtually every city and town across the United States.

If what you want is a job in a large, music-related company, however, your hometown may not be the place to be. That's because the big record labels and music publishing companies—and the companies that serve them—are pretty much centralized in just three locations: New York City, Los Angeles, and Nashville. Unfortunately, you won't find too many big music companies outside of these three cities.

New York City has been one of the centers of the American music industry since the late 1880s, through the Tin Pan Alley and Brill Building eras of the twentieth century, to today. Many music publishers and record labels continue to be based there; NYC is also home to several music-related magazines, such as *Blender* and *Rolling Stone*.

Los Angeles is the West Coast equivalent of New York City, home to the biggest record labels and their associated publishing companies. It's also home to the TV and movie industries, which provide lots of work to musicians and music companies. Los Angeles is also host to a number of still-thriving recording studios, so there's some work for producers, engineers, and studio musicians.

Nashville, of course, is the home of country music, and is home to all manner of music publishers, record labels, talent agencies, and the like that cater to country artists and audiences. It's also a big recording hub, and one of the few places left where studio musicians and professional songwriters both flourish.

That doesn't mean that there aren't music scenes outside of these three cities; there are many local and regional music hubs across America. But nowhere else has the same concentration of music-related *businesses*, the big companies that employ most of the nonmusicians in the music business.

If you want to find work at a record label or music publishing company, then, you're advised to move to one of these three major cities. While some work might exist in Chicago or Miami, the bulk of the jobs are on either coast or in Nashville. That's just the way it is.

The Least You Need to Know

- ◆ Music publishing companies seek out songwriters and then manage the use of their clients' songs.

- ◆ The A&R/creative department scouts and signs new talent, and then works to place clients' songs with other artists and record producers.

- ◆ Similarly, the licensing department works to license songs for TV shows, movies, commercials, and the like.

- ◆ The production/editorial department publishes sheet music that is then sold and promoted by the sales and marketing departments.

- ◆ The rights administration department deals with contractual and legal issues.

- ◆ The accounting and royalty departments track, collect, and pay all royalties due.

Part 5

The Legal Side of the Music Business

Copyrights, licenses, and royalties, oh my! There are a lot of legal issues for professional musicians, from simple gig contracts to complicated music publishing deals. Learn how to negotiate your way through the legal maze—and get what's rightfully yours.

Chapter 23

The Business of Contracts

In This Chapter

◆ Understanding contracts

◆ When you need a contract

◆ How to negotiate a contract

◆ Common contractual clauses

◆ How to spot a bad deal

The legal side of the music business is all about contracts. You deal with contracts when you agree to perform at a given venue. You deal with contracts when you sign with a record label. You deal with contracts when you sign with a music publishing company. You deal with contracts if you license your music for use in movies or TV shows. You even deal with contracts—or you should, anyway—when you form a band.

Contracts, contracts, everywhere. But if you're not a lawyer, how do you navigate your way through the maze of legal terms of clauses? While it's always advisable to consult with an entertainment attorney, you have every reason to become a little knowledgeable yourself about all the legal whys and wherefores—the better to keep from being taken advantage of.

What a Contract Is

Every interaction you have with another person, organization, company, or venue is a contractual interaction—whether or not you have anything written down on paper. You agree to do something for another person or entity, in return for that person or entity doing something for you.

For example, a simple contract for playing a club date can be summed up as you agree to play at the club on a given date; in return, the club will pay you a specified number of dollars. Put that in writing, and you have a formal contract.

Smart Business

You can have verbal contracts, of course, where you and the other party essentially have a handshake agreement to do what you need to do. However, while verbal agreements are legally binding, they're difficult to enforce; that's because it's difficult if not impossible to prove who agreed to what. It's always better to have a written contract, even for what appear to be small issues.

A contract should be written, with all the main details spelled out within the body of the contract. In fact, the more details you can include, the better; try to think of all contingencies—anything that might come up—and put them on paper, too.

Smart Business

If you find a clause in the contract that needs to be changed, strike out the original wording, write in the new section, and initial the new section in the margin.

The contract needs to be signed and dated by both parties. You could go to the trouble to have a contract notarized, but that's not really necessary to establish its legal status. Just sign it and date it, and make sure the other party does, too.

Once you sign a contract, you should keep a copy of it on file in case something goes wrong—either you or the other party doesn't deliver as promised. Then you can use the contract to take legal action against the nonperforming party.

When Do You Need a Contract?

Writing and negotiating a contract can be a pain in the posterior, especially if you don't have any prior legal training. Why can't you just make a verbal agreement and be done with it?

As stated, you need a signed contract to protect yourself from nonperformance of the other party. And he needs the contract to protect himself if you don't perform. If someone doesn't do something they promised to do, a signed contract gives you incontrovertible proof of what each of you agreed to do. Without a contract, the issue can devolve into a "he said, she said" situation, with neither of you agreeing on (or able to prove) even the most basic facts.

That said, here are the typical situations for which you need to have a signed contract:

◆ **Performances:** It doesn't matter whether you're playing a small wedding reception or a big concert at a major stadium—both parties need to agree on performance and payment terms, and put that agreement in contractual form.

◆ **Tours:** A tour is just a series of performances, and as such you'll need a series of contracts, one with each venue along the tour—along with master contracts for the tour's booking agent, promoter, and such. In addition, you'll need contracts to lease or purchase all the equipment you use for the tour—instruments, sound reinforcement, lighting, you name it—as well as for any backing musicians, roadies, and stagehands you employ.

◆ **Recording:** When you record at a professional studio, you'll need to sign a contract with the studio. You may also need separate contracts with the record's producer and engineer, and with any studio musicians you use.

◆ **Sales and distribution:** The music you record has to be distributed, which means signing contracts with independent distributors, large retailers, music download services—you name it. A contract may also be necessary between you and the CD duplicator, and with any graphic designers, artists, and other artists you use to create the CD cover and liner notes.

◆ **Signing with a record label:** Of course, distribution is part of the deal if you sign with a major record label—and there's a big contract involved when you sign. This may be the longest and most important contract of your entire career, involving all aspects of your music.

◆ **Signing with a music publishing company:** Likewise, when you sign with a music publishing company to represent your songs, you sign a contract describing just what it is the publisher does and owns and how much you get paid.

◆ **Licensing your music:** If you're fortunate enough to get a song placed in a TV show, movie, or commercial, you'll need to sign a contract stipulating just what's involved in the licensing.

◆ **Forming a band:** When you form a band, you need to specify who does what, how much each person gets paid, and what happens if the band breaks up. I know this isn't what you want to think about when you're first starting out, but it's extremely important to put all of this on paper from day one.

◆ **Assembling your team:** Every member of your team—your manager, your agent, your business manager, your webmaster—needs to be under a signed contract. This extends to the minor but still important members of your team, including instrument techs, roadies, sound people, and such.

Okay, so that's a lot of contracts to deal with. Virtually every new project you start—performing or recording—needs to be accompanied by the necessary contracts.

Negotiating a Contract

How do you decide what's included in a given contract? Well, it helps to start out with some sort of boilerplate text, which you can then modify to the specifics of the situation.

The details of a contract are sometimes dictated by one party, but are just as often negotiated. An example of a dictated detail might be the royalty split between you and your publishing company. They split royalties 50/50 with all their clients; that's just part of the deal. A negotiated detail might be the rate you charge to play a specific gig; you might start out asking $5,000, the promoter might offer up $3,000, and you eventually agree to play for $4,000.

Smart Business

You can find boilerplate contracts of various types at 101 Music Biz Contracts (www.musiccontracts101.com), MusicContracts.com (www.musiccontracts.com), and MusicLegalForms.com (www.musiclegalforms.com).

That's the whole point of negotiations—to get to a mutually acceptable point. It's not a fair negotiation if one party has unreasonable influence; for example, if a club owner says, "You'll never work in this town again if you don't accept my rate," and can back up his threat. Negotiations have to be entered into in good faith, and should create results that both parties can live with.

At some point it helps to bring in legal counsel to advise on the pending contract. For big contracts, you may want your lawyer in the room helping you negotiate. For other contracts, it may suffice to have the lawyer put the terms you negotiate into proper legal format. For still other contracts, all you need might be for your lawyer to look over the contract you negotiated just to make sure all the i's are dotted and the t's are crossed.

If you sign what amounts to a boilerplate contract—that is, a contract you've previously approved and used and haven't changed at all—then you may not need to engage the services of your lawyer. Assuming that your attorney approved the boilerplate and that you haven't edited it, then his prior approval should suffice.

Understanding the Various Parts of a Contract

You're not a lawyer, and shouldn't be expected to write a detailed legal contract. That said, you should be able to understand the contracts you sign, which means becoming familiar with the various parts and *clauses* that are common in entertainment industry contracts.

def•i•ni•tion

A **clause** is a section or paragraph in a contract.

To that end, here are some of the clauses you're likely to encounter in various music-related contracts:

- ◆ **Header:** The top of the contract should display your (or your business's) name, address, telephone number, and e-mail address.

- ◆ **Signature and date:** The bottom of the contract should include space for both parties to sign and date the thing.

- ◆ **Compensation:** This is how much you expect to get paid (or to pay) for services rendered. The compensation should spell out the exact compensation, whether in the form of a flat fee, royalty, or whatever. The contract should also define the terms of payment—do you get it all in advance, or some up-front and some later, and if so, when? This section should also state to whom the payment goes— to one of the band members, to the booking agent, to the band's manager, or what.

- ◆ **Definition of performance:** This clause defines what the artist or the other party is expected to do to earn the agreed-upon compensation. Performance contracts should provide a clear, concise description of the nature of the performance, the number of musicians involved, the number of sets, the length of each set, and so forth. For employment contracts (such as with the band's manager), spell out the exact duties the other party is expected to provide.

◆ **Location, date, and time:** For performance contracts, when and where are you performing?

◆ **Merchandising rights:** Also for performance contracts, can the artist sell his merchandise at the venue? If so, does the venue (or promoter) receive a cut of merchandise sales?

◆ **Meals, transportation, and lodging:** For tour-related contracts, who is responsible for the artist's expenses during the tour? Who arranges these particulars, and what does the artist expect to receive?

◆ **Equipment, sound, and production:** For both performance and recording contracts, what musical, sound, and lighting equipment will the venue or recording studio provide—and for what additional cost?

◆ **Acts of God:** This is a fairly standard clause necessary to protect both parties in the event of a major disaster preventing the contract from being fulfilled.

◆ **Cancellation:** Separate from the Acts of God clause, this clause details who is owed what if either party cancels the contract.

◆ **Exclusivity:** Does the artist agree to contract exclusively with the other party—or vice versa? Some types of contracts, such as those with major labels, are by nature exclusive; others not.

You won't find all these clauses in every contract. Some clauses are specific to certain types of contracts; other clauses might not be necessary in every situation. But you need to be familiar with each of these clauses for when you do encounter them. As in all things, it's better to be informed than to be ignorant.

Smart Business

Given all the various clauses that you can and probably should include in your contracts, you should also strive to keep your contracts as simple as possible. Try to avoid unnecessary legalese, instead wording your contracts in plain English whenever you can. The goal is to spell out the terms of the contract in a way that is easy for all parties to understand and accept.

When a Contract Is Broken

Even if you're diligent about negotiating and signing contracts, you can still run into trouble if the other party doesn't uphold his part of the deal. This most often occurs when you play a gig and don't get paid.

So you have a contract that says the other party is supposed to do something—like pay you—but the other party doesn't do this. What recourse do you have at this point?

When one party doesn't uphold his part of a contract, you can sue that party for the payment due. That means taking that person to court, typically *small claims court*. You present your case (and the original contract) to the judge, the other party does the same, and the judge makes a judgment. If the judgment is in your favor, the other party is obligated to pay whatever the judge says he must pay—typically the amount detailed in the contract, sometimes with court costs added in.

def•i•ni•tion

A **small claims court** is one where low-dollar disputes are resolved relatively quickly and inexpensively. The dollar amounts heard in small claims courts differ from state to state, with the top limits ranging from $1,500 (Kentucky) to $25,000 (Tennessee).

You can take this legal action yourself (it's not that difficult, especially for small claims court) or with the help of an attorney. Just make sure you have all the necessary documents, including the original contract, as well as documentation of what you did and the other party didn't.

Of course, just because you get a judgment against the other party doesn't mean you'll actually get paid. The court can only rule; it can't enforce. So if the other party doesn't want to pay, there's not a lot you can do. Likewise, if the other party simply doesn't have the money, you can't get something he doesn't have.

As you can see, enforcing a contract can be a bit of a crapshoot. If a club owner or promoter wants to shaft you, he can—or at least make your life difficult in trying to recover what's legally yours. If the dollar amount involved is low enough, you may decide it's not worth the trouble pursuing. Or you may want to go after the offending party like a bulldog. It's your choice.

How Do I Spot a Bad Deal?

Lots of folks out there are eager to take advantage of unsuspecting musicians. That's why you need to run your contracts—the bigger ones, especially—by a trusted lawyer before you sign on the dotted line.

You should also develop a nose for bad deals. You need to be able to spot the signs of a rip-off as early as possible in the process, before you sign your life away. With that in mind, here are some signs that a pending deal might not be all that it appears to be:

♦ **A manager, agent, PR company, or other third party asks you to pay an up-front fee for them to represent you.** Legitimate players are paid when they perform; asking for the money up-front is the sign of a "cash and dash" artist.

♦ **You're asked to put up your own money to play a gig.** This is charity, my friend, not good business. Musicians should *never* pay to play—and that includes paying a promoter for the "privilege" of performing on a given bill.

♦ **The other party pushes you to use their lawyer, not yours.** This is the sign of a con artist trying to stack the deck; his lawyer is in on the con. This is why you always want your own lawyer looking at things, not an attorney for the other side.

♦ **The percentages are out of whack.** Throughout this book I've given you some typical ranges for the most common percentage splits. Beware any deal that falls significantly outside these ranges. For example, never pay more than 20 percent to a manager, and never accept less than 50 percent for a music publishing deal. No matter how famous the other party thinks he is, don't pay more than you should.

♦ **You turn over all your rights.** The shadiest characters are those that want to own what should be rightfully yours. That includes performers and producers who want to be listed as songwriters, and thus share your copyright to a song. When you sign over your rights, you're losing legal status—and a lot of potential income.

♦ **It sounds too good to be true.** Sometimes you can't put your finger on it but a deal just doesn't feel right. Trust your instincts; if a deal sounds too good to be true, it probably is.

If you're not sure about a deal, walk away. And don't fall for the "if you don't sign right now, it goes away" ploy. There's no deal so important and so urgent that you can't take the time to think it over—and have it looked over by a trusted attorney.

The Least You Need to Know

◆ A contract is a binding legal agreement that spells out what each party will do.

◆ You need a contract to document any major interaction you have with other parties—performances, tours, recordings, distribution, music publishing, even forming a band.

◆ You can often start with a boilerplate (preprepared) contract and then alter it as you negotiate specific terms.

◆ Most contracts contain similar clauses, detailing the terms of performance and payment.

Chapter 24

The Business of Copyrights and Royalties

In This Chapter

- How copyright works
- How to deal with copyright infringement
- Different types of licenses and royalties: mechanical, performance, synchronization, print, display, and foreign
- When you need to pay royalties on the music you perform and record

One way to make money as a musician is to license your songs for various uses and then collect the licensing income, typically in the form of royalties. Licensing is different for songs than it is for sound recordings; in most instances, a songwriter has more licensing opportunities than do artists recording those songs.

To fully benefit from licensing opportunities, you need to know a little bit about copyrights, licenses, and royalties. You can then determine just how much income you can generate from the music you write and record.

How Copyright Works

Let's start with the concept of *copyright*. Virtually any piece of music you create is intellectual property, which can be—and automatically is—copyrighted. You can copyright songs that you write, of course, as well as recordings you make of those songs.

It's easy to understand how a song is intellectual property; it's a piece of music, often with lyrics, that one or more persons create. When you record a song, you own the copyright on the recording you create; the copyright on the song itself, of course, is still owned by the song's writer(s).

def•i•ni•tion

Copyright is the right given by law to the creator of a work to determine who may publish, copy, and distribute that work.

Different Types of Copyright

Because songs differ from sound recordings, and because each can be used in a variety of ways, the U.S. Copyright Act of 1976 provides for six different types of rights. Which rights a copyright owner has depends on the type of work involved.

> **Behind the Music**
>
> Copyright law differs significantly from country to country. We discuss U.S. copyright law in this book; consult local sources to better understand the copyright law in other countries.

The six types of rights granted by U.S. copyright law are as follows:

◆ **Make copies or records.** Songwriters hold the right to make copies or records of their songs. Makers of recordings also hold the right to make copies of their recordings.

◆ **Distribute copies or records.** Making a copy or recording is different from distributing the copies or recordings you make. Songwriters hold the right to distribute copies or records of their songs. Makers of recordings also hold the right to distribute their recordings.

◆ **Prepare derivative works.** A derivative work is a new work based on one or more existing works. For example, writing new lyrics for an existing song is a derivative work, as is sampling an existing recording for a new recording. The right to prepare derivative works applies to both songs and sound recordings.

◆ **Perform publicly.** This right, sometimes called the public performance right, applies only to songs, not to sound recordings. A public performance can be a live performance of a song by a cover band or playing a recording of a song over the radio or on a public speaker system. Songwriters hold the right to perform their songs publicly, and collect royalties when others perform their songs. Note, however, that only a song can be licensed for public performance. A sound recording has no protection against being played publicly; performers, then, earn no royalties when their recordings are played on the radio or in public.

◆ **Perform publicly by digital audio transmission.** This right applies only to recordings played over the Internet and on satellite and cable radio stations; songs are not included, as they are already protected under the general right to perform publicly. This is the only performance right granted to sound recordings.

◆ **Display publicly.** This final right applies only to songs, and involves the reproduction of music or lyrics in print or on the Internet.

Behind the Music

A song (called a *musical work* in the Copyright Act) is a melody, chords, and any accompanying lyrics. A sound recording is the recorded performance of a song. A single song can be recorded multiple times by multiple artists. Copyright law recognizes a copyright in the song and a separate copyright in the song recording.

Performance rights for digital audio transmissions (Internet, cable, and satellite) were created in 1995, via the Digital Performance Right in Sound Recordings Act. Before this act was passed, recordings could be played on the Internet (and on satellite and cable radio) with no royalties due.

The following table details which rights apply to songs and to sound recordings:

Copyright Owner's Rights in Songs and Sound Recordings

Exclusive Right	Song	Sound Recording
Make copies or records	Yes	Yes
Distribute copies or records	Yes	Yes
Prepare derivative works	Yes	Yes
Perform publicly	Yes	No
Perform publicly by digital audio transmission	No	Yes
Display publicly	Yes	No

When Copyright Begins

In the United States, a song is copyrighted as soon as you write it, and a recording is copyrighted as soon as you record it. You don't have to register the song or recording with the U.S. Copyright Office in order to hold the copyright, but that is the best way to obtain *proof* of copyright. Registration provides additional protection in court in case someone does infringe your work. (Learn more about filing for copyright in Chapter 15.)

To register the copyright for a work, go to www.copyright.gov, or write to the following address:

U.S. Copyright Office
101 Independence Ave. S.E.
Washington, DC 20559-6000

How long does a copyright last? In the United States, a copyrighted work has protection under the law for the life of the creator, *plus* 75 years after his or her death. So if a songwriter wrote a song in 1990 and passed away in 2005, the copyright doesn't expire until 2080. (After the songwriter's death, the copyright is held by the songwriter's estate.)

Dealing with Copyright Infringement

Of what value is a copyright? It's not just about ownership; it's also about collecting royalties when your song or recording is used by another artist. If your work is used without permission, that's called copyright infringement, and you have legal recourse to recover damages due.

Let's take the concept of a copyrighted song first. You write a song, it's yours, and you deserve all royalties due for the use of that song. If another artist happens to copy the melody of your song in a song he writes, that's stealing, and you're owed any royalties he earns from that work.

As an example of this sort of copyright infringement, look no further than George Harrison's "My Sweet Lord." In this famous instance, it was alleged that the ex-Beatle based the melody of his 1969 song on the melody of "He's So Fine," a previous song written by Ronald Mack and made famous by the Chiffons in 1963. The courts found that Harrison indeed did infringe on the copyright for "He's So Fine," and he was ordered to surrender the appropriate royalties earned to the original song's copyright holder.

Behind the Music

In the case of "My Sweet Lord," it was the copyright on the song that was infringed, not the copyright on the Chiffons' recording. Harrison didn't copy the previous recording; he copied part of the song.

Interestingly, it's not infringement to write a song or make a record that parodies an existing song or recording. Parody is a fair use of copyrighted material, and is allowed under the law.

Infringement of a copyrighted song is different from infringement of a copyrighted recording. In the latter instance, a new recording would have to incorporate pieces of a previous recording—without the permission of the previous recording's copyright holder.

A good example of this type of copyright infringement is "Ready to Die," a song by the late rapper Notorious B.I.G. This song sampled a piece of the 1992 recording "Singing in the Morning" by the Ohio Players, without prior permission. A jury found that this was indeed copyright infringement, and ordered payment of $4.2 million in damages to two companies that own the rights to the Ohio Players recording.

Behind the Music

Sampling of existing recordings is common in rap and hip hop music. To use a sample, however, you must obtain permission from the copyright holder of the previous recording, or risk legal action. Another alternative is to use samples from so-called sample libraries, recorded expressly and provided for royalty-free usage.

Understanding Types of Licenses and Royalties

Copyright is important not just because it establishes legal ownership of a work, but also because it determines royalties to be paid for use of that work. In essence, the copyright is the source of future revenue for a songwriter or recording artist.

Revenue is generated when the copyright holder issues a *license* for the use of a copyrighted work. There are five different types of licenses that can be issued, based on different uses of a musical work. These licenses include the following.

def•i•ni•tion

A **license** is the official authorization to use a copyrighted work.

- **Mechanical licenses,** which involve making a recording of a song.

- **Performance licenses,** which involve performing a song (or playing a recording) in public.

- **Synchronization licenses,** which involve using a song in a visual medium, such as TV or movies.

- **Print licenses,** which involve distributing your song in printed form (sheet music, typically).

- **Foreign licenses,** which involve distributing your song outside of the United States.

We'll discuss each of these licenses and corresponding royalties in turn.

Mechanical Licenses

Mechanical licenses are for the use of songs, and mechanical royalties are paid to songwriters and their publishing companies. A mechanical license gives a record company, musician, or other party the right to reproduce your song on a record, CD, digital download, or other media. The person recording your song doesn't have to obtain your permission to make the recording; he does, however, have to pay a compulsory mechanical license for the use of your song.

> **Behind the Music**
>
> It's called a mechanical license because the very first recordings were actually piano rolls, which were created by mechanically punching holes in the paper rolls.

The party recording your song pays the song's copyright owner a set fee, called the *statutory rate*. As of 2009, the mechanical royalty rate is 9.1¢ per song for each CD, tape, download, or other recording sold. If the recording is more than five minutes long, the rate is 1.75¢ per minute per recording. So if someone makes a four-minute recording of your song, you get 9.1¢; if another artist makes a six-minute recording of your song, you get 10.5¢ (that's 1.75¢ × 6 minutes).

If a recording artist doesn't want to pay the statutory rate, he can negotiate a different rate with the song's copyright holder. This is common when a major artist records a song from a beginning songwriter; to get his work recorded, the songwriter will often agree to a lower royalty rate, or even a single flat fee for use of the song.

The mechanical royalty is paid to the songwriter's publisher, or to the songwriter himself if he doesn't have a publisher. If a publisher is involved, the songwriter and the publisher typically split this amount between the two of them.

> ### Behind the Music
>
> The statutory rate changes over time, as set by the U.S. Copyright Office. Mechanical royalties are the same for the sale of music in any format. It doesn't matter whether a consumer buys a CD or audio tape, or whether he downloads a song from iTunes or some other online store, the same 9.1¢ royalty is due.
>
> Many music publishers use a company called the Harry Fox Agency to negotiate and issue their mechanical licenses, and to collect the corresponding royalties. This company charges a fee equal to 4.5 percent of the mechanical royalties it collects.

Performance Licenses

Like mechanical licenses, performance licenses are for songs, and performance royalties are paid to songwriters and their publishing companies. A performance license gives a venue or company the right to reproduce or play your song in public. It doesn't matter whether your song is being played by a live band in a bar or if a recorded version of your song is played over the radio or via store speakers; these are both forms of public performance.

As such, any location that plays music must obtain a performing rights license for the songs (live or recorded) played on premises. In addition, radio stations, television stations, and Internet radio stations must also obtain performing rights licenses and pay royalties to the copyright owners of the songs they play.

> ### Behind the Music
>
> With the exception of Internet, satellite, and cable play, performing rights apply only to songs, not to recordings. So for example, when a recording is played on a traditional radio station, the songwriter earns a performance royalty, but the recording artist doesn't. For digital reproduction only, royalties are also paid to the musicians performing on the recording.

> ### Behind the Music
>
> Venues pay performance royalties, not the artists playing the tunes. So if you're in a cover band, you don't have to pay anything to play those tunes live. (You would have to pay the songwriter if you recorded the songs, however.) The clubs you play, however, have to pay a performing royalty for the songs you and other musicians play in those clubs.

In practice, performing rights are managed by one of three large performing rights organizations (PRO): ASCAP, BMI, or SESAC. These are the three U.S.-based organizations; different PROs exist elsewhere in the world.

A PRO issues blanket licenses to companies and venues that play live or recorded music in a public setting. That includes music broadcasters, such as radio and television stations, as well as concert halls, clubs, hotels, restaurants, even retail stores with Muzak running in the background. By paying a blanket license fee, these companies and establishments can then play whatever music they want without having to account for all the individual songwriters of the songs they play.

The PROs keep track of all the music that is played, and then pay performance royalties to songwriters based on the number of times that person's songs are played. Actually, they pay the royalties to the songwriter's publishing company, which takes its split and passes on the rest to the songwriter.

Synchronization Licenses

Synchronization licenses (*synch licenses*, for short) are for both songs and recordings. Synchronization license fees or royalties are paid to both songwriters and the musicians who recorded the song.

Behind the Music
It's called a synchronization license because the licensed music is synchronized with visual images in film or on the TV screen.

A synchronization license authorizes a third party to use your song in movies, TV shows, and commercials. Synchronization royalties or fees are always paid to the copyright owner of the song itself; if an existing sound recording is used, synchronization fees must be paid to the recording's copyright owners, as well.

Synchronization fees are typically negotiated between the copyright owner and the licensee. Rates vary from a few thousand dollars for the short use of a song in a TV show to tens of thousands of dollars for major use of a song in a big-time motion picture.

Print Licenses

A print license authorizes the sale or distribution of your song in printed form. Obviously, a print license is issued only for songs, not for sound recordings, because it's the songs (the music and words) that are printed, typically in sheet music or music books. The distributor of the sheet music typically pays a royalty to the song's copyright owner for each unit sold.

Foreign Licenses

All of the rights just discussed are *domestic* rights—that is, they apply within the United States. The same licenses (mechanical, performance, synchronization, and print) are also issued in foreign countries.

To make things easier to administer, copyright owners typically retain agents, called subpublishers, located in each country outside the United States where the song is exploited. These subpublishers collect fees based on 15 to 25 percent of royalties collected for their work in issuing licenses in their respective territories.

Paying Royalties

If you're a songwriter, then, you have all sorts of rights and get all sorts of royalties when your songs are recorded, performed, printed, or whatever. But as a performer, how do you know when you need to pay royalties on the songs you play or record?

Royalties for Live Performances

When it comes to performing other people's songs, as most cover bands do, there's good news and bad news. The bad news is that yes, royalties do need to be paid to the songwriters of the songs you perform. The good news is that you, the cover musicians, don't have to pay it.

That's because performance royalties, which is what we're talking about here, are paid by the *venue* where the songs are performed, not by the performers. Performing musicians do not have to pay performance royalties; clubs, concert halls, lounges, you name it, do have to pay royalties.

That's why just about every venue that plays live music takes out a performing rights license with the big performing rights organizations: ASCAP, BMI, and SESAC. This blanket license covers them when the musicians they hire play cover tunes. The venue pays the royalties to the PROs, the PROs pay the royalties to the publishing companies, and the publishing companies pay their songwriters. The musicians who play songs by other songwriters are in the clear.

> ### Behind the Music
>
> If you own a venue that has live music, you could be proactive about contacting ASCAP and BMI to seek a performing rights license—or you could wait for them to knock on your door, which they will. The PROs tend to be a tad aggressive (some would say overaggressive) in making sure that any and all places where music is played are signed up for their licensing programs.

Royalties for Recordings

That's not the case when you record someone else's songs. In this instance, the copyright owner of the recording owes the songwriters mechanical royalties on each copy of that recording sold. So I guess, technically, you don't pay royalties when you make a recording; instead, you pay royalties when you sell copies of that recording.

> ### Behind the Music
>
> The Fox agency has special licensing terms if you think you'll be selling fewer than 2,500 copies or downloads of a song. Above that number, you'll have to report exact sales for the royalty calculations.

Who pays these royalties? If you record for a big record label, the label will handle sales tracking and royalty payments. It comes out of your profits, at the end of the day, but the label handles all the paperwork.

If, on the other hand, you're doing your own distribution, for either CDs or digital downloads, then you're responsible for paying royalties to the writers of all the songs on your recording. The way it works is that you contact the Harry Fox Agency (www.harryfox.com) and request a mechanical license for each song you record. (That you didn't write yourself, of course.) The agency will then walk you through the process of reporting sales and paying royalties due; you pay the royalties to the Fox agency, they pay them to the publishing companies, and the publishing companies share them with their songwriters.

Should Performers Be Paid for Radio Play?

The whole music-licensing and royalty system was constructed to compensate songwriters for their work. Performers, however, do not have the same rights and do not receive near the amount of royalty income as do songwriters. Is that fair?

One of the major concerns has to do with performance royalties, particularly for radio play. Songwriters receive performance royalties when their songs are played on the radio; the musicians who make the recording do not.

The music industry has typically explained this away by claiming, rightly or wrongly, that radio play promotes record sales, and performers do receive royalties for the records they sell. This doesn't explain why songwriters receive radio royalties, but, hey, why get in the way of a good story?

That said, there is a new movement afoot to add copyright protection (and royalty payments) to the performers of recordings played over the radio. A new recording industry group, called the musicFIRST Coalition, is pushing for Congress to make terrestrial radio stations pay performance royalties to recording artists. Not surprisingly, the National Association of Broadcasters is opposed to this move—and the radio industry has a lot of clout in Congress.

What Congress decides is impossible to predict at this juncture. Personally, I tend to agree with House Judiciary Chairman Patrick Leahy, who believes that this bill could correct a glaring inequity. "When we listen to music," Leahy stated, "we are enjoying the intellectual property of two creative artists—the songwriter and the performer."

As both a songwriter and a performer, I couldn't have put it any better myself. Isn't it time that all of us are rewarded for our creative work?

The Least You Need to Know

- ◆ A song is automatically copyrighted when it is written; a recording is automatically copyrighted when it is recorded. (That said, proof of copyright is created when you register the work with the U.S. Copyright Office.)

- ◆ Mechanical royalties are earned for a songwriter when a song is recorded and that recording is then sold—via CD, tape, or digital download.

- ◆ Performance royalties are earned for a songwriter when a song is performed live or a recording of that song is played on the radio or in other venues.

- ◆ Synchronization royalties are earned when a song or recording is used in film, television, or other visual media.

- ◆ Print royalties are earned when a song is reproduced in sheet music format.

- ◆ Foreign licenses are granted for the use of a song or recording outside of the United States.

- ◆ Clubs and other venues pay performance royalties for cover songs played by the artists they employ; artists and their record labels pay mechanical royalties for cover songs they record.

Glossary

360-degree deal An agreement, typically with a major record label, that gives the label a cut of all the artist's activities—not just record sales.

A&R Artists and Repertoire, the department of a record company responsible for finding and grooming new artists.

advance An up-front payment to an artist that is charged against an artist's royalties.

advertising Typically a paid activity whose purpose is to inform potential customers about products and services.

agent See *booking agent*.

artist manager See *personal manager*.

ASCAP The American Society of Composers, Authors, and Publishers, one of the largest performing rights organizations in the United States.

attorney An individual licensed to practice law who represents his or her clients in various legal matters.

Big Four The four major worldwide record companies today: EMI Group, Sony BMG Entertainment, Universal Music Group, and Warner Music Group.

BMI Broadcast Music, Inc., one of the largest performing rights organizations in the United States.

booker   See *booking agent*.

booking agent   An individual or firm who finds jobs for people and groups in the entertainment business.

budget   An estimate of expected income and expenditures for a future period of time.

business manager   An individual who helps an artist with financial planning, investment decisions, tax matters, monitoring of income from contracts, and other financial matters.

business plan   A written document used to develop, grow, and manage a business.

clause   A section or paragraph in a contract.

composer   An individual who writes music, not words.

contract   A formal record of the terms negotiated between two parties.

copyright   The right given by law to the creator of a work to determine who may publish, copy, and distribute that work.

copyright infringement   The unauthorized use of a copyrighted work; typically the recording or performance of a song without paying royalties due.

corporation   A type of business entity legally separate from the persons who form the business; the corporation is typically owned by one or more shareholders who own stock in the company.

cross-collateralize   Also known as cross-deduction, the act of applying the terms of a contract across multiple projects.

derivative work   A new musical work based on one or more existing works.

digital audio transmission   Nontraditional audio broadcast media, including cable and satellite radio, as well as the Internet.

digital audio workstation (DAW)   A software program that enables you to record your music on a personal computer to a digital file.

digital download   See *download*.

distributor   A company that serves as a middleman between the label or artist and the retail store, distributing the label's products to individual retail stores.

download   The process of obtaining a song, in the form of a digital audio file, from a site on the Internet. A track downloaded from the Internet is also called a download.

engineer   The individual who supervises the technical aspects of a recording session and makes the actual recording.

file-sharing site   A website offering illegal music downloads.

Harry Fox Agency   The company responsible for tracking and collecting mechanical royalties for most U.S. record labels.

IFPI   The International Federation of the Phonographic Industry, an organization that represents the interests of the recording industry worldwide.

illegal download   A copyrighted recording that is downloaded from the Internet for free, without the proper royalties being paid to the copyright owners, typically from a file-sharing or file-swapping website.

independent artist   An artist that is not signed to one of the Big Four major labels.

independent label   Any record label that is not affiliated in any way with one of the Big Four major-label conglomerates.

Internet radio station   A website or online service that streams specific genres of music to listeners.

jingle   A simple song about a product or service, used in a commercial message.

keyword   A word or phrase that people use as part of their queries on Google and other search sites.

lawyer   See *attorney*.

license   The official authorization to use a copyrighted work.

licensee   The party that licenses use of a copyright.

licensor   The party that owns a copyright and issues licenses for use of that work.

lyricist   An individual who writes words to songs.

major label   Any record label associated with one of the Big Four record companies.

manager   See *personal manager*.

marketing   The act of presenting products or services in such a way as to make them desirable.

mastering   The process of readying recorded and mixed tracks for final release.

mechanical license   The authorization to make a recording of a song.

mechanical royalty   The payment for recording a song, due to the song's copyright holder—typically the songwriter.

merchandising   The exchange of goods for an agreed-upon sum of money.

mixing   The process of assembling the individual tracks, adjusting volume levels, adding effects, and the like for a recording.

music industry   Those individuals and companies involved with making and selling music.

music publishing company   A company that contracts with songwriters to promote their songs to other artists, create sheet music of their songs, and collect all royalties due when those songs are recorded, sold, or performed.

musical work   Per the U.S. Copyright Act, a song—melody, chords, and accompanying lyrics.

online music store   A website offering legal music downloads for a fee.

online subscription service   A website that lets listeners subscribe to all the music they can listen to for a monthly fee.

partnership   A type of business entity formed by a contract between two or more co-owners.

patronage   The support, often financial, that one individual or organization bestows on another.

pay-per-click (PPC) advertising   Online advertising in which the advertiser pays only when someone clicks on the link within the ad.

performance license   See *performing rights license.*

performance royalty   See *performing rights royalty.*

performing rights license   The authorization to publicly perform or play a song.

performing rights organization   Also known as a PRO, a company or organization charged with tracking and collecting payments for the performance of musical works. The three largest PROs in the United States are ASCAP, BMI, and SESAC.

performing rights royalty   The payment for playing a song, due to the song's copyright holder—typically the songwriter.

personal manager   An individual who guides the professional career of an artist in the entertainment business.

preproduction   The planning done before a recording session.

print license   The authorization to reproduce a song in printed format.

print royalty   The payment for printing sheet music or lyrics for a song, due to the song's copyright holder—typically the songwriter.

PRO   See *performing rights organization.*

producer   The person in charge of a recording session, responsible for every aspect of the recording.

production music   See *stock music.*

promoter   An individual or company who contracts with artists for a given venue, and then promotes the artists' shows.

promotion   The act of disseminating information about a product, service, or brand.

public relations   See *publicity.*

publicist   An individual who is responsible for generating and managing publicity for an individual, group, or organization.

publicity   The act of spreading word to a large audience, using primarily free media.

record producer   See *producer.*

recording engineer   See *engineer.*

RIAA   The Recording Industry Association of America, an organization that represents the recording industry—primarily the big record labels—in the United States.

royalty   Payment made to the holder of a copyright for the use of that copyrighted work.

SESAC   The Society of European Stage Authors and Composers, the third-largest performing rights organization in the United States.

social network   A website that enables virtual communities of people who share interests, activities, or other connections.

sole proprietorship   A type of business entity owned by a single person and that legally has no separate existence from its owner.

songwriter   An individual who writes songs, typically both words and music.

statutory rate   The official rate, set by the U.S. Copyright Office, for mechanical royalties.

stock music   Royalty-free music used in television, film, commercials, and other media.

stock music library   A firm that licenses stock music to third parties.

studio musician   A performer who specializes and is paid for playing on other musician's recordings.

synchronization license   The authorization to use a song in a visual medium, such as television or movies.

synchronization royalty   The payment for using a song in a visual medium. In all cases, synchronization royalties are due to the song's copyright owner; if an existing recording is used, royalties are also due to the recording's copyright owner.

talent agent   See *booking agent.*

ticket agency   A firm that handles the selling of tickets for a venue or event.

venue   A facility for the performance of live music.

venue operator   An individual who manages entertainment for a venue and coordinates with artists, promoters, and booking agents.

webmaster   An individual who creates and manages the content and organization of a website.

Index

GROSSET'S
ITALIAN
PHRASE BOOK
AND DICTIONARY
FOR TRAVELERS

PHRASES Most useful in every travel situation.
PRONUNCIATION GUIDES Complete and easy to use.
DICTIONARY Over 2000 basic words.
MENU READER Local foods and native dishes.
SIGNS AND NOTICES Street, airport, and road signs.
CONVERSION TABLES Weights, measures, sizes.

CONVENIENT INDEX / SELF-PRONUNCIATIONS

GROSSET'S

ITALIAN

PHRASE BOOK
AND
DICTIONARY

by Charles A. Hughes

GROSSET & DUNLAP, INC.
A National General Company

New York

Published simultaneously in Canada

Library of Congress Catalog Card No.: 75-144062
ISBN: 0-448-00653-7
Printed in the U.S.A.

CONTENTS

INTRODUCTION

In this phrase book for travel in Italy, we have tried to incorporate features that will make it convenient and easy for you to use in actual situations. Every phrase and word is translated into proper Italian and then respelled to guide you in its pronunciation.

The book is also "programmed" to help you with two of the basic problems of the novice in a language — an inability to comprehend the spoken word and a certain hesitancy in speaking out. To solve the first problem, questions have been avoided, to the extent possible, in the phrases. When they could not be avoided, they have been worded so that a yes or no answer may be expected. And sometimes, when even this solution is impossible, the anticipated answer is given. To solve the problem of hesitancy, the contents of the book have been arranged so that a minimal command of basic phrases, salutations, weather, numbers-time, statements of need and desire, may be acquired in the first sections. The pronunciation guides printed under the Italian translations should also give you confidence that you will be understood. If your listener should indicate that he doesn't understand, merely try again. A slight mispronunciation is no embarrassment.

Finally, to aid you in finding a phrase that you wish to use, the Dictionary has been partially indexed. The Dictionary itself is comprehensive enough so that you will not lack the basic words for any usual situation.

TIPS ON PRONUNCIATION AND ACCENT

The pronunciation of each word in this phrase book is indicated by a respelling that approximates the sounds of Italian, according to the following system:

The vowels:

ah	Pronounced like "a" in f*a*ther
eh	Pronounced like "ay" in m*ay*be
e	Pronounced like "e" in m*e*t
ee	Pronounced like "ee" in s*ee*n
o	Pronounced like "o" in b*o*y
oh	Pronounced like "o" in *o*ver
oo	Pronounced like "oo" in s*oo*n
ah-ee	Pronounced like the pronoun *I* or the word *eye*
ow	Pronounced like "ow" in n*ow*
wah	Pronounced like "wa" in *wa*ter
woh	Pronounced like "wo" in *wo*n't
oy	Pronounced like "oy" in b*oy*

Consonants are sounded approximately as in English, with these exceptions:

"c" before "a," "o" and "u" sounds like "c" in *c*an; it is represented in the pronunciations by "k."

"c" before "e" and "i" sounds like "ch" in *ch*urch.

"ch" sounds like "k" in s*k*ate.

"g" before "a," "o" and "u" sounds like "g" in *g*o.

"g" before "e" and "i" sounds like "g" in *g*em or "j" in *j*oy.

"gh" sounds like "g" in *g*o.

"gl" sounds like "lli" in mi*lli*on.

"gn" sounds like "ny" in ca*ny*on.

"h" is always silent.

"r" is always trilled.

"s" between vowels and before voiced consonants sounds like "z" in *z*ebra.

"s" when it is initial, or is doubled in writing, or comes before voiceless consonants sounds like "ss" in mi*ss*.

"z" sounds like "ts" in ca*ts* or like "dz" in a*dz*e.

All consonants written double in Italian are pronounced twice as long as their single counterparts.

In the pronunciations, the stress or main accent in a word is indicated by an accent mark (') after the stressed syllable.

brother, fratello *frah-tel'-loh*
four, quattro *kwaht'-troh*
city, città *cheet-tah'*
lightning, fulmine *fool'-mee-neh*

Salutations and Greetings

Even before you learn anything else in a foreign language, you will want to learn how to greet people. Here are some short expressions that you will find easy to learn and to use when you meet people in a foreign land or along the way, perhaps on the ship or the plane.

Good morning.
Buon giorno.
Bwon jor'-noh

Good day.
Buon giorno
Bwon jor'-noh.

Good afternoon.
Buon giorno.
Bwon jor'-noh.

Good evening.
Buona sera.
Bwoh'-nah seh'-rah.

Good-bye.
Addio.
Ad-dee'-yoh.

Good-night.
Buona notte.
Bwoh'-nah not'-teh.

How are you?
Come sta?
Ko'-meh stah?

Well, thank you. And you?
Bene, grazie. E Lei?
Beh'-neh, grah'-tsee-yeh. Eh leh'-ee?

How is Mr. . . . ?
Come sta il signor . . . ?
Ko'-meh stah eel seen-yor' . . ?

How is Mrs. . . . ?
Come sta la signora . . . ?
Ko'-meh stah lah seen-yoh'-rah . . . ?

Is Miss . . . well?
Sta bene la signorina . . . ?
Stah beh'-neh lah seen-yoh-ree'-nah . . . ?

May I present my wife?
Posso presentare mia moglie?
Pos'-soh preh-zen-tah'-reh mee'-yah mo'-lyeh?

This is my husband.
Questo è mio marito.
Kwehs'-toh e mee'-yoh mah-ree'-toh.

Pleased to meet you.
Piacere di conoscerla.
Pyah-che'-reh dee ko-no'-sher-lah.

This is my friend.
Questo è il mio amico (m).
*Kwehs'-toh e eel mee'-yoh
ah-mee'-koh.*

This is my friend.
Questa è la mia amica (f).
*Kwehs'-tah e lah mee'-yah
ah-mee'-kah.*

This is my mother and my father.
Questa è mia madre e questo è mio padre.
*Kwehs'-tah e mee'-yah mah'-dreh eh kwes'-toh e mee'-yoh
pah'-dreh.*

This is my sister and my brother.
Questa è mia sorella e questo è mio fratello.
*Kwes'-tah e mee'-yah so-rel'-lah eh kwes'-toh e mee'-yoh
frah-tel'-loh.*

Is this your daughter?
È questa Sua figlia?
*E kwes'-tah soo'-ah feel'-
yah?*

Is this your son?
È questo Suo figlio?
*E kwes'-toh soo-oh feel'-
yoh?*

I hope that we will meet again.
Spero che ci incontriamo di nuovo.
Spe'-roh keh chee een-kon-tree-yah'-moh dee nwoh'-voh.

I'll be seeing you.
Arrivederci.
Ahr-ree-veh-der'-chee.

I'll see you tomorrow.
Ci vediamo domani.
*Chee veh-dee-yah'-moh
doh-mah'-nee.*

Excuse me.
Mi scusi.
Mee skoo'-zee.

Pardon me.
Scusi.
Skoo'-zee.

I'm very sorry.
Mi dispiace molto. / Mi rincresce molto.
*Mee dees-pyah'-cheh mol'-toh. / Mee reen-kre'-sheh mol'-
toh*

Don't mention it.
Non c'è di che.
Non che dee keh.

You're welcome.
Prego.
Preh'-goh.

With pleasure.
Con piacere.
Kon pyah-cheh'-reh.

Please.
Per favore. / Per piacere.
Per fah-voh'-reh. / Per pyah-cheh'-reh.

Good luck!
Buona fortuna.
Bwoh'-nah for-too'-nah!

The Weather

The weather is one thing everyone has in common, and it is a universal topic of conversation. The phrases given here — combined with a bit of added vocabulary — are easily mastered.

It's nice weather today.
Oggi fa bel tempo.
Oj'-jee fah bel tem'-poh.

It's bad weather today.
Oggi fa brutto tempo.
Oj'-jee fah broot'-toh tem'-poh.

It's cold.
Fa freddo.
Fah frehd'-doh.

It's warm.
Fa caldo.
Fah kahl'-doh.

Is it raining?
Piove?
Pyo'-veh'!

Yes, it's raining.
Sì, piove.
See, pyo'-veh.

No, it's not raining.
No, non piove.
Noh, non pyo'-veh.

It's snowing.
Nevica.
Neh'-vee-kah.

It rains (snows) here every day.
Qui piove (nevica) tutti i giorni.
Kwee pyo'-veh (neh'-vee-kah) toot'-tee ee jor'-nee.

It's beginning to rain (to snow).
Comincia a piovere (nevicare).
Ko-meen'-chah ah pyo'-veh-reh (neh-vee-kah'-reh).

It often rains (snows) here.
Qui piove (nevica) spesso.
Kwee pyo'-veh (neh'-vee-kah) spes'-soh.

It will rain (snow) tomorrow.
Domani pioverà (nevicherà).
Doh-mah'-nee pyo-ve-rah' (neh-vee-ke-rah').

It rained (snowed) yesterday.
Ha piovuto (nevicato) ieri.
Ah pyo-voo'-toh (neh-vee-kah'-toh) ye'-ree.

It has stopped raining (snowing).
Ha cessato di piovere (nevicare).
Ah ches-sah'-toh dee pyo'-ve-reh (neh-vee-kah'-reh).

It's windy.
Tira vento.
Tee'-rah ven'-toh.

There's a lot of fog.
C'è molta nebbia.
Che mol'-tah nehb'-byah.

The sun is rising.
Il sole si leva.
Eel so'-leh see leh'-vah.

The sun is setting.
Il sole tramonta.
Eel so'-leh trah-mon'-tah.

How is the weather?
Che tempo fa?
Keh tem'-poh fah?

I need an umbrella.
Ho bisogno d'un ombrello.
Oh bee-zo'-nyoh doon om-brel'-loh.

I see . . .	I like . . .	I'm afraid of . .
Vedo . . .	Mi piace . . .	Ho paura di . . .
Veh'-doh . . .	*Mee pyah'-cheh...*	*Ah pah-oo'-rah dee . . .*

the rain.
la pioggia.
lah pyoj'-jah.

the wind.
il vento.
eel ven'-toh.

the snow.
la neve.
lah neh'-veh.

the ice.
il ghiaccio.
eel gyahch'-choh.

the sky.
il cielo.
eel chyeh'-loh.

the sun.
il sole.
eel soh'-leh.

the moon.
la luna.
la loo'-nah.

the stars.
le stelle.
leh stel'-leh.

a star.
una stella.
oo'-nah stel'-lah.

a rainbow.
un arcobaleno.
oon ahr-koh-bah-leh'-noh.

a cloud.
una nuvola.
oo'-nah noo'-voh-lah.

the clouds.
le nuvole.
leh noo'-voh-leh.

the lightning.
il fulmine, i lampi.
eel fool'-mee-neh, ee lahm'-pee.

the thunder.
il tuono.
eel twoh'-noh.

the storm.
la tempesta, il temporale.
lah tem-pe'-stah, eel tem-poh-rah'-leh.

Will it be cool there?
Farà fresco là?
Fah-rah' fres'-koh lah?

Will it be damp there?
Ci sarà umidità?
Chee sah-rah' oo-mee-dee-tah'?

Should I take a sweater?
Dovrei prendere un maglione?
Dov-reh'-ee pren'-deh-reh oon mah-lyoh'-neh?

a jacket?
una giacca?
oo'-nah jahk'-kah?

a raincoat?
un impermeabile?
oon eem-per-meh-yah'-bee-leh?

It's lightning.
Lampeggia.
Lahm-pej'-jah.

It's thundering.
Tuona.
Twoh'-nah.

Warm weather.
Tempo caldo.
Tem'-poh kahl'-doh.

Cold weather.
Tempo freddo.
Tem'-poh frehd'-doh.

Warm water.
Acqua calda.
Ahk'-kwah kahl'-dah.

Hot water.
Acqua caldissima.
Ahk'-kwah kahl-dees'-see-mah.

Cold water.
Acqua fredda.
Ahk'-kwah frehd'-dah.

General Expressions

In this section you will find the most useful expressions — the ones you will use over and over again. They are the phrases that you should have on the tip of the tongue, ready for immediate use — particularly those that express desire or volition. Here they have been kept short for easy acquisition and speedy communication. You will see them appear again and again in other sections of this book, where they are used in particular situations.

What is your name?
Come si chiama Lei?
Ko'-meh see kyah'-mah leh'-ee?

My name is . . .
Mi chiamo . . .
Mee kyah'-moh . . .

What is his (her) name?
Come si chiama lui (lei)?
Ko'-meh see kyah'-mah loo'-ee (leh'-ee)?

I don't know.
Non lo so.
Non loh soh.

His (her) name is . . .
Si chiama . . .
See kyah'-mah . . .

Do you know him (her)?
Lo (La) conosce?
Loh (lah) ko-no'-sheh?

Yes, I know him (her).
Sí, lo (la) conosco.
See, loh (lah) ko-nos'-koh.

No, I don't know him (her).
No, non lo (la) conosco.
Noh, non loh (lah) ko-nos'-koh.

I know you.
La conosco.
Lah ko-nos'-koh.

Where do you live?
Dove abita Lei?
Do'-veh ah'-bee-tah leh'-ee?

I live here.
Abito qui.
Ah'-bee-toh kwee.

At which hotel are you staying?
A quale albergo scende?
Ah kwah'-leh ahl-ber'-goh shen'-deh?

She's a beautiful woman.
È una bella donna.
E oo'-nah bel'-lah don'-nah.

She's a pretty girl.
È una ragazza graziosa.
E oo'-nah rah-gaht'-tsah grah-tsyoh'-zah.

He's a handsome man.
È un bell'uomo.
E oon bel-lwoh'-moh.

I love you.
Ti amo.
Tee ah'-moh.

I love her.
L'amo.
Lah'-moh.

I love him.
Lo amo.
Loh ah'-moh.

Do you know where he lives?
Sa dove lui abita?
Sah do'-veh loo'-ee ah'-bee-tah?

Do you speak English?
Parla Lei inglese?
Pahr'-lah leh'-ee een-gleh'-zeh?

Please say it in English.
Lo dica in inglese, per favore.
Loh dee'-kah een een-gleh'-zeh, per fah-voh'-reh.

Is there anyone here who speaks English?
C'è qualcuno qui che parla inglese?
Che kwahl-koo'-noh kwee keh pahr'-lah een-gleh'-zeh?

Do you understand?
Capisce?
Kah-pee'-sheh?

Yes, I understand.
Sì, capisco.
See, kah-pees'-koh.

No, I don't understand.
No, non capisco.
Noh, non kah-pees'-koh.

I understand a little.
Capisco un poco.
Kah-pees'-koh oon poh'-koh.

I don't understand everything.
Non capisco tutto.
Non kah-pees'-koh toot'-toh.

Please speak more slowly.
Parli più lentamente (adagio), per favore.
Pahr'-lee pyoo len-tah-men'-teh (ah-dah'-joh) per fah-voh'-reh.

Please repeat.
Ripeta, per favore.
Ree-peh'-tah, per fah-voh'-reh.

What did you say?
Che cosa ha detto?
Keh ko'-zah ah det'-toh?

How do you say that in Italian?
Come si dice questo in italiano?
Ko'-meh see dee'-cheh kwes'-toh een ee-tah-lyah'-noh?

What does that mean?
Che significa questo?
Keh see-nyee'-fee-kah kwes'-toh?

What do you mean?
Che vuol dire?
Keh vwohl dee'-reh?

You are right (wrong).
Lei ha ragione (torto).
Leh'-ee ah rah-joh'-neh (tor'-toh).

He is right (wrong).
Lui ha ragione (torto).
Loo'-ee ah rah-joh'-neh (tor'-toh).

Without doubt.
Senza dubbio.
Sehn'-tsah doob'-byoh.

Where are you going?
Dove va Lei? Dove va?
Do'-veh vah leh'-ee?

Where is he going?
Dove va lui? Dove va?
Do'-veh vah loo'-ee?

Where are we going?
Dove andiamo?
Do'-veh ahn-dyah'-moh?

I will wait here.
Aspetterò qui.
Ah-spet-te-roh' kwee.

How long must I wait?
Quanto tempo devo aspettare?
Kwahn'-toh tem'-poh deh'-voh ah-spet-tah'-reh?

Wait here until I come back.
Aspetti qui finchè torni.
Ah-spet'-tee kwee feen-keh' tor'-nee.

Come here.
Venga qua.
Ven'-gah kwah.

Is it near here?
È qui vicino?
E kwee vee-chee'-noh?

Come in.
Avanti.
Ah-vahn'-tee.

Is it far from here?
È lontano da qui?
E lon-tah'-noh dah kwee?

Bring me . . .
Mi porti . . .
Mee por'-tee . . .

Tell me . . .
Mi dica . . .
Mee dee'-kah . . .

Give me . . .
Mi dia . . .
Mee dee'-yah . . .

Show me . . .
Mi mostri . . .
Mee mos'-tree . . .

Send me . . .
Mi mandi . . .
Mee mahn'-dee . . .

Write to me . . .
Mi scriva . . .
Mee skree'-vah . .

I need . . .
Ho bisogno di . . .
Oh bee-zo'-nyoh dee . . .

I would like . . .
Vorrei . . .
Vor-reh'-ee . . .

I want . . .
Voglio (Desidero) . . .
Vo'-lyoh (deh-zee'-de-roh) . . .

I don't want . . .
Non voglio (desidero) . .
Non vo'-lyoh (deh-zee'-de-roh) . . .

I can do that.
Posso fare questo.
Pos'-soh fah'-reh kwes'-toh.

I cannot do that.
Non posso fare questo.
Non pos'-soh fah'-reh kwes'-toh.

Have you . . . ?
Ha Lei . . . ?
Ah leh'-ee . . . ?

Are you . . . ?
È Lei . . . ?
E leh'-ee . . . ?

Where is . . . ?
Dov'è . . . ?
Do-ve' . . . ?

Where are . . . ?
Dove sono . . . ?
Do'-veh soh'-noh . . . ?

It's possible.
È possibile.
E pos-see'-bee-leh.

It's impossible.
E impossibile.
È eem-pos-see'-bee-leh.

Emergencies

You will probably never need to use any of the brief
cries, entreaties, or commands that appear here, but
accidents do happen, items may be mislaid or stolen,
and mistakes do occur. If an emergency does arise, it
will probably be covered by one of these expressions.

Help!
Aiuto! Al soccorso!
*Ah-yoo'-toh! Ahl sok-kor'-
soh!*

Stop!
Alt! Fermate!
Ahlt! Fer-mah'-teh!

Help me!
Mi aiuti!
Mee ah-yoo'-tee!

Hurry up!
Faccia presto!
Fahch'-chah pres'-toh!

There has been an accident!
C'è stato un incidente!
*Che stah'-toh oon een-
chee-den'-teh!*

Look out!
Attenzione!
Aht-ten-tsyoh'-neh!

Send for a doctor!
Faccia venire un medico!
Fahch'-chah veh-nee'-reh oon meh'-dee-koh!

Poison!
Veleno!
Veh-leh'-noh!

Fire!
Fuoco!
Fwoh'-koh!

Police!
Polizia!
Poh-lee-tsee'-yah!

What happened?
Che cosa è successo?
Keh ko'-zah e sooch-chehs'-soh?

What's the matter?
Che c'è?
Keh che?

Don't worry!
Non si preoccupi!
Non see preh-ok'-koo-pee!

I missed the train (bus) (plane).
Ho perduto il treno (autobus) (aeroplano).
Oh per-doo'-toh eel treh'-noh (ow-toh-boos') (ah-eh-roh-plah'-noh).

I've been robbed!
Sono stato derubato!
Soh'-noh stah'-toh deh-roo-bah'-toh!

That man stole my money!
Quell'uomo mi ha rubato il denaro!
Kwel-lwoh'-moh mee ah roo-bah'-toh eel deh-nah'-roh!

Call the police!
Chiami la polizia!
Kyah'-mee lah poh-lee-tseo'-yah!

I have lost my money!
Ho perduto il mio denaro!
Oh per-doo'-toh eel mee-yoh deh-nah'-roh!

I have lost my passport!
Ho perduto il mio passaporte!
Oh per-doo'-toh eel mee'-yoh pahs-sah-por'-teh!

It's an American (British) passport.
È un passaporte americano (inglese).
E oon pahs-sah-por'-teh ah-meh-ree-kah'-noh (een-gleh'-zeh).

Stay where you are!
Rimanete dove siete!
Ree-mah-neh'-teh do'-veh sye'-teh!

Don't move!
Non si muova!
Non see mwoh'-vah!

Signs and Notices

You could probably get along in a foreign land without speaking a word if only you could read the signs and notices that are posted and displayed as directions and advertising. A sign is an immediate communication to him who can read it, and the pronunciation doesn't matter. Here are the messages of some common signs. Some will help you to avoid embarrassment, and others danger. And some of them will merely make life more pleasant.

A DESTRA, To the right
A SINISTRA, To the left
ALT, Stop
ALLARME D'INCENDIO, Fire alarm
APERTO, Open
APPARTAMENTI MOBIGLIATI D'AFFITTARE
   Furnished rooms to let
ASCIUGAMANI, Hand towels

ASPETTATE, Wait
ATTENZIONE, Caution
AVANTI, Go
AVVISO, Warning
CALDO, Warm
CASSIERE, Cashier
CHIESA, Church
CHIUSO, Closed
COLLINA, Hill
CURVA, Curve
CURVA PERICOLOSA, Dangerous curve
DEVIAZIONE, Detour
DIVIETO DI SOSTA, No parking
DONNE, Women
ENTRATA, Entrance
ENTRATA LIBERA, Admission free
È PERICOLOSO, It's dangerous
È PROIBITO PASSARE, No thoroughfare
È VIETATO L'INGRESSO, Keep out
È VIETATO FUMARE, No smoking
FREDDO, Cold
GABINETTO, Lavatory, toilet
INCROCIO FERROVIA, Railroad crossing
INCROCIO PERICOLOSO, Dangerous crossroad
INFORMAZIONI, Information
INGRESSO, Entrance
LAVORI IN CORSO, Men working
LA VIA CHIUSA, No thoroughfare
LIBERO, Free
NON BEVETE L'ACQUA, Do not drink the water
NON ENTRATE, Do not enter
NON GIRATE A DESTRA, No right turn
NON GIRATE A SINISTRA, No left turn

NON TOCCATE, Do not touch
OCCUPATO, Occupied
PEDAGGIO, Toll
PERICOLO, Danger
PONTE STRETTO, Narrow bridge
POSTEGGIO, Parking
PROIBITO, Forbidden
RALLENTARE, Slow, Go slow
RITIRATA, Toilet
SALA D'ASPETTO, Waiting room
SALA DA PRANZO, Dining room
SCUOLA, School
SENSO UNICO, One way
SIGNORE, Women
SIGNORI, Men
SI PERMETTE FUMARE, Smoking allowed
SPINGETE, Push
STANZA DA BAGNO, Bathroom
STRADA STRETTA, Narrow road
SUONATE, Ring
TENETE LA DESTRA, Keep to the right
TIRATE, Pull
UOMINI, Men
USCITA, Exit
VIETATO, Forbidden
VIETATO IL POSTEGGIO, No parking

Numbers, Time and Dates

You may only want to count your change or make an appointment or catch a train, but you will need to know the essentials of counting and telling time if you wish to stay on schedule, buy gifts, or pay for accommodations. In Europe, you should remember, time is told by a twenty-four hour system. Thus 10 P.M. in Italy is 2200 and 10:30 P.M. is 2230.

Cardinal Numbers

one
uno, una, un, un'
oo'-noh, oo'-nah, oon, oon'

two
due
doo'-eh

three
tre
tre

four
quattro
kwaht'-troh

five
cinque
cheen'-kweh

six
sei
seh'-ee

seven
sette
set'-teh

eight
otto
ot'-toh

nine
nove
no'-veh

ten
dieci
dyeh'-chee

eleven
undici
oon'-dee-chee

twelve
dodici
do'-dee-chee

thirteen
tredici
tre'-dee-chee

fourteen
quattordici
kwaht-tor'-dee-chee

fifteen
quindici
kween'-dee-chee

sixteen
sedici
seh'-dee-chee

seventeen
diciassette
dee-chahs-set'-teh

eighteen
diciotto
dee-chot'-toh

nineteen
diciannove
dee-chahn-no'-veh

twenty
venti
ven'-tee

twenty-one
ventuno
ven-too'-noh

twenty-two
ventidue
ven-tee-doo'-eh

thirty
trenta
tren'-tah

thirty-one
trentuno
tren-too'-noh

forty
quaranta
kwah-rahn'-tah

fifty
cinquanta
cheen-kwahn'-tah

sixty
sessanta
ses-sahn'-tah

seventy
settanta
set-tahn'-tah

eighty
ottanta
ot-tahn'-tah

ninety
novanta
no-vahn'-tah

one hundred
cento
chen'-toh

two hundred
duecento
doo-eh-chen'-toh

three hundred
trecento
tre-chen'-toh

five hundred
cinquecento
cheen-kweh-chen'-toh

one thousand
mille
meel'-leh

one million
un milione
oon mee-lyoh'-neh

nineteen hundred seventy- . . .
mille novecento settanta- . . .
meel'-leh no-veh-chen'-toh set-tahn'-tah- . . .

one man
un uomo
oon woh'-moh

one woman
una donna
oo'-nah don'-nah

one child
un bambino (un fanciullo)
*oon bahm-bee'-noh (fahn-
chool'-loh)*

two children
due bambini (fanciulli)
*doo'-eh bahm-bee'-nee
(fahn-chool'-lee).*

two women
due donne
doo'-eh don'-neh

two men
due uomini
doo'-eh woh'-mee-nee

Some Ordinal Numbers

the first
il primo
eel pree'-moh

the second
il secondo
eel seh-kon'-doh

the third
il terzo
eel ter'-tsoh

the fourth
il quarto
eel kwahr'-toh

the fifth
il quinto
eel kween'-toh

the sixth
il sesto
eel ses'-toh

the seventh
il settimo
eel set'-tee-moh

the eighth
l'ottavo
lot-tah'-voh

the ninth
il nono
eel noh'-noh

the tenth
il decimo
eel deh'-chee-moh

the first man
il primo uomo
eel pree'-moh woh'-moh

the first woman
la prima donna
lah pree'-mah don'-nah

the first child
il primo bambino
eel pree'-moh bahm-bee'-noh

the fifth floor
il quinto piano
eel kween'-toh pyah'-noh

the third day
il terzo giorno
eel ter'-tsoh johr'-noh

the fourth street
la quarta strada
lah kwahr'-tah strah'-dah

the second building
il secondo edifizio
eel seh-kohn'-doh eh-dee-fee'-tsyoh

Telling Time

What time is it?
Che ora è?
Keh oh'-rah e?

It's one o'clock.
È l'una.
E loo'-nah.

It's two o'clock.
Sono le due.
Soh'-noh leh doo'-eh.

It's a quarter after two.
Sono le due e un quarto.
*Soh'-noh leh doo'-eh eh
oon kwahr'-toh.*

It's half-past two.
Sono le due e mezza.
Soh'-noh leh doo'-eh eh med'-dzah.

It's a quarter till two.
Sono le due meno un quarto.
Soh'-noh leh doo'-eh meh'-noh oon kwahr'-toh.

It's ten after two.
Sono le due e dieci.
*Soh'-noh leh doo'-eh eh
dyeh'-chee.*

It's ten till two.
Sono le due meno dieci.
*Soh'-noh leh doo'-eh meh'-
noh dyeh'-chec.*

It's five o'clock.
Sono le cinque.
Soh'-noh leh cheen'-kweh.

It's ten o'clock.
Sono le dieci.
Soh'-noh leh dyeh'-chee.

It's noon.
È mezzogiorno.
E med-dzoh-jor'-noh.

It's midnight.
È mezzanotte.
E med-dzah-not'-teh.

It's early.
È presto.
E pre-stoh.

It's late.
È tardi.
E tahr'-dee.

one second
un secondo
oon seh-kon'-doh

five seconds
cinque secondi
cheen'-kweh seh-kon'-dee

one minute
un minuto
oon mee-noo'-toh

five minutes
cinque minuti
cheen'-kweh mee-noo'-tee

one quarter hour
un quarto d'ora
oon kwahr'-toh doh'-rah

one half hour
una mezz'ora
oo'-nah med-dzoh'-rah

one hour
un'ora
oon oh'-rah

five hours
cinque ore
cheen'-kweh oh'-reh

At what time are you leaving?
A che ora parte?
Ah keh oh'-rah pahr'-teh?

When do you arrive?
Quando arriva?
Kwahn'-doh ahr-ree'-vah?

When do you arrive?
Quando arriva?
Kwahn'-doh ahr-ree'-vah?

When will we arrive?
Quando arriveremo?
Kwahn'-doh ahr-ree-veh-reh'-moh?

When shall we meet?
Quando ci incontreremo?
Kwahn'-doh chee een-kon-treh-reh'-moh?

Meet me here at five o'clock.
M'incontri qui alle cinque.
Meen-kon'-tree kwee ahl'-leh cheen'-kweh.

At what time do you get up?
A che ora si alza?
Ah keh oh'-rah see ahl'-tsah?

At what time do you go to bed?
A che ora si corica?
Ah keh oh'-rah see koh'-ree-kah?

Dates

today
oggi
oj'-jee

tomorrow
domani
doh-mah'-nee

yesterday
ieri
ye'-ree

one day
un giorno
oon jor'-noh

two days
due giorni
doo'-eh jor'-nee

five days
cinque giorni
cheen'-kweh jor'-nee

the day after tomorrow
dopo domani
doh'-poh doh-mah'-nee

the day before yesterday
l'altro ieri
lahl'-troh ye'-ree

the morning
la mattina
lah maht-tee'-nah

the afternoon
il pomeriggio
eel poh-me-reej'-joh

the evening
la sera
lah seh'-rah

the night
la notte
lah not'-teh

the week
la settimana
lah set-tee-mah'-nah

the month
il mese
eel meh'-zeh

the year
l'anno
lahn'-noh

last week
la settimana scorsa
lah set-tee-mah'-nah skor'-sah

last month
il mese scorso
eel meh'-zeh skor'-soh

last year
l'anno scorso
lahn'-noh skor'-soh

this week
questa settimana
kwes'-tah set-tee-mah'-nah

this month
questo mese
kwes'-toh meh'-zeh

this year
quest'anno
kwest-ahn'-noh

next week
la settimana ventura (prossima)
lah set-tee-mah'-nah ven-too'-rah (pros'-see-mah)

next month
il mese venturo (prossimo)
eel meh'-zeh ven-too'-roh (pros'-see-moh)

next year
l'anno venturo (prossimo)
lahn'-noh ven-too'-roh (pros'-see-moh)

this morning
stamattina
stah-maht-tee'-nah

yesterday morning
ieri mattina
ye'-ree maht-tee'-nah

tomorrow morning
domani mattina
doh-mah'-nee maht-tee'-nah

this evening
stasera
stah-seh'-rah

yesterday evening
ieri sera
ye'-ree seh'-rah

tomorrow evening
domani sera
doh-mah'-nee seh'-rah

every day
tutti i giorni (ogni giorno)
toot'-tee ee jor'-nee (oh'-nyee jor'-noh)

two days ago
due giorni fa
doo'-oh jor'-nee fah

The Days of the Week

Monday
lunedì
loo-neh-dee'

Tuesday
martedì
mahr-teh-dee'

Wednesday
mercoledì
mer-koh-leh-dee'

Thursday
giovedì
joh-veh-dee'

Friday
venerdì
ve-ner-dee'

Saturday
sabato
sah'-bah-toh

Sunday
domenica
doh-meh'-nee-kah

The Months of the Year

January
gennaio
jen-nah'-yoh

February
febbraio
feb-brah'-yoh

March
marzo
mahr'-tsoh

April
aprile
ah-pree'-leh

May
maggio
mahj'-joh

June
giugno
joo'-nyoh

July
luglio
loo'-lyoh

August
agosto
ah-go'-stoh

September
settembre
set-tem'-breh

October
ottobre
ot-to'-breh

November
novembre
no-vem'-breh

December
dicembre
dee-chem'-breh

The Seasons

the spring
la primavera
lah pree-mah-veh'-rah

the summer
l'estate
le-stah'-teh

the autumn
l'autunno
low-toon'-noh

the winter
l'inverno
leen-ver'-noh

Changing Money

Whether poet or businessman, you will need cash as you travel. Sooner or later every traveler meets the problem of how to manage the exchange. The following phrases cover most situations you will encounter. You will help yourself if you obtain the latest official exchange rate before you leave home, and it can do no harm if you familiarize yourself with the sizes, shapes, and even colors of the various coins and bills. It is wise, too, to take along a small amount of the foreign currency for immediate use on arrival.

Where is the nearest bank?
Dov'è la banca più vicina?
Do-ve' lah bahn'-kah pyoo vee-chee'-nah?

Please write the address.
Scriva l'indirizzo, per piacere
Skree'-vah leen-dee-reet'-tsoh, per pyah-cheh'-reh.

I would like to cash this check.
Vorrei incassare quest'assegno.
Vor-reh'-ee een-kahs-sah'-reh kwest-ahs-seh'-nyoh.

Will you cash this check?
Vuole scontarmi quest'assegno?
Vwoh'-leh skon-tahr'-mee kwest-ahs-seh'-nyoh?

Do you accept travelers' checks?
Accettate assegni di viaggio?
Ahch-chet-tah'-teh ahs-seh'-nyee dee vyahj'-joh?

I want to change some money.
Voglio cambiare del denaro.
Voh'-lyoh kahm-byah'-reh del deh-nah'-roh.

What kind?
Che specie?
Keh speh'-chyeh?

Dollars.	**Pounds.**
Dollari.	Libbre.
Dol'-lah-ree.	*Leeb'-breh.*

What is the rate of exchange for the dollar (pound)?
Qual'è il cambio in dollari (libbre)?
Kwahl-e' eel kahm'-byoh een dol'-lah-ree (leeb'-breh)?

Your passport, please.
Il Suo passaporto, per piacere.
Eel soo'-woh puhs sah-por'-toh, per pyah-cheh'-reh.

How much do you wish to change?
Quanto desidera cambiare?
Kwahn'-toh deh-zee'-deh-rah kahm-byah'-reh?

I want to change ten dollars.
Voglio cambiare dieci dollari.
Voh'-lyoh kahm-byah'-reh dyah'-chee dol'-lah-ree.

Go to that clerk's window.
Vada allo sportello di quell'impiegato.
Vah'-dah ahl'-loh spor-tel'-loh dee kwel'-leem-pyeh-gah'-toh.

Here's the money.
Ecco il denaro.
Ek'-koh eel deh-nah'-roh.

Please give me some small change.
Per piacere, mi dia della moneta spicciola.
Per pyah-cheh'-reh, mee dee'-yah del'-lah moh-neh'-tah speech'-choh-lah.

Here's your change.
Ecco il resto.
Ek'-koh eel res'-toh.

Please count to see if it's right.
Lo conti, per favore, per vedere se è giusto.
Loh kon'-tee, per fah-voh'-reh, per veh-deh'-reh seh e joos'-toh.

Please sign this receipt.
Firmi questa ricevuta, per piaccre.
Feer'-mee kwes'-tah ree-cheh-voo'-tah, per pyah-cheh'-reh.

Can I change money here at the hotel?
Posso cambiare denaro qui in albergo?
Pos'-soh kahm-byah'-reh deh-nah'-roh kwee een ahl-ber'-goh?

I'm expecting some money by mail.
Aspetto denaro per la posta.
Ah-spet'-toh deh-nah'-roh per lah pos'-tah.

Customs

Your first experience with Italian may be with the personnel or fellow passengers on a ship or a plane, but you will really begin to use the language when you come to customs. Here are some phrases that will speed your entry into the country and get you on your way again.

Have you anything to declare?
Ha qualcosa da dichiarare?
Ah kwahl-ko'-zah dah dee-kyah-rah'-reh?

I have nothing to declare.
Non ho niente da dichiarare.
Non oh nyen'-teh dah dee-kyah-rah'-reh.

Your passport, please.
Il passaporto, prego.
Eel pahs-sah-por'-toh, preh'-goh.

Here is my passport.
Ecco il mio passaporto.
Ek'-koh eel mee'-yoh pahs-sah-por'-toh.

Are these your bags?
Sono queste le Sue valige?
Soh'-noh kwes'-teh leh soo'-weh vah-lee'-jeh?

Yes, and here are the keys.
Sì, ed ecco le chiavi.
See, ed ek'-koh leh kyah'-vee.

Open this box.
Apra questa scatola.
Ah'-prah kwes'-tah skah'-toh-lah.

Close your bags.
Chiuda le valige.
Kyoo'-dah leh vah-lee'-jeh.

Have you any cigarettes or tobacco?
Ha delle sigarette o tabacco?
Ah del'-leh see-gah-ret'-teh oh tah-bahk'-koh?

I have only some cigarettes.
Ho soltanto qualche sigaretta.
Oh sol-tahn'-toh kwahl'-keh see-gah-ret'-teh.

You must pay duty.
Lei deve pagare dazio.
Leh'-ee deh'-veh pah-gah'-reh dah'-tsyoh.

They are for my personal use.
Sono per il mio uso personale.
Soh'-noh per eel mee'-yoh oo'-zoh per-soh-nah'-leh.

How much must I pay?
Quanto devo pagare?
Kwahn'-toh deh'-voh pah-gah'-reh?

You must pay . . .
Deve pagare . . .
Deh'-veh pah-gah'-reh . . .

May I go now?
Posso andare adesso?
Pos'-soh ahn-dah'-reh ah-dehs'-soh?

Is that all?
Questo è tutto?
Kwes'-toh e toot'-toh?

Porter, please carry this luggage.
Facchino, per piacere, porti questo bagaglio.
Fahk-kee'-noh, per pyah-cheh'-reh por'-tee kwes'-toh bah-gahl'-yoh.

At the Hotel

Your accommodations may be a deluxe hotel, a modest hotel, a pension, or whatever, but it is important to be able to express your needs to be sure you get what you want. Outside of the cities, of course, few people are likely to be able to help you if you do not speak Italian, so we have given you the most useful expressions to cover most situations. They may make the difference between getting the room you want and having to settle for something less.

Which is the best hotel?
Qual'è il miglior albergo?
Kwahl-e' eel meel-yohr' ahl-ber'-goh?

This is a good hotel.
Questo è un buon albergo.
Kwes'-toh e oon bwon ahl-ber'-goh.

I like this hotel.
Mi piace quest'albergo.
Mee pyah'-cheh kwest-ahl-ber'-goh.

I would like to have a room here.
Vorrei prendere una camera qui.
Vor-reh'-ee pren'-de-reh oo'-nah kah'-meh-rah kwee.

A single room.
Una camera a un letto.
*Oo'-nah kah'-meh-rah ah
   oon let'-toh.*

A double room.
Una camera a due letti.
*Oo'-nah kah'-meh-rah ah
   doo'-eh let'-tee.*

A room with (without) bath.
Una camera con (senza) bagno.
Oo'-nah kah'-meh-rah kon (sehn'-tsah) bah'-nyoh.

May I see the room?
Posso vedere la camera?
*Pos'-soh veh-deh'-reh lah
   kah'-meh-rah?*

Is there a shower?
C'è una doccia?
Che oo'-nah doch'-chah?

This is a large room.
Questa è una camera grande.
Kwes'-tah e oo'-nah kah'-meh-rah grahn'-deh.

This room is too small.
Questa camera è troppo piccola.
Kwes'-tah kah'-meh-rah e trop'-poh peek'-koh-lah.

The room faces the street.
La camera dà sulla strada.
Lah kah'-meh-rah dah sool'-lah strah'-dah.

Do you have a quieter room?
Ha una camera più silenziosa?
Ah oo'-nah kah'-meh-rah pyoo see-len-tsyoh'-rah?

Do you have a room with a view of the ocean (court)?
Ha una camera con vista sull'oceano (sul cortile)?
*Ah oo'-nah kah'-meh-rah kon vees'-tah sool loh-cheh'-
   ah-noh (sool kor-tee'-leh)?*

What is the price of this room?
Qual'è il prezzo di questa camera?
Kwahl-e' eel preht'-tsoh dee kwes'-tah kah'-meh-rah?

That's much too expensive.
È troppo cara.
E trop'-poh kah'-rah.

That's very good.
È molto buono.
E mol'-toh bwoh'-noh.

Does the price include breakfast?
È compresa la prima colazione nel prezzo?
Eh kom-preh'-zah lah pree'-mah koh-lah-tsyoh'-neh nel pret'-tsoh?

Do you have a restaurant in the hotel?
C'è un ristorante nell'albergo?
Cheh oon rees-toh-rahn'-teh nel-lahl-ber'-goh?

Must we eat our meals in the hotel restaurant?
Dobbiamo mangiare i pasti nel ristorante dell'albergo?
Dob-byah'-moh mahn-jah'-reh ee pahs'-tee nel rees-toh-rahn'-teh del-lahl-ber'-goh?

Where is the dining room?
Dov'è la sala da pranzo?
Do-ve' lah sah'-lah dah prahn'-dzoh?

We will stay here.
Rimarremo qui.
Ree-mahr-reh'-moh kwee.

How long will you stay?
Quanto tempo rimarrà?
Kwahn'-toh tem'-poh ree-mahr-rah'?

I will stay three weeks.
Rimarrò tre settimane.
Ree-mahr-roh'-tre set-tee-mah'-neh.

We will stay three weeks.
Rimarremo tre settimane.
Ree-mahr-reh'-moh tre set-tee-mah'-neh.

Please fill out this card.
Riempia questa carta, per favore.
Ree-em-pee'-yah kwes'-tah kahr'-tah, per fah-voh'-reh.

My key, please.
La mia chiave, prego.
Lah mee'-yah kyah'-veh, preh'-goh.

What number, sir?
Che numero, signore?
Keh noo'-me-roh, see-nyoh'-reh?

I have lost my key.
Ho perduto la mia chiave.
Oh per-doo'-toh lah mee'-yah kyah'-veh.

Where is the elevator?
Dov'è l'ascensore?
Do-ve' lah-shen-soh'-reh?

Where is the key to my room?
Dov'è la chiave della mia camera?
Do-ve' lah kyah'-veh del'-lah mee-yah kah'-meh-rah?

Take my suitcase to my room.
Porti la mia valigia alla mia camera.
Por'-tee lah mee'-yah vah-lee'-jah ahl'-lah mee'-yah kah'-meh-rah.

Where is the bathroom?
Dov'è la stanza da bagno?
Do-ve' lah stahn'-tsah dah bah'-nyoh?

Open the window, please.
Apra la finestra, per favore.
Ah'-prah lah fee-nes'-trah, per fah-voh'-reh.

Close the window, please.
Chiuda la finestra, per favore.
Kyoo'-dah lah fee-nes'-trah, per fah-voh'-reh.

Please call the chambermaid.
Chiami la cameriera, per favore.
Kyah'-mee lah kah-meh-ree-ye'-rah, per fah-voh'-reh.

I want to have these shirts washed.
Desidero far lavare queste camice.
Deh-zee'-de-roh fahr lah-vah'-reh kwes'-teh kah-mee'-cheh.

This is not my handkerchief.
Questo non è il mio fazzoletto.
Kwes'-toh non e eel mee'-yoh faht-tsoh-let'-toh.

I want a towel and some soap.
Desidero un asciugamano e del sapone.
Deh-zee'-de-roh oon ah-shoo-gah-mah'-noh eh del sah-poh'-neh.

I want a clean towel.
Voglio un asciugamano pulito.
Vohl'-yoh oon ah-shoo-gah-mah'-noh poo-lee'-toh.

Please wake me at seven o'clock.
Per favore, mi svegli alle sette.
Per fah-voh'-reh, mee zve'-lyee ahl'-leh set'-teh.

We are leaving tomorrow.
Partiamo domani.
Pahr-tyah'-moh doh-mah'-nee.

Take my luggage down.
Faccia scendere il mio bagaglio.
Fahch'-chah shen'-de-reh eel mee'-yoh bah-gahl'-yoh.

Are there any letters for me?
Ci sono delle lettere per me?
Chee soh'-noh del'-leh let'-te-reh per meh?

I need some postage stamps.
Ho bisogno di alcuni francobolli.
Oh bee-zoh'-nyoh dee ahl-koo'-nee frahn-koh-bol'-lee.

Using the Telephone

Many visitors to foreign lands avoid using the telephone when they should not. Of course, gesturing and pointing are of no avail when you cannot see the person to whom you are speaking and have to depend entirely on what you hear and say. Still, it is possible to communicate if you make an effort. If there is difficulty, remember to ask the other person to speak slowly. It's your best assurance that the message will get through.

Where is there a telephone?
Dove c'è un telefono?
Do'-veh che oon te le'-foh-noh?

I would like to telephone.
Vorrei telefonare.
Vor-reh'-ee te-le-foh-nah'-reh.

I would like to make a (long-distance) call to . . .
Vorrei fare una telefonata (interurbana) a . . .
Vor-reh'-ee fah'-reh oo'-nah te-le-foh-nah'-tah (een-ter-oor-bah'-nah) ah . .

What is the telephone number?
Qual'è il numero telefonico?
Kwahl-e' eel noo'-me-roh te-le-foh'-nee-koh?

Where is the telephone book?
Dov'è l'elenco telefonico?
Do-ve' leh-lehn'-koh te-le-foh'-nee-koh?

My number is . . .
Il mio numero è . . .
Eel mee'-yoh noo'-me-roh eh . . .

Operator!
Telefonista!
Te-le-foh-nees'-tah!

I want number . . .
Desidero il numero . . .
Deh-zee'-de-roh eel noo'-me-roh . . .

Can I dial this number?
Posso fare questo numero?
Pos'-soh fah'-reh kwes'-toh noo'-me-roh?

How much is a telephone call to . . . ?
Quanto costa una chiamata telefonica a . . . ?
Kwahn'-toh kos'-tah oo'-nah kyah-mah'-tah te-le-foh'-nee-kah ah . . . ?

I am ringing.
Sto suonando.
Stoh swoh-nahn'-doh.

Please do not hang up.
Un momento, per favore.
Oon moh-men'-toh, per fah-voh'-reh.

Deposit coins.
Depositi della moneta.
Deh-poh'-zee-tee del'-lah moh-neh'-tah.

They do not answer.
Non rispondono.
Non ree-spon'-doh-noh.

Please dial again.
Faccia il numero di nuovo, per piacere.
Fahch'-chah eel noo'-me-roh dee nwoh'-voh, per pyah-cheh'-reh.

The line is busy.
La linea è occupata.
Lah lee'-neh-yah e ok-koo-pah'-tah.

Who is speaking?
Chi parla?
Kee pahr'-lah?

May I speak to . . . ?
Posso parlare con . . . ?
Pos'-soh pahr-lah'-reh kon . . . ?

He (she) is not in.
Non c'è.
Non che.

Please speak more slowly.
Parli più lentamente (adagio), per favore.
Pahr'-lee pyoo len-tah-men'-teh (ah-dah'-joh), per fah-voh'-reh.

Getting Around by Taxi and Bus

The drivers of taxis and buses almost never speak English, which may be fortunate when you relish a few peaceful moments. However, you will have to tell them where you're going, or want to go, and for that we've provided some handy phrases.

Call a taxi, please.
Chiami un tassì, per piacere.
Kyah'-mee oon tahs-see', per pyah-cheh'-reh.

Put my luggage into the taxi.
Metta il mio bagaglio nel tassì.
Met'-tah eel mee'-yoh bah-gahll'-yoh nel tahs-see'.

Driver, are you free?
Autista, è libero?
Ow-tees'-tah, e lee'-be-roh?

Where do you wish to go?
Dove desidera andare?
Do'-veh deh-zee'-de-rah ahn-dah'-reh?

Drive to the railroad station (airport).
Mi conduca alla stazione ferroviaria (all'aeroporto).
Meek on-doo'-kah ahl'-lah stah-tsyoh'-neh fer-roh-vee'-yah-ree-yah (ahll-ah-eh-roh-por'-toh).

How much is the ride from here to the hotel?
Quanto costa la passeggiata da qui all'albergo?
Kwahn'-toh kos'-tah lah pahs-sehj-jah'-tah dah kwee ahl-ahl-ber'-goh?

Stop here!
Fermi qui!
Fer'-mee kwee!

I want to get out here.
Voglio scendere qui.
Vohl'-yoh shen'-de-reh kwee.

Wait until I come back.
Aspetti finchè torni.
Ahs-pet'-tee feen-keh' tor'-nee.

Wait for me here.
Mi aspetti qui.
Mee ahs-pet'-tee kwee.

Drive a little farther.
Vada un po' più avanti.
Vah'-dah oon po pyoo ah-vahn'-tee.

Please drive carefully.
Vada con cura, per favore.
Vah'-dah kon koo'-rah, per fah-voh'-reh.

Please drive slowly.
Vada adagio, per favore.
Vah'-dah ah-dah'-joh, per fah-voh'-reh.

Turn to the left (right) here.
Giri a sinistra (destra) qui.
Jee'-ree ah see-nees'-truh (des'-trah) kwee.

Drive straight ahead.
Vada sempre diritto.
Vah'-dah sem'-preh dee-reet'-toh.

How much is the fare?
Quanto è la tariffa?
Kwahn'-toh e lah tah-reef'-fah?

Which bus goes downtown?
Quale autobus va al centro della città?
*Kwah'-leh ow-toh-boos' vah ahl chen'-troh del'-lah cheet-
tah'?*

Bus number . . .
L'autobus numero . . .
Low-toh-boos' noo'-me-roh . . .

Does the bus stop here?
L'autobus si ferma qui?
Low-toh-boos' see fer'-mah kwee?

Which bus goes to . . . ?
Quale autobus va a . . . ?
Kwah'-leh ow-toh-boos' vah ah . . . ?

Get on the bus here.	**Get off the bus here.**
Salga nell'autobus qui.	Scenda dall'autobus qui.
Sahl'-gah nell-ow-toh-boos'	*Shen'-dah dahll-ow-toh-*
kwee.	*boos' kwee.*

Please tell me when we arrive at . . . street.
Mi dica, per piacere, quando arriveremo alla via . . .
*Mee dee'-kah per pyah-cheh'-reh kwahn'-doh ahr-ree-ve-
reh'-moh ahl'-lah vee'-yah . . .*

Does this bus go to the museum?
Va quest'autobus al museo?
Vah kwest-ow-toh-boos' ahl moo-zeh'-oh?

Where must I transfer?
Dove devo trasferire?
Do'-veh deh'-voh trahs-fe-ree'-reh?

When does the last bus leave?
Quando parte l'ultimo autobus?
Kwahn'-doh pahr'-teh lool'-tee-moh ow-toh-boos'?

Eating and Drinking

Merely going abroad is thrill enough for some persons; for others the high points are likely to be the hours spent at the table. Getting to know and appreciate the national cuisine and learning how to order native dishes are extra thrills for many travelers. Here, to the phrases that are necessary to order your meals, we have added a menu reader of the most typical dishes of the cuisine in the countries where Italian is spoken.

I'm hungry.
Ho fame.
Oh fah'-meh.

I'm thirsty.
Ho sete.
Oh seh'-teh.

Are you hungry?
Ha fame?
Ah fah'-meh?

Are you thirsty?
Ha sete?
Ah seh'-teh?

I'm not hungry.
Non ho fame.
Non oh fah'-meh.

I'm not thirsty.
Non ho sete.
Non oh seh'-teh.

Do you want to eat now?
Vuole mangiare adesso?
Vwoh'-leh mahn-jah'-reh ah-dehs'-soh?

Let's eat now.
Mangiamo adesso.
Mahn-jah'-moh ah-dehs'-soh.

Where is there a good restaurant?
Dove c'è un buon ristorante?
Do'-veh che oon bwon ree-stoh-rahn'-teh?

The meals.
I pasti.
Ee pahs'-tee.

breakfast
la prima colazione
lah pree'-mah koh-lah-tsyoh'-neh

lunch
la seconda colazione
lah seh-kon'-dah koh-lah-tsyoh'-neh

dinner
il pranzo
eel prahn'-dzoh

supper
la cena
lah cheh'-nah

At what time is breakfast (lunch, dinner)?
A che ora si serve la prima colazione (la seconda colazione, il pranzo)?
Ah keh oh'-rah see ser'-veh lah pree'-mah koh-lah-tsyoh'-neh (lah seh-kon'-dah koh-lah-tsyoh'-neh, eel prahn'-dzoh)?

I want breakfast in my room.
Desidero la prima colazione nella mia camera.
Deh-zee'-deh-roh lah pree'-mah koh-lah-tsyoh'-neh nel'-lah mee'-yah kah'-mee-rah.

I would like . . .
Vorrei . . .
Vor-reh'-ee . . .

eggs uova *woh'-vah*	**fried eggs** uova fritte, uova alpiatto *woh'-vah freet'-teh, woh'-vah ahl pyaht'-toh*
scrambled eggs uova strapazzate *woh'-vah strah-pahd-dzah'-teh*	**two soft-boiled eggs** due uova bollite *doo'-eh woh'-vah bol-lee'-teh*
a poached egg un uovo affogato *oon woh'-voh ahf-foh-gah'-toh*	**bacon** pancetta, lardo *pahn-chet'-tah, lahr'-doh*
bread and butter pane e burro *pah'-neh eh boor'-roh*	**black coffee** caffè nero *kahf-fe' neh'-roh*
coffee with milk caffè latte *kahf-fe' laht'-teh*	**coffee without milk** caffè senza latte *kahf-fe' sehn'-tsah laht'-teh*
milk il latte *el laht'-teh*	**tea** il tè *eel te*
ham prosciutto *proh-shoot'-toh*	**cold meat** carne fredda *kahr'-neh frehd'-dah*
rolls panini *pah-nee'-nee*	

Breakfast is ready.
La prima colazione è servita.
Lah pree'-mah koh-lah-tsyoh'-neh e ser-vee'-tah.

Dinner is being served.
Il pranzo è servito.
Eel prahn'-dzoh e ser-vee'-toh.

A table for two, please.
Una tavola per due, per favore.
Oo'-nah tah'-voh-lah per doo'-eh, per fah-voh'-reh.

Where is the waitress?
Dov'è la cameriera?
Do-ve' lah kah-me-ree-yeh'-rah?

Waiter (waitress), the menu, please.
Cameriere (cameriera), la lista, per favore.
Kah-me-ree-yeh'-reh (kah-me-ree-yeh'-rah), lah lees'-tah, per fah-voh'-reh.

Waiter, please bring an ashtray.
Cameriere, porti un portacenere, per favore.
Kah-me-ree-yeh'-reh, por'-tee oon por-tah-cheh'-neh-reh, per fah-voh'-reh.

What do you recommend?
Che raccomanda? / Che mi consiglia?
Keh rahk-koh-mahn'-dah? / Keh mee kon-seel'-yah?

Do you recommend . . . ?
Raccomanda . . . ? / Mi consiglia . . . ?
Rahk-koh-mahn'-dah . . . ? / Mee kon-seel'-yah . . . ?

Bring me some coffee now, please.
Mi porti un po' di caffè adesso, per favore.
Mee por'-tee oon po dee kahf-fe' ah-dehs'-soh, per fah-voh'-reh.

More butter, please.
Più burro, per favore.
Pyoo boor'-roh, per fah-voh'-reh.

Bring some more sugar.
Porti più zucchero.
Por'-tee pyoo dzook'-ke-roh.

Bring me a glass of water, please.
Mi porti un bicchiere d'acqua, per favore.
Mee por'-tee oon beek-kee-ye'-reh dahk'-kwah, per fah-voh'-reh.

This coffee is cold.
Questo caffè è freddo.
Kwes'-toh kahf-fe' e frehd'-doh.

Do you take milk and sugar?
Prende latte e zucchero?
Pren'-deh laht'-teh eh dzook'-ke-roh?

The Condiments

the salt	**the pepper**
il sale	il pepe
eel sah'-leh	*eel peh'-peh*
the sugar	**the oil**
lo zucchero	l'olio
loh dzook'-ke-roh	*loh'-lyoh*
the vinegar	
l'aceto	
lah-cheh'-toh	
the mustard	
il senape, la mostarda	
eel seh'-nah-peh, lah mos-tahr'-dah	

No sugar, thank you.
Niente zucchero, grazie.
Nyen'-teh dzook'-ke-roh, grah'-tsee-yeh.

We eat only fruit for breakfast.
Mangiamo solo frutta alla prima colazione.
Mahn-jah'-moh soh'-loh froot'-tah ahl'-lah pree'-mah koh-lah-tsyoh'-neh.

This butter is not fresh.
Questo burro non è fresco.
Kwes'-toh boor'-roh non e fres'-koh.

This milk is warm.
Questo latte è caldo.
Kwes'-toh laht'-teh e kahl'-doh.

This milk is sour.
Questo latte è acido.
Kwes'-toh laht'-teh e ah'-chee-doh.

I would like a glass of cold milk.
Vorrei un bicchiere di latte freddo.
Vor-reh'-ee oon beek-kee-ye'-reh dee laht'-teh frehd'-doh.

Foods and Beverages

the fish
il pesce
eel peh'-sheh

fruit
la frutta
lah froot'-tah

the meat
la carne
lah kahr'-neh

the water
l'acqua
lahk'-kwah

vegetables
i legumi
ee leh-goo'-mee

the beer
la birra
lah beer'-rah

the wine
il vino
eel vee'-noh

the bread
il pane
eel pah'-neh

Another cup of coffee?
Un'altra tazza di caffè?
Oon ahl'-trah taht'-tsah dee kahf-fe'?

Another cup of tea?
Un'altra tazza di tè?
Oon ahl'-trah taht'-tsah dee te?

Do you want some more tea?
Vuole più tè?
Vwoh'-leh pyoo te?

Nothing more, thank you.
Nient'altro, grazie.
Nyent-ahl'-troh, grah'-tsee-yeh.

At what time are the meals in this hotel?
A che ora si servono i pasti in quest'albergo?
Ah keh oh'-rah see ser'-voh-noh ee pahs'-tee een kwest-ahl-ber'-goh?

We dine at seven o'clock.
Pranziamo alle sette.
Prahn-dzyah'-moh ahl'-leh set'-teh.

---

the cheese
il formaggio
eel for-mahj'-joh

the milk
il latte
eel laht'-teh

the butter
il burro
eel boor'-roh

the honey
il miele
eel myeh'-leh

the jam
la confettura
lah kon-fet-too'-rah

the salad
l'insalata
leen-sah-lah'-tah

the soup
la zuppa, la minestra
lah dzoop'-pah, lah mee-nes'-trah

Here they dine at eight o'clock.
Qui mangiano alle otto.
Kwee mahn'-jah-noh ahl'-leh ot'-toh.

Please reserve a table for us.
Prenoti una tavola per noi, per piacere.
Preh-noh'-tee oo'-nah tah'-voh-lah per noy, per pyah-cheh'-reh.

Do you want soup?
Vuole zuppa?
Vwoh'-leh dzoop'-pah?

The Setting

a spoon
un cucchiaio
oon kook-kee-ah'-ee-yoh

a small spoon
un cucchiaino
oon kook-kee-ah-ee'-noh

a knife
un coltello
oon kol-tel'-loh

a small knife
un coltello piccolo
oon kol-tel'-loh peek'-koh-loh

a fork
una forchetta
oo'-nah for-ket'-tah

a small fork
una forchetta piccola
oo'-nah for-ket'-tah peek'-koh-lah

a plate
un piatto
oon pyaht'-toh

a tray
un vassoio
oon vahs-soh'-yoh

a napkin
un tovagliolo
oon toh-vahl-yoh'-loh

Bring me a fork (a knife, a spoon).
Mi porti una forchetta (un coltello, un cucchiaio).
Mee por'-tee oo'-nah for-ket'-tah (oon kol-tel'-loh, oon kook-kee-ah'-ee-yoh).

This fork is dirty.
Questa forchetta è sporca.
Kwes'-tah for-ket'-tah e spor'-kah.

This spoon isn't clean.
Questo cucchiaio non è pulito.
Kwes'-toh kook-kee-ah'-ee-yoh non e poo-lee'-toh.

Please bring me a napkin.
Mi porti un tovagliolo, per favore.
Mee por'-tee oon toh-vahl-yoh'-loh, per fah-voh'-reh.

I would like a glass of wine.
Vorrei un bicchiere di vino.
Vor-reh'-ee oon beek-kee-ye'-reh dee vee'-noh.

A glass of red (white) wine.
Un bicchiere di vino rosso (bianco).
Oon beek-kee-ye'-reh dee vee'-noh ros'-soh (byahn'-koh).

A bottle of wine.
Una bottiglia di vino.
Oo'-nah bot-teel'-yah dee vee'-noh.

This wine is too warm.
Questo vino è troppo caldo.
Kwes'-toh vee'-noh e trop'-poh kahl'-doh.

A half-bottle.
Una mezza bottiglia.
Oo'-nah med'-dzah bot-teel'-yah.

Please bring some ice.
Porti un po' di ghiaccio, per favore.
Por'-tee oon po dee gyahch'-choh, per fah-voh'-reh.

I didn't order this.
Non ho ordinato questo.
Non oh or-dee-nah'-toh kwes'-toh.

A glass of beer.
Un bicchiere di birra.
Oon beek-kee-ye'-reh dee beer'-rah.

A bottle of beer.
Una bottiglia di birra.
Oo'-nah bot-teel'-yah dee beer'-rah.

To your health!
Alla Sua (Vostra) salute!
Ahl'-lah Soo'-wah (Vos'-trah) sah-loo'-teh!

Enjoy your meal!
Buon appetito!
Bwon ahp-peh-tee'-toh!

This tablecloth is not clean.
Questa tovaglia non è pulita.
Kwes'-tah toh-vahl'-yah non e poo-lee'-tah.

Do you eat fish?
Mangia pesce?
Mahn'-jah peh'-sheh?

He doesn't eat meat.
Lui non mangia carne.
Loo'-ee non mahn'-jah kahr'-neh.

I don't eat dessert.
Io non mangio dolci.
Ee'-yoh non mahn'-joh dohl'-chee.

He would like some ice cream.
Vorrebbe gelato.
Vor-reb'-beh jeh-lah'-toh.

Waiter, the check, please.
Cameriere, il conto, per favore.
Kah-me-ree-yeh'-reh, eel kon'-toh, per fah-voh'-reh.

How much do I owe you?
Quento Le devo?
Kwahn'-toh Leh deh'-voh?

Is the tip included?
È compreso il servizio?
*E kom-preh-zoh eel ser-
vee'-tsee-yoh?*

Where do I pay?
Dove pago?
Do'-veh pah'-goh?

At the cashier's booth.
Alla cassa.
Ahl'-lah kahs'-sah.

I have already paid.
Ho già pagato.
Oh jah pah-gah'-toh.

Here is a tip.
Ecco una mancia.
Ek'-koh oo'-nah mahn'-chah.

I left the tip on the table.
Ho lasciato la mancia sulla tavola.
Oh lah-shah'-toh lah mahn'-chah sool'-lah tah'-voh-lah.

There is a mistake in the bill.
C'è uno sbaglio nel conto.
Che oo'-noh zbahl'-yoh nel kon'-toh.

Menu
Reader

Zuppe ed Antipasti Soups and Appetizers

Antipasto (*ahn-tee-pahs'-toh*) Hor d'oeuvres.

Brodo (*broh'-doh*) Consomme.

Minestrone (*mee-nes-troh'-neh*) Vegetable soup with various regional additions.

Pastina in brodo (*pahs-tee'-nah een broh'-doh*) Pasta in soup broth.

Zuppa alla pavese (*dzoop'-pah ahl'-lah pah-veh'-zeh*) Egg soup.

Zuppa di pesce (*dzoop'-pah dee peh'-sheh*) Fish soup.

Farinacei Pasta Dishes

Cannelloni (*kahn-nel-loh'-nee*) Meat-filled pasta, baked in cheese and tomato sauce.

Ravioli alla fiorentina (*rah-vyoh'-lee ahl'-lah fyoh-ren-tee'-nah*) Cheese ravioli.

alla vegetariana (*ahl'-lah veh-jeh-tah-ree-yah'-nah*) Ravioli with tomato sauce.

fatti in casa (*faht-tee een kah-zah*) Home-made ravioli.

Spaghetti alla Bolognese (*spah-get'-tee ahl'-lah boh-lohn-yeh'-zeh*) Spaghetti with meat sauce.

alla bosaiola (*ahl'-lah boh-zah-yoh'-lah*) Spaghetti with tuna, mushrooms and cheese.

alla carbonara (*ahl'-lah kahr-boh-nah'-rah*) Spaghetti cooked in egg and bacon.

al pomodoro (*ahl poh-moh-doh'-roh*) Spaghetti with tomato sauce.

al sugo di carne (*ahl soo'-goh dee kahr'-neh*) Spaghetti with meat sauce.

alle vongole (*ahl-leh von-goh-leh*) Spaghetti with clam sauce.

Taglierini, fettuccine (*tahl-yeh-ree'-nee, fet-tooch-chee'-neh*) Noodles.

Pesce Fish

Acciughe (*ahch-choo'-geh*) Anchovies.

Aragosta (*ah-rah-gos'-tah*) Lobster.

Filetto di sogliola (*fee-let'-toh dee sohl'-yoh-lah*) Filet of sole.

Fritto misto (*freet'-toh mees'-toh*) Assorted tiny fried fish. Italian specialty.

Gamberi (*gahm'-beh-ree*) Shrimps.

Ostriche (*os'-tree-keh*) Oysters.

Sgombro (*zgom'-broh*) Mackerel.

Tonno (*ton'-noh*) Tuna fish.

Trotta (*trot'-tah*) Trout.

Carne Meat

Bistecca (*bees-tek'-kah*) Steak.

all'inglese (*ahl-leen-gleh'-zeh*) Rare.

ben cotta (*ben kot'-tah*) Well done.

Cervello (*cher-vel'-loh*) Brains.

Cotoletta alla bolognese (*koh-toh-let'-tah ahl'-lah boh-lohn-yeh'-zeh*) Veal cutlet with melted cheese.

  alla Milanese (*ahl'-lah mee-lah-neh'-zeh*) Breaded veal cutlet

Fegato (*feh'-gah-toh*) Liver.

Maiale (*mah-yah'-leh*) Pork.

Manzo lesso (*mahn'-dzoh les'-soh*) Boiled beef.

Pancetta (*pahn-chet'-tah*) Bacon.

Pollo alla cacciatora (*pol'-loh ahl'-lah kahch-chah-toh'-rah*) Stewed chicken.

  alla diavolo (*ahl'-lah dyah'-voh-loh*) Chicken broiled with herbs.

Prosciutto (*proh-shoot'-toh*) Thinly sliced, dark spicy ham.

Rosbif (*roz-beef'*) Roast beef.

Salsicce (*sahl-seech'-cheh*) Sausages.

Saltimbocca (*sahl-teem-bok'-kah*) Veal and ham dish. Italian specialty.

Spezzatino di manzo (*spet-tsah-tee'-noh dee mahn'-dzoh*) Beef stew.

Vitello al forno (*vee-tel'-loh ahl for'-noh*) Roast veal.

Verdura ed Insalata Vegetables and Salads

Asparagi (*ahs-pah'-rah-jee*) Asparagus.

Carciofi (*kahr-choh'-fee*) Artichokes.

Cavolo (*kah'-voh-loh*) Cabbage.

Cetrioli (*cheh-tree-yoh'-lee*) Cucumbers.

Cipolle (*chee-pol'-leh*) Onions.

Fagiolini (*fah-joh-lee'-nee*) String beans.

Finocchio (*fee-nok'-kyoh*) Type of celery.

Funghi (*foon'-gee*) Mushrooms.

Insalata mista (*een-sah-lah'-tah mees'-tah*) Mixed salad.

Insalata verde (*een-sah-lah'-tah ver'-deh*) Lettuce salad.

Lattuga (*laht-too'-gah*) Lettuce.

Melanzana (*meh-lahn-dzah'-nah*) Eggplant.

Olive (*oh-lee'-veh*) Olives.

Peperoni (*peh-peh-roh'-nee*) Green peppers.

Pomodori (*poh-moh-doh'-ree*) Tomatoes.
Spinaci (*spee-nah'-chee*) Spinach.
Zucchini (*dzook-kee'-nee*) Summer squash.

Frutte e Dolci Fruits and Desserts

Ananasso (*ah-nah-nahs'-soh*) Pineapple.
Arance (*ah-rahn'-cheh*) Oranges.
Banane (*bah-nah'-neh*) Bananas.
Cassata (*kahs-sah'-tah*) Ice cream with fruit.
Ciliegie (*chee-lee-yeh'-jeh*) Cherries.
Composta di frutta (*kom-pos'-tah dee froot'-tah*) Stewed
  fruit.
Formaggio (*for-mahj'-joh*) Cheese.
Gelato (*jeh-lah'-toh*) Ice cream.
Mela (*meh'-lah*) Apple.
Pasticceria (*pahs-teech-cheh-ree'-yah*) Pastry.
Pesca alla melba (*pes'-kah ahl'-lah mel'-bah*) Peach melba.
Pere (*peh'-reh*) Pears.
Pompelmo (*pom-pel'-moh*) Grapefruit.
Torta (*tor'-tah*) Cake.
Uva (*oo'-vah*) Grapes.

Bibite Beverages

Acqua (*ahk'-kwah*) Water.
Aranciata (*ah-rahn-chah'-tah*) Orangeade.
Birra (*beer'-rah*) Beer.
Caffè (*kahf-feh'*) Coffee.
  caffè latte (*kahf-feh' laht'-teh*) Coffee with milk.
Latte (*laht'-teh*) Milk.
Limonata (*lee-moh-nah'-tah*) Lemonade.
Sherry dolce (*sher'-ree dol'-cheh*) Sweet sherry.
Sherry secco (*sher'-ree sek'-koh*) Dry sherry.
Succhi di frutta (*sook'-kee dee froot'-tah*) Fruit juices.
Tè (*teh*) Tea.
Vino bianco (*vee'-noh byahn'-koh*) White wine.
Vino rosso (*vee'-noh ros'-soh*) Red wine.

Shopping

Shopping abroad is always an adventure and frequently a delight. It's not only the varied merchandise that you may buy to take home as gifts, but the sheer pleasure of making yourself understood. It's important to know, and to be able to explain, exactly what it is that you want since, obviously, you won't be able to trot downtown a week later to make an exchange. You'll discover, too, that sizes and weights are different; so we have included conversion tables here. Here are the typical questions that you or the salesman might ask or the statements you may make during your shopping trips.

I would like to go shopping.
Vorrei fare delle compre.
Vor-reh'-ee fah'-reh del'-leh kom'-preh.

At what time do the stores open?
A che ora si aprono i negozi?
Ah keh oh'-rah see ah'-proh-noh ee neh-goh'-tsee?

At what time do the stores close?
A che ora si chiudono i negozi?
Ah keh oh'-rah see kyoo'-doh-noh ee neh-goh'-tsee?

Where is there . . . ?
Dove c'è . . . ?
Do'-veh che . . . ?

an antique shop.
un negozio di antichità.
oon neh-goh'-tsyoh dee ahn-tee-kee-tah'.

a book store.
una libreria.
oo'-nah lee-bre-ree'-yah.

a candy store.
una confetteria.
oo'-nah kon-fet-te-ree'-yah.

a department store.
un grande magazzino.
oon grahn'-deh mah-gahd-dzee'-noh.

a dressmaker.
una sarta.
oo'-nah sahr'-tah.

a druggist.
un droghiere.
oon droh-gyeh'-reh.

a drugstore.
una farmacia.
oo'-nah fahr-mah-chee'-yah.

a florist.
un fioraio.
oon fee-yoh-rah'-yoh.

a grocery.
una bottega di comestibili.
oo'-nah bot-teh'-gah dee ko-mes-tee'-bee-lee.

a greengrocer.
un verduraio.
oon ver-doo-rah'-yoh.

May I help you?
Posso servirLe?
Pos'-soh ser-veer'-leh?

Will you help me, please?
Per piacere, mi aiuterà?
Per pyah-cheh'-reh, mee ah-yoo-te-rah'?

Are you being served? (m)
È stato servito?
Eh stah'-toh ser-vee'-toh?

Are you being served? (f)
È stata servita?
E stah'-tah ser-vee'-tah?

What do you wish?
Che cosa desidera?
Keh ko'-zah deh-zee'-deh-rah?

---

a hat shop.
una cappelleria.
oo'-nah kahp-pel-le-ree'-yah.

a jewelry store.
una gioielleria.
oo'-nah joy-el-le-ree'-yah.

a perfumery.
una profumeria.
oo'-nah proh-fee-me-ree'-yah.

a photography shop.
un negozio di fotografia.
oon neh-goh'-tsyoh dee foh-toh-grah-fee'-yah.

a shoe store.
una calzoleria.
oo'-nah kahl-tsoh-le-ree'-yah.

a tailor.
un sarto.
oon sahr'-toh.

a tobacconist.
una tabaccaio.
oo'-nah tah-bahk-kah'-yoh.

a toy store.
un negozio di giocattoli.
oon neh-goh'-tsyoh dee joh-kaht'-toh-lee.

a watchmaker.
un orologiaio.
oon oh-roh-loh-jah'-yoh.

I would like . . .
Vorrei . . .
Vor-reh'-ee . . .

---

a brassiere.
un reggipetto.
oon rej-jee-pet'-toh.

a handkerchief.
un fazzoletto.
oon faht-tshoh-let'-toh.

panties.
mutandine.
moo-tahn-dee'-neh.

shoes.
scarpe.
skahr'-peh.

a skirt.
una gonna.
oo'-nah gon'-nah.

socks.
calzette.
kahl-tset'-teh.

a suit.
un abito.
oon ah'-bee-toh.

a tie.
una cravatta.
oo'-nah krah-vaht'-tah.

underwear.
biancheria.
byahn-ke-ree'-yah.

gloves.
dei guanti.
deh'-ee gwahn'-tee.

a hat.
un cappello.
oon kahp-pel'-loh.

a shirt.
una camicia.
oo'-nah kah-mee'-chah.

shorts.
mutande.
moo-tahn'-deh.

a slip.
una sottana.
oo'-nah sot-tah'-nah.

stockings.
calze.
kahl'-tseh.

a sweater.
un maglione.
oon mah-lyoh'-neh.

an undershirt.
una camiciola.
oo'-nah kah-mee'-choh-lah.

I would like to buy . . .
Vorrei comprare . . .
Vor-reh'-ee kom-prah'-reh . . .

a battery.
una batteria.
oo'-nah baht-te-ree'-yah.

a camera.
una macchina fotografica.
*oo'-nah mahk'-kee-nah
foh-toh-grah'-fee-kah.*

film.
pellicola, film.
pel-lee'-koh-lah, feelm.

flashbulbs.
lampadine fotografiche.
*lahm-pah-dee'-neh foh-
toh-grah'-fee-keh.*

a pen.
una penna.
oo'-nah pen'-nah.

a pencil.
una matita.
oo'-nah mah-tee'-tah.

postcards.
cartoline postali.
*kahr-toh-lee'-neh pos-
tah'-lee.*

stamps.
francobolli.
frahn-koh-bol'-lee.

lotion.
lozione.
loh-tsyoh'-neh.

powder.
cipria.
cheep'-ree-yah.

razor blades.
lame da rasoio.
*lah'-meh dah rah-zoh'-
yoh.*

shampoo.
shampoo, frizionamento.
*shahm-poo', free-tsyoh-
nah-men'-toh.*

shaving cream.
crema da barba.
kreh'-mah dah bahr'-bah.

soap.
sapone.
sah-poh'-neh.

toothbrush.
spazzolino da denti.
*spaht-tshoh-lee'-noh dah
den'-tee.*

toothpaste.
pasta dentifricia.
*pahs'-tah den-tee-free'-
chah.*

Do you sell . . . ?
Vendete . . . ?
Ven-deh'-teh . . . ?

Do you have . . . ?
Ci avete . . . ?
Chee ah-veh'-teh . . . ?

Please show me some . . .
Per piacere, mi mostri . . .
Per pyah-cheh'-reh, mee mos'-tree . . .

What size, please?
Che misura, per favore?
Keh mee-zoo'-rah, per fah-voh'-reh?

Try on these . . .
Provi questi . . .
Proh'-vee kwes'-tee . . .

How much does it cost?
Quanto costa?
Kwahn'-toh kos'-tah?

How much do they cost?
Quanto costano?
Kwahn'-toh kos'-tah-noh?

That is too expensive.
Questo è troppo caro.
Kwes'-toh e trop'-poh kah'-roh.

That is cheap.
Questo è a buon mercato.
Ques'-toh e ah bwon mer-kah'-toh.

I like this one.
Questo mi piace.
Kwes'-toh mee pyah'-cheh.

I will take this one.
Prenderò questo.
Pren-de-roh' kwes'-toh.

---

cigar.
sigaro.
see'-gah-roh.

cigarettes.
sigarette.
see-gah-ret'-teh.

flint.
pietra focaia.
pye'-trah foh-kah'-yah.

fluid.
benzina.
ben-dzee'-nah.

lighter.
accendi-sigari.
ahch-cheh'-dee-see'-gah-ree.

matches.
fiammiferi.
fee-yahm-mee'-fe-ree.

I don't like this color.
Questo colore non mi piace.
Kwes'-toh koh-loh'-reh non mee pyah'-cheh.

I prefer it in . . .
Lo preferisco in . . .
Loh preh-fe-rees'-koh een . . .

black	**blue**	**brown**	**gray**
nero	azzurro	bruno, marrone	grigio
neh'-roh	*ahd-dzoor'-roh*	*broo'-noh, mahr'-roh'-neh*	*gree'-joh*

green	**red**	**white**	**yellow**
verde	rosso	bianco	giallo
ver'-deh	*ros'-soh*	*byahn'-koh*	*jahl'-loh*

dark		**light**	
scuro		chiaro	
skoo'-roh		*kyah'-roh*	

Sale
Vendita
Ven'-dee-tah

For Sale
Da vendere
Dah ven'-deh-reh

Clearance Sale
Vendita a stralcio, svendita
Ven'-dee-tah ah strahl'-choh, sven'-dee-tah

This dress is too short.
Questo vestito è troppo corto.
Kwes'-toh ves-tee'-toh e trop'-poh kor'-toh.

This skirt is too long.
Questa gonna è troppo lunga.
Kwes'-tah gon'-nah e trop'-poh loon'-gah.

I would like to see a white shirt.
Vorrei vedere una camicia bianca.
Vor-reh'-ee veh-deh'-reh oo'-nah kah-mee'-chah byan'-kah.

He would like to see some white shirts.
Lui vorrebbe vedere alcune camice bianche.
Loo'-ee vor-reb'-beh veh-deh'-reh ahl-koo'-neh kah-mee'-cheh byan'-keh.

The sleeves are too wide.
Le maniche sono troppo larghe.
Leh mah'-nee-keh soh'-noh trop'-poh lahr'-geh.

The sleeves are too narrow.
Le maniche sono troppo strette.
Leh mah'-nee-keh soh'-noh trop'-poh stret'-teh.

I would like to see some shoes.
Vorrei vedere delle scarpe.
Vor-reh'-ee veh-deh'-reh del'-leh skahr'-peh.

A pair of black (brown) shoes.
Un paio di scarpe nere (marroni).
Oon pah'-yoh dee skahr'-peh neh'-reh (mahr-roh'-nee).

Try this pair on.	**They are too narrow.**
Provi questo paio.	Sono troppo strette.
Proh'-vee kwes'-toh pah'-yoh.	*Soh'-noh trop'-poh stret'-teh.*

They are too (tight, loose, long, short).
Sono troppo (strette, sciolte, lunghe, corte).
Soh'-noh trop'-poh (stret'-teh, shol'-teh, loon'-geh, kor'-teh).

They are not big enough.
Non sono abbastanza grandi.
Non soh'-noh ahb-bahs-tahn'-tsah grahn'-dee.

Do you sell cigarettes?
Vendete sigarette?
Ven-deh'-teh see-gah-ret'-teh?

Do you have matches?
Avete fiammiferi?
Ah-veh'-teh fee-yahm-mee'-fe-ree?

I want to buy needles, pins, and some thread.
Voglio comprare aghi, spilli e del filo.
Vohl'-yoh kom-prah'-reh ah'-gee, speel'-lee eh del fee'-loh.

How many do you want?
Quanti ne vuole?
Kwahn'-tee neh vwoh'-leh?

Anything else?
Qualche altra cosa?
Kwahl'-keh ahl'-trah ko'-zah?

No, thank you. That's all.
No, grazie. Questo è tutto.
Noh, grah'-tsee-yeh. Kwes'-toh e toot'-toh.

I'll take it (them) with me.
Lo (Li) prenderò con me.
Loh (lee) pren-de-roh' kon meh.

Will you wrap it, please?
Vuole avvolgerlo, per favore?
Vwoh'-leh ahv-vol'-jer-loh, per fah-voh'-reh?

Send it to the hotel.
Lo mandi in albergo.
Loh mahn'-dee een ahl-ber'-goh.

Pack it (them) for shipment to . . .
Lo (Li) impacchi per spedizione a . . .
Loh (lee) eem-pahk'-kee per speh-dee-tsyoh'-neh ah . . .

Here is the bill.
Ecco la fattura.
Ek'-koh lah faht-too'-rah.

Is there a discount?
C'è uno sconto?
Cheh oo'-noh skon'-toh?

I will pay cash.
Pagherò in denaro contante.
Pah-ge-roh' een deh-nah'-roh kon-tahn'-teh.

CLOTHING SIZE CONVERSIONS: *Women*

Dresses, Suits and Coats

American:	8	10	12	14	16	18
British:	30	32	34	36	38	40
Continental:	36	38	40	42	44	46

Blouses and Sweaters

American:	32	34	36	38	40	42	44
British:	34	36	38	40	42	44	46
Continental:	40	42	44	46	48	50	52

Stockings

American & British:	8	8½	9	9½	10	10½	11
Continental:	35	36	37	38	39	40	41

Shoes

American:	5	5½	6	6½	7	7½	8	8½	9
British:	3½	4	4½	5	5½	6	6½	7	7½
Continental:	35	35	36	37	38	38	38½	39	40

Gloves

American, British and Continental sizes are the same.

CLOTHING SIZE CONVERSIONS: *Men*

Suits, Sweaters and Overcoats

American & British:	34	36	38	40	42	44	46	48
Continental:	44	46	48	50	52	54	56	58

Shirts

American & British:	14	14½	15	15½	16	16½	17	17½
Continental:	36	37	38	39	40	41	42	43

Socks

American and British:	9½	10	10½	11	11½	12	12½
Continental:	39	40	41	42	43	44	45

Shoes

American:	7	7½	8	8½	9	9½	10	10½	11	11½
British:	6½	7	7½	8	8½	9	9½	10	10½	11
Continental:	39	40	41	42	43	43	44	44	45	45

Getting Around by Automobile

Since few attendants who work at garages and stations speak English, some ability in Italian will be very useful. Your car will need gasoline, of course, and probably some regular servicing. And should there be some problem with it, a lot of time and energy will be saved if you can explain your needs.

I would like to hire a car.
Vorrei noleggiare una macchina.
Vor-reh'-ee noh-lej-jah'-reh oo'-nah mahk'-kee-nah.

How much does a car cost per day?
Quanto costa una macchina al giorno?
Kwahn'-toh kos'-tah oo'-nah mahk'-kee-nah ahl jor'-noh?

How much per kilometer?
Quanto per chilometro?
Kwahn'-toh per kee-loh'-meh-troh?

Is gasoline expensive in this country?
È cara la benzina in questo paese?
E kah'-rah lah ben-dzee'-nah een kwes'-toh pah-eh'-zeh?

Is there a deposit?
C'è un deposito?
Cheh oon deh-poh'-zee-toh?

I would like a car with seatbelts and an outside mirror, please.
Vorrei una macchina con cinture di posto e uno specchio esteriore, per favore.
Vor-reh'-ee oo'-nah mahk'-kee-nah kon cheen-too'-reh dee pos'-toh eh oo'-noh spek'-kyoh es-te-ree-yoh'-reh, per fah-voh'-reh.

I will (will not) take the car out of the country.
Prenderò (Non prenderò) la macchina fuori del paese.
Pren-deh-roh' (non pren-deh-roh') lah mahk'-kee-nah fwoh'-ree del pah-eh'-zeh.*

I want to leave it in . . .
Voglio lasciarla a . . .
Vohl'-yoh lah-shahr'-lah ah . . .

How much is the insurance per day?
Quanto è l'assicurazione al giorno?
Kwahn'-toh eh las-see-koo-rah-tsyoh'-neh ahl jor'-noh?

Here is the registration and the key.
Ecco la registrazione e la chiave.
Ek'-koh lah reh-jees-trah-tsyoh'-neh eh lah kyah'-veh.

Where is there a gas station?
Dove c'è una pompa di benzina?
Do'-veh che oo'-nah pom'-pah dee ben-dzee'-nah?

a garage?
un'autorimessa, un garage?
oon ow-toh-ree-mes'-sah, oon gah-rah'-jeh?

Fill it up.
Lo riempia.
Loh ree-em-pee'-yah.

Premium.
Superiore.
Soo-peh-ree-yoh'-reh.

Regular.
Ordinario.
Ord-dee-nah'-ree-yoh.

I want twenty liters of gasoline.
Voglio venti litri di benzina.
Vohl'-yoh ven'-tee lee'-tree dee ben-dzee'-nah.

I also need some oil.
Anche mi occorre un po' d'olio.
Ahn'-keh mee ok-kor'-reh oon po doh'-lyoh.

Please put in some water.
Metta dentro un po' d'acqua, per favore.
Met'-tah den'-troh oon po dahk'-kwah, per fah-voh'-reh.

Wash the car, please.
Lavi la macchina, per piacere.
Lah'-vee lah mahk'-kee-nah, per pyah-cheh'-reh.

Please inspect the tires.
Esamini le gomme (i pneumatici), per favore.
*Eh-zah-mee'-nee leh gom'-meh (ee pneh-oo-mah'-tee-chee),
    per fah-voh'-reh.*

Put in some air.
Metta dentro un po' d'aria.
*Met'-tah den'-troh oon po
    dah'-ree-yah.*

Is there a mechanic here?
C'è un meccanico qui?
*Che oon mek-kah'-nee-koh
    kwee?*

Can you fix a flat tire?
Può riparare una gomma forata?
Pwoh ree-pah-rah'-reh oo'-nah gom'-mah foh-rah'-tah?

How long will it take?
Quanto tempo ci vorrà?
Kwahn'-toh tem'-poh chee vor-rah'?

Have you a road map?
Ha una carta stradale?
Ah oo'-nah kahr'-tah strah-dah'-leh?

Where does this road go to?
Dove va questa strada?
Do'-veh vah kwes'-tah strah'-dah?

Is this the road to . . . ?
È questa la strada per . . . ?
E kwes'-tah lah strah'-dah per . . ?

Is the road good?
È buona la strada?
E bwoh'-nah lah strah'-dah?

A narrow road.
Una strada stretta.
Oo'-nah strah'-dah stret'-tah.

A wide road.
Una strada larga.
Oo'-nah strah'-dah lahr'-gah.

A narrow bridge.
un ponte stretto.
Oon pon'-teh stret'-toh.

A bad road.
Una cattiva strada.
Oo'-nah kaht-tee'-vah strah'-dah.

This road is slippery when it's wet.
Questa strada è scivolosa quando è bagnata.
Kwes'-tah strah'-dah e shee-voh-loh'-zah kwahn'-doh e bah-nyah'-tah.

Is there a speed limit here?
C'è un limite di velocità qui?
Che oon lee'-mee-teh dee veh-loh-chee-tah' kwee?

You were driving too fast.
Lei conduceva troppo veloce.
Leh'-ee kon-doo-cheh'-vah trop'-poh veh-loh'-cheh.

You must pay the fine.
Lei deve pagare la multa.
Leh'-ee deh'-veh pah-gah'-reh lah mool'-tah.

May I leave the car here?
Posso lasciare la macchina qui?
Pos'-soh lah-sha'-reh lah mahk'-kee-nah kwee?

May I park here?
Posso parcheggiare qui?
Pos'-soh pahr-kehj-jah'-reh kwee?

Where is the nearest garage?
Dov'è l'autorimessa più vicina?
Do-ve' low-toh-ree-mes'-sah pyoo vee-chee'-nah?

This car isn't running well.
Questa macchina non va bene.
Kwes'-tah mahk-kee'-nah non vah beh'-neh.

I have a driver's license.
Ho un patente.
Oh oon pah-ten'-teh.

Please check . . .
Per piacere, esamini . . .
Per pyah-cheh'-reh eh-zah-mee'-nee . . .

Can you fix it?
Può ripararlo?
Pwoh ree-pah-rahr'-loh?

How long will it take?
Quanto tempo ci vorrà?
Kwahn'-toh tem'-poh chee vor-rah'?

Your car is ready.
La Sua macchina è pronta.
Lah Soo'-wah mahk'-kee-nah e pron'-tah.

Drive carefully!
Conduca con cura!
Kon-doo'-kah kon koo'-rah!

Please wipe the windshield.
Per piacere, pulisca la parabrezza.
Per pyah-cheh'-reh, poo-lees'-kah lah pah-rah-bret'-tsah.

I don't know what the matter is.
Non so ciò che c'è.
Non soh choh keh che.

I think it's . . .	Is it . . . ?
Credo che è	È . . . ?
Creh'-doh keh e . . .	*E . . . ?*

the accelerator.	**the air filter.**
l'acceleratore.	il filtro d'aria.
lahch-cheh-leh-rah-toh'-reh.	*eel feel'-troh dah'-ree-yah.*
the battery.	**the brakes.**
la batteria.	i freni.
lah baht-teh-ree'-yah.	*ee freh'-nee.*
the carburetor.	**the clutch.**
il carburatore.	la frizione.
eel kahr-boo-rah-toh'-reh.	*lah free-tsyoh'-neh.*
the lights.	**the motor.**
i fari.	il motore.
ee fah'-ree.	*eel moh-toh'-reh.*
the spark plugs.	**the tires.**
le candele.	le gomme, i pneumatici.
leh kahn-deh'-leh.	*leh gom'-meh, ee pneh-oo-mah'-tee-chee.*
the wheel.	**the wheels.**
la ruota.	le ruote.
lah rwoh'-tah.	*leh rwoh'-teh.*
the front wheel.	**the back wheel.**
la ruota anteriore.	la ruota posteriore.
lah rwoh'-tah ahn-te-ree-yoh'-reh.	*lah rwoh'-tah pos-te-ree-yoh'-reh.*

Priority road ahead

Some International Road Signs

 = RED

= BLUE

= BLACK

Stop

Dangerous curve

Right curve

Double curve

Intersection

Intersection with secondary road

Railroad crossing
with gates

Railroad crossing
without gates

Road work

Pedestrian
crossing

Children

Road narrows

Uneven road

Slippery road

Traffic circle
ahead

Danger

Closed to
all vehicles

No entry

No left turn

No U turn

Overtaking
prohibited

Speed limit

Customs

No parking

Direction to
be followed

Traffic circle

No parking

Getting Around by Train

The railroad is the most frequently used means of transportation by travelers abroad. Schedules and timetables are usually readily understandable — if they are available and visible — but otherwise, in arranging your travel by train, you will need to use some of these phrases.

The railroad station.
La stazione ferroviaria.
Lah stah-tsyoh'-neh fer-roh-vee-yah'-ree-yah.

The train.
Il treno.
Eel treh'-noh.

Drive to the railroad station.
Mi conduca alla stazione ferroviaria.
Mee kon-doo'-kah ahl'-lah stah-tsyoh'-neh fer-roh-vee-yah'-ree-yah.

I need a porter.
Mi occorre un facchino.
Mee ok-kor'-reh oon fahk-kee'-noh.

Porter, here is my luggage.
Facchino, ecco il mio bagaglio.
Fahk-kee'-noh, ek'-koh eel mee'-yoh bah-gahl'-yoh.

These are my bags.
Queste sono le mie valige.
Kwes'-teh soh'-noh leh mee'-yeh vah-lee'-jeh.

Here are the baggage checks.
Ecco gli scontrini.
Ek'-koh lyee skon-tree'-nee.

Where is the ticket window?
Dov'è lo sportello dei biglietti?
Do-ve' loh spor-tel'-loh deh'-ee bee-lyet'-tee?

Have you a timetable?
Avete un orario?
Ah-veh'-teh oon oh-rah'-ree-yoh?

When does the train leave?
Quando parte il treno?
Kwahn'-doh pahr'-teh eel treh'-noh?

From which platform?
Da che piattaforma?
Dah keh pyaht-tah-for'-mah?

I want to check this baggage.
Desidero registrare questo bagaglio.
Deh-zee'-de-roh reh-jees-trah'-reh kwes'-toh bah-gahl'-yoh.

I must pick up a ticket.
Devo prendere un biglietto.
Deh-voh pren'-de-reh oon bee-lyet'-toh.

I want a ticket to . . .
Voglio un biglietto per . . .
Vohl'-yoh oon bee-lyet'-toh per . . .

First class.
Prima classe.
Pree'-mah klahs'-seh.

Second class.
Seconda classe.
Seh-kon'-dah klahs'-seh.

One way.
Andata solo.
Ahn-dah'-tah soh'-loh.

Round trip.
Andata e ritorno.
Ahn-dah'-tah eh ree-tor'-noh.

Is there a dining car?
C'è una carrozza ristorante?
Che oo'-nah kahr-rot'-tsah rees-toh-rahn'-teh?

Does this train go to . . . ?
Va questo treno a . . . ?
Vah kwes'-toh treh'-noh ah . . . ?

Does this train stop at . . . ?
Si ferma questo treno a . . . ?
See fer'-mah kwes'-toh treh'-noh ah . . . ?

Is the train late?
È in ritardo il treno?
E een ree-tahr'-doh eel treh'-noh?

Is this seat occupied?
È occupato questo posto?
E ok-koo-pah'-toh kwes'-toh pos'-toh?

What is the name of this station?
Come si chiama questa stazione?
Ko'-meh see kyah'-mah kwes'-tah stah-tsyoh'-neh?

How long do we stop here?
Quanto tempo ci fermiamo qui?
Kwahn'-toh tem'-poh chee fer-myah'-moh kwee?

May I open the window?
Posso aprire il finestrino?
Pos'-soh ah-pree'-reh eel fee-nes-tree'-noh?

Please close the door.
Per piacere, chiuda lo sportello.
Per pyah-cheh'-reh, kyoo'-dah loh spor-tel'-loh.

I have missed the train!
Ho perduto il treno!
Oh per-doo'-toh eel treh'-noh!

When does the next train leave?
Quando parte il prossimo treno?
Kwahn'-doh pahr'-teh eel pros'-see-moh treh'-noh?

Where is the waiting room?
Dov'è la sala d'aspetto?
Do-ve' lah sah'-lah dahs-pet'-toh?

Where is the lavatory?
Dov'è il gabinetto?
Do-ve' eel gah-bee-net'-toh?

The train is arriving now.
Il treno arriva adesso.
Eel treh'-noh ahr-ree-vah ah-dehs'-soh.

Tickets, please.
I biglietti, prego.
Ee bee-lyet'-tee, preh'-goh.

All aboard!
In carrozza!
Een kahr-rot'-tsah!

The train is leaving.
Il treno è in partenza.
Eel treh'-noh e een pahr-tehn'-tsah.

Arrivals.
Arrivi.
Ahr-ree'-vee.

Departures.
Partenze.
Pahr-tehn'-tseh.

Express train.
Il treno diretto. / Direttissimo.
Eel treh-noh dee-ret'-toh. / Dee-ret-tees'-see-moh.

Local train.
Il treno accelerato.
Eel treh'-noh ahch-cheh-leh-rah'-toh.

Getting Around by Ship and Plane

If you go abroad on a ship or airplane, your first chance to use your Italian will come in transit. Being able to speak with the personnel can be an exciting start to a journey. They will be more helpful, too, if you make an effort to speak to them in their language. And your efforts will be rewarded.

There's the harbor (the port).
Ecco il porto.
Ek'-koh eel por'-toh.

Where is the pier?
Dov'è il molo?
Do-ve' eel moh'-loh?

When does the ship sail?
Quando parte la nave?
Kwahn'-doh pahr'-teh lah nah'-veh?

Let's go on board!
Andiamo a bordo!
Ahn-dyah'-moh ah bor'-doh!

Where is cabin number . . . ?
Dov'è la cabina numero . . . ?
Do-ve' lah kah-bee'-nah noo'-me-roh . . . ?

Is this my cabin?
È questa la mia cabina?
E kwes'-tah lah mee'-yah kah-bee'-nah?

Steward, do you have the key to my cabin?
Cameriere, ha la chiave della mia cabina?
*Kah-meh-ree-ye'-reh, ah lah kyah'-veh del'-lah mee'-yah
kah-bee'-nah?*

I'm looking for the dining room.
Cerco la sala da pranzo.
Cher'-koh lah sah'-lah dah prahn'-dzoh.

We want a table for two.
Vogliamo una tavola per due.
Vohl-yah'-moh oo'-nah tah'-voh-lah per doo'-eh.

A first-class cabin.
Una cabina di prima classe.
Oo'-nah kah-bee'-nah dee pree'-mah klahs'-seh.

A second-class cabin.
Una cabina di seconda classe.
Oo'-nah kah-bee'-nah dee seh-kon'-dah klahs'-seh.

Let's go on deck.
Andiamo sul ponte.
Ahn-dyah' moh sool pon'-teh.

I would like a deck chair.
Vorrei una sedia a sdraio.
Vor-reh'-ee oo'-nah seh'-dyah ah zdrah'-yoh.

I would like to eat by the swimming pool.
Vorrei mangiare vicino alla piscina.
Vor-reh'-ee mahn-jah'-reh vee-chee'-noh ahl'-lah pee-shee'-nah.

The ship arrives at seven o'clock.
La nave arriva alle sette.
Lah nah'-veh ahr-ree'-vah ahl'-leh set'-teh.

When do we go ashore?
Quando scendiamo a terra?
Kwahn'-doh shen-dyah'-moh ah ter'-rah?

Where is the gangplank?
Dov'è la passerella (lo scalandrone)?
Do-ve' lah pahs-se-rel'-lah (loh skah-lahn-droh'-neh)?

The landing card, please.
Il permesso (cartoncino) di sbarco, prego.
Eel 'per-mes'-soh (kahr-ton-chee'-noh) dee zbahr'-koh, preh'-goh.

I wasn't seasick at all!
Non avevo mal di mare affatto!
Non ah-veh'-voh mahl dee mah'-reh ahf-faht'-toh!

Have a good trip!
Buon viaggio!
Bwon vyahj'-joh!

I want to go to the airport.
Voglio andare all'aeroporto.
Vohl'-yoh ahn-dah'-reh ahll-ah-eh-roh-por'-toh.

Drive me to the airport.
Mi conduca all'aeroporto.
Mee kon-doo'-kah ahll-ah-eh-roh-por'-toh.

When does the plane leave?
Quando parte l'aeroplano?
Kwahn'-doh pahr'-teh lah-eh-roh-plah'-noh?

When does it arrive?
Quando arriva?
Kwahn'-doh ahr-ree'-vah?

Flight number . . . leaves at . . .
Il volo numero . . . parte alle . . .
Eel voh'-loh noo'-me-roh . . . pahr'-teh ahl'-leh . . .

From which gate?
Da che porta?
Dah keh por'-tah?

I want to reconfirm my flight.
Voglio riconfirmare il mio volo.
Vohl'-yoh ree-kon-feer-mah'-reh eel mee'-yoh voh'-loh.

Ticket, please.
Il biglietto, prego.
Eel bee-lyet'-toh, preh'-goh.

Boarding pass, please.
Il permesso d'imbarco, prego.
Eel per-mes'-soh deem-bahr'-koh, preh'-goh.

Please fasten your seat belts.
Attaccate le cinture, prego.
Aht-tahk-kah'-teh leh cheen-too'-reh, preh'-goh.

No smoking.
Vietato fumare.
Vyeh-tah'-toh foo-mah'-reh.

Stewardess, a small pillow, please.
Hostess, un guanciale piccolo, per piacere.
Ohs-tess, oon gwahn-chah'-leh peek'-koh-loh, per pyah-cheh'-reh.

I fly to Europe every year.
Io volo all'Europa ogni anno.
Ee'-yoh voh'-loh ahll-eh-oo-roh'-pah oh'-nyee ahn'-noh.

The airplane is taking off!
L'aeroplano decolla.
Lah-eh-roh-plah'-noh deh-kol'-lah.

Is a meal served during this flight?
Si serve un pasto durante questo volo?
See ser'-veh oon pahs'-toh doo-rahn'-teh kwes'-toh voh'-loh?

The airplane will land in ten minutes.
L'aeroplano atterrerà fra dieci minuti.
Lah-eh-roh-plah'-noh aht-ter-re-rah' frah dyeh'-chee mee-noo'-tee.

There will be a delay.
Ci sarà un ritardo.
Chee sah-rah' oon ree-tahr'-doh.

There's the runway!
Ecco la pista!
Ek'-koh lah pees'-tah!

We have arrived.
Siamo arrivati.
Syah'-moh ahr-ree-vah'-tee.

Health

We hope you will never need the phrases you will find in this section; but emergencies do arise, and sickness does overwhelm. Since a physician's diagnosis often depends on what you, the patient, can tell him, you will want to make your woes clearly understood. If you have a chronic medical problem, you will want to have prescriptions or medical descriptions of the difficulty in hand or translated before you leave on your trip.

I need a doctor.
Ho bisogno d'un medico.
Oh bee-zoh'-nyoh doon meh'-dee-koh.

Send for a doctor.
Faccia venire un medico.
Fahch'-chah veh-nee'-reh oon meh'-dee-koh.

Send for a doctor.
Mandi chiamare un medico.
Mahn'-dee kyah-mah'-reh oon meh'-dee-koh.

Are you the doctor?
È Lei il medico?
E leh'-ee eel meh'-dee-koh?

What is the matter with you?
Che cosa ha?
Keh ko'-zah ah?

I don't feel well.
Non mi sento bene.
Non mee sen'-toh beh'-neh.

I am sick.
Sono ammalato (*m*) / ammalata (*f*).
Soh'-noh ahm-mah-lah'-toh (m) / -tah (f).

How long have you been sick?
Da quanto tempo è ammalato?
Dah kwahn'-toh tem'-poh e ahm-mah-lah'-toh?

I have a headache.
Ho mal di testa.
Oh mahl dee tes'-tah.

Where is the hospital?
Dov'è l'ospedale?
Do-ve' los-peh-dah'-leh?

Is there a drugstore near here?
C'è una farmacia qui vicino?
Che oo'-nah fahr-mah-chee'-yah kwee vee-chee'-noh?

I have a stomach ache.
Ho mal di stomaco.
Oh mahl dee stoh'-mah-koh.

Where does it hurt?
Dove Le duole?
Do'-veh leh dwoh'-leh?

My leg hurts.
La gamba mi fa male.
Lah gahm'-bah mee fah mah'-leh.

My finger is bleeding.
Il mio dito sanguina.
Eel mee'-yoh dee'-toh sahn'-gwee-nah.

Do I have a fever?
Ho una febbre?
Oh oo'-nah feb'-breh?

---

the arm, the arms
il braccio, le braccia
eel brahch'-choh, leh brahch-chah.

the back
la schiena
lah skyeh'-nah

the bladder
la vescica
lah veh-shee'-kah

the bone
l'osso
los'-soh

the chest
il petto
eel pet'-toh

the ear, the ears
l'orecchio, gli orecchi
loh-rek'-kyoh, lyee oh-rek'-kee.

the elbow
il gomito
eel goh'-mee-toh

the eye, the eyes
l'occhio, gli occhi
lok'-kyoh, lyee ok'-kee

the face
il viso, la faccia
eel vee'-zoh, lah fahch'-chah

the finger
il dito
eel dee'-toh

the foot, the feet
il piede, i piedi
eel pyeh'-deh, ee pyeh'-dee

the forehead
la fronte
lah fron'-teh

I have burned myself.
Mi sono bruciato (*m*) / bruciata (*f*).
Mee soh'-noh broo-chah'-toh (m) / -tah (f).

You must stay in bed.
Deve stare a letto.
Deh'-veh stah'-reh ah let'-toh.

How long?
Quanto tempo?
Kwahn'-toh tem'-poh?

---

the hair
i capelli
ee kah-pel'-lee

my hair
i miei capelli
ee myeh'-ee kah-pel'-lee

the hand, the hands
la mano, le mani
lah mah'-noh, leh mah'-nee

the head
la testa
lah tes'-tah

the heart
il cuore
eel kwoh'-reh

the hip
l'anca
lahn'-kah

the joint
la giuntura
lah joon-too'-rah

the kidneys
i reni
ee reh'-nee

the knee
il ginocchio
eel jee-nok'-kyoh

the leg, the legs
la gamba, le gambe
lah gahm'-bah, leh gahm'-beh

the liver
il fegato
eel feh'-gah-toh

the lung, the lungs
il polmone, i polmoni
eel pol-moh'-neh, ee pol-moh'-nee

At least two days.
Al meno due giorni.
Ahl meh'-noh doo'-eh jor'-nee.

Show me your tongue.
Mi mostri la lingua.
Mee mos'-tree lah leen'-gwah.

---

the mouth
la bocca
lah bok'-kah

the muscle
il muscolo
eel moos'-koh-loh

the neck
il collo
eel kol'-loh

the nose
il naso
eel nah'-zoh

the shoulder
la spalla
lah spahl'-lah

the skin
la pelle
lah pel'-leh

the skull
il cranio
eel krah'-nyoh

the spine
la spina dorsale
lah spee'-nah dor-sah'-leh

the stomach
lo stomaco
loh stoh'-mah-koh

the thigh
la coscia
lah ko'-shah

the throat
la gola
lah goh'-lah

the thumb
il pollice
eel pol'-lee-cheh

the toe
il dito del piede
eel dee'-toh del pyeh'-deh

the tooth, the teeth
il dente, i denti
eel den'-teh, ee den'-tee

the waist
la vita
lah vee'-tah

the wrist
il polso
eel pol'-soh

Lie down.
Si corichi.
See koh'-ree-kee.

Get up.
Si alzi.
See ahl'-tsee.

I have a cold.
Sono raffreddato (*m*) / raffreddata (*f*).
Soh'-noh rahf-frehd-dah'-toh (m) / -tah (f).

Do you smoke?
Fuma?
Foo'-mah?

Yes, I smoke.
Sì, fumo.
See, foo'-moh.

No, I don't smoke.
No, non fumo.
Noh, non foo'-moh.

Do you sleep well?
Dorme bene?
Dor'-meh beh'-neh?

No, I don't sleep well.
No, non dormo bene.
Noh, non dor'-moh beh'-neh.

I cough frequently.
Tossisco spesso.
Tos-sees'-koh spehs'-soh.

Take this medicine three times a day.
Prenda questa medicina tre volte al giorno.
Pren'-dah kwes'-tah meh-dee-chee'-nah tre vol'-teh ahl jor'-noh.

Here is a prescription.
Ecco una prescrizione.
Ek'-koh oo'-nah preh-skree-tsyoh'-neh.

Can you come again tomorrow?
Può venire di nuovo domani?
Pwoh veh-nee'-reh dee nwoh'-voh doh-mah'-nee?

Yes, I can come.
Sì, posso venire.
See, pos'-soh veh-nee'-reh.

I will come later.
Verrò più tardi.
Ver-roh' pyoo tahr'-dee.

He's a good doctor.
Lui è un buon medico.
*Loo'-ee e oon bwon meh'-
dee-koh.*

Sightseeing

No phrase book can possibly supply you with all the phrases you might want in the infinite number of situations, emotions, likes, and dislikes you will encounter in your travels. The basics are here, but they can only be a beginning. The dictionary at the back of this book will supply you with a larger vocabulary to use with the phrases given here. In addition, local bilingual or multilingual guides are usually very helpful in supplying other language information concerning a given situation. If an unusual phrase is required, ask him and it will be given to you gladly.

I would like to go sightseeing.
Vorrei girare per vedere delle curiosità.
Vor-reh'-ee jee-rah'-reh per veh-deh'-reh del'-leh koo-ree-yoh-zee-tah'.

How long does the tour last?
Quanto tempo dura il giro?
Kwahn'-toh tem-poh doo'-rah eel jee'-roh?

It lasts three hours.
Dura tre ore.
Doo'-rah tre oh'-reh.

Are you the guide?
È Lei la guida?
E leh'-ee lah gwee'-dah?

What is the name of this place?
Come si chiama questo luogo?
Ko'-meh see kyah'-mah kwes'-toh lwoh'-goh?

Are the museums open today?
Sono aperti i musei oggi?
Soh'-noh ah-per'-tee ee moo-zeh'-ee oj'-jee?

No, the museums are closed today.
No, i musei sono chiusi oggi.
Noh, ee moo-zeh'-ee soh'-noh kyoo'-zee oj'-jee.

The stores are open.
I negozi sono aperti.
Ee neh-goh'-tsee soh'-noh ah-per'-tee.

I would like to visit an art museum.
Vorrei visitare un museo d'arte.
Vor-reh'-ee vee-zee-tah'-reh oon moo-zeh'-oh dahr'-teh.

Is there an exhibition there now?
C'è un' esposizione lì adesso?
Che oon es-poh-zee-tsyoh'-neh lee ah-des'-soh?

I would like to see the city.
Vorrei vedere la città.
Vor-reh'-ee veh-deh'-reh lah cheet-tah'.

What is the name of that church?
Come si chiama quella chiesa?
Ko'-meh see kyah'-mah kwel'-lah kyeh'-zah?

May we go in?
Possiamo entrare?
Pos-syah'-moh en-trah'-reh?

Is the old church closed this morning?
È chiusa la vecchia chiesa stamattina?
E kyoo'-zah lah vek'-kyah kyeh'-zah stah-maht-tee'-nah?

Will it be open this evening?
Sarà aperta stasera?
Sah-rah' ah-per'-tah stah-seh'-rah?

This is the main square of the city.
Questa è la piazza principale della città.
Kwes'-tah e lah pyaht'-tsah preen-chee-pah'-leh del'-lah cheet-tah'.

May I take pictures here?
Posso fare delle fotografie qui?
Pos'-soh fah'-reh del'-leh fot-toh-grah-fee'-yeh kwee?

We have walked a lot.
Abbiamo camminato molto.
Ahb-byah'-moh kahm-mee-nah'-toh mol'-toh.

I am tired.
Sono stanco (*m*) / stanca (*f*).
Soh'-noh stahn'-koh (m) / -kah (f).

Let's sit down.
Sediamoci.
Seh-dyah'-moh-chee.

Where does this street lead to?
Dove va questa strada?
Do'-veh vah kwes'-tah strah'-dah?

To the cathedral.
Alla cattedrale.
Ahl'-lah kaht-teh-drah'-leh.

What is that monument?
Qual'è quel monumento?
Kwahl-e' kwel moh-noo-men'-toh?

Is that a theater?
È quello un teatro?
E kwel'-loh oon teh-yah'-troh?

It's a movie house.
È un cinema.
E oon chee'-neh-mah.

What is the name of this park?
Come si chiama questo parco?
Ko'-meh see kyah'-mah kwes'-toh pahr'-koh?

We cross the street here.
Attraversiamo la strada qui.
Aht-trah-ver-syah'-moh lah strah'-dah kwee.

Will we visit a castle?
Visiteremo un castello?
Vee-zee-teh-reh'-moh oon kahs-tel'-loh?

We will visit a palace.
Visiteremo un palazzo.
Vee-zee-teh-reh'-moh oon pah-laht'-tsoh.

Who lives in this palace?
Chi abita questo palazzo?
Kee ah'-bee-tah kwes'-toh pah-laht'-tsoh?

Nobody lives here.
Nessuno abita qui.
Nes-soo'-noh ah'-bee-tah kwee.

What is the name of this river?
Come si chiama questo fiume?
Ko'-meh see kyah'-mah kwes'-toh fyoo'-meh?

This is the longest bridge in the city.
Questo è il ponte più lungo della città.
Kwes'-toh e eel pon'-teh pyoo loon'-goh del'-lah cheet-tah'.

There's too much water in the boat.
C'è tropp'acqua nella barca.
Che trop-pahk'-kwah nel'-lah bahr'-kah.

Is our hotel near the river?
È il nostro albergo vicino al fiume?
E eel nos'-troh ahl-ber'-goh vee-chee'-noh ahl fyoo'-meh?

This is the shopping center.
Questo è il centro di compre.
Kwes'-toh e eel chen'-troh dee kom'-preh.

Is it far from here to the beach?
È lontano da qui alla spiaggia?
E lon-tah'-noh dah kwee ahl'-lah spyahj'-jah?

I would like to go swimming this morning.
Vorrei andare a fare il bagno stamattina.
Vor-reh'-ee ahn-dah'-reh ah fah'-reh eel bah'-nyoh stah-maht-tee'-nah.

If it doesn't rain, we'll go there.
Se no piove, ci andremo.
Seh non pyo'-veh, chee ahn-dreh'-moh.

Thank you for an interesting tour.
Grazie per un giro interessante.
Grah'-tsee-yeh per oon jee'-roh een-te-res-sahn'-teh.

Thank you very much for it.
La ringrazio molto.
Lah reen-grah'-tsyoh mol'-toh.

I like it.	**I liked it.**
Mi piace.	Mi è piaciuto.
Mee pyah'-cheh.	*Mee e pyah-choo'-toh.*

DICTIONARY

Some Tips On Italian Grammar

Gender Nouns in Italian are either masculine or feminine. This is important to know since the form of other parts of speech (articles, adjectives, pronouns) depends on whether they modify or appear in connection with a masculine or feminine noun. The indefinite and definite articles and adjectives, always agree with the noun in number and gender.

As a rule, nouns ending in "o" are masculine and those ending in "a" are feminine. Nouns ending in "e" in the singular may be either masculine or feminine, and the correct gender must be learned when the word is first encountered.

The definite articles (*the*) are *il* for the masculine singular nouns beginning with a single consonant (except "z") or with two consonants (except "s" plus consonant), and *lo* for masculine singular nouns beginning with "z" or with "s" plus consonant. The definite article *l'* is used before masculine and feminine singular nouns beginning with a vowel. The definite article *la* is used before feminine singular nouns beginning with a consonant or consonants. In plural nouns, *i* replaces the article *il*, and *gli* replaces *lo* and *l'* with masculine nouns. *Le* replaces *la* and *l'* with feminine noune. Notice the following:

il fiume (the river)	i fiumi (the rivers)
il vestito (the dress)	i vestiti (the dresses)
l'uomo (the man)	gli uomini (the men)
lo zio (the uncle)	gli zii (the uncles)
lo spillo (the pin)	gli spilli (the pins)
la donna (the woman)	le donne (the women)
l'acqua (the water)	le acque (the waters)

The indefinite articles (*a, an*) are *un* or *uno* for masculine singular nouns and *una* for feminine singular nouns.

un fiume (a river)
una donna (a woman)

Adjectives vary in gender according to the nouns they modify. Notice the following:

un fiume lung*o* (a long river)
fiumi lungh*i* (long rivers)
una spiaggia lung*a* (a long beach)
spiagge lungh*e* (long beaches)

When a woman or girl speaks of herself or refers to another female, the feminine form of the adjective must be used:

Sono ammalato.	**I am sick.** (a man speaking)
Sono ammalata.	**I am sick.** (a woman speaking)
È ammalato.	**He is sick.**
È ammalata.	**She is sick.**
Sono ammalati.	**They are sick.** (men or men and women)
Sono ammalate.	**They are sick.** (women only)

Plurals The plurals of nouns and adjectives are formed by substituting *-i* for masculine singular *-o* and masculine and feminine singular *-e*. Feminine plurals substitute *-e* for singular *-a*.

mela (apple)	mele (apples)
dente (tooth)	denti (teeth)
libro (book)	libri (books)
arancia (orange)	arance (oranges)
ponte (bridge)	ponti (bridges)
matita (pencil)	matite (pencils)

Word Order The order of words in Italian is much the same as in English, with two prime exceptions. In Italian the adjective usually follows the noun:

un fiume lungo	**a long river**
lo spillo piccolo	**the small pin**
il vestito nero	**the black dress**

And the indirect and direct object pronouns, in an affirmative statement, precede the verb:

He gave me the money.	Mi ha dato il denaro.
He gave it to me.	Me l'ha dato.

Verbs Person is indicated in Italian verbs by endings attached to the verb stem. In regular verbs, the verb stem is got by dropping the *-are*, *-ere*, and *-ire* from the infinite form. (Some verb stems are irregular.) Notice the following:

parl*are*, **to speak**
parl*o*, **I speak**
parl*a*, **he, she speaks; you** (polite) **speak**
parl*iamo*, **we speak**
parl*ate*, **you** (pl., polite) **speak**
parl*ano*, **they speak**

prend*ere*, **to take**
prend*o*, **I take**
prend*e*, **he, she takes; you** (polite) **take**
prend*iamo*, **we take**
prend*ete*, **you** (pl., polite) **take**
prend*ono*, **they take**

part*ire*, **to leave**
part*o*, **I leave**
part*e*, **he, she leaves; you** (polite) **leave**
part*iamo*, **we leave**
part*ite*, **you** (pl., polite) **leave**
part*ono*, **they leave**

fin*ire*, **to finish**
fin*isco*, **I finish**
fin*isce*, **he, she finishes; you** (polite) **finish**
fin*iamo*, **we finish**
fin*ite*, **you** (pl., polite) **finish**
fin*iscono*, **they finish**

There is a set of personal subject pronouns that indicate person with verbs, but they are used largely for emphasis:

parlo, I speak	io parlo, *I* speak
ho parlato, I spoke	io ho parlato, *I* spoke
parlano, they speak	essi parlano, *they* speak

The reflexive pronouns used with reflexive verbs (those ending in -*si* in the Dictionary) follow the same rule for word order given above.

a, uno, una, un, un' *oo'-noh, oo'nah, oon, oon*
able: to be able, potere *poh-teh'-reh*
aboard, a bordo *ah bor'-doh*
about *adv.,* quasi *kwah'-zee*
about *prep.,* circa *cheer'-kah*
above, sopra *soh'-prah*
abroad, all'estero *ahl-les'-te-roh*
absolutely, assolutamente *ahs-soh-loo-tah-men'-teh*
accelerate, accelerare *ahch-cheh-leh-rah'-reh*
accelerator, acceleratore *ahch-cheh-leh-rah-toh'-reh*
accent *n.,* accento *ahch-chen'-toh*
accept *v.,* accettare *ahch-chet-tah'-reh* [31]
accident, incidente *een-chee-den'-teh* [14]
according to, secondo *seh-kon'-doh*
account *n.,* conto *kon'-toh*
ache *n.,* dolore *doh-loh'-reh*
ache *v.,* far male, dolere *fahr mah'-leh, doh-leh'-reh*
acquaintance, conoscenza *koh-noh-shehn'-tsah*
across, attraverso *aht-trah-ver'-soh*
act *n.,* atto *aht'-toh*
act [do] *v.,* agire, fare *ah-jee'-reh, fah'-reh;* [drama],
   recitare *reh-chee-tah'-reh*
active, attivo *aht-tee'-voh*
actor, attore *aht-toh'-reh*
actress, attrice *aht-tree'-cheh*
actual, attuale *aht-too-ah'-leh*
add, sommare, aggiungere *som-mah'-reh, ahj-joon'-geh-
   reh*
address *n.,* indirizzo *een-dee-reet'-tsoh* [30]
admiration, ammirazione (f) *ahm-mee-rah-tsyoh'-neh*
admire, ammirare *ahm-mee-rah'-reh*
admission, ammissione (f) *ahm-mees-syoh'-neh*
admit, ammettere *ahm-met'-teh-reh*
adorable, adorabile *ah-doh-rah'-bee-leh*
advance *v.,* avanzare *ah-vahn-tsah'-reh*
advantage, vantaggio *vahn-tahj'-joh*

adventure, avventura *ahv-ven-too'-rah*
advertisement, pubblicità *poob-blee-chee-tah'*
advice, consiglio *kon-seel'-yoh*
advise, consigliare *kon-seel-yah'-reh*
affectionate, affettuoso *ahf-fet-too-oh'-zoh*
afraid: to be afraid, aver paura *ah-vehr' pah-oo'-rah*
after, dopo *doh'-poh*
afternoon, pomeriggio *poh-meh-reej'-joh*
afterwards, dopo *doh'-poh*
again, di nuovo *dee nwoh'-voh*
against, contro *kon'-troh*
age, età *eh-tah'*
agent, agente *ah-jen'-teh*
ago, fa *fah*
agree: to be in accord, essere d'accordo *es'-seh-reh dahk-kor'-doh*
agreeable [pleasing], gradevole *grah-deh'-voh-leh*
agreement, accordo *ahk-kohr'-doh*
ahead: straight ahead, sempre diritto *sem'-preh dee-reet'-toh*
air, aria *ah'-ree-yah* [74]
air filter, filtro d'aria *feel'-troh dah'-ree-yah*
air line, linea acrea *lee'-neh-yah ah-eh'-reh-yah*
airmail, posta aerea *pos'-tah ah-eh'-reh-yah*
airplane, aereo, aeroplano *ah-eh'-reh-oh, ah-eh-roh-plah'-noh* [89, 90]
airport, aeroporto *ah-eh-roh-por'-toh* [45, 88]
alarm, allarme (m) *ahl-lahr'-meh*
alarm clock, sveglia *zvehl'-yah*
alcohol, alcool *ahl-koh-ohl'*
alike, simile, somigliante *see'-mee-leh, soh-meel-yahn'-teh*
alive, vivo *vee'-voh*
all, tutto *toot'-toh* **not at all** [none], niente affatto *nyen'-teh ahf-faht'-toh*; [it's nothing], non c'è di che *non che dee keh* **after all,** dopo tutto *doh'-poh toot'-toh*

allergy, allergia *ahl-ler-jee'-yah*
allow, permettere *per-met'-teh-reh*
almond, mandorla *mahn'-dor-lah*
almost, quasi *kwah'-zee*
alone, solo *soh'-loh*
along, lungo *loon'-goh*
already, già *jah* [57]
also, anche *ahn'-keh*
altar, altare (m) *ahl-tah'-reh*
alter, modificarsi *moh-dee-fee-kahr'-see*
alteration [of clothing], alterazione *ahl-teh-rah-tsyoh'-neh*
although, sebbene, benchè *seb-beh'-neh, ben-keh'*
altogether, interamente *een-teh-rah-men'-teh*
always, sempre *sem'-preh*
am: I am, sono, sto, io sono *soh'-noh, stoh, ee'-yoh soh'-noh*
ambassador, ambasciatore (m) *ahm-bah-shah-toh'-reh*
American, americano *ah-meh-ree-kah'-noh*
amount, somma *som'-mah*
amusement, divertimento *dee-ver-tee-men'-toh*
amusing, divertente *dee-ver-ten'-teh*
an, uno, una, un, un' *oo'-noh, oo'-nah, oon, oon*
and, e, ed *eh, ehd*
anger *n.,* rabbia, collera *rahb'-byah, kol'-leh-rah*
angry, arrabbiato, adirato *ahr-rahb-byah'-toh, ah-dee-rah'-toh*
animal, animale (m) *ah-nee-mah'-leh*
ankle, caviglia *kah-veel'-yah*
announce, anunziare *ah-noon-tsyah'-reh*
annoy, annoiare *ahn-noh-yah'-reh*
another, un altro, un'altra *oon ahl'-troh, oon ahl'-trah*
answer *n.,* risposta *rees-pos'-tah*
answer *v.,* rispondere *rees-pon'-deh-reh* [42]
antique shop, negozio di antichità *neh-goh'-tsyoh dee ahn-tee-kee-tah'*
anxious, ansioso *ahn-syoh'-zoh*

any, alcuno *ahl-koo'-noh*
anyone, chiunque *kee-yoon'-kweh*
anyhow, comunque, in ogni modo *koh-moon'-kweh, een on'-yee moh'-doh*
anything, qualunque cosa, qualsiasi cosa *kwah-loon'-kweh ko'-zah, kwahl-see'-yah-zee ko'-zah*
anywhere, dovunque, ovunque *doh-voon'-kweh, oh-voon'-kweh*
apartment, appartamento *ahp-pahr-tah-men'-toh*
apologize, scusarsi *skoo-zahr'-see*
apology, apologia *ah-poh-loh-jee'-yah*
appear, apparire *ahp-pah-ree'-reh*
appendicitis, appendicite *ahp-pen-dee-chee'-teh*
appendix, appendice *ahp-pen'-dee-cheh*
appetite, appetito *ahp-peh-tee'-toh*
appetizer, antipasto *ahn-tee-pahs'-toh*
apple, mela *meh'-lah*
appointment, appuntamento *ahp-poon-tah-men'-toh*
appreciate, apprezzare *ahp-pret-tsah'-reh*
approve, approvare *ahp-proh-vah'-reh*
approximately, approssimativamente *ahp-pros-see-mah-tee-vah-men'-teh*
April, aprile *ah-pree'-leh*
arch, arco *ahr'-koh*
architect, architetto *ahr-kee-tet'-toh*
architecture, architettura *ahr-kee-tet-too'-rah*
are: you are, tu sei, Lei è *too say, leh'-ee e*   **you** (pl), **they are,** voi siete, essi sono *voy syeh'-teh, es'-see soh'-noh*   **we are,** noi siamo *noy syah'-moh*
area, area *ah'-reh-yah*
argue, disputare *dees-poo-tah'-reh*
arm, braccio *brahch'-choh*
around, intorno *een-tor'-noh*
arrange, regolare *reh-goh-lah'-reh*
arrest *v.,* arrestare *ahr-res-tah'-reh*
arrival, arrivo *ahr-ree'-voh* [85]

arrive, arrivare *ahr-ree-vah'-reh* [25, 46, 85, 87, 88, 90]
art, arte (f) *ahr'-teh* [99]
artichoke, carciofo *kahr-choh'-foh*
article, articolo *ahr-tee'-koh-loh*
artificial, artificiale *ahr-tee-fee-chah'-leh*
artist, artista *ahr-tees'-tah*
as, come *ko'-meh*
ashamed, vergognoso *ver-gon-yoh'-zoh*
ashore, a terra *ah ter'-rah* [88]
ashtray, portacenere (m) *por-tah-cheh'-neh-reh* [50]
ask, domandare *doh-mahn-dah'-reh*
asleep, addormentato *ahd-dor-men-tah'-toh*
asparagus, asparagi (m, pl) *ahs-pah'-rah-jee*
aspirin, aspirina *ahs-pee-ree'-nah*
assist, assistere *ahs-sees'-teh-reh*
assistant, assistente *ahs-sees-ten'-teh*
associate *n.,* socio *soh'-choh*
association, associazione (f) *ahs-soh-chah-tsyoh'-neh*
assure, assicurare *ahs-see-koo-rah'-reh*
at *prep.,* a, ad *ah, ahd*
Atlantic, Atlantico *aht-lahn'-tee-koh*
attach, accludere *ahk-kloo'-deh-reh*
attain [reach], ottenere *ot-teh-neh'-reh*
attempt *v.,* provare, tentare *proh-vah'-reh, ten-tah'-reh*
attend, attendere, assistere *aht-ten'-deh-reh, ahs-sees'-teh-reh*
attention, attenzione (f) *aht-ten-tsyoh'-neh*
attract, attirare *aht-tee-rah'-reh*
audience, udienza *oo-dyen'-tsah*
August, agosto *ah-gos'-toh*
aunt, zia *dzee'-yah*
author, autore (m) *ow-toh'-reh*
authority, autorità *ow-toh-ree-tah'*
automobile, automobile (f), macchina *ow-toh-moh'-bee-leh, mahk'-kee-nah*
autumn, autunno *ow-toon'-noh*

available, disponibile *dees-poh-nee'-bee-leh*
avenue, via, viale (m) *vee'-yah, vee-yah'-leh*
avoid, evitare *eh-vee-tah'-reh*
await, aspettare *ah-spet-tah'-reh*
awake *adj.,* sveglio *zvehl'-yoh*
awake *v.,* svegliarsi *zvehl-yahr'-see*
away, via, lontano *vee'-yah, lon-tah'-noh*
axle, asse (f) *ahs'-seh*

baby, bambino, bimbo *bahm-bee'-noh, beem'-boh*
bachelor, celibe (m) *cheh'-lee-beh*
back *adv.,* dietro *dyeh'-troh* **to go back,** tornare *tohr-nah'-reh*
back *n.,* schiena *skyeh'-nah*
bacon, pancetta, lardo *pahn-chet'-tah, lahr'-doh*
bad, cattivo *kaht-tee'-voh*
badly, male *mah'-leh*
bag, sacco, borsa *sahk'-koh, bor'-sah*; [suitcase], valigia *vah-lee'-jah* [34, 83]
baggage, bagaglio *bah-gahl'-yoh* [83]
baggage check, scontrino *skon-tree'-noh* [83]
bakery, panetteria *pah-net-teh-ree'-yah*
balcony, galleria, balcone (m) *gahl-leh-ree'-yah, bahl-koh'-neh*
ball, palla *pahl'-lah*
banana, banana *bah-nah'-nah*
band [music], banda *bahn'-dah*
bandage, benda *ben'-dah*
bank, banca *bahn'-kah* [30]
bar, bar (m) *bahr*
barber, barbiere (m) *bahr-byeh'-reh*
bargain *n.,* occasione (f) *ok-kah-zyoh'-neh*
basket, cestino *ches-tee'-noh*
bath, bagno *bahn'-yoh* [37]
bathe, bagnarsi, fare il bagno *bahn-yahr'-see, fah'-reh eel bahn'-yoh*

bathing suit, costume da bagno (m) *kos-too'-meh dah bahn'-yoh*

bathroom, stanza da bagno *stahn'-tsah dah bahn'-yoh* [39]

battery, batteria *baht-teh-ree'-yah*

bay, baia *bah'-yah*

be, essere, stare *es'-seh-reh, stah'-reh*

beach, spiaggia *spyahj'-jah* [102]

beans, fagioli *fah-joh'-lee*

beard, barba *bahr'-bah*

beautiful, bello *behl'-loh* [10]

beauty parlor, salone di bellezza *sah-loh'-neh dee bel-leht'-tsah*

because, perchè *per-keh'*

become, diventare *dee-ven-tah'-reh*

bed, letto *let'-toh* [94] **to go to bed,** andare al letto *ahn-dah'-reh ahl let'-toh*

bedroom, camera da letto *kah'-meh-rah dah let'-toh*

bee, ape (f) *ah'-peh*

beef, manzo *mahn'-dzoh*

beefsteak, bistecca *bee-stek'-kah*

beer, birra *beer'-rah* [56]

beet, barbabietola *bahr-bah-byeh'-toh-lah*

before [time], prima (di) *pree'-mah (dee)*; [place], davanti a *dah-vahn'-tee ah*

begin, cominciare *ko-meen-chah'-reh*

beginning, principio *preen-chee'-pyoh*

behind, dietro a *dyeh'-troh ah*

believe, credere *kreh'-deh-reh*

bell, campana *kahm-pah'-nah*

belong, appartenere *ahp-pahr-teh-neh'-reh*

belt, cintura *cheen-too'-rah* [73, 89]

beside, accanto a, al lato di *ahk-kahn'-toh ah, ahl lah'-toh dee*

besides, inoltre, di più *een-ohl'-treh, dee pyoo*

best, ottimo *ot'-tee-moh*

better *adj.*, migliore *meel-yoh'-reh*
better *adv.*, meglio *mehl'-yoh*
between, tra, fra *trah, frah*
big, grande, grosso *grahn'-deh, gros'-soh* [69]
bill, conto *kon'-toh* [57]
bird, uccello *ooch-chel'-loh*
birth, nascita *nah'-shee-tah*
birthday, compleanno *kom-pleh-ahn'-noh*
bit: a bit, un poco *oon poh'-koh*
bite *v.*, mordere *mor'-deh-reh*
black, nero *neh'-roh*
blanket, coperta *koh-per'-tah*
bleed, sanguinare *sahn-gwee-nah'-reh* [93]
blind, cieco *chyeh'-koh*
blister, bolla *bol'-lah*
block *n.*, masso *mahs'-soh*
blonde, biondo *byon'-doh*
blood, sangue (m) *sahn'-gweh*
blouse, blusa, camicetta *bloo'-zah, kah-mee-chet'-tah*
blue, azzurro *ahd-dzoor'-roh*
board: room and board, camera con vitto *kah'-meh-rah kon veet'-toh*
boarding house, pensione (f) *pen-syoh'-neh*
boarding pass, permesso d'imbarco *per-mes'-soh deem-bahr'-koh* [89]
boat, barca *bahr'-kah* [101]
body, corpo *kor'-poh*
boil *v.*, bollire *bol-lee'-reh*
bone, osso *os'-soh*
book, libro *leeb'-roh*
bookstore, libreria *leeb-reh-ree'-yah*
booth, cabina *kah-bee'-nah*
boot, stivale (m) *stee-vah'-leh*
border *n.*, frontiera, confine (m) *fron-tyeh'-rah, kon-fee'-neh*

born, nato *nah'-toh*

borrow, prendere a prestito *pren'-deh-reh ah pres'-tee-toh*

both, tutti e due (m), tutte e due (f) *toot'-tee eh doo'-eh, toot'-teh eh doo'-eh*

bottle, bottiglia *bot-teel'-yah* [55, 56]

bottle opener, cavatappi (m) *kah-vah-tahp'-pee*

bottom, fondo *fon'-doh*

box, scatola *skah'-toh-lah* [34]

boy, ragazzo *rah-gaht'-tsoh*

bracelet, braccialetto *brahch-chah-let'-toh*

brake *n.,* freno *freh'-noh*

brandy, acquavite (m), cognac *ahk-kwah-vee'-teh, kon-yahk'*

brassiere, reggipetto *rej-jee-pet'-toh*

brave, coraggioso *koh-rahj-joh'-zoh*

bread, pane (m) *pah'-neh*

break *v.,* rompere *rom'-peh-reh*

breakfast, prima colazione (f) *pree'-mah koh-lah-tsyoh'-neh* [38, 48, 50, 52]

breast, seno *seh'-noh*

breath, respiro *res-pee'-roh*

breathe, respirare *res-pee-rah'-reh*

bridge, ponte (m) *pon'-teh* [101]

bright, chiaro *kyah'-roh*

bring, portare *por-tah'-reh* [13, 50, 51, 55]

broken, rotto *rot'-toh*

brother, fratello *frah-tel'-loh* [3]

brown, marrone, bruno *mahr-roh'-neh, broo'-noh*

bruise *n.,* bernoccolo *ber-nok'-koh-loh*

brush *n.,* spazzola *spaht'-tsoh-lah*

brunette, bruno *broo'-noh*

build *v.,* costruire *kos-troo-ee'-reh*

building, edifizio *eh-dee-fee'-tsyoh*

burn *n.,* bruciatura *broo-chah-too'-rah*

burn *v.,* bruciare *broo-chah'-reh* [94]

burst, scoppiare *skop-pyah'-reh*
bus, autobus, pullman *ow'-toh-boos, pool'-mahn* [15, 46]
business, affari (m, pl) *ahf-fah'-ree*
busy, occupato *ok-koo-pah'-toh* [43]
but, ma *mah*
butter, burro *boor'-roh* [49, 50, 51]
button, bottone (m) *bot-toh'-neh*
buy, comprare *kom-prah'-reh* [66, 70]
by, da *dah*

cabbage, cavolo *kah'-voh-loh*
cabin, cabina *kah-bee'-nah* [86, 87]
café, caffè (m) *kahf-feh'*
cake, torta *tor'-tah*
call *n.,* chiamata *kyah-mah'-tah* [41, 42]
call *v.,* chiamare *kyah-mah'-reh* [15, 40, 44]
camera, macchina fotografica *mahk'-kee-nah foh-toh-grah'-fee-kah*
can *n.,* latta *laht'-tah*
can: to be able, potere *poh-teh'-reh* **I can,** posso *pos'-soh*
canal, canale (m) *kah-nah'-leh*
cancel *v.,* annullare *ahn-nool-lah'-reh*
candy, caramella, dolci *kah-rah-mel'-lah, dol'-chee*
candy store, confetteria *kon-fet-teh-ree'-yah*
capital, capitale (f) *kah-pee-tah'-leh*
car, automobile (f), macchina *ow-toh-moh'-bee-leh, mahk'-kee-nah* [72, 73, 74, 76]
carburetor, carburatore (m) *kahr-boo-rah-toh'-reh*
card, cartolina *kahr-toh-lee'-nah*
care, *n.,* cura *koo'-rah*
care *v.,* preoccuparsi (di) *preh-ok-koo-pahr'-see (dee)*
careful, cauto *kow'-toh*
carpet, tappeto *tahp-peh'-toh*
carrot, carota *kah-roh'-tah*
carry, portare *por-tah'-reh* [35]
cash *n.,* denaro contante *deh-nah'-roh kon-tahn'-teh* [70]

cashier, cassiere (m) *kahs-syeh'-reh* [57]

castle, castello *kahs-tehl'-loh* [101]

cat, gatto *gaht'-toh*

catch *v.,* prendere, acchiappare *pren'-deh-reh, ahk-kyahp-pah'-reh*

cathedral, cattedrale (f), duomo *kaht-teh-drah'-leh, dwoh'-moh* [100]

Catholic, cattolico *kaht-toh'-lee-koh*

catsup, salsa di pomodori *sahl'-sah dee poh-moh-doh'-ree*

cattle, bestiame (m) *bes-tee-yah'-meh*

cauliflower, cavolfiore (m) *kah-vol-fyoh'-reh*

caution, precauzione (f) *preh-kow-tsyoh'-neh*

cave, caverna, grotta *kah-ver'-nah, grot'-tah*

ceiling, soffitto *sof-feet'-toh*

celery, sedano *seh'-dah-noh*

cellar, cantina *kahn-tee'-nah*

cemetary, cimitero *chee-mee-teh'-roh*

center, centro *chen'-troh*

centimeter, centimetro *chen-tee'-meh-troh*

century, secolo *seh'-koh-loh*

ceremony, cerimonia *cheh-ree-moh-nee'-yah*

certain, certo *cher'-toh*

certainly, certo *cher'-toh*

chair, sedia *seh'-dyah* [87]

chambermaid, cameriera *kah-me-ree-yeh'-rah* [40]

champagne, sciampagna *shahm-pahn'-yah*

chance *n.,* caso, azzardo *kah'-zoh, ahd-dzahr'-doh*

change [coins], cambio *kahm'-byoh* [32]

change *v.,* cambiare *kahm-byah'-reh* [31, 32]

chapel, cappella *kahp-pehl'-lah*

charge *v.,* mettere sul conto *met'-teh-reh sool kon'-toh*

charming, grazioso, incantevole *grah-tsyoh'-zoh, een-kahn-teh'-voh-leh*

chauffeur, autista (m) *ow-tees'-tah*

cheap, a buon mercato *ah bwon mer-kah'-toh* [67]

check *n.*, assengo *ahs-sehn'-yoh* [31] **traveler's check,** assegno di viaggio *ahs-sehn'-yoh dee vyahj'-joh* [31]

check [one's luggage], spedire una valigia *speh-dee'-reh oo'-nah vah-lee'-jah* [83]

check [inspect], esaminare, verificare *eh-zah-mee-nah'-reh, veh-ree-fee-kah'-reh* [76]

cheek, guancia *gwahn'-chah*

cheese, formaggio *fohr-mahj'-joh*

cherry, ciliegia *chee-lee-yeh'-jah*

chest, petto *pet'-toh*

chicken, pollo *pol'-loh*

child, bambino, fanciullo *bahm-bee'-noh, fahn-chool'-loh*

chin, mento *men'-toh*

chocolate, cioccolata *chok-koh-lah'-tah*

choose, scegliere *shehl'-yeh-reh*

chop, costoletta *kos-toh-let'-tah*

Christmas, Natale (m) *nah-tah'-leh*

church, chiesa *kyeh'-zah* [99, 100]

cigar, sigaro *see'-gah-roh*

cigarette, sigaretta *see-gah-ret'-tah* [34, 70]

cinema, cinema *chee'-neh-mah*

circle, circolo *cheer'-koh-loh*

citizen, cittadino *cheet-tah-dee'-noh*

city, città *cheet-tah'* [99, 100, 101]

class, classe (f) *klahs'-seh* **first class,** prima classe *pree'-mah klahs'-seh* **second class,** seconda classe *seh-kon'-dah klahs'-seh*

classify, classificare *klahs-see-fee-kah'-reh*

clean *adj.,* pulito *poo-lee'-toh* [40, 55, 56]

clean *v.,* pulire *poo-lee'-reh*

cleaners, lavanderia a secco *lah-vahn-deh-ree'-yuh ah sek'-koh*

clear, chiaro *kyah'-roh*

climb, salire, arrampicarsi *sah-lee'-reh, ahr-rahm-pee-kahr'-see*

clock, orologio *oh-roh-lohj'-joh*

close [near], vicino *vee-chee'-noh*

close *v.,* chiudere *kyoo'-deh-reh* [34, 39, 62, 84, 99, 100]

closed, chiuso *kyoo'-zoh* [99, 100]

closet, armadio *ahr-mah'-dyoh*

cloth, tela *teh'-lah*

clothes, vestiti *ves-tee'-tee*

cloud, nuvola *noo'-voh-lah* [7]

clutch [of a car], frizione (f) *free-tsyoh'-neh*

coast, costa *kos'-tah*

coat, cappotto, soprabito *kahp-pot'-toh, soh-prah'-bee-toh*

cocktail, cocktail *kok'-tehl*

coffee, caffè (m) *kahf-feh'* [49, 50, 51, 53]

cognac, cognac (m) *kon-yahk'*

coin, moneta *moh-neh'-tah* [42]

cold *adj.,* freddo *frehd'-doh* [51, 52] **I am cold,** ho freddo *oh frehd'-doh* **it is cold,** fa freddo *fah frehd'-doh*

cold *n.,* raffreddore (m) *rahf-frehd-doh'-reh* [96]

collar, colletto *kol-let'-toh*

collect, raccogliere *rahk-kohl'-yeh-reh*

collection, collezione (f) *kol-leh-tsyoh'-neh*

college, università, collegio *oo-nee-ver-see-tah', kol-lehj'-joh*

collide, scontrarsi *skon-trahr'-see*

color, colore (m) *koh-loh'-reh* [68]

comb, pettine (m) *pet'-tee-neh*

come, venire *veh-nee'-reh* [12, 96, 97]

comfortable, comodo *koh'-moh-doh*

company, compagnia, ditta *kom-pahn-yee'-yah, deet'-tah*

comparison, paragone (m), confronto *pah-rah'-goh-neh, kon-fron'-toh*

compartment, compartimento *kom-pahr-tee-men'-toh*

complain, lamentarsi, lagnarsi *lah-men-tahr'-see, lahn-yahr'-see*

complete *adj.,* completo *kom-pleh'-toh*

compliment *n.*, complimento *kom-plee-men'-toh*

concert, concerto *kon-cher'-toh*

condition, condizione (f) *kon-dee-tsyoh'-neh*

confuse, confondere *kon-fon'-deh-reh*

congratulations, congratulazioni (f, pl) *kon-grah-too-lah-tsyoh'-nee*

connect, connettere *kon-net'-teh-reh*

consent *v.*, consentire *kon-sen-tee'-reh*

consider, considerare *kon-see-deh-rah'-reh*

constipated, costipato *kos-tee-pah'-toh*

consul, console (m) *kon'-soh-leh*

consulate, consolato *kon-soh-lah'-toh*

contagious, contagioso *kon-tah-joh'-zoh*

contain, contenere *kon-teh-neh'-reh*

contented, contento *kon-ten'-toh*

continue, continuare *kon-tee-noo-ah'-reh*

contrary, contrario *kon-trah'-ree-yoh*   **on the contrary**, al contrario *ahl kon-trah'-ree-yoh*

convenient, conveniente *kon-veh-nyen'-teh*

conversation, conversazione (f) *kon-ver-sah-tsyoh'-neh*

cook *n.*, cuoco *kwoh'-koh*

cook *v.*, cuocere *kwoh'-cheh-reh*

cool, fresco *fres'-koh* [8]

copy, copia *koh'-pyah*

corkscrew, cavatappi (m) *kah-vah-tahp'-pee*

corn, frumento *froo-men'-toh*

corner, angolo *ahn'-goh-loh*

correct *adj.*, corretto *kor-ret'-toh*

cost *n.*, costo *kos'-toh*

cost *v.*, costare *kos-tah'-reh* [67, 72]

cotton, cotone (m) *koh-toh'-neh*

cough *n*, tosse (f) *tos'-seh*

cough *v.*, tossire *tos-see'-reh* [96]

count *v.*, contare *kon-tah'-reh* [32]

country [nation], paese (m) *pah-eh'-zeh* [73]; [not city], campagna *kahm-pahn'-yah*

courage, coraggio *koh-rahj-joh*

course, corso *kor'-soh* **of course,** certo *cher'-toh* **main course,** piatto principale *pyaht'-toh preen-chee-pah'-leh*

court, tribunale (m) *tree-boo-nah'-leh*

courtyard, cortile (m) *kor-tee'-leh* [37]

cover *v.*, coprire *koh-pree'-reh*

cow, vacca, mucca *vahk'-kah, mook'-kah*

crab, granchio *grahn'-kyoh*

cramp, crampo *krahm'-poh*

crazy, pazzo, matto *paht'-tsoh, maht'-toh*

cream, crema, panna *kreh'-mah, pahn'-nah*

cross *n.*, croce (f) *kroh'-cheh*

cross *v.*, attraversare *aht-trah-ver-sah'-reh* [101]

crossing, incrocio *een-kroh'-choh;* [by ship], traversata *trah-ver-sah'-tah*

crossroads, incrocio, bivio *een-kroh'-choh, bee'-vee-yoh*

crowd, folla *fol'-lah*

cry *v.*, piangere *pyahn-jeh'-reh*

cucumber, cetriolo *cheh-tree-yoh'-loh*

cup, tazza *taht'-tsah* [53]

curve, curva *koor'-vah*

custard, crema *kreh'-mah*

customer, cliente (m) *klee-yen'-teh*

customs, dogana *doh-gah'-nah*

cut [injury], piaga *pyah'-gah*

cut *v.*, tagliare *tahl-yah'-reh*

cutlet, costoletta *kos-toh-let'-tah*

daily *adj.*, quotidiano *kwoh-tee-dyah'-noh*

daily *adv.*, ogni giorno *oh'-nyee johr'-noh*

damage *v.*, danneggiare *dahn-nehj-jah'-reh*

damaged, danneggiato *dahn-nehj-jah'-toh*

damp, umido *oo'-mee-doh* [8]

dance *n.*, ballo *bahl'-loh*

dance *v.*, ballare *bahl-lah'-reh*

danger, pericolo *peh-ree'-koh-loh*

dangerous, pericoloso *peh-ree-koh-loh'-zoh*

dare *v.,* osare *oh-zah'-reh*

dark, scuro, buio *skoo'-roh, boo'-ee-yoh*

darkness, oscurità *oh-skoo-ree-tah'*

date [time], data *dah'-tah;* [appointment], appuntamento *ahp-poon-tah-men'-toh*

daughter, figlia *feel'-yah* [3]

day, giorno *johr'-noh* **per day, a day,** al giorno *ahl johr'-noh*

dead, morto *mor'-toh*

dear [endearment], caro *kah'-roh*

December, dicembre *dee-chem'-breh*

decide, decidere *deh-chee'-deh-reh*

deck, ponte *pon'-teh* [87]

declare, dichiarare *dee-kyah-rah'-reh* [33]

deep, profondo *proh-fon'-doh*

deer, cervo *cher'-voh*

delay *n.,* ritardo *ree-tahr'-doh* [90]

delicious, delizioso *deh-lee-tsyoh'-zoh*

delighted, felicissimo *feh-lee-chees'-see-moh*

deliver, consegnare *kon-sehn-yah'-reh*

dentist, dentista (m) *den-tees'-tah*

deodorant, deodorante (m) *deh-oh-doh-ruhn'-teh*

department store, grande magazzino *grahn'-deh mah-gahd-dzee'-noh*

departure, partenza *pahr-tehn'-tsah* [85]

deposit *v.,* depositare *deh-poh-zee-tah'-reh* [42]

descend, scendere *shen'-deh-reh*

describe, descrivere *deh-skree'-veh-reh*

desert *n.,* deserto *deh-zer'-toh*

desert *v.,* disertare, abbandonare *dee-zer-tah'-reh, ahb-bahn-doh-nah'-reh*

desire *v.,* desiderare *deh-zee-deh-rah'-reh*

desk, scrivania *skree-vah-nee'-yah*

dessert, dessert, dolci *dehs-ser', dohl'-chee* [56]

destroy, distruggere *dee-strooj'-jeh-reh*

detour, deviazione (f) *deh-vee-yah-tsyoh'-neh*

develop, sviluppare *zvee-loop-pah'-reh*

dial *v.,* fare il numero *fah'-reh eel noo'-meh-roh* [42, 43]

diamond, diamante (m) *dee-yah-mahn'-teh*

diaper, pannilino *pahn-nee-lee'-noh*

diarrhea, diarrea *dee-yahr-reh'-yah*

dictionary, dizionario *dee-tsee-yoh-nah'-ree-yoh*

die, morire *moh-ree'-reh*

difference, differenza *deef-feh-rehn'-tsah*

different, differente *deef-feh-rehn'-teh*

difficult, difficile *deef-fee'-chee-leh*

dine, pranzare *prahn-dzah'-reh* [53]

dining car, carrozza ristorante *kahr-rot'-tsah rees-toh-rahn'-teh* [84]

dining room, sala da pranzo *sah'-lah dah prahn'-dzoh* [38, 87]

dinner, pranzo *prahn'-dzoh* [48, 50]

direct, diretto *dee-ret'-toh*

direction, direzione (f) *dee-reh-tsyoh'-neh*

director, direttore (m) *dee-reht-toh'-reh*

dirty, sporco *spor'-koh* [55]

disappear, sparire *spah-ree'-reh*

discount *n.,* sconto *skon'-toh* [70]

discuss, discutere *dee-skoo'-teh-reh*

disease, malattia *mah-laht-tee'-yah*

dish, piatto *pyaht'-toh*

disinfect, disinfettare *dee-seen-fet'-tah-reh*

distance, distanza *dee-stahn'-tsah*

district, distretto *dee-stret'-toh*

disturb, disturbare *dee-stoor-bah'-reh*

divorced, divorziato *dee-vohr-tsyah'-toh*

do, fare *fah'-reh* **how do you do?** come sta? *ko'-meh stah*

dock, molo *moh'-loh*

doctor, medico, dottore *meh'-dee-koh, dot-toh'-reh* [51, 91]

dog, cane (m) *kah'-neh*

doll, bambola *bahm'-boh-lah*

dollar, dollaro *dol'-lah-roh* [31]
done, fatto *faht'-toh*
donkey, asino *ah'-zee-noh*
door, porta *por'-tah*
dose, dose (f) *doh'-zeh*
double, doppio *dop'-pyoh*
doubt, dubbio *doob'-byoh* **without doubt,** senza dubbio *sehn'-tsah doob'-byoh* **no doubt,** nessun dubbio *nes-soon' doob'-byoh*
down, giù *joo* **to go down,** scendere *shen'-deh-reh*
downtown, centro città *chen'-troh chee-tah'* [46]
dozen, dozzina *dod-dzee'-nah*
drawer, cassetto *kahs-set'-toh*
dress *n.,* vestito *ves-tee'-toh* [68]
dress [oneself], vestirsi *ves-teer'-see*
dressmaker, sarta *sahr'-tah*
drink *n.,* bibita, bevanda *bee'-bee-tah, beh-vahn'-dah*
drink *v.,* bere *beh'-reh*
drive *v.,* condurre *kon-door'-reh* [45, 75, 76]
driver, autista *ow-tees'-tah* [44]
drop *v.,* lasciar cadere *lah-shar' kah-deh'-reh*
druggist, farmacista (m) *fahr-mah-chees'-tah*
drugstore, farmacia *fahr-mah-chee'-yah* [92]
drunk, ubriaco *oo-bree-yah'-koh*
dry, secco *sek'-koh*
duck, anitra *ah'-nee-trah*
during, durante *doo-rahn'-teh*
dust, polvere (f) *pol'-veh-reh*
duty, dovere (m) *doh-veh'-reh* [34]
dysentery, dissenteria *dees-sen-teh-ree'-yah*

each ciascuno, ciascun *chahs-koo'-noh, chahs-koon'*
each one, ciascuno *chahs-koo'-noh*
eager, avido *ah'-vee-doh*
ear, orecchio *oh-rek'-kyoh*
earache, mal d'orecchi *mahl doh-rek'-kee*

early, presto, di buon'ora *pres'-toh, dee bwon-oh'-rah* [24]

earn, guadagnare *gwah-dahn-yah'-reh*

earrings, orecchini *oh-rek-kee'-nee*

earth, terra *ter'-rah*

easily, facilmente *fah-cheel-men'-teh*

east, est (m) *est*

Easter, Pasqua *pahs'-kwah*

easy, facile *fah'-chee-leh*

eat, mangiare *mahn-jah'-reh* [38, 48, 52, 56, 87]

edge, orlo *ohr'-loh*

egg, uovo *woh'-voh*

eight, otto *ot'-toh*

eighteen, diciotto *dee-chot'-toh*

eighth, ottavo *ot-tah'-voh*

eighty, ottanta *ot-tahn'-tah*

either, l'uno o l'altro *loo'-noh oh lahl'-troh*

either . . . or . . . , o . . . o . . . *oh . . . oh . . .*

elbow, gomito *goh'-mee-toh*

electric, elettrico *eh-let'-tree-koh*

elevator, ascensore (m) *ah-shen-soh'-reh* [39]

eleven, undici *oon'-dee-chee*

else: nobody else, nessun altro *nes-soon' ahl'-troh* **nothing else,** nient'altro *nyent-ahl'-troh* **something else,** qualcosa d'altro *kwahl-ko'-zah dahl'-troh*

elsewhere, altrove *ahl-troh'-veh*

embark, imbarcarsi *eem-bahr-kahr'-see*

embarrassed, imbarazzato *eem-bah-rahd-dzah'-toh*

embassy, ambasciata *ahm-bah-shah'-tah*

embrace *v.,* abbracciare *ahb-brach-chah'-reh*

emergency, emergenza *eh-mer-jehn'-tsah*

empty, vuoto *vwoh'-toh*

end *n.,* fine (f) *fee'-neh*

engaged [busy], occupato *ok-koo-pah'-toh*

engine, motore (m) *moh-toh'-reh*

English, inglese *een-gleh'-zeh* [11]

enjoy godere *goh-deh'-reh*

enormous, enorme *eh-nohr'-meh*

enough, abbastaza *ahb-bahs-tahn'-tsah* **that's enough,** basta *bahs-tah*

enter, entrare *en-trah-reh*

entertaining, divertente *dee-ver-ten'-teh*

entire, intero *een-teh'-roh*

entrance, entrata, ingresso *en-trah'-tah, een-gres'-soh*

envelope, busta *boos'-tah*

equal, uguale *oo-gwah'-leh*

equipment, equipaggiamento *eh-kwee-pahj-jah-men'-toh*

error, errore (m) *er-roh'-reh*

Europe, Europa *eh-oo-roh'-pah*

even *adv.,* anche, perfino *ahn'-keh, per-fee'-noh*

even [number], pari *pah'-ree*

evening, sera *seh'-rah* [100] **good evening,** buona sera *bwoh'-nah seh'-rah*

ever, sempre, mai *sem'-preh, mah'-ee*

every, ogni *ohn'-yee*

everyone, ognuno *ohn-yoo'-noh*

everything, ogni cosa, tutto *ohn'-yee ko'-zah, toot'-toh*

everywhere, dappertutto *dahp-per-toot'-toh*

evidently, evidentemente *eh-vee-den-teh-men'-teh*

exact, esatto *eh-zaht'-toh*

examination, esame (m) *eh-zah'-meh*

examine, esaminare *eh-zah-mee-nah'-reh*

example, esempio *eh-zem'-pyoh* **for example,** per esempio *per eh-zem'-pyoh*

excellent, eccellente *ech-chel-len'-teh*

except, eccetto *ech-chet'-toh*

exchange *v.,* cambiare, scambiare *kahm-byah'-reh, skahm-byah'-reh*

exchange rate, cambio *kahm'-byoh* [31]

excursion, escursione (f) *es-koor-zyoh'-neh*

excuse *v.,* scusare *skoo-zah'-reh* **excuse me,** (mi) scusi *(mee) skoo'-zee*

exercise, esercizio *eh-zer-chee'-tsyoh*

exhibition, esposizione (f) *es-poh-zee-tsyoh'-neh* [99]
exit, uscita *oo-shee'-tah*
expect, sperare *speh-rah'-reh* [32]
expensive, costoso, caro *kos-toh'-zoh, kah'-roh* [38, 67]
explain, spiegare *spyeh-gah'-reh*
explanation, spiegazione (f) *spyeh-gah-tsyoh'-neh*
export v., esportare *es-por-tah'-reh*
express adj., espresso *es-pres'-soh*
extra, extra, suppletivo *es'-trah, soop-pleh-tee'-voh*
extraordinary, straordinario *strah-ohr-dee-nah'-ree-yoh*
eye, occhio *ok'-kyoh*

face, faccia, viso *fahch-chah, vee'-zoh*
factory, fabbrica *fahb'-bree-kah*
faint v., svenire *zveh-nee'-reh*
fair [market], fiera *fyeh'-rah*
fall [season], autunno *ow-toon'-noh*
fall n., caduta *kah-doo'-tah*
fall v., cadere *kah-deh'-reh*
false, falso *fahl'-soh*
family, famiglia *fah-meel'-yah*
famous, famoso *fah-moh'-zoh*
fan, ventilatore (m), ventaglio *ven-tee-lah-toh'-reh, ven-tahl'-yoh*
far, lontano *lon-tah'-noh* **so far,** così lontano *ko-see' lon-tah'-noh* **how far is it?** a quanta distanza è? *ah kwahn'-tah dees-tahn'-tsah eh?*
fare [cost], tariffa *tah-reef'-fah* [45]
farewell, addio *ahd-dee'-yoh*
farm, podere (m), fattoria *poh-deh'-reh, faht-toh-ree'-yah*
farmer, agricoltore (m) *ah-gree-kol-toh'-reh*
farther, più lontano *pyoo lon-tah'-noh*
fashion, moda *moh'-dah*
fast [quick], veloce *veh-loh'-cheh*
fasten, attaccare *aht-tahk-kah'-reh* [89]

fat, grasso *grahs'-soh*
father, padre *pah'-dreh* [3]
father-in-law, suocero *swoh'-cheh-roh*
fault, colpa *kol'-pah*
favor, favore (m) *fah-voh'-reh*
favorite *adj. & n.,* favorito *fah-voh-ree'-toh*
fear: to be afraid, temere, aver paura *teh-meh'-reh, ah-vehr' pah-oo'-rah*
feather, piuma, penna *pyoo'-mah, pen'-nah*
February, febbraio *feb-brah'-yoh*
fee, onorario *oh-noh-rah'-ree-yoh*
feel, sentire *sen-tee'-reh* [92]
feeling, sentimento *sen-tee-men'-toh*
female, femmina *fem'-mee-nah*
fence, steccato *stek-kah'-toh*
fender, parafango *pah-rah-fahn'-goh*
ferry [boat], nave-traghetto *nah'-veh trah-get'-toh*
fever, febbre (f) *feb'-breh* [93]
few, pochi, poche *poh'-kee, poh'-keh*
field, campo *kahm'-poh*
fifteen, quindici *kween'-dee-chee*
fifth, quinto *kween'-toh*
fifty, cinquanta *cheen-kwahn'-tah*
fight *n.,* lotta *lot'-tah*
fight *v.,* combattere *kom-baht'-teh-reh*
fill *v.,* riempire *ree-em-pee'-reh* [39, 74]
filling [for a tooth], piombatura *pyom-bah-too'-rah*
film, pellicola, film *pel-lee'-koh-lah, feelm*
final, finale *fee-nah'-leh*
finally, finalmente *fee-nah'-men'-teh*
find, trovare *troh-vah'-reh*
fine *adj.,* bene *beh'-neh*
fine *n.,* multa *mool'-tah* [75]
finger, dito *dee'-toh* [93]
finish *v.,* finire *fee-nee'-reh*
fire, fuoco *fwoh'-koh* [15]

first, primo *pree'-moh* **first class,** prima classe *pree'-mah klahs'-seh* [83, 87]

fish, pesce (m) *peh'-sheh* [56]

fish *v.,* pescare *pes-kah'-reh*

fish-bone, lisca *lees'-kah*

fit [seizure], convulsione (f) *kon-vool-syoh'-neh*

fit *v.,* andar bene *ahn-dahr' beh'-neh*

fitting [of a garment], prova *proh'-vah*

five, cinque *cheen'-kweh*

fix *v.,* reparare, aggiustare *reh-pah-rah-reh, ahj-joos-tah'-reh* [74, 76]

flag, bandiera *bahn-dyeh'-rah*

flashbulb, lampadina fotografica *lahm-pah-dee'-nah fot-toh-grah'-fee-kah*

flat, piano *pyah'-noh*

flat tire, gomma forata *gom'-mah foh-rah'-tah* [74]

flavor, sapore (m) *sah-poh'-reh*

flight, volo *voh'-loh* [88, 89, 90]

flint, pietra focaia *pyeh'-trah foh-kah'-yah*

flirt *v.,* civettare *chee-vet-tah'-reh*

flood, inondazione (f) *ee-non-dah-tsyoh'-neh*

floor, pavimento *pah-vee-men'-toh;* [storey], piano *pyah'-noh*

florist, fioraio *fyoh-rah'-yoh*

flower, fiore (m) *fyoh'-reh*

fluid, fluido, liquido *floo-ee'-doh, lee'-kwee-doh*

fly [insect], mosca *mos'-kah*

fly *v.,* volare *voh-lah'-reh* [89]

fog, nebbia *nehb'-byah* [6]

follow, seguire *seh-gwee-reh*

food, cibo, vitto *chee'-boh, veet'-toh*

foot, piede (m) *pyeh'-deh*

for, per *per*

forbid, proibire, vietare *proh-ee-bee'-reh, vyeh-tah'-reh*

forbidden, proibito, vietato *proh-ee-bee'-toh, vyeh-tah'-toh*

forehead, fronte (f) *fron'-teh*
foreign, estero, straniero *es'-teh-roh, strah-nyeh'-roh*
foreigner, straniero, forestiere *strah-nyeh'-roh, foh-res-tyeh'-reh*
forest, selva, foresta *sel'-vah, foh-res'-tah*
forget, dimenticare *dee-men-tee-kah'-reh*
forgive, perdonare *per-doh-nah'-reh*
fork, forchetta *fohr-ket'-tah* [55]
form, forma *for'-mah*
former, precedente *preh-cheh-den'-teh*
formerly, prima *pree'-mah*
fort, forte (m) *for'-teh*
fortunate, fortunato *for-too-nah'-toh*
fortunately, fortunatamente *for-too-nah-tah-men'-tah*
forty, quaranta *kwah-rahn'-tah*
forward, avanti *ah-vahn'-tee*
fountain, fontana *fon-tah'-nah*
four, quattro *kwaht'-troh*
fourteen, quattordici *kwaht-tor'-dee-chee*
fourth, quarto *kwahr'-toh*
fracture *n.,* frattura *fraht-too'-rah*
fragile, fragile *frah'-jee-leh*
free, libero *lee'-beh-roh* [44]
freedom, libertà *lee-ber-tah'*
freeze, gelare *jeh-lah'-reh*
frequently, frequentemente *freh-kwen-teh-men'-teh*
fresh, fresco *fres'-koh* [52]
Friday, venerdì *ve-ner-dee'*
fried, fritto *freet'-toh*
friend, amico *ah-mee'-koh,* [2]
friendly, amichevole *ah-mee-keh'-voh-leh*
from, da *dah*
front, fronte (f) *fron'-teh* **in front of,** davanti a *dah-vahn'-tee ah*
frozen, congelato *kon-jeh-lah'-toh*
fruit, frutta *froot'-tah* [52]

full, pieno *pyeh'-noh*

fun, divertimento *dee-ver-tee-men'-toh*

function, funzione (f) *foon-tsyoh'-neh*

funnel, imbuto *eem-boo'-toh*

funny, comico *koh'-mee-koh*

fur, pelo *peh'-loh*

furnished, ammobiliato *ahm-moh-bee-lee-yah'-toh*

furniture, mobili *moh'-bee-lee*

further, inoltre, di più *een-ol'-treh, dee pyoo*

future, futuro, avvenire (m) *foo-too'-roh, ahv-veh-nee'-reh*

gain *v.,* guadagnare *gwah-dahn-yah'-reh*

gamble *v.,* giocare *joh-kah'-reh*

game, gioco *joh'-koh*

gangplank, passerella, scalandrone (m) *pahs-seh-rehl'-lah, skah-lahn-droh'-neh* [88]

garage, autorimessa *ow-toh-ree-mes'-sah* [73, 76]

garden, giardino *jahr-dee'-noh*

garlic, aglio *ahl'-yoh*

gas, gas *gahs*

gasoline, benzina *ben-dzee'-nah* [73, 74]

gas station, stazione di servizio *stah-tsyoh'-neh dee ser-vee'-tsyoh* [73]

gate, cancello, porta *kahn-chel'-loh, por'-tah* [89]

gather [collect], raccogliere *rahk-kol'-yeh-reh*

gay, gaio *gah'-yoh*

general *adj.,* generale *jeh-neh-rah'-leh* **generally, in general,** generalmente *jeh-neh-rahl-men'-teh*

generous, generoso *jeh-neh-roh'-zoh*

gentleman, signore *seen-yoh'-reh*

get, ottenere *ot-teh-neh'-reh* **get in, get on,** salire *sah-lee'-reh* [46] **get off,** scendere *shen'-deh-reh* [46] **get up,** alzarsi *ah-tsahr'-see* [96]

gift, regalo *reh-gah'-loh*

gin, gin *jeen*

girl, ragazza *rah-gaht'-tsah* [10]

give, dare *dah'-reh* [13, 32]

glad, contento *kon-ten'-toh*

gladly, con piacere, volentieri *kon-pyah-cheh'-reh, voh-len-tyeh'-ree*

glass [for drinking], bicchiere *beek-kyeh'-reh* [51, 52, 55]

glasses [for the eyes], occhiali (m, pl) *ok-kyah'-lee*

glove, guanto *gwahn'-toh*

go, andare *ahn-dah'-reh* [12, 35, 44, 46, 88, 102] **go back,** tornare *tohr-nah'-reh* **go in,** entrare *en-trah'-reh* **go out,** uscire *oo-shee'-reh*

God, Dio *dee'-yoh*

gold, oro *oh'-roh*

good, buono *bwoh'-noh*

good-bye, arrivederci *ahr-ree-veh-der'-chee*

government, governo *goh-ver'-noh*

grandfather, nonno *non'-noh*

grandmother, nonna *non'-nah*

grape(s), uva *oo'-vah*

grapefruit, pompelmo *pom-pel'-moh*

grass, erba *er'-bah*

grateful, grato *grah'-toh*

gray, grigio *gree'-joh*

grease *n.*, grasso *grahs'-soh*

great, grande *grahn'-deh*

green, verde *ver'-deh*

grocery, bottega bi comestibili *bot-teh'-gah dee koh-mes-tee'-bee-lee*

ground, terra *ter'-rah*

group, gruppo *groop'-poh*

grow, crescere *kreh'-sheh-reh*

guard *n.*, guardia *gwahr'-dyah*

guest, ospite (m) *os'-pee-teh*

guide *n.*, guida *gwee'-dah* [99]

guilty, colpevole *kol-peh'-voh-leh*

guitar, chitarra *kee-tahr'-rah*

gum [chewing], gomma da masticare *gom'-mah dah mahs-tee-kah'-reh*

gun, fucile (m) *foo-chee'-leh*

habit, abitudine (f) *ah-bee-too'-dee-neh*

hair, capelli (m, pl) *keh-pel'-lee*

haircut, taglio di capelli *tahl'-yoh dee kah-pel'-lee*

hairdresser, parrucchiere (m) *pahr-rook-kyeh'-reh*

hairpin, forcella *for-chel'-lah*

half *adj.*, mezzo *med'-dzoh*

half *n.*, metà *meh-tah'*

hall, corridoio *kor-ree-doh'-yoh*

ham, proscuitto *proh-shoot'-toh*

hand, mano (f) *mah'-noh*

handkerchief, fazzoletto *faht-tsoh-let'-toh* [40]

hand-made, fatto a mano *faht'-toh ah mah'-noh*

handsome, bello *bel'-loh* [10]

hang, impiccare *eem-peek-kah'-reh* **hang up**, appendere *ahp-pen-deh'-reh*

hanger [for clothing], attaccapanni *aht-tahk-kah-pahn'-nee*

happen, succedere *sooch-cheh'-deh-reh* [15]

happy, felice *feh-lee'-cheh*

harbor, porto *por'-toh* [86]

hard, duro *doo'-roh*

hardly, appena *ahp-peh'-nah*

harm *n.*, male (m) *mah'-leh*

harm *v.*, far male *fahr mah'-leh*

harmful, nocivo *noh-chee'-voh*

haste, fretta *fret'-tah*

hat, cappello *kahp-pel'-loh*

hat shop, cappelleria *kahp-pel-leh-ree'-yah*

hate *v.*, odiare *oh-dee-yah'-reh*

have, avere *ah-veh'-reh* **I have**, ho *oh* **have you?** ha Lei? *ah leh'-ee*

he, egli, lui *ehl'-yee, loo'-ee*

head, testa *tes'-tah*

headache, mal di testa *mahl dee tes'-tah* [92]

health, salute (f) *sah-loo'-teh* [56]

hear, udire, sentire *oo-dee'-reh, sen-tee'-reh*

heart, cuore (m) *kwoh'-reh*

heat *n.,* calore (m) *kah-loh'-reh*

heavy, pesante *peh-zahn'-teh*

heel, tacco *tahk'-koh*

hello, ciao, buon giorno *chow, bwon johr'-noh*

help *n.,* aiuto, soccorso *ah-yoo'-toh, sok-kor'-soh*

help *v.,* aiutare *ah-yoo-tah'-reh* [14, 64]

helpful, soccorevole *sok-kor-reh'-voh-leh*

hem *n.,* orlo *ohr'-loh*

hen, gallina *gahl-lee'-nah*

her, la, lei *lah, leh'-ee*

here, qui, qua *kwee, kwah*

hers, suo, sua *soo'-oh, soo'-ah*

high, alto *ahl'-toh*

hill, collina *kol-lee'-nah*

him, lo, lui *loh, loo'-ee*

hip, anca *ahn'-kah*

hire, noleggiare *noh-lej-jah'-reh* [72]

his, suo, sua *soo'-oh, soo'-ah*

history, storia *stoh' ree-yah*

hit *v.,* colpire *kol-pee'-reh*

hold, tenere *teh-neh'-reh*

hole, buco *boo'-koh*

holiday, giorno festivo, giorno di festa *johr'-noh fes-tee'-voh, johr'-noh dee fes'-tah*

holy, santo *sahn'-toh*

home, casa *kah'-zah*

honest, onesto *oh-nes'-toh*

honey [food], miele (m) *myeh'-leh*

honor, onore (m) *oh-noh'-reh*

hope *n.,* speranza *speh-rahn'-tsah*

hope *v.,* sperare *speh-rah'-reh* [3]

horn [automobile], tromba *trom'-bah*

hors d'oeuvres, antipasto *ahn-tee-pahs'-toh*

horse, cavallo *kah-vahl'-loh*

hospital, ospedale (m) *os-peh-dah'-leh* [92]

host, oste (m) *os'-teh*

hot, caldo *kahl'-doh*

hotel, albergo *ahl-ber'-goh* [10, 32, 36, 38, 45, 53, 70, 102]

hour, ora *oh'-rah*

house, casa *kah'-zah*

how, come *ko'-meh* **how are you?** come sta? *ko'-meh stah* **how far?** quanto lontano? *kwahn'-toh lon-tah'-noh* **how long?** quanto tempo? *kwahn'-toh tem'-poh* **how many?** quanti? quante? *kwahn'-tee, kwahn'-teh* **how much?** quanto? *kwahn'-toh*

hug *n.,* abbraccio *ahb-brahch'-choh*

human, umano *oo-mah'-noh*

humid, umido *oo'-mee-doh*

hundred, cento *chen'-toh*

hunger, fame (f) *fah'-meh*

hungry: to be hungry, aver fame *ah-vehr' fah'-meh* [47, 48]

hurry *v.,* affrettarsi *ahf-fret-tahr'-see* **to be in a hurry,** aver fretta *ah-vehr' fret'-tah*

hurt, far male *fahr mah'-leh* [93]

husband, marito *mah-ree'-toh* [2]

I, io *ce'-yoh*

ice, ghiaccio *gyahch'-choh* [55]

ice cream, gelato *jeh-lah'-toh* [56]

idea, idea *ee-deh'-yah*

identification, identificazione (f) *ee-den-tee-fee-kah-tsyoh'-neh*

if, se *seh*

ill, ammalato *ahm-mah-lah'-toh*

illegal, illegale *eel-leh-gah'-leh*

illness, malattia *mah-laht-tee'-yah*

imagine, immaginare, figurarsi *eem-mah-jee-nah'-reh, fee-goo-rahr'-see*

immediately, immediatamente, subito *eem-meh-dee-yah-tah-men'-teh, soo'-bee-toh*

important, importante *eem-por-tahn'-teh*

impossible, impossibile *eem-pos-see'-bee-leh* [13]

improve, migliorare *meel-yoh-rah'-reh*

improvement, miglioramento *meel-yoh-rah-men'-toh*

in, in *een*

incident, incidente (m) *een-chee-den'-teh*

included, incluso, compreso *een-kloo'-zoh, kom-preh'-zoh* [57]

incomplete, incompleto *een-kom-pleh'-toh*

inconvenient, inconveniente *een-kon-veh-nyen'-teh*

incorrect, inesatto *een-eh-zaht'-toh*

increase *v.,* aumentare *ow-men-tah'-reh*

incredible, incredibile *een-kreh-dee'-bee-leh*

indeed, in verità *een veh-ree-tah'*

independence, indipendenza *een-dee-pen-den'-tsah*

independent, indipendente *een-dee-pen-den'-teh*

indicate, indicare *een-dee-kah'-reh*

indigestion, indigestione (f) *een-dee-jes-tyoh'-neh*

indoors, dentro *den'-troh*

industrial, industriale *een-doos-tree-yah'-leh*

inexpensive, a buon mercato *ah bwon mehr-kah'-toh*

infection, infezione (f) *een-feh-tsyoh'-neh*

infectious, infettivo *een-fet-tee'-voh*

inform, informare *een-fohr-mah'-reh*

information, informazioni (f, pl) *een-fohr-mah-tsyoh'-nee*

injection, iniezione (f) *een-yeh-tsyoh'-neh*

injury, ferita, danno, lesione (f) *feh-ree'-tah, dahn'-noh, leh zyoh'-neh*

injustice, ingiustizia *een-joos-tee'-tsyah*

ink, inchiostro *een-kyohs'-troh*

inn, taverna *tah-ver'-nah*

inquire, domandare, informarsi *doh-mahn-dah'-reh, een-fohr-mahr'-see*

inside, dentro *den'-troh*

insist, insistere *een-sees'-teh-reh*

inspect, ispezionare *ee-speh-tsee-yoh-nah'-reh*

instead of, invece di *een-veh'-cheh dee*

institution, istituzione (f) *ee-stee-toot-syoh'-neh*

insurance, assicurazione (f) *ahs-see-koo-rah-tsyoh'-neh*

insure, assicurare *ahs-see-koo-rah'-reh*

intelligent, intelligente *een-tel-lee-jen'-teh*

intend, intendere *een-ten'-deh-reh*

intense, intenso *een-ten'-soh*

intention, intenzione (f) *een-ten-tsyoh'-neh*

interest *n.,* interesse (m) *een-teh-res'-seh*

interest *v.,* interessare *een-teh-res-sah'-reh*

interesting, interessante *een-teh-res-sahn'-teh* [102]

intermission, intervallo *een-ter-vahl-loh*

internal, interno *een-ter'-noh*

international, internazionale *een-ter-nah-tsee-yoh-nah'-leh*

interpret, interpretare *een-ter-preh-tah'-reh*

interpreter, interprete (m) *een-ter'-preh-teh*

interview *n.,* intervista *een-ter-vees'-tah*

into, in *een*

introduce, presentare *preh-zen-tah'-reh*

introduction, presentazione (f) *preh-zen-tah-tsyoh'-neh*

investigate, investigare *een-ves-tee-gah'-reh*

invitation, invito *een-vee'-toh*

invite, invitare *een-vee-tah'-reh*

iron [for ironing], ferro da stiro *fer'-roh dah stee'-roh*

iron [metal], ferro *fer'-roh*

iron *v.,* stirare *stee-rah'-reh*

is: è, sta *eh, stah* **he is,** lui è *loo'-ee eh* **she is,** lei è *leh'-ee eh* **it is,** è *eh*

island, isola *ee'-zoh-lah*

itch *v.,* prudere *proo'-deh-reh*

jacket, giacca *jahk'-kah* [8]

jail, carcere (m) *kahr'-cheh-reh*

jam, confettura *kon-fet-too'-rah*

January, gennaio *jen-nah'-yoh*

jaw, mandibola *mahn-dee'-boh-lah*

jelly, gelatina *jeh-lah-tee'-nah*

jewelry, gioielli (m, pl) *joh-yel'-lee*

jewelry store, gioielleria *joh-yel-leh-ree'-yah*

job, compito, lavoro *kom'-pee-toh, lah-voh'-roh*

joke, scherzo *sker'-tsoh*

juice, succo *sook'-koh*

July, luglio *lool'-yoh*

jump *v.,* saltare *sahl-tah'-reh*

June, giugno *joon'-yoh*

just, giusto *joos'-toh*

justice, giustizia *joos-tee'-tsee-yah*

keep, mantenere *mahn-teh-neh'-reh*

key, chiave (f) *kyah'-veh* [34, 39, 73, 87]

kidneys, reni *reh'-nee*

kill, uccidere, ammazzare *och-chee'-deh-reh, ahm-mahd-dzah'-reh*

kilogram, chilogrammo *kee-loh-grahm'-moh*

kilometer, chilometro *kee-loh'-me-troh* [72]

kind *adj.,* gentile *jen-tee'-leh*

kind *n.,* specie (f) *speh'-chyeh* [31]

king, re *reh*

kiss *n.,* bacio *bah'-choh*

kiss *v.,* baciare *bah-chah'-reh*

kitchen, cucina *koo-chee'-nah*

knee, ginocchio *jee-nok'-kyoh*

knife, coltello *kol-tel'-loh* [55]

knock *v.,* bussare *boos-sah'-reh*

know [something], sapere *sah-peh'-reh* [9]; [someone], conoscere *koh-noh'-sheh-reh* [10]

laborer, lavoratore (m), operaio *lah-voh-rah-toh'-reh, oh-peh-rah'-yoh*

lace, merletto *mer-let'-toh*

ladies' room, gabinetto da signore *gah-bee-net'-toh dah seen-yoh'-reh*

lady, signora *seen-yoh'-rah*

lake, lago *lah'-goh*

lamb, agnello *an-yel'-loh*

lame, zoppo *dzop'-poh*

lamp, lampada *lahm'-pah-dah*

land *n.,* terra *ter'-rah*

land *v.,* atterrare *aht-ter-rah'-reh* [90]

landing card, cartoncino (permesso) di sbarco *kahr-ton-chee'-noh (per-mes'-soh) dee zbahr'-koh* [88]

language, lingua *leen'-gwah*

large, grande, grosso *grahn'-deh, gros'-soh*

last *adj.,* ultimo *ool'-tee-moh*

last *v.,* durare *doo-rah'-reh* [99]

late, tardi *tahr'-dee* [24, 84]

laugh *v.,* ridere *ree'-deh-reh*

laughter, riso *ree'-zoh*

laundry, lavanderia *lah-vahn-deh-ree'-yah*

lavatory, gabinetto *gah-bee-net'-toh* [85]

law, legge (f) *lej-jeh*

lawyer, avvocato *ahv-voh-kah'-toh*

lazy, pigro *peeg'-roh*

lead *v.,* condurre *kon-door'-reh*

leaf, foglia *fohl'-yah*

leak *n.,* perdita *per'-dee-tah*

learn, imparare *eem-pah-rah'-reh*

least, minimo *mee'-nee-moh*

leather, cuoio *kwoh'-yoh*

leave, partire, andarsene *pahr-tee'-reh, ahn-dahr'-seh-neh* [25, 40, 46, 83, 85, 88]

left, sinistro *see-nees'-troh* [45]

leg, gamba *gahm'-bah* [93]

lemon, limone (m) *lee-moh'-neh*

lend, prestare *pres-tah'-reh*

length, lunghezza *loon-get'-tsah*

lens, lente (f) *len'-teh* **contact lens,** lente (f) *len'-teh*

less, meno *meh'-noh*

let, lasciare *lah-shah'-reh*

letter, lettera *let'-teh-rah* [40]

lettuce, lattuga *laht-too'-gah*

liberty, libertà *lee-ber-tah'*

library, biblioteca *bee-blee-oh-teh'-kah*

license, licenza, patente (f) *lee-chen'-tsah, pah-ten'-teh* [76]

lie [untruth], bugia, menzogna *boo-jee'-yah, men-tsohn'-yah*

lie: to lie down, coricarsi *koh-ree-kahr'-see* [96]

life, vita *vee'-tah*

lift *v.,* sollevare *sol-leh-vah'-reh*

light [weight], leggero *lej-jeh'-roh*; [color], chiaro *kyah'-roh*

light *n.,* luce (f) *loo'-cheh*

lighter [cigarette], accendi-sigari (m) *ahch-chen'-dee see'-gah-ree*

lightning, lampo, fulmine (m) *lahm'-poh, fool'-mee-neh* [00]

like *adv.,* come *ko'-meh*

like *v.,* piacere a *pyah-cheh'-reh ah* [7, 36, 67, 102] **I would like,** vorrei *vor-reh'-ee* [37, 52, 69, 98]

line, linea *lee'-neh-ah*

linen, lino *lee'-noh*

lip, labbro *luhb'-broh*

lipstick, matita per le labbra *mah-tee'-tah per leh lahb'-brah*

liqueur, liquore (m) *lee-kwoh'-reh*

list, lista *lees'-tah*

listen, ascoltare *ahs-kol-tah'-reh*

liter, litro *leet'-roh* [74]

little, piccolo *peek'-koh-loh* **a little,** un poco *oon poh'-koh* [11]

live *v.,* vivere, abitare *vee'-veh-reh, ah-bee-tah'-reh* [10]

liver, fegato *feh'-gah-toh*

lobby, atrio *ah'-tree-yoh*

lobster, aragosta *ah-rah-gos'-tah*

long, lungo *loon'-goh* [68, 69]

look *v.,* guardare *gwahr-dah'-reh*

loose, sciolto *shol'-toh* [69]

lose, perdere *per'-deh-reh* [16, 39]

lost, perduto *per-doo'-toh*

lot: a lot of, molto *mol'-toh*

lotion, lozione (f) *loh-tsyoh'-neh*

loud, ad alta voce *ahd ahl'-tah voh'-cheh*

love *n.,* amore (m) *ah-moh'-reh*

love *v.,* amare *ah-mah'-reh* [10]

low, basso *bahs'-soh*

lubricate *v.,* lubricare *loo-bree-kah'-reh*

luck, fortuna *for-too'-nah* **good luck,** buona fortuna *bwoh'-nah for-too'-nah*

lucky, fortunato *for-too-nah'-toh* **to be lucky,** essere fortunato *es'-seh-reh for-too-nah'-toh*

luggage, bagaglio *bah-gahl'-yoh* [35, 40, 44, 48]

lunch, seconda colazione *seh-kon'-dah koh-lah-tsyoh'-neh* [48]

lung, polmone (m) *pol-moh'-neh*

machine, macchina *mahk'-kee-nah*

madam, signora *seen-yoh'-rah*

magazine, rivista *ree-vees'-tah*

mail *n.,* posta *pos'-tah* [32]

mailbox, buca da lettere, cassetta postale *boo'-kah dah let'-teh-reh, kahs-set'-tah pos-tah'-leh*

main, principale *preen-chee-pah'-leh* **main course,** piatto principale *pyaht'-toh preen-chee-pah'-leh*

major, maggiore *mahj-joh'-reh*

make, fare *fah'-reh*

male, maschio, maschile (m) *mahs'-kyoh, mahs-kee'-leh*

man, uomo *woh'-moh* [10, 15]

manager, gerente (m), *direttore* (m) *jeh-ren'-teh, dee-ret-toh'-reh*

manicure, manicure (f) *mah-nee-koo'-reh*

manner, maniera *mah-nyeh'-rah*

manufactured, fabbricato *fahb-bree-kah'-toh*

many, molti, molte *mol'-tee, mol'-teh*

nap, carta geografica *kahr'-tah jeh-oh-grah'-fee-kah* [75]

marble, marmo *mahr'-moh*

March, marzo *mahr'-tsoh*

mark, marca *mahr'-kah*

market, mercato *mer'-kah-toh*

marketplace, mercato *mer-kah'-toh*

marmalade, marmellata *mahr-mel-lah'-tah*

married, sposato *spoh-zah'-toh*

marry, sposarsi *spoh-zahr'-see*

marvelous, meraviglioso *meh-rah-veel-yoh'-zoh*

mass [church], messa *mes'-sah*

massage *n.*, massaggio *mahs-sahj'-joh*

match, fiammifero *fyahm-mee'-feh-roh* [70]

material, materiale (m) *mah-teh-ree-yah'-leh*

matter: no matter, non importa *non eem-por'-tah* **what is the matter?** che c'è? *keh cheh*

May, maggio *mahj'-joh*

may, potere *poh-teh'-reh* **I may**, posso *pos'-soh* **may I?** posso? *pos'-soh*

maybe, forse *for'-seh*

me, me, mi *meh, mee* **to me**, mi, mc *mee, meh*

meal, pasto *pahs'-toh* [38, 48, 53, 90]

mean *v.*, significare, voler dire *seen-yee-fee-kah'-reh, voh-lehr' dee'-reh* [12]

measure *n.*, misura *mee-zoo'-rah*

measure *v.*, misurare *mee-zoo-rah'-reh*

meat, carne (f) *kahr'-neh* [56]
mechanic, meccanico *mek-kah'-nee-koh* [74]
medicine, medicina *meh-dee-chee'-nah* [96]
medium, medio *meh'-dyoh*
meet, incontrare *een-kon-trah'-reh* [3]
melon, melone (m) *meh-loh'-neh*
member, membro *mem'-broh*
memory, memoria *meh-moh'-ree-yah*
mend, rammendare *rahm-men-dah'-reh*
men's room, gabinetto per signori *gah-bee-net'-toh per seen-yoh'-ree*
mention *v.,* menzionare *men-tsee-yoh-nah'-reh*
menu, lista *lees'-tah* [50]
message, messaggio *mes-sahj-joh*
messenger, messaggero *mes-sahj-jeh'-roh*
metal, metallo *meh-tahl'-loh*
meter [measure], metro *meh'-troh*
middle, mezzo *med'-dzoh*
midnight, mezzanotte *med-dzah-not'-teh* [24]
mild, mite *mee'-teh*
milk, latte (m) *laht'-teh* [52, 53]
milliner, modista *moh-dees'-tah*
million, milione *meel-yoh'-neh*
mind, mente (f) *men'-teh*
mine, mio *mee'-yoh*
mineral, minerale *mee-neh-rah'-leh*
mineral water, acqua minerale *ahk'-kwah mee-neh-rah'-leh*
minute, minuto *mee-noo'-toh*
mirror, specchio *spek'-kyoh* [73]
misfortune, disgrazia *dees-grah'-tsee-yah*
Miss, signorina *seen-yoh-ree'-nah*
missing, manca, mancante *mahn'-kah, mahn-kahn'-teh*
mistake *n.,* sbaglio *zbahl'-yoh* [57]
mistaken, sbagliato *zbah-lyah'-toh*
mix *v.,* mescolare *mes-koh-lah'-reh*

mixed, mescolato, misto *mes-koh-lah'-toh, mees'-toh*

model, modello *moh-del'-loh*

modern, moderno *moh-der'-noh*

modest, modesto *moh-des'-toh*

moment, momento *moh-men'-toh*

Monday, lunedì *loo-neh-dee'*

money, denaro *deh-nah'-roh* [15, 31, 32]

money order, vaglia *vahl'-yah*

monk, monaco *moh'-nah-koh*

month, mese (m) *meh'-zeh* **per month, a month,** al mese *ahl meh'-zeh*

monument, monumento *moh-noo-men'-toh* [101]

moon, luna *loo'-nah* [7]

more, più *pyoo*

morning, mattina, mattino *maht-tee'-nah, maht-tee'-noh* [100] **good morning,** buon giorno *bwon johr'-noh*

mosquito, zanzara *dzahn-dzah'-rah*

mosquito net, zanzariera *dzahn-dzah-ree-yeh'-rah*

most, il più (m), la più (f) *eel pyoo, lah pyoo* **most of,** la maggior parte di, la maggioranza di *lah mahj-johr' pahr'-teh dee, lah mahj-joh-rahn'-tsah dee*

mother, madre *mah'-dreh* [3]

motion, mozione (f), moto, movimento *moh-tsyoh'-neh, moh'-toh, moh-vee-men'-toh*

motor, motore (m) *moh-toh'-reh*

mountain, montagna *mon-tahn'-yah*

mouth, bocca *bok'-kah*

move *v.*, muovere, trasferire *mwoh'-veh-reh, trahs-feh-ree'-reh* [16]

movie, cinema (m) *chee'-neh-mah* [101]

Mr., signore *seen-yoh'-reh*

Mrs., signora *seen-yoh'-rah*

much, molto, molta *mol'-toh, mol'-tah* **very much,** moltissimo *mol-tees'-see-moh* **too much,** troppo *trop'-poh* **how much?** quanto? *kwahn' toh*

mud, fango *fahn'-goh*

muffler, silenziatore (m) *see-len-tsee-yah-toh'-reh*
muscle, muscolo *moos'-koh-loh*
museum, museo *moo-zeh'-oh* [46, 99]
mushroom, fungo *foon'-goh*
music, musica *moo'-zee-kah*
musician, musicista *moo-zee-chees'-tah*
must, dovere *doh-veh'-reh* **I must,** devo *deh'-voh*
mustache, baffi (pl) *bahf'-fee*
mustard, mostarda, senape (m) *mos-tahr'-dah, seh'-nah-peh*
mutton, montone (m) *mon-toh'-neh*
my, mio *mee'-yoh*
myself, io stesso *ee'-yoh stes'-soh*

nail [fingernail], unghia *oon'-gyah*
nailfile, lima da unghie *lee'-mah dah oon'-gyeh*
naked, nudo *noo'-doh*
name, nome (m) *noh'-meh* [9, 10] **last name,** cognome (m) *kon-yoh'-meh* **what is your name?** come si chiama Lei? *ko'-meh see kyah'-mah leh'-se* **my name is . . . ,** mi chiamo . . . *mee kyah'-moh . . .*
napkin, tovagliolo *toh-vahl-yoh'-loh* [55]
narrow, stretto *stret'-toh* [69, 75]
nation, nazione (f) *nah-tsyoh'-neh*
national, nazionale *nah-tsyoh-nah'-leh*
nationality, nazionalità *nah-tsyoh-nah-lee-tah'*
native, nativo *nah-tee'-voh*
natural, naturale *nah-too-rah'-leh*
naturally, naturalmente *nah-too-rahl-men'-teh*
nature, natura *nah-too'-rah*
near, vicino *vee-chee'-noh*
nearly, circa, quasi *cheer'-kah, kwah'-zee*
necessary, necessario *neh-chehs-sah'-ree-yoh*
neck, collo *kol'-loh*
necklace, collana *kol-lah'-nah*
necktie, cravatta *krah-vaht'-tah*

need *v.*, aver bisogno di *ah-vehr' bee-zon'-yoh dee*
  I need, ho bisogno di, mi occorre *oh bee-zon'-yoh dee,*
  mee ok-kor'-reh
needle, ago *ah'-goh* [70]
neighbor, vicino *vee-chee'-noh*
neighborhood, vicinato *vee-chee-nah'-toh*
neither . . . nor . . . , nè . . . nè . . . *neh . . . neh . . .*
nephew, nipote (m) *nee-poh'-teh*
nerve, nervo *ner'-voh*
nervous, nervoso *ner-voh'-zoh*
never, mai, non . . . mai . . . *mah'-ee, non . . . mah'-ee*
nevertheless, tuttavia *toot-tah-vee'-yah*
new, nuovo *nwoh'-voh*
news, notizia, notizie *noh-tee'-tsyah, noh-tee'-tsyeh*
newspaper, giornale (m) *johr-nah'-leh*
next *adj.,* prossimo *pros'-see-moh*
next, *adv.,* quindi *kween'-dee* [85]
nice, simpatico *seem-pah'-tee-koh*
niece, nipote (f) *nee-poh'-teh*
night, notte (f) *not'-teh*   **good night,** buona notte *bwoh'-
nah not'-teh*
nightclub, locale notturno (m) *loh-kah'-leh not-toor'-noh*
nightgown, camicia da notte *kah-mee'-chah dah not'-teh*
nine, nove *noh'-veh*
nineteen, diciannove *dee-chahn-noh'-veh*
ninety, novanta *noh-vahn'-tah*
ninth, nono *noh'-noh*
no, no *noh*
noise, rumore (m) *roo-moh'-reh*
noisy, rumoroso *roo-moh-roh'-zoh*
none, nessuno *nes-soo'-noh*
noodles, taglierini (m,pl), fettuccine (f, pl) *tahl-yeh-ree'-
nee, fet-tooch-chee'-neh*
noon, mezzogiorno *med-dzoh-johr'-noh* [24]
no one, nessuno *nes-soo'-noh*
north, nord (m) *nord*

northeast, nord-est *nord-est'*
northwest, nord-ovest *nord-oh'-vest*
nose, naso *nah'-zoh*
not, non *non*
notebook, quaderno *kwah-dehr'-noh*
nothing, niente *nyen'-teh* **nothing else,** nient'altro *nyent-ahl'-troh*
notice *n.,* avviso *ahv-vee'-zoh*
notice *v.,* notare *noh-tah'-reh*
notify, notificare *noh-tee-fee-kah'-reh*
novel [book], romanzo *roh-mahn'-dzoh*
November, novembre *noh-vem'-breh*
novocaine, novocaina *noh-voh-kah-ee'-nah*
now, adesso, ora *ah-des'-soh, oh'-rah*
nowhere, in nessun luogo *een nes-soon' lwoh'-goh*
number, numero *noo'-meh-roh* [39, 42, 88]
nun, monaca *moh'-nah-kah*
nurse, infermiera *een-fer-myeh'-rah*
nursemaid, governante (f) *goh-ver-nahn'-teh*
nut, nuts, noce, noci (f) *noh'-cheh, noh'-chee*

obey, obbedire *ob-beh-dee'-reh*
obliged, obbligato *ohb-blee-gah'-toh*
obtain, ottenere *ot-teh-neh'-reh*
obvious, ovvio *ov'-vyoh*
occasionally, occasionalmente, di tempo in tempo *ok-kah-zyoh-nahl-men'-teh, dee tem'-poh een tem'-poh*
occupation, occupazione (f) *ok-koo-pah-tsyoh'-neh*
occupied, occupato *ok-koo-pah'-toh* [86]
ocean, oceano *oh-cheh'-ah-noh* [37]
October, ottobre *ot-toh'-breh*
odd [unusual], raro *rah'-roh*
odd [number], dispari *dees'-pah-ree*
of, di *dee*
offer *v.,* offrire *of-free'-reh*
office, ufficio *oof-fee'-choh*

official *adj.*, ufficiale *oof-fee-chah'-leh*

often, spesso *spes'-soh*

oil, olio *oh'-lyoh* [74]

old, vecchio, anziano *vek'-kyoh, ahn-tsyah'-noh*

olive, oliva *oh-lee'-vah*

omelet, frittata, omeletta *freet-tah'-tah, oh-meh-let'-tah*

on, su *soo*

once, una volta *oo'-nah vol'-tah*

one, uno, un, una, un' *oo'-noh, oon, oo'-nah, oon*

one-way [street], senso unico *sen'-soh oo'-nee-koh*;
[ticket], solo andata *soh'-loh ahn-dah'-tah* [84]

onion, cipolla *chee-pol'-lah*

only, soltanto, solamente *sol-tahn'-toh, soh-lah-men'-teh*

open *adj.*, aperto *ah-per'-toh* [100]

open *v.*, aprire *ah-pree'-reh* [34, 39, 62, 84, 99, 100]

opera, opera *oh'-peh-rah*

operation, operazione (f) *oh-peh-rah-tsyoh'-neh*

operator [telephone], telefonista, centralino *teh-leh-foh-nees'-tah, chen-trah-lee'-noh*

opinion, opinione (f) *oh-pee-nyoh'-neh*

opportunity, occasione, opportunità (f) *ok-kah-zyoh'-neh, oppor-too-nee-tah'*

opposite, opposto *op-pos'-toh*

optician, ottico *ot'-tee-koh*

or, o, od *oh, ohd*

orange, arancia *ah-rahn'-chah*

order *v.*, ordinare *or-dee-nah'-reh* [56] **in order to,** per
per

ordinary, ordinario *or-dee-nah'-ree-yoh*

oriental, orientale *oh-ree-en-tah'-leh*

original, originale *oh-ree-jee-nah'-leh*

ornament, ornamento *or-nah-men'-toh*

other, altro *ahl'-troh*

ought, dovere *doh-veh'-reh*

our, ours, nostro, il nostro *nos'-troh, eel nos'-troh*

out *adv.*, fuori *fwoh'-ree*

outdoor, all'aperto *ahl-lah-per'-toh*
out of order, non funziona *non foon-tsyoh'-nah*
outside *adv.,* fuori *fwoh'-ree* **outside of,** fuori di *fwoh'-ree dee*
over [ended] *adj.,* finito *fee-nee'-toh*
over [above] *prep.,* sopra *so'-prah*
overcharge *n.,* prezzo eccessivo *pret'-tsoh ech-ches-see'-voh*
overcoat, soprabito *so-prah'-bee-toh*
overcooked, troppo cotto *trop'-poh kot'-toh*
overhead, in alto, di sopra *een ahl'-toh, dee so'-prah*
overturn, capovolgere *kah-poh-vol'-jeh-reh*
owe, dovere *doh-veh'-reh* [56]
own *adj.,* proprio *proh'-pree-yoh*
owner, proprietario *proh-pree-yeh-tah'-ree-yoh*
oyster, ostrica *os'-tree-kah*

pack *v.,* impaccare *eem-pahk-kah'-reh* [70]
package, pacco *pahk'-koh*
page, pagina *pah'-jee-nah*
paid, pagato *pah-gah'-toh*
pain, dolore (m) *doh-loh'-reh*
paint, pittura *peet-too'-rah*
paint *v.,* dipingere *dee-peen'-jeh-reh*
painting, pittura *peet-too'-rah*
pair, paio *pah'-yoh* [69]
palace, palazzo *pah-laht'-tsoh* [101]
pale, pallido *pahl'-lee-doh*
palm, palmo *pahl'-moh*
pants, pantaloni (m, pl) *pahn-tah-loh'-nee*
paper, carta *kahr'-tah*
parcel, pacco *pahk'-koh*
pardon, scusa *skoo'-zah* **pardon me,** mi scusi *mee skoo'-zee*
parents, genitori *jeh-nee-toh'-ree*
park, parco *pahr'-koh* [101]

park [a car] *v.*, posteggiare, parcheggiare *pos-tej-jah'-reh, pahr-kej-jah'-reh* [76]

parsley, prezzemolo *pred-dzeh'-moh-loh*

part, parte (f) *pahr'-teh*

part [leave], partire *pahr-tee'-reh*

particular, particolare *pahr-tee-koh-lah'-reh*

partner [business], socio, *soh'-choh*

party, festa *fes'-tah*

pass *v.*, passare *pahs-sah'-reh*

passage, passaggio *pahs-sahj'-joh*

passenger, passeggero *pahs-sej-jeh'-roh*

passport, passaporto *pahs-sah-por'-toh* [16, 31, 33, 34]

past *adj. & n.*, passato *pahs-sah'-toh*

pastry, pasticceria *pahs-teech-cheh-ree'-yah*

path, sentiero *sen-tyeh'-roh*

patient *adj. & n.*, paziente *pah-tsyen'-teh*

pay *v.*, pagare *pah-gah'-reh* [34 ,57, 75] **to pay cash,** pagare in contante *pah-gah'-reh een kon-tahn'-teh* [70]

payment, pagamento *pah-gah-men'-toh*

pea, pisello *pee-zel'-loh*

peace, pace (f) *pah'-cheh*

peaceful, pacifico *pah-chee'-fee-koh*

peach, pesca *pes'-kah*

peak, picco *peek'-koh*

peanut, arachide (f) *ah-rah'-kee-deh*

pear, pera *peh'-rah*

pearl, perla *per'-lah*

peasant, contadino *kon-tah-dee'-noh*

peculiar, strano *strah'-noh*

pen, penna *pen'-nah* **fountain pen,** penna stilografica *pen'-nah stee-loh-grah'-fee-kah*

penalty, pena *peh'-nah*

pencil, matita *mah-tee'-tah*

penny, centesimo *chen-teh'-zee-moh*

people, gente (f) *jen'-teh*

pepper [spice], pepe (m) *peh'-peh*

peppermint, menta *men'-tah*

per, al, alla *ahl, ahl'-lah*

perfect, perfetto *per-fet'-toh*

performance, rappresentazione (f) *rahp-preh-zen-tah-tsyoh'-neh*

perfume, profumo *proh-foo'-moh*

perfumery, profumeria *proh-foo-meh-ree'-yah*

perhaps, forse *for'-seh*

period, periodo *peh-ree'-oh-doh*

permanent, permanente *per-mah-nen'-teh*

permission, permesso *per-mes'-soh*

permit *v.,* permettere *per-met'-teh-reh*

person, persona *per-soh'-nah*

personal, personale *per-soh-nah'-leh* [34]

perspiration, sudore (m) *soo-doh'-reh*

petrol, petrolio *peh-trohl'-yoh*

petticoat, sottoveste (f) *sot-toh-ves'-teh*

pharmacist, farmacista (m) *fahr-mah-chees'-tah*

pharmacy, farmacia *fahr-mah-chee'-yah*

photograph, fotografia *foh-toh-grah-fee'-yah*

photographer, fotografo *foh-toh'-grah-foh*

photography, fotografia *foh-toh-grah-fee'-yah*

photography shop, negozio di fotografia *neh-goh'-tsyoh dee foh-toh-grah-fee'-yah*

piano, pianoforte (m) *pee-yah-noh-for'-teh*

pick up, cogliere *kohl'-yeh-reh*

picture, quadro *kwah'-droh*

pie, torta *tor'-tah*

piece, pezzo *pet'-tsoh*

pier, molo *moh'-loh* [86]

pig, maiale, porco *mah-yah'-leh, por'-koh*

pigeon, piccione (m) *peech-choh'-neh*

pile, catasta, mucchio *kah-tahs'-tah, mook'-kyoh*

pill, pillola *peel'-loh-lah*

pillar, pilastro *pee-lahs'-troh*

pillow, guanciale (m) *gwahn-chah'-leh* [89]

pilot, pilota (m) *pee-loh'-tah*

pin, spillo *speel'-loh* [70]   **safety pin,** spillo di sicurezza *speel'-loh dee see-koo-ret'-tsah*

pineapple, ananasso *ah-nah-nahs'-soh*

pink, rosa *roh'-zah*

pipe [tobacco], pipa *pee'-pah*

place *n.,* posto, luogo *pos'-toh, lwoh'-goh* [99]

place *v.,* mettere, collocare *met'-teh-reh, kol-loh-kah'-reh*

plain [simple], semplice *sem'-plee-cheh*

plan *n.,* piano *pyah'-noh*

plant, pianta *pyahn'-tah*

plastic, plastico *plahs'-tee-koh*

plate, piatto *pyaht'-toh*

platform, piattaforma *pyaht-tah-for'-mah* [83]

play *v.,* giocare *joh-kah'-reh*

pleasant, piacevole *pyah-cheh'-voh-leh*

please [suit or satisfy], piacere a *pyah-cheh'-reh ah*   **if you please,** per favore, per piacere *per fah-voh'-reh, per pyah-cheh'-reh*

pleasure, piacere (m) *pyah-cheh'-reh* [4]

plenty of, molto, molti *mol'-toh, mol'-tee*

plum, susina *soo-zee'-nah*

pneumonia, polmonite (f) *pohl-moh-nee'-teh*

poached, cotto in camicia *kot'-toh een kah-mee'-chah*

pocket, tasca *tahs'-kah*

pocketbook [wallet], portafoglio *por-tah-fohl'-yoh*; [purse], borsa *bor'-sah*

point *n.,* punto *poon'-toh*

poison, veleno *veh-leh'-noh*

poisonous, velenoso *veh-leh-noh'-zoh*

police, polizia (f) *poh-lee-tsee'-yah* [15]

policeman, poliziotto, carabiniere (m) *poh-lee-tsee-yot'-toh, kah-rah-bee-nyeh'-reh*

police station, questura *kwes-too'-rah*

political, politico *poh-lee'-tee-koh*

pond, stagno *stahn'-yoh*

pool, piscina *pee-shee'-nah*
poor, povero *poh'-veh-roh*
popular, popolare *poh-poh-lah'-reh*
pork, carne di maiale (f) *kahr'-neh dee mah-yah'-leh*
port, porto *por'-toh* [86]
porter, facchino *fahk-kee'-noh* [35, 82, 83]
portrait, ritratto *ree-traht'-toh*
position, posizione (f) *poh-zee-tsyoh'-neh*
positive, positivo *poh-zee-tee'-voh*
possible, possibile *pos-see'-bee-leh* [13]
possibly, possibilmente *pos-see-beel-men'-teh*
postage, affrancatura *ahf-frahn-kah-too'-rah*
postage stamp, francobollo *frahn-koh-bol'-loh* [40]
postcard, cartolina postale *kahr-toh-lee'-nah pos-tah'-leh*
post office, ufficio postale *oof-fee'-choh pos-tah'-leh*
potato, patata *pah-tah'-tah*
pound [money], libbra *leeb'-brah* [31]
powder, cipria *cheep'-ree-yah*
power, potenza *poh-ten'-tsah*
powerful, potente *poh-ten'-teh*
practical, pratico *prah'-tee-koh*
practice *n.,* pratica *prah'-tee-kah*
prayer, preghiera *preh-gyeh'-rah*
precious, prezioso *preh-tsyoh'-zoh*
prefer, preferire *preh-feh-ree'reh*
preferable, preferibile *preh-feh-ree'-bee-leh*
pregnant, incinta *een-cheen'-tah*
premier, primo ministro *pree'-moh mee-nees'-troh*
preparation, preparazione (f) *preh-pah-rah-tsyoh'-neh*
prepare, preparare *preh-pah-rah'-reh*
prepay, pagare anticipatamente *pah-gah'-reh ahn-tee-chee-pah-tah-men'-teh*
prescription, prescrizione (f) *preh-skree-tsyoh'-neh* [96]
present [gift], regalo *reh-gah'-loh*; [time], attuale *aht-too-ah'-leh*
present *v.,* regalare *reh-gah-lah'-reh* [2]

press [clothes] *v.*, stirare *stee-rah'-reh*
pressure, pressione (f) *pres-syoh'-neh*
pretty, bello, grazioso *bel'-loh, grah-tsyoh'-zoh* [10]
prevent, prevenire *preh-veh-nee'-reh*
previous, precedente *preh-cheh-den'-teh*
price, prezzo *pret'-tsoh* [38]
priest, prete *preh'-teh*
principal, principale *preen-chee-pah'-leh*
prison, prigione (f) *pree-joh'-neh*
prisoner, prigioniero *pree-joh-nyeh'-roh*
private, privato *pree-vah'-toh*
prize, premio *preh'-myoh*
probable, probabile *proh-bah'-bee-leh*
probably, probabilmente *proh-bah-beel-men'-teh*
problem, problema (m) *proh-bleh'-mah*
produce *v.*, produrre *proh-door'-reh*
production, produzione (f) *proh-doo-tsyoh'-neh*
profession, professione (f) *proh-fes-syoh'-neh*
professor, professore (m) *proh-fes-soh'-reh*
profit, profitto *proh-feet'-toh*
program *n.*, programma (m) *proh-grahm'-mah*
progress *n.*, progresso *proh-gres'-soh*
promenade, passeggiata *pahs-sej-jah'-tah*
promise *n.*, promessa *proh-mes'-sah*
prompt, pronto *pron'-toh*
pronunciation, pronunzia *proh-noon'-tsyah*
proof, prova *proh'-vah*
proper, appropriato *ahp-proh-pree-yah'-toh*
property, proprietà *proh-pree-eh-tah'*
proposal, proposta *proh-pos'-tah*
proprietor, proprietario *proh-pree-eh-tah'-ree-yoh*
prosperity, prosperità *proh-speh-ree-tah'*
protect, proteggere *proh-tej'-jeh-reh*
protection, protezione (f) *proh-teh-tsyoh'-neh*
protestant, protestante *proh-tes-tahn'-teh*
proud, orgoglioso *ohr-gohl-yoh'-zoh*

provide, provvedere *prov-veh-deh'-reh*
province, provincia *proh-veen'-chah*
provincial, provinciale *proh-veen-chah'-leh*
provision, disposizione (f) *dees-poh-zee-tsyoh'-neh*
prune, prugna secca, prugna *proon'-yah sek'-kah, proon'-nyah*
public, pubblico *poob'-blee-koh*
publish, pubblicare *poob-blee-kah'-reh*
pull *v.,* tirare *tee-rah'-reh*
pump, pompa *pom'-pah*
punish, punire *poo-nee'-reh*
pupil, alunno *ah-loon'-noh*
purchase *n.,* compera *kom'-peh-rah*
purchase *v.,* comprare *kom-prah'-reh*
pure, puro *poo'-roh*
purple, porpora *por'-poh-rah*
purpose *n.,* scopo *skoh'-poh*
purse, borsa *bor'-sah*
purser, commissario *kom-mees-sah'-ree-yoh*
push *v.,* spingere *speen'-jeh-reh*
put, mettere *met'-teh-reh* [74]

quality, qualità *kwah-lee-tah'*
quantity, quantità *kwahn-tee-tah'*
quarrel *n.,* alterco *ahl-ter'-koh*
quarrel *v.,* litigare *lee-tee-gah'-reh*
quarter *adj. & n.,* quarto *kwahr'-toh*
queen, regina *reh-jee'-nah*
question *n.,* domanda *doh-mahn'-dah*
quick, rapido, veloce *rah'-pee-doh, veh-loh'-cheh*
quickly, rapidamente *rah-pee-dah-men'-teh*
quiet, quieto, silenzioso *kwee-eh'-toh, see-len-tsyoh'-zoh* [38]
quite, molto, del tutto *mol'-toh, del toot'-toh*

radio, radio (f) *rah'-dyoh*

railroad, ferrovia *fer-roh-vee'-yah*

railroad car, vagone (m), carrozza *vah-goh'-neh, kahr-rot'-tsah*

railroad station, stazione ferroviaria *stah-tsyoh'-neh fer-roh-vee-yah'-ree-yah* [45, 82]

rain *n.*, pioggia *pyoj'-jah* [7]

rain *v.*, piovere *pyoh'-veh-reh* [102] **it's raining,** piove *pyoh'-veh*

rainbow, arcobaleno *ahr-koh-bah-leh'-noh* [7]

raincoat, impermeabile (m) *eem-per-meh-ah'-bee-leh* [8]

raise *v.*, sollevare *sol-leh-vah'-reh*

rapidly, rapidamente *rah-pee-dah-men'-teh*

rare, raro *rah-roh*

rash *n.*, eruzione cutanea (f) *eh-roo-tsyoh'-neh koo-tah-neh'-ah*

raspberry, lampone (m) *lahm-poh'-neh*

rate, tariffa *tah-reef'-fah*

rather, piuttosto, abbastanza *pyoot-tos'-toh, ahb-bahs-tahn'-tsah*

raw, crudo *kroo'-doh*

razor, rasoio *rah-zoh'-yoh*

razor blade, lametta (per la barba) *lah-met'-tah (per lah bahr'-bah)*

reach *v.*, raggiungere *rahj-joon'-jeh-reh*

read, leggere *lej'-jeh-reh*

ready, pronto *pron'-toh* [75]

real, vero *veh'-roh*

really, veramente *veh-rah-men'-teh*

rear, di dietro *dee dyeh'-troh*

reason *n.*, ragione (f) *rah-joh'-neh*

reasonable, ragionevole *rah-joh-neh'-voh-leh*

receipt, ricevuta *ree-cheh-voo'-tah* [32]

receive, ricevere *ree-cheh'-veh-reh*

recent, recente *reh-chen'-teh*

reception desk, ricevimento *ree-cheh-vee-men'-toh*

recognize, riconoscere *ree-koh-noh'-sheh-reh*

recommend, raccomandare *rahk-koh-mahn-dah'-reh* [50]

reconfirm [a flight], riconfirmare *ree-kon-feer-mah'-reh* [89]

recover, guarire *gwah-ree'-reh*

red, rosso *ros'-soh*

reduce, ridurre *ree-door'-reh*

reduction, riduzione (f) *ree-doo-tsyoh'-neh*

refreshments, rinfreschi (m, pl) *reen-fres'-kee*

refund *v.,* rimborsare *reem-bohr-sah'-reh*

refuse *v.,* rifiutare *ree-fyoo-tah'-reh*

region, regione (f) *reh-joh'-neh*

register *n.,* registro *reh-jees'-troh*

register [a letter], raccomandare *rahk-koh-mahn-dah'-reh*; [at a hotel], iscriversi sul registro *ees-kree'-vehr-see sool reh-jees'-troh*

regret *v.,* dispiacersi *dees-pyah-chehr'-see*

regular, regolare *reh-goh-lah'-reh*

regulation, regolamento *reh-goh-lah-men'-toh*

relative [kin], parente (m) *pah-ren'-teh*

religion, religione (f) *reh-lee-joh'-neh*

remark *n.,* osservazione (f) *os-ser-vah-tsyoh'-neh*

remember, ricordarsi di *ree-kor-dahr'-see dee*

remove, rimuovere *ree-mwoh'-veh-reh*

renew, rinnovare *reen-noh-vah'-reh*

rent *v.,* affittare *ahf-feet-tah'-reh*

repair *v.,* riparare *ree-pah-rah'-reh*

repeat *v.,* ripetere *ree-peh'-teh-reh* [11]

replace [put back], ricollocare *ree-kol-loh-kah'-reh*

reply *n.,* risposta *rees-pos'-tah*

republic, repubblica *reh-poob'-blee-kah*

request *v.,* chiedere *kyeh'-deh-reh*

rescue *v.,* salvare *sahl-vah'-reh*

reservation, prenotazione (f) *preh-noh-tah-tsyoh'-neh*

reserve *v.,* prenotare, riservare *preh-noh-tah'-reh, ree-zer-vah'-reh* [54]

reserved, riservato *ree-zer-vah'-toh*

residence, residenza *reh-zee-den'-tsah*

resident, residente *reh-zee-den'-teh*

responsible, responsabile *reh-spon-sah'-bee-leh*

rest *n.,* riposo *ree-poh'-zoh*

rest *v.,* riposarsi *ree-poh-zahr'-see*

restaurant, ristorante (m) *rees-toh-rahn'-teh* [38, 48]

restless, irrequieto *eer-reh-kwee-eh'-toh*

rest room, gabinetto *gah-bee-net'-toh*

result *n.,* risultato *ree-zool-tah'-toh*

return *v.,* ritornare, tornare *ree-tohr-nah'-reh, tohr-nah'-reh*

return ticket, biglietto di ritorno *beel-yet'-toh dee ree-tohr'-noh*

review *n.,* rivista *ree-vees'-tah*

reward, ricompensa *ree-kom-pen'-sah*

rib, costola *kos'-toh-lah*

ribbon, nastro *nahs'-troh*

rice, riso *ree'-zoh*

rich, ricco *reek'-koh*

ride *n.,* corsa, passeggiata *kor'-sah, pahs-sej-jah'-tah* [45]

right [correct], corretto *kor-ret'-toh* **to be right,** aver ragione *ah-vehr' rah-joh'-neh* [12] **all right,** molto bene, va bene *mol'-toh beh'-neh, vah beh'-neh*

right [direction], a destra *ah des'-trah*

ring *n.,* anello *ah-nel'-loh*

ring *v.,* suonare *swoh-nah'-reh* [44]

ripe, maturo *mah-too'-roh*

rise *v.,* sorgere *sor'-jeh-reh*

river, fiume (m) *fyoo'-meh* [101, 102]

road, strada, cammino *strah'-dah, kahm-mee'-noh* [75]

roast, arrosto *ahr-rohs'-toh*

rob, rubare *roo-bah'-reh* [15]

robber, ladro *lah'-droh*

rock, roccia *roch'-chah*

roof, tetto *tet'-toh*

roll [bread], panino *pah-nee'-noh*

roll *v.*, rotolare *roh-toh-lah'-reh*

room [of a house], stanza, camera *stahn'-tsah, kah'-meh-rah* [7]; [in a hotel], camera *kah'-meh-rah* [37, 38, 48]

rope, corda *kor'-dah*

rose, rosa *roh'-zah*

rouge, rossetto *ros-set'-toh*

rough, ruvido, aspro *roo'-vee-doh, ahs'-proh*

round, rotondo *roh-ton'-doh*

round trip, andata e ritorno *ahn-dah'-tah eh ree-tor'-noh* [84]

royal, reale *reh-ah'-leh*

rubber, gomma *gom'-mah*

rude, rude, rozzo, sgarbato *roo'-deh, rot'-tsoh, zgahr-bah'-toh*

rug, tappeto *tahp-peh'-toh*

ruin *v.*, rovinare *roh-vee-nah'-reh*

rum, rum (m) *room*

run *v.*, correre *kor'-reh-reh*

runway, pista *pees'-tah* [90]

sad, triste *trees'-teh*

safe, sicuro *see-koo'-roh*

safety pin, spillo di sicurezza *speel'-loh dee see-koo-ret'-tsah*

sail *v.*, navigare, veleggaiare, partire *nah-vee-gah'-reh, veh-lej'-jah-reh, pahr-tee'-reh* [86]

sailor, marinaio *mah-ree-nah'-yoh*

saint, santo *sahn'-toh*

salad, insalata *een-sah-lah'-tah*

sale, vendita *ven'-dee-tah* [68] **for sale**, da vendere *dah ven'-deh-reh*

salesgirl, venditrice (f) *ven-dee-tree'-cheh*

salesman, commesso, venditore *kom-mes'-soh, ven-dee-toh'-reh*

salmon, salmone (m) *sahl-moh'-neh*

salt, sale (m) *sah'-leh*

same, stesso *stes'-soh* **the same as,** lo stesso come *loh stes'-soh ko'-meh*

sample *n.,* campione (m) *kahm-pyoh'-neh*

sand, sabbia *sahb'-byah*

sandwich, panino imbottito *pah-nee'-noh eem-bot-tee'-toh*

sanitary, sanitario *sah-nee-tah'-ree-yoh*

sanitary napkin, pannilino igienico *pahn-nee-lee'-noh ee-jyeh'-nee-koh*

satin, raso *rah'-zoh*

satisfactory, soddisfacente *sod-dees-fah-chen'-teh*

satisfied, soddisfatto *sod-dees-faht'-toh*

satisfy, soddisfare *sod-dees-fah'-reh*

Saturday, sabato *sah'-bah-toh*

sauce, salsa *sahl'-sah*

saucer, piattino *pyaht-tee'-noh*

sausage, salsiccia *sahl-seech'-chah*

save, risparmiare *rees-pahr-myah'-reh*; [rescue], salvare *sahl-vah'-reh*

say, dire *dee'-reh* [11]

scale, bilancia *bee-lahn'-chah*

scar *n.,* cicatrice (f) *chee-kah-tree'-cheh*

scarce, scarso *skahr'-soh*

scarcely, appena *ahp-peh'-nah*

scare *v.,* spaventare *spah-ven-tah'-reh*

scarf, sciarpa *shahr'-pah*

scenery, paesaggio *pah-eh-zahj'-joh*

scent *n.,* promfumo, fiuto *proh-foo'-moh, fyoo'-toh*

schedule *n.,* orario *oh-rah'-ree-yoh*

school, scuola *skwoh'-lah*

science, scienza *shyen'-tsah*

scientist, scienziato *shyen-tsyah'-toh*

scissors, forbici (f, pl) *for'-bee-chee*

scratch *n.,* graffio *grahf'-fyoh*

sculpture, scultura *skool-too'-rah*

sea, mare (m) *mah'-reh*

seafood, pesce e frutti di mare *peh'-sheh eh froot'-tee dee mah'-reh*

seagull, gabbiano *gahb-byah'-noh*

seam, cucitura *koo-chee-too'-rah*

seaport, porto di mare *por'-toh dee mah'-reh*

search v., cercare *cher-kah'-reh*

seasick, soffrendo mal di mare *sof-fren'-doh mahl dee mah'-reh* [88]

season, stagione (f) *stah-joh'-neh*

seat, posto *pos'-toh* [84]

second, secondo *seh-kon'-doh* **second class,** seconda classe *seh-kon'-dah klahs'-seh* [83, 87]

secret adj. & n., segreto *seh-greh'-toh*

secretary, segretario *seh-greh-tah'-ree-yoh*

section sezione (f) *seh-tsyoh'-neh*

see, vedere *veh-deh'-reh* [3, 7, 99]

seem, sembrare, parere *sem-brah'-reh, pah-reh'-reh*

select v., scegliere *shehl'-yeh-reh*

selection, selezione (f) *seh-leh-tsyoh'-neh*

self, stesso, stessa *stes'-soh, stes'-sah*

sell, vendere *ven'-deh-reh* [67, 70]

send, mandare, spedire *mahn-dah'-reh, speh-dee'-reh* [13, 70]

sensible, ragionevole *rah-joh-neh'-voh-leh*

separate adj., separato *seh-pah-rah'-toh*

separate v., separare *seh-pah-rah'-reh*

September, settembre (m) *set-tem'-breh*

series, serie (f) *seh'-ree-yeh*

serious, serio *seh'-ree-yoh*

servant, servo, domestico *ser'-voh, doh-mes'-tee-koh*

serve v., servire *ser-vee'-reh* [50, 64, 90]

service, servizio *ser-vee'-tsee-yoh*

service charge, spese di servizio (f, pl) *speh'-zeh dee ser-vee'-tsee-yoh*

set [fixed], fissato *fees-sah'-toh*

set [place] *v.*, mettere *met'-teh-reh*
seven, sette *set'-teh*
seventeen, diciassette *dee-chahs-set'-teh*
seventh, settimo *set'-tee-moh*
seventy, settanta *set-tahn'-tah*
several, parecchi *pah-rek'-kee*
severe, severo *seh-veh'-roh*
sew, cucire *koo-chee'-reh*
shade, ombra *om'-brah*
shampoo, shampoo *shahm-poo'*
shape *n.*, forma *for'-mah*
share *v.*, condividere *kon-dee-vee'-deh-reh*
shark, pescecane (m) *peh-sheh-kah'-neh*
sharp, affilato, aguzzo *ahf-fee-lah'-toh, ah-goot'-tsoh*
shave *v.*, farsi la barba, radersi *fahrsee lah bahr'-bah, rah'-der-see*
shaving cream, crema per la barba *kreh'-mah per lah bahr'-bah*
she, ella, essa, lei *el'-lah, es'-sah, leh'-ee*
sheep, pecora *peh'-koh-rah*
sheet [of paper], foglio *fohl'-yoh* **bedsheet,** lenzuolo *len-tswoh'-loh*
shellfish, frutti di mare *froot'-tee dee mah'-reh*
shelter, rifugio *ree-foo'-joh*
sherry, vino di Xeres *vee'-noh dee sheh'-rehs*
shine *v.*, lustrare *loos-trah'-reh*
ship *n.*, nave (f) *nah'-veh* [86, 87]
ship *v.*, spedire *speh-dee'-reh* [70]
shirt, camicia *kah-mee'-chah* [40, 69]
shiver *v.*, tremare *treh-mah'-reh*
shock *n.*, colpo *kol'-poh*
shoe, scarpa *skahr'-pah* [69]
shoelace, laccio *lahch'-choh*
shoeshine, lustro di scarpe *loos'-troh dee skahr'-peh*
shoestore, calzoleria *kahl-tsoh-leh-ree'-yah*
shoot *v.*, sparare *spah-rah'-reh*

shop *n.*, negozio *neh-goh'-tsyoh*

shop: to go shopping, fare delle compere *fah'-reh del'-leh kom'-peh-reh* [62]

shopping center, centro di compere *chen'-troh dee kom'-peh-reh* [102]

shore, sponda, riva *spon'-dah, ree'-vah*

short, corto *kor'-toh* [68, 69]

shorts, mutande (f, pl) *moo-tahn'-deh*

shoulder, spalla *spahl'-lah*

show *n.*, spettacolo *spet-tah'-koh-loh*

show *v.*, mostrare *mos-trah'-reh* [13, 67, 95]

shower [bath], doccia *doch'-chah* [37]

shrimp, gambero *gahm'-beh-roh*

shut *adj.*, chiuso *kyoo'-zoh*

shut *v.*, chiudere *kyoo'-deh-reh*

shy, timido *tee'-mee-doh*

sick, ammalato *ahm-mah-lah'-toh* [92]

side, lato, fianco *lah'-toh, fyahn'-koh*

sidewalk, marciapiede (m) *mahr-chah-pyeh'-deh*

sight, vista *vees'-tah*

sightseeing, girare per vedere le curiosità *jee-rah'-reh per veh-deh'-rah leh koo-ree-yoh-zee-tah'* [98]

sign *n.*, insegna *een-sehn'-yah*

sign *v.*, firmare *feer-mah'-reh* [32]

signature, firma *feer'-mah*

silence, silenzio *see-len-tsee'-yoh*

silent, silenzioso *see-len-tsee-yoh'-zoh*

silk, seta *seh'-tah*

silly, sciocco, stolto *shok'-koh, stol'-toh*

silver, argento *ahr-jen'-toh*

similar, simile *see'-mee-leh*

simple, semplice *sem'-plee-cheh*

since, da, dacchè, siccome *dah, dahk-keh', seek-ko'-meh*

sing, cantare *kahn-tah'-reh*

single, singolo *seen'-goh-loh*

sir, signore *seen-yoh'-reh*

sister, sorella *soh-rel'-lah* [3]
sit, sedersi *seh-dehr'-see* [100]
situation, situazione (f) *see-too-ah-tsyoh'-neh*
six, sei *seh'-ee*
sixteen, sedici *seh'-dee-chee*
sixth, sesto *ses'-toh*
sixty, sessanta *ses-sahn'-tah*
size, misura, *mee-zoo'-rah* [67]
skilled, skillful, abile *ah'-bee-leh*
skin, pelle (f) *pel'-leh*
skirt, gonna, gonnella *gon'-nah, gon-nel'-lah* [68]
skull, cranio *krah'-nee-yoh*
sky, cielo *chyeh'-loh*
sleep *n.,* sonno *son'-noh*
sleep *v.,* dormire *dor-mee'-reh* [96]
sleeve, manica *mah'-nee-kah* [69]
slice *n.,* fetta *fet'-tah*
slice *v.,* affettare *ahf-fet-tah'-reh*
slight, leggero *lej-jeh'-roh*
slip [garment], sottogonna *sot-toh-gon'-nah*
slip *v.,* scivolare *shee-voh-lah'-reh*
slippers, pantofole (f, pl) *pahn-toh'-foh-leh*
slippery, sciovoloso, sdruccievole *shee-voh-loh'-zoh, zdrooch-chyeh'-voh-leh* [75]
slow, lento *len'-toh*
slowly, lentamente, adagio, pian piano *len-tah-men'-teh, ah-dah'-joh, pyahn pyah'-noh* [11, 45]
small, piccolo *peek'-koh-loh*
smart, svelto *zvel'-toh*
smell *n.,* odore *oh-doh'-reh*
smell *v.,* odorare *oh-doh-ruh'-reh*
smile *n.,* sorriso *sor-ree'-zoh*
smile *v.,* sorridere *sor-ree'-deh-reh*
smoke *n.,* fumo *foo'-moh*
smoke *v.,* fumare *foo-mah'-reh* [89, 96]
smooth, liscio *lee'-shoh*

snack, spuntino *spoon-tee'-noh*

snow, neve (f) *neh'-veh* **it's snowing,** nevica *neh'-vee-kah*

so, così *koh-see'* **so as,** così che *koh-see' keh* **so that,** affinchè *ahf-feen-keh'*

soap, sapone (m) *sah-poh'-neh* [40]

social, sociale *soh-chah'-leh*

sock, calzino *kahl-tsee'-noh*

soda, soda *soh'-dah*

soft, soffice, morbido, molle *sof'-fee-cheh, mor'-bee-doh, mol'-leh*

sold, venduto *ven-doo'-toh*

solid, solido *soh'-lee-doh*

some, del, della, dei *del, del'-lah, deh'-ee*

somehow, in qualche modo *een kwahl'-keh moh'-doh*

someone, qualcuno *kwahl-koo'-noh*

something, qualche cosa, qualcosa *kwahl'-keh ko'-zah, kwahl-ko'-zah*

sometimes, qualche volta *kwahl'-keh vol'-tah*

somewhere, in qualche luogo *een kwahl'-keh lwoh'-goh*

son, figlio *feel'-yoh* [3]

song, canzone (f) *kahn-tsoh'-neh*

soon, fra poco *frah poh'-koh*

sore *adj.,* dolente *doh-len'-teh*

sore throat, mal di gola *mahl dee goh'-lah*

sorrow, afflizione (f) *ahf-flee-tsyoh'-neh*

sorry: to be sorry, dispiacere a, rincrescere a *dees-pyah-cheh'-reh ah, reen-kreh'-sheh-reh ah* [3] **I'm sorry,** mi dispiace, mi rincresce *mee dees-pyah'-cheh, mee reen-kreh'-sheh*

sort, sorta *sor'-tah*

soul, anima *ah'-nee-mah*

sound *n.,* suono *swoh'-noh*

soup, zuppa, minestra *dzoop'-pah, mee-nes'-trah* [54]

sour, agro, acido *ah'-groh, ah'-chee-doh* [52]

south, sud (m) *sood*

southeast, sud-est *sood-est'*

southwest, sud-ovest *sood-oh'-vest*

souvenir, ricordo *ree-kor'-doh*

space, spazio *spah'-tsee-yoh*

speak, parlare *pahr-lah'-reh* [43] **do you speak English?** parla Lei inglese? *pahr'- leh'-ee een-gleh'-zeh*

special, speciale *speh-chah'-leh*

specialty, specialità *speh-chah'-lee-tah*

speed, velocità *veh-loh-chee-tah'* [75]

spell *v.,* sillabare, scrivere *seel-lah-bah'-reh, skree'-veh-reh*

spend, spendere *spen'-deh-reh*

spicy, piccante *peek-kahn'-teh*

spinach, spinaci (m, pl) *spee-nah'-chee*

spine, spina dorsale *spee'-nah dor-sahl'-leh*

splendid, splendido *splen'-dee-doh*

spoiled, guasto *gwah'-toh*

spoon, cucchiaio *kook-kee-yah'-yoh* [55]

spot *n.,* macchia *mahk'-kee-yah*

sprain *n.,* storta *stor'-tah*

spring [season], primavera *pree-mah-veh'-rah*

spring [water], sorgente (f) *sor-jen'-teh*

springs [of a car], molla *mol'-lah*

square *adj.,* quadrato *kwah-drah'-toh*

square [public], piazza *pyaht'-tsah* [100]

stairs, scala *skah'-lah*

stamp, francobollo *frahn-koh-bol'-loh* [40]

stand *v.,* stare in piedi *stah'-reh een pyeh'-dee*

star, stella *stel'-lah* [7]

starch, amido *ah'-mee-doh*

start *n.,* principio *preen-chee'-pyoh*

start *v.,* cominciare *kom-een-chah'-reh*

state, stato *stah'-toh*

stateroom, cabina *kah-bee'-nah*

station, stazione (f) *stah-tsyoh'-neh* [82]

statue, statua *stah'-too-ah*

stay *v.,* stare, rimanere *stah'-reh, ree-mah-neh'-reh* [16, 38, 39, 94]

steak, bistecca *bees-tek'-kah*

steal *v.,* rubare *roo-bah'-reh* [15]

steel, acciaio *ahch-chah'-yoh*

steep, erto *er'-toh*

step, passo, gradino *pahs'-soh, grah-dee'-noh*

stew, stufato *stoo-fah'-toh*

steward, cameriere (m) *kah-mee-ree-yeh'-reh* [87]

stick *n.,* stecco *stek'-koh*

stiff, rigido *ree'-jee-doh*

still [quiet], tranquillo *trahn-kweel'-loh*

still [yet], tuttavia, eppure *toot-tah-vee'-yah, ep-poo'-reh*

sting *n.,* puntura *poon-too'-rah*

sting *v.,* pungere *poon'-jeh-reh*

stockings, calze (f, pl) *kahl'-tseh*

stolen, rubato *roo-bah'-toh*

stomach, stomaco *stoh'-mah-koh* [92]

stone, pietra *pyeh'-trah*

stop *n.,* fermata *fer-mah'-tah*

stop *v.,* fermarsi *fer-mahr'-see* [14, 45 46, 84]

store *n.,* negozio *neh-goh'-tsyoh* [62, 99]

storey, piano *pyah'-noh*

storm, tempesta, temporale (m) *tem-pes'-tah, tem-poh-rah'-leh*

story, storia *stoh'-ree-yah*

straight, diritto *dee-reet'-toh*

straight ahead, sempre diritto *sem'-preh dee-reet'-toh* [45]

strange, strano *strah'-noh*

stranger, straniero *strah-nyeh'-roh*

strawberry, fragola *frah'-goh-lah*

stream, corrente (f) *kor-ren'-teh*

street, strada, via *strah'-dah, vee'-yah* [37, 46, 100, 101]

streetcar, tranvia *trahn-vee'-yah*

strength, forza *for'-tsah*

string, spago *spah'-goh*

strong, forte *for'-teh*

structure, struttura *stroot-too'-rah*

student, studente *stoo-den'-teh*

study *v.,* studiare *stoo-dee-yah'-reh*

style, stile (m) *stee'-leh*

suburb, sobborgo, dintorni (m, pl) *sob-bor'-goh, deen-tor'-nee*

succeed [follow], seguire *seh-gwee'-reh;* [attain one's goal], riuscire *ree-oo-shee'-reh*

success, successo *sooch-ches'-soh*

such, tale *tah'-leh*

suddenly, improvvisamente, ad un tratto *eem-prov-vee-zah-men'-teh, ahd oon traht'-toh*

suffer, soffrire *sof-free'-reh*

sufficient, sufficiente *soof-fee-chyen'-teh*

sugar, zucchero *dzook'-keh-roh* [51, 52]

suggest, suggerire *sooj-jeh-ree'-reh*

suggestion, suggerimento *sooj-jeh-ree-men'-toh*

suit, vestito, abito *vest-tee'-toh, ah'-bee-toh*

suitcase, valigia *vah-lee'-jah* [39]

summer, estate (f) *es-tah'-teh*

sun, sole (m) *soh'-leh* [6]

sunburned, bruciato dal sole *broo-chah'-toh dahl soh'-leh*

Sunday, domenica *doh-meh'-nee-kah*

sunglasses, occhiali da sole *ok-kyah'-lee dah soh'-leh*

sunny, soleggiato *soh-lej-jah'-toh*

supper, cena *chen'-nah* [51]

sure, sicuro *see-koo'-roh*

surface, superficie (f) *soo-per-fee'-chyeh*

surprise *n.,* sorpresa *sor-preh'-zah*

surprise *v.,* sorprendere *sor-pren'-deh-reh*

suspect *v.,* sospettare *soh-spet-tah'-reh*

suspicion, sospetto *sos-pet'-toh*

sweater, maglione di lana (m) *mahl-yoh'-neh dee lah'-nah* [8]

sweep, spazzare, scopare *spaht-tsah'-reh, skoh-pah'-reh*

sweet, dolce *dol'-cheh*

swim, nuotare *nwoh-tah'-reh* [102]

swollen, gonfiato *gon-fyah'-toh*
sword, spada *spah'-dah*

table, tavola *tah'-voh-lah* [50, 54, 57, 87]
tablecloth, tovaglia *toh-vahl'-yah* [56]
tailor, sarto *sahr'-toh*
take, prendere *pren'-deh-reh* [51, 67] **take off,** decollare *deh-kol-lah'-reh* [89]
talk, parlare *pahr-lah'-reh*
tall, alto *ahl'-toh*
tank, serbatoio *ser-bah-toh'-yoh*
taste *n.*, gusto *goos'-toh*
taste *v.*, assaggiare, gustare, saporare *ahs-saj-jah'-reh, goos-tah'-reh, sah-poh-rah'-reh*
tax *n.*, tassa *tahs'-sah*
taxi, tassì *tahs-see'* [44]
tea, tè (m) *teh* [53]
teach, insegnare *een-sehn-yah'-reh*
teacher, maestro *mah-ehs'-troh*
tear [drop], lagrima *lah'-gree-mah*
tear *v.*, strappare *strahp-pah'-reh*
teaspoon, cucchiaino *kook-kyah-ee'-noh*
teeth, denti (m, pl) *den'-tee*
telegram, telegramma (m) *teh-leh-grahm'-mah*
telephone, telefono *teh-leh'-foh-noh* [41]
telephone booth, cabina telefonica *kah-bee'-nah teh-leh-foh'-nee-kah*
telephone operator, telefonista, centralino *teh-leh-foh-nees'-tah, chen-trah-lee'-noh*
television, televisione (f) *teh-leh-vee-zyoh'-neh*
tell, dire, raccontare *dee'-reh, rahk-kon-tah'-reh* [13, 46]
temperature, temperatura *tem-peh-rah-too'-rah*
temple, tempio *tem'-pyoh*
temporary, provvisorio *prov-vee-zoh'-ree-yoh*
ten, dieci *dyeh'-chee*
tent, tenda *ten'-dah*

tenth, decimo *deh'-chee-moh*

test, prova *proh'-vah*

than, di, che *dee, keh*

thank, ringraziare *reen-grah-tsyah'-reh*   **thank you,** grazie *grah'-tsee-yeh*

thankful, grato *grah'-toh*

that *adj.*, quello, quel, quell', quella *kwel'-loh, kwel, kwel, kwel'-lah*

that *conj.*, che *keh*

that *pron.*, quello, quella *kwel'-loh, kwel'-lah*

the, il, la, l', lo i, le, gli *eel, lah, l, loh, ee, leh, lyee*

theater, teatro *teh-ah'-troh* [101]

theft, furto *foor'-toh*

their, loro *loh'-roh*

theirs, loro *loh'-roh*

them, loro, li, le *loh'-roh, lee, leh*

then, allora *ahl-loh'-rah*

there *adv.*, lì, là, ci *lee, lah, chee*   **there is, there are,** c'è, ci sono *cheh, chee soh'-noh*

therefore, perciò *per-choh'*

thermometer, termometro *ter-moh'-meh-troh*

these *adj.*, & *pron.*, questi, queste *kwes'-tee, kwes'-teh*

they, loro, essi, esse *loh'-roh, es'-see, es'-seh*

thick, spesso *spes'-soh*

thigh, coscia *koh'-shah*

thin, sottile, magro *sot-tee'-leh, mah'-groh*

thing, cosa *ko'-zah*

think, pensare *pen-sah'-reh*

third, terzo *ter'-tsoh*

thirst, sete *seh'-teh*

thirsty: to be thirsty, aver sete *ah-vehr' seh'-teh* [47, 48]

thirteen, tredici *treh'-dee-chee*

thirty, trenta *tren'-tah*

this *adj.*, questo, questa, quest' *kwes'-toh, kwes'-tah, kwest*

this *pron.*, questo, questa *kwes'-toh, kwes'-tah*

those *adj.*, quelli, quelle, quegli, quei *kwel'-lee, kwel'-leh, kwel'-yee, kweh'-ee*

those *pron.*, quelli, quelle *kwel'-lee, kwel'-leh*

thoroughfare, strada principale *strah'-dah preen-chee-pah'-leh*

thousand, mille *meel'-leh*

thread, filo *fee'-loh* [70]

three, tre *treh*

throat, gola *goh'-lah*

through *prep.*, per, attraverso *per, aht-trah-ver'-soh*

through [finished], finito *fee-nee'-toh*

throw, lanciare, gettare *lahn-chah'-reh, jet-tah'-reh*

thumb, pollice (m) *pol'-lee-cheh*

thunder, tuono *twoh'-noh*

Thursday, giovedì *joh-veh-dee'*

ticket, biglietto *beel-yet'-toh* [83, 85, 89]

ticket office, sportello dei biglietti *spor-tel'-loh deh'-ee beel-yet'-tee* [83]

tie [bind], legare *leh-gah'-reh*

tight, stretto *stret'-toh* [69]

tighten, stringere *streen'-jeh-reh*

till, fino a, finchè *fee'-noh ah, feen-keh'*

time, tempo, volta *temp'-poh, vol'-tah* **what time is it?** che ora è? *keh oh'-reh eh* **on time,** a tempo *ah tem'-poh*

timetable, orario *oh-rah'-ree-yoh* [83]

tip [money], mancia *mahn'-chah* [57]

tire [of a car], gomma, pneumatico *gom'-mah, pneh-oo-mah'-tee-koh* [74]

tire *v.*, stancarsi *stahn-kahr'-see*

tired, stanco *stahn'-koh* [100]

to, a, ad *ah, ahd*

toast, pane tostato *pah'-neh tos-tah'-toh*

tobacco, tabacco *tah-bahk'-koh* [34]

tobacconist, tabaccaio *tah-bahk-kah'-yoh*

today, oggi *oj'-jee* [5, 99]

toe, dito del piede *dee'-toh del pyeh'-deh*

together, insieme *een-syeh'-meh*

toilet, gabinetto *gah-bee-net'-toh*

toilet paper, carta igienica *kahr'-tah ee-jyeh'-nee-kah*

tomato, pomodoro *poh-moh-doh'-roh*

tomorrow, domani *doh-mah'-nee* [3, 6, 40, 96]

tongue, linqua *leen'-gwah* [95]

tonight, questa notte, stasera *kwes'-tah not'-teh, stah-seh'-rah*

tonsils, tonsille (f, pl) *ton-seel'-leh*

too [excessive], troppo *trop'-poh;* [also], anche *ahn'-keh*

tooth, dente (m) *den'-teh*

toothache, dolor di denti *doh-lohr' dee den'-tee*

toothbrush, spazzolino da denti *spaht-tsoh-lee'-noh dah den'-tee*

toothpaste, pasta dentifricia *pahs'-tah den-tee-free'-chah*

top, cima *chee'-mah*

torn, strappato *strahp-pah'-toh*

total, totale *toh-tah'-leh*

touch *v.*, toccare *kok-kah'-reh*

tough, duro, resistente *doo'-roh, reh-zees-ten'-teh*

tour, giro *jee'-roh* [99, 102]

tow, rimorchiare *ree-mor-kyah'-reh*

toward, verso *ver'-soh*

towel, asciugamano *ah-shoo-gah-mah'-noh* [40]

town, città *sheet-tah'*

toy, giocattolo *joh-kaht'-toh-loh*

toy shop, negozio di giocattoli *neh-goh'-tsyoh dee joh-kaht'-toh-lee*

trade, commercio *kom-mer'-choh*

traffic, traffico *trahf'-fee-koh*

train, treno *treh'-noh* [15, 82, 83, 84, 85]

transfer *v.*, trasferire *trahs-feh-ree'-reh* [46]

translate, tradurre *trah-door'-reh*

translation, traduzione (f) *trah-doo-tsyoh'-neh*

translator, traduttore (m), traduttrice (f) *trah-doot-toh'-reh, trah-doot-tree'-cheh*

transmission, trasmissione (f) *trahz-mees-syoh'-neh*

transportation, trasporto *trahs-por'-toh*

travel *v.,* viaggiare *vyahj-jah'-reh*

traveler, viaggiatore (m) *vyahj-jah-toh'-reh*

traveler's check, assegno di viaggio *ahs-sehn'-yoh dee vyahj'-joh* [31]

tray, vassoio *vahs-soh'-yoh*

tree, albero *ahl'-beh-roh*

trip, viaggio *vyahj'-joh* [88]

tropical, tropicale *troh-pee-kah'-leh*

trousers, pantaloni (m, pl) *pahn-tah-loh'-nee*

truck, camione (m) *kah-myoh'-neh*

true, vero *veh'-roh*

trunk, baule (m) *bah-oo'-leh*

truth, verità *veh-ree-tah'*

try *v.,* tentare, cercare di *ten-tah'-reh, cher-kah'-reh dee* **try on,** provarsi *proh-vahr'-see* [67, 69]

Tuesday, martedì *mahr-teh-dee'*

turn *n.,* giro, voltata *jee'-roh, vol-tah'-tah*

turn *v.,* girare *jee-rah'-reh* [45]

twelve, dodici *doh'-dee-chee*

twenty, venti *ven'-tee*

twice, due volte *doo'-eh vol'-teh*

twin beds, letti gemelli *let'-tee jeh-mel'-lee*

two, due *doo'-eh*

ugly, brutto *broot'-toh*

umbrella, ombrello *om-brel'-loh* [6]

uncle, zio *dzee'-yoh*

uncomfortable, scomodo *skoh'-moh-doh*

unconscious, inconscio, privo di sensi *een-kon'-shoh, pree'-voh dee sen'-see*

under *prep.*, sotto *sot'-toh*
underneath *prep.*, disotto *dee-sot'-toh*
undershirt, camiciola *kah-mee-choh'-lah*
understand, capire *kah-pee-reh* [11]
underwear, maglia *mahl'-yah*
undress *v.*, svestirsi *zves-teer'-see*
unequal, ineguale *een-eh-gwah'-leh*
unfair, ingiusto *een-joos'-toh*
unfortunate, sfortunato *sfor-too-nah'-toh*
unhappy, infelice *een-feh-lee'-cheh*
unhealthy, malsano *mahl-sah'-noh*
United States, Stati Uniti (m, pl) *stah'-tee oo-nee'-tee*
university, università *oo-nee-ver-see-tah'*
unless, a meno che *ah meh'-noh keh*
unlucky, sfortunato *sfor-too-nah'-toh*
unpack, disfare le valige, sballare *dees-fah'-reh leh vah-lee'-jeh, zbahl-lah'-reh*
unpleasant, spiacevole *spyah-cheh'-voh-leh*
unsafe, non sicuro *non see-koo'-roh*
until, fino a, finchè *fee'-noh ah, feen-keh'*
untrue, falso *fahl'-soh*
unusual, insolito *een-soh'-lee-toh*
up, su *soo*
upper, superiore *soo-peh-ree-yoh'-reh*
upstairs, sopra *soh'-prah*
urgent, urgente *oor-jen'-teh*
us, noi, ci *noy, chee*
use *n.*, uso *oo'-zoh* [34]
use *v.*, usare *oo-zah'-reh*
useful, utile *oo'-tee-leh*
useless, inutile *een-oo'-tee-leh*
usual, usuale, solito *oo-zoo-ah'-leh, soh'-lee-toh*

vacant, libero *lee'-beh-roh*
vacation, vacanze (f, pl) *vah-kahn' tseh*

vaccination, vaccinazione (f) *vahch-chee-nah-tsyoh'-neh*
valuable, prezioso, di valore *preh-tsyoh'-zoh, dee vah-loh'-reh*
value *n.,* valore (m) *vah-loh'-reh*
vanilla, vaniglia *vah-neel'-yah*
variety, varietà *vah-ree-eh-tah'*
veal, vitello *vee-tel'-loh*
vegetables, legumi (m, pl) *leh-goo'-mee*
very, molto *mol'-toh*
vest, panciotto *pahn-chot'-toh*
victim, vittima *veet'-tee-mah*
view *n.,* veduta, vista *veh-doo'-tah, vees'-tah* [37]
village, villaggio *veel-lahj'-joh*
vinegar, aceto *ah-cheh'-toh*
visa, visto *vees'-toh*
visit *n.,* visita *vee'-zee-tah*
visit *v.,* visitare *vee-zee-tah'-reh* [99, 101, 103]
voice, voce (f) *voh'-cheh*
volcano, vulcano *vool-kah'-noh*
voyage *n.,* viaggio *vyahj'-joh*

waist, vita *vee'-tah*
wait *v.,* aspettare *ahs-pet-tah'-reh* [12, 45]
waiter, cameriere (m) *kah-meh-ree-yeh'-reh* [50, 56]
waiting room, sala d'aspetto *sah'-lah dahs-pet'-toh* [85]
waitress, cameriera *kah-meh-ree-yeh'-rah* [50]
wake up, svegliare, svegliarsi *zvehl-yah'-reh, zvehl-yahr'-see*
walk *n.,* passeggiata *pahs-sej-jah'-tah*
walk *v.,* camminare *kahm-mee-nah'-reh* [100]
wall, muro, parete (f) *moo'-roh, pah-reh'-teh*
wallet, portafogli (m) *por-tah-fohl'-yee*
want *v.,* volere *voh-leh-reh* **I want,** voglio *vohl'-yoh*
warm, caldo *kahl'-doh* [52, 55]
warn, avvertire *ahv-ver-tee'-reh*

warning, avvertimento, avvertenza *ahv-ver-tee-men'-toh, ahv-ver-ten'-tsah*

wash *v.,* lavare *lah-vah'-reh* [40, 74]

wasp, vespa *ves'-pah*

watch *n.,* orologio *oh-roh-loh'-joh*

watch *v.,* guardare, osservare *gwahr-dah'-reh, os-ser-vah'-reh*

water, acqua *ahk'-kwah* [8, 51, 74]

waterfall, cascata *kahs-kah'-tah*

wave [ocean], onda *on'-dah*

way [manner], maniera, modo *mah-nyeh'-rah, moh'-doh*

we, noi *noy*

weak, debole *deh'-boh-leh*

wear *v.,* indossare, portare *een-dos-sah'-reh, por-tah'-reh*

weather, tempo *tem'-poh* [5, 6, 7]

Wednesday, mercoledì *mer-koh-leh-dee'*

week, settimana *set-tee-mah'-nah* [38, 39]

weigh, pesare *peh-zah'-reh*

weight, peso *peh'-zoh*

welcome *n.,* benvenuto *ben-veh-noo'-toh*

well, bene *beh'-neh* **well done** [food], ben cotto *ben kot'-toh*

well [for water], pozzo *pot'-tsoh*

west, ovest (m) *oh'-vest*

wet, bagnato *bahn-yah'-toh* [75]

what *interr.,* che? che cosa? *keh, keh ko'-zah* **what else?** che altro? *keh ahl'-troh?*

wheel, ruota *rwoh'-tah*

when, quando *kwahn'-doh*

whenever, ogni volta che *ohn'-yee vol'-tah keh*

where, dove *do'-veh* **where is, where are,** dov'è, dove sono *do-ve', do'-veh soh'-noh*

wherever, dovunque *do-voon'-kweh*

which *interr.,* quale? *kwah'-leh?*

while, mentre *men'-treh*

whip *n.*, frusta *froos'-tah*
white, bianco *byahn'-koh* [69]
who *interr.*, chi? *kee*
who [*rel.*,] che *keh*
whole, intero *een-teh'-roh*
whom *interr.*, chi? *kee*
whose *interr.*, di chi? *dee kee*
why *interr.*, perchè? *per-keh'*
wide, largo *lahr'-goh* [69, 75]
width, larghezza *lahr-get'-tsah*
wife, moglie (f) *mohl'-yeh* [2]
wild, selvaggio *sel-vahj'-joh*
willing, disposto a *dees-pos'-toh ah*
win *v.*, vincere *veen'-cheh-reh*
wind, vento *ven'-toh* [6, 7]
window, finestra *fee-nes'-trah* [39, 84]
windshield, parabrezza *pah-rah-bret'-tsah* [76]
wine, vino *vee'-noh* [55]   **red wine,** vino rosso *vee'-noh ros'-soh*   **white wine,** vino bianco *vee'-noh byahn'-koh*
wing, ala *ah'-lah*
winter, inverno *een-ver'-noh*
wipe, pulire *poo-lee'-reh* [76]
wise, saggio *sahj'-joh*
wish *n.*, desiderio, augurio *deh-zee-deh'-ree-yoh, ow-goo'-ree-yoh*
wish *v.*, desiderare *deh-zee-deh-rah'-reh* [44, 64]
with, con *kon*
without, senza *sen'-tsah*
woman, donna *don'-nah* [10]
wonderful, meraviglioso *meh-rah-veel-yoh'-zoh*
wood, legno *lehn'-yoh*
woods, bosco *bos'-koh*
wool, lana *lah'-nah*
word, parola *pah-roh'-lah*
work *n.*, lavoro *lah-voh'-roh*
work *v.*, lavorare *lah-voh-rah'-reh*

world, mond *moon'-doh*
worried, preoccupato *preh-ok-koo-pah'-toh*
worse, peggiore, peggio *pej-joh'-reh, pej'-joh*
worth, valore *vah-loh'-reh*
wound [injury], ferita *feh-ree'-tah*
wrap *v.,* avvolgere *ahv-vol'-jeh-reh* [70]
wrist, polso *pol'-soh*
wristwatch, orologio da polso *oh-roh-loh'-joh dah pol'-soh*
write, scrivere *skree'-veh-reh* [13, 30]
writing, scrittura *skreet-too'-rah*
wrong: to be wrong, aver torto *ah-vehr' tor'-toh* [12]

x ray, raggi x *rahj'-jee eh-kees*

yard, cortile (m) *kor-tee'-leh*
year, anno *ahn'-noh* [89]
yellow, giallo *jahl'-loh*
yes, sì *see*
yesterday, ieri *yeh'-ree* [6]
yet, ancora *ahn-koh'-rah*
you, Lei, voi, tu *leh'-ee, voy, too*
young, giovane *joh'-vah-neh*
your, yours, suo, sua, vostro, vostra, tuo, tua *soo'-oh, soo'-ah vos'-troh, vos'-trah, too'-oh, too'-ah*

zero, zero *dzeh'-roh*
zipper, chiusura lampo *kyoo-zoo'-rah lahm'-poh*

CONVERSION TABLES

Length
1 centimetro (cm) = 0.39 inch
1 metro (m) = 39.36 inches
1 chilometro (km) = 0.62 mile
1 inch = 2.54 cm.
1 foot = 0.30 m.
1 mile = 1.61 km.

Weight
1 grammo (gm) = 0.04 ounce
1 kilo (kg) = 2.20 pounds
1 ounce = 28.35 gm.
1 pound = 453.59 gm.

Volume
1 litro = 0.91 dry quart
1 litro = 1.06 liquid quarts
1 pint liquid = 0.47 liter
1 US quart liquid = 0.95 liter
1 US gallon = 3.78 liters

Temperature
Celsius (°C):	−17.8	0	10	20	30	37	37.8	100
Fahrenheit (°F):	0	32	50	68	86	98.6	100	212